INDIA'S FOREIGN POLICY IN THE 21ST CENTURY

INDIA'S FOREIGN POLICY IN THE 21ST CENTURY

Edited by
V.D. Chopra

Publications
KALPAZ PUBLICATIONS
DELHI-110052

India's Foreign Policy in the 21st Century

ISBN: 81-7835-500-0

First Published in 2006, reprint 2017 in India by
Kalpaz Publications
C-30, Satyawati Nagar, Delhi-110052
E-mail : kalpaz@hotmail.com
Ph- 011-47034999, 9811692060

Laser Typesetting at : Master Computers, Delhi
Printed at : Salasar Imaging System, Delhi

Contents

Preface

India in the early 21st century has become a focus of international attention more than ever before. During the last century, since India became politically independent, it witnessed tremendous changes in the socio-economic base of the country and thereupon in its political structure – political system and political parties. It had its own bearing on the international developments. It is for instance of historic importance that when in 1947, India became an independent sovereign state, it ushered a new era of decolonisation. British empire, the biggest colonial empire of the world was confronted with liberation movements in country after country. A large number of countries in the world became independent. In this sense when the last British soldier left the shores of India, it marked the beginning of a new phase in the history of our planet. There is something more to it. The various Afro-Asian countries which were ruled by colonial powers, united and a new Afro-Asian solidarity movement developed, in which India played a leading role.

In the pyramid of world powers in 1947, India was perhaps at the rock bottom. However, within a short span of three to four decades, India pushed forward its position in this period and became a most developed country among the developing countries. It started exerting its political, moral and material influence on the course of human history. The role played by India in 1971 in the liberation struggle of Bangladesh changed the geopolitics and correlation of the world forces. India demonstrated that it can face the challenge of the world's biggest powers and play an independent role. In this sense, since early 1970s India became an important influential factor.

In fact, the last four decades will go down in the history as an era of change, a change unprecedented in scale and depth, particularly after early 1990s of the last century, when after the collapse of the Soviet Union, it embarked on a new path of economic regeneration and building relations with other countries. This has altered the entire course of history of the Indian people because they have not only become masters of their destiny, but have already begun to play a significant role, influencing world events and moulding world-situation. It is, therefore, but natural that every major power in the world has started watching India from close quarters.

India is the seventh largest country in the world and next to China has the highest population on our planet. It is well marked off from the rest of Asia by mountains and seas, which give the country a distinct geographical identity. Bounded by the great Himalayas in the north, it stretches southwards and at the Tropic of Cancer, shrinks off into the Indian Ocean.

Such a vast country and that too being so densely populated and lying entirely in the northern hemisphere, obviously has a strategic position in the geopolitics of the present day world. A casual look at India's geographical location on the world map immediately brings home the fact of her enviable importance. The Himalayas and other lofty mountain ranges of Muztagh Ata, Aghil and Kunlun to the north of Kashmir and south-eastern portion of Zanskar mountains to the east of Himachal Pradesh form India's northern boundary. She is adjoined in the north by China, Nepal and Bhutan. A series of mountain ranges in the east separate India from Myanmar. Also in the east, lies Bangladesh, bounded by the Indian States of West Bengal, Assam, Meghalaya, Tripura and Mizoram. In the northwest, Afghanistan and Pakistan border on India. South of the Tropic of Cancer, the country tapers off into the Indian Ocean between the Arabian Sea on the West and the Bay of Bengal on the East. The Gulf of Mannar and the Palk Strait separate India from Sri Lanka. The Andaman and Nicobar Islands in the Bay of Bengal and Lakshadweep in the Arabian Sea are parts of the territory of India.

Geopolitical location and its population apart, one thing that stands out clearly and unmistakably is that long before most parts of the world had embarked upon the path of civilisation, India could already boast of culture and progress with millennia of human endeavour behind it. Perhaps these civilisations flourished in the third millennium before Christ. The mystery of the ancient Indian culture remains a mystery even today, because the distinction between 'history' and 'prehistory' is peculiarly elusive in her case. None can fully reconstruct the story of the culture that once thrived in this great country. Though writing was known and employed in India in the third and second millennia B.C., the exclusive script has yet to be deciphered in a meaningful way. It is a recognised fact, however, that along with Persia, Mesopotamia, and Egypt, India was one of the most important centres on the globe where the civilisation processes were initiated and matured.

No wonder then, India and its cultural achievements had started shaping the evolution of human thought, even during the unrecorded periods of history, by forging contacts with other areas and peoples.

It is this India, which once again has begun to remake human history and this process is building relations with all the countries.

In this book, various scholars and specialists have critically examined the new contours of India's foreign policy. I express my deep gratitude to them for their cooperation in compiling this book. I must also express my thanks to Mr. Manohar Singh Batra for his help in giving shape to the manuscript of the book. I must also compliment the senior members of the staff of the Gyan Publishing House/Kalpaz Publications, Delhi for their cooperation.

V.D. Chopra

List of Contributors

1.	Mr. Rajindar Sachar	Chief Justice (Retd.) High Court of Delhi, UN Special Rapporteur on Housing; Member, U.N. Sub-Commission on Prevention of Discrimination and Protection of Minorities (Ex.)
2.	Prof. V.P. Dutt	Former Pro-Vice-Chancellor of Delhi University and Former Member of Parliament, Leading Expert on International Affairs.
3.	Air Commodore (Retd.) Jasjit Singh	Director, Centre for Strategic and International Studies, New Delhi, Director, Institute for Defence Studies and Analyses (Ex.)
4.	Prof. R.R. Sharma	Former Vice-Chancellor of Jammu University, Dean, School of International Studies, Jawaharlal Nehru University, New Delhi, Leading Expert on International Affairs.
5.	Brigadier (Retd.) Chandra B. Khanduri	Well-known author on Military History and Strategy, Expert on the UNPKOs Developments.
6.	Prof. K.R. Singh	Former Professor, School of International Studies, Jawaharlal Nehru University, New Delhi.
7.	Mr. Ashwini Kumar	Formerly of Indian Police Service. Held several High Ranking posts.
8.	Prof. B.K. Shrivastava	Former Professor, Centre for American Studies, Jawaharlal Nehru University, New Delhi and Expert on the United States.

9.	Dr. Gulshan Sachdeva	Associate Professor, School of International Studies, Jawaharlal Nehru University, New Delhi.
10.	Mr. V.D. Chopra	Former Chief Editor, Patriot Daily and Link Weekly; Vice-President of International Institute for Asia-Pacific Studies, New Delhi and a well-known author.
11.	Dr. Jagdish P. Sharma	Associate Professor, Department of African Studies, University of Delhi and Expert on Afro-Arab and Asian Affairs.
12.	Professor Kalim Bahadur	Former Professor, Jawaharlal Nehru University, New Delhi and an Expert on Pakistan.
13.	Mr. Manohar Singh Batra	Former Deputy Director General, All India Radio and Commentator on International Affairs.
14.	Major General (Retd.) Afsir Karim	Security Expert and Editor, Aakrosh, Journal on Terrorism.
15.	Prof. A.K. Pasha	Chairman, Centre for West Asian and African Studies, School of International Studies, Jawaharlal Nehru University, New Delhi and Expert on Gulf Countries.
16.	Dr. Parmanand	Associate Professor in Political Science, University of Delhi and Hony. Director, South Asian Studies Foundation, New Delhi.
17.	Dr. Sita Kaushik	Reader, Department of Political Science, Kalindi College, Delhi University.
18.	Dr. Udai Bhanu Singh	Research Fellow, Institute for Defence Studies and Analyses, New Delhi.
19.	Dr. R.K. Wadhwa	Asstt. Professor, Indian Institute of Foreign Trade, New Delhi.

1

India's Foreign Policy

Rajindar Sachar

Foreign policy in the 21st Century is going to be very different from what it was when India became independent. At that time there were well-known two blocks, the USA and the USSR. India's foreign policy rightly did not wish to become a part of either of the two blocks and evolved what is known as a non-aligned group of nations. Notwithstanding this, our tilt sometimes a little too much in form of USSR like the unfortunate tilt towards USSR when it invaded Afghanistan in 1980, the disastrous consequences which since followed and our keeping silent when Russian troops moved into Hungary in 1956 made a claim of our independent policy somewhat blunt. We were, however, able along with other non-aligned leaders like Tito of Yugoslavia, Sokrano of Indonesia and Nasser of Egypt to help project the concept of non-aligned policy.

This broad arrangement continued with minor ups and downs till a very serious change came about with the collapse of the Soviet Union in 1989. By this time USA had become a single superpower. Russia which, after the breakup of USSR was expected to keep some kind of a balance, unfortunately because of its internal contradictions and economic collapse, was not able to keep up the pressure.

There was of course the other aspect of Europe trying to come together. The European Nations' efforts to make and have European Union strong and big so that it would be able to challenge USA in various matters, has unfortunately, not succeeded fully at present, because of their own internal differences. That influence is also going to now lessen because of the rejection of referendum on constitution by France and the Netherlands. Apparently, this will stoke the ambition of USA to behave irresponsibly and to act like a Don ignoring completely the sensitivities and the interests of other nations.

A conflict looming large before India's foreign policy relations is the proposal for expansion of the Security Council. The Group of 4—India, Brazil, Germany and Japan are putting forth a proposal for expansion of the Security Council and their inclusion as permanent members. They have even softened their approach on not having Veto rights straightaway, but leaving an interval of at least 15-20 years for this. USA in brazen partisan manner has opposed this matter being taken up in the current UN Assembly and is pressurizing the other countries to veto it. This opposition, apart from anything, is really aimed at India and Germany.

The opposition by USA to Germany, apart from the fact that the US was undecided about the overall enlargement plan, and it can be feasible but it has considered its bottomline was clear enough: Germany was not welcome to join the club. And if people thought that had something to do with continuing US resentments over Chancellor Gerhard Schroeder's outspoken opposition to the Iraq war, then they might not be all that wrong. It would be wrong strategy for India to move away from the group of four, for the apprehension that USA being against Germany, India remaining in the Group may damage its chance. But then India should have the confidence that it cannot be ignored at international plank notwithstanding USA's opposition.

Maybe, USA does not want India's potential which every one is now conceding at international level to be enhanced further by inclusion in the Security Council. Maybe, it is sending a message to Pakistan who, unfortunately, notwithstanding some relaxations in India-Pakistan relations seems to be against India's inclusion in the Security Council. China is also opposing, more so, because it feels that if Japan and India are included, its sole monopoly from Asia will suffer. Naturally, we want good relations with China. It will be one of the challenges of the 21st century's Foreign Policy as to how to combine our self-interest and justify our posture of wanting to play a bigger role in the international arena and at the same time not spoil our relations with China and Pakistan. This needs a very delicate handling and understanding that whatever the position of India, it will never be hostile to the interests of Pakistan or China. Rather, we need to create an atmosphere in which China should feel that it would play even a greater role if it, along with India, Pakistan and Japan, were to form a workable understanding on major issues which, in any case, are common more to these countries than to the interests of USA. In that connection, one was not very happy at the arms supply from USA in the shape of a pact which India signed with USA, but also for manufacturing advanced improved version of F-16. To be drawn into arms manufacturing with USA does not fit with India's Foreign Policy of settling the matters peacefully and of creating a world without conflicts. The danger of joint arms manufacturing is that one is drawn interminably into the orbit of USA, which can have serious consequences in our independent relationship with China and also, especially for the upcoming countries like Brazil and Venezuela.

Another strain is in the attitude of USA to Iran. European Union wants to engage Iran in talks so that a flash point is not reached. But USA is adopting the same tactic of false statements as used with Iraq about danger of nuclearisation from Iran, when neutral international opinion is not willing to go along with it as it is not convinced of the material relied upon by USA which is suspect.

India has never been a favourite with USA nor, in my view, have we to try to cater to that status. Rather India, in the past, has had comfortable relationship bordering on the mildly hostile with the USA. But since last few years and because of rapid opening up of the Indian economy (one is not happy at the undiluted way in which it is done and which could have serious consequences, but then that is a different aspect to be considered separately). But, at present USA has, because of its potential of market in India, somewhat changed its tone and has at least lessened its hostile stance. This stand has been encouraged a little by somewhat over-indulgence by the various policies of the Central Government, namely its cooperative approach even in the matter of USA's arms supply, joint military exercises and other exchange of delicate information.

The further domination of USA in the wake of 9/11 has made matters worse. USA is now impervious to the UN pressure. It treats even the Secretary General's pleas with disdain. USA's venture in Afghanistan met with some opposition but it was not strong enough to prevent it. The neo-conservatives in the US are ruling therein and have now embarked upon a programme of action and international behaviour wedded to the sole objective of how best it will serve USA's interests even by causing damage to world peace or the world economy. So much now is the indifference of USA that it is continuing with its Iraq policy and occupation of Iraq notwithstanding the evidence beyond any doubt that the excuse of WMD being stored by

Iraq and the danger of their being used by Saddam Hussein was a deliberate and false cover-up. It was so unashamedly done that the officials of USA did not even feel embarrassed to put it on record (which documents have now become public) that this whole attack was in the planning for almost a year immediately after Bush had got re-elected. The whole venture of Iraq must be understood in the context of oil diplomacy that is now the sole determining feature of USA's foreign policy, which has to be kept in view by all countries, especially by India when deciding its foreign policy for the 21st Century. The latest example of this is to be seen in the strong statement of the US Secretary of State Condleeza Rice threatening Pakistan not to enter into an agreement between India, Iran and Pakistan to supply Iran's gas to India. There is so much of brazenness and contempt with other nations that USA's Secretary of State has made no secret of the fact that if Pakistan goes through this project, it will affect Washington's relations with Islamabad. Of course, so far as India is concerned, though there may not be publicly stated opposition to it, but the fact that India-Iran pipeline cannot be worked at an economic advantage unless Pakistan is a party to it. At present, with good relations between India and Pakistan on the rise, Pakistan is more than willing especially considering that it could earn upto £600 million a year from this pipeline which agreement is to be for 25 years on this £4 billion pipeline. The reason that interests of the big gas companies are being affected is really what determines the American policy. That is why Ms. Condleeza Rice only wants Pakistan against joining this India-Iran project but has, without any embarrassment suggested Pakistan to think of the alternative gas from Qatar and Turkmenistan, which are being handled by USA oil companies. Naturally, Iran is justifiably angry because its Oil Minister has publicly stated that it is unreasonable to prevent India and Pakistan from accessing gas from Iran. Here then is one of the challenges to our foreign policy experts because to give in to pressure by USA is such an important matter of our national economy that it could send wrong signals to the world. India needs to tell the USA straightaway that though it wants a friendly relationship with USA, it cannot allow the latter to suggest policies which will damage and delay the economic uplift of the country.

One of the touchy and delicate matters of our Foreign Policy is our approach to Myanmar. For some time now Indian government is quite silent on the release of leaders like Aung San Suu Kyi. Maybe, in its own interests considering that there are portions in Myanmar which are the headquarters of the armed insurgents operating in North-East, India has to walk a little delicately. But an impression should not be given as if we have completely jettisoned the pro-democratic movements in Myanmar. If UN Secretary General and Norwegian Nobel Committee can demand her release, it is incumbent on democratic India to extend its support on this demand. There is, thus, no reason why India which is such a close and friendly neighbour to Myanmar, should not use its influence with understanding to seek the release of its leaders.

India's Foreign Policy must give top-most priority to improving relations with Pakistan. The recent controversy on Advani vis-a-vis Jinnah's role in the sub-continent has been an unfortunate one not in the sense that it may lead to weakening of BJP (if this was so, I would certainly welcome this development). My worry is that the Congress, without properly appreciating the significance, jumped into a controversy of whether Mr. Jinnah was a secular leader or not and whether he was responsible for partition. I believe it is a totally uncalled for controversy. Quaid-e-Azam is the founder of Pakistan and deserves all respect like Gandhiji does in our country. Gandhiji and Jinnah are the icons of their respective countries. There may be an indepth and critical study by historians and serious political scientists on the respective merits and demerits of the contribution by Gandhiji and Jinnah, but I think it is not in the interest of our countries that politicians or media hacks should fall in the trap of discussing the merits and demerits of their contribution during the freedom struggle and of their work pre-1947 and purporting to give them honour or dishonour for any of their political thoughts. These are not matters into which political parties have any business to enter into, nor are they relevant at this stage. Pakistan is an established reality. Howsoever it came into being (may be the concern of social scientists and as a matter of fact many even in Pakistan are doing studies on it) but so far as the integrity and inalterability of Pakistan as an independent sovereign country is concerned, it cannot even brook a moment's denial. The Indian government must not forget this angle in internal unnecessary jibes with the opposition. Rather it must unequivocally reiterate as a solemn pledge that the integrity and sovereignty of Pakistan is a sacred and an established reality and accepted by India and that our foreign policy is based on a friendship between two independent countries with an effort to make both these states stronger. One should expect that the ruling party takes this stand unequivocally, because it is justifiably engaged in improving relations with Pakistan and taking reasonably positive steps towards it. It needs to be accepted that without real and genuine open friendship and goodwill between India and Pakistan, neither of the countries can play any worthwhile role in the international field. It is, therefore, in the interest of both the countries not to, in any way, spoil the atmosphere if we really want to be counted as a rising force in the world.

2

Foreign Policy in 21st Century: An Overview

V.P. Dutt

India's foreign policy must be in accord with the developing international situation, otherwise it would function in a vacuum. The chief characteristic of the international situation in the 21st Century is its utter complexity. This complexity can almost be bewildering, requiring all the skills and resources of diplomacy to cope with it. Almost every major country is following a dual, if not triple, stance towards the other major powers. China towards USA, USA towards China, USA towards Russia, USA towards Europe, Europe towards USA, Japan towards China, China towards Japan, Japan towards Russia and Russia almost toward everyone except India.

Let us first take China towards USA and vice versa to examine their contrasting statements, actions and attitudes. Beijing is supposed to be emerging as a rival to USA and often in their writings the most trenchant criticism is reserved for the Americans. Yet, take a speech by Director-General of the Chinese Foreign Ministry's Asian Affairs Department, Cui Tiankai who said in Hong Kong early this year that Beijing had no desire to squeeze the US presence out of Asia as part of its quest to promote stronger regional integration and cooperation. China, he said, would continue to welcome America's strong presence in the region, as long as it remained a positive influence. "We recognize the US long history and interests. There is no intention to drive out the US".[1]

This statement comes in the context of Beijing's efforts to set up mechanisms of cooperation with other Asian countries, including a free trade agreement with the Association of South East Asian Nations

(ASEAN). Beijing is also a strong supporter of the forthcoming East Asia Summit to be held in Malaysia to be attended by the leaders of South-East Asian Nations as well as Japan, China and South Korea. Mr. Cui said that Washington should consider Asian regional integration a win-win situation, because it would lead to greater stability in the region, thereby serving US interests.

Yet, on the other hand, Beijing's view of US policies was forcefully expressed by former Vice-Premier and senior foreign policy adviser, Qian Qichian, in the *China Daily* where he accused USA of the arrogance of unilateralism. In a similar way, Wang Yichou, Editor of Yellow Book of International Politics, speaking of the past year, described it as one of spreading terrorists attacks and failed US unilateralist policy. A well-known Chinese scholar said in a symposium in New Delhi that even though China ostensibly had a strategic relationship with USA, "in our hearts we do not feel any such strategic partnership".

The US approach towards China is no less dubiously complex. On the one hand a velvet glove; on the other hand continued efforts at containment of China. On the surface, US Deputy Secretary of State, Robert Zoellick described as "foolish any policy to contain Chinese influence and expressed US intent on deepening economic and political ties with ASEAN but without trying to contain China's rising influence in the region.[2]

It should not be overlooked that China today is the second largest holder of US treasury bonds, Japan being the first. Japan holds some $ 841 billion in US treasury bonds and China nearly $ 400 billion. We may also note in passing that 70 per cent of South Korea's foreign exchange is held in US treasury bonds. The United States is able to continue running a huge deficit chiefly because of these inflows of foreign money, particularly from Asia.

The United States is among the top economic partners of China. Exports to the US are about 5½ times imports from the US: $ 16 billion a month in exports compared to $ 2.8 billion in imports, leaving a trade imbalance approaching $ 200 billion a year—or about a third of the entire US deficit.[3] It may be noted that Chinese trade surplus with the United States now equals slightly more than a 10th of its entire economic output—an extraordinary figure by any reckoning. China, in fact, is a huge beneficiary of American consumer appetites, but at the same time profoundly dependent on them. It has been pointed out by an analyst that China needs secure sea-lanes for its ever-rising oil imports, and like the rest of Asia, it implicitly relies on the American Navy to keep the tankers safe.[4] The United States is also dependent on China for registering any progress on the North Korean nuclear issue.

On the other side of the picture, the United States is sounding loud alarms over Chinese military build-up and leaning heavily on Europe not to lift the embargo on arms supply to China. The CIA in its annual assessment of worldwide threats released on 26 February 2005 warned that Chinese military modernization was tilting the balance of power in the Taiwan Straits, increasing the threat to US forces in the region. The report said that China was making determined military and diplomatic efforts to "counter what it sees as US efforts to contain or encircle China". The report indicated that the CIA was paying growing attention to potential military threat amid China's growing economic ties with its neighbours and the United States and particularly referred to increase in Chinese ballistic missiles deployed across the Taiwan Straits and the improvements in the Chinese nuclear and conventional capabilities.[5]

Let us take the United States and Europe. The war between "old Europe" and America is over, but the old friendship is history too. A number of things have happened after the collapse of the Soviet Union starting the process of estrangement between Western Europe and Washington. With the demise of the Soviet Union, Western Europeans no longer needed American strategic protection. The United States also did not require the European strategic space as before. America was unbound, no longer contained and constrained by another superpower, and began to wield its raw power more liberally than before. But there has also been what has been called the "great sobering up". America's adversaries learnt that they could defy but not dethrone the last remaining superpower, and the last remaining superpower also learnt that it could slice through the Iraqi army without much damage to it but could not win the peace all by itself.

A similar duality is noticeable in the relationship between China and Japan, equally important for the peace of Asia and the world. Politics is never far below the surface of Sino-Japanese relations, and the first and the second largest economies of Asia are in some trouble over the spat around recent history. The Chinese believe that Japan has not sincerely reflected over its past aggression against many Asian countries, particularly China, and this impression is being fortified by the recent history textbooks issued in Japan that the Chinese believe gloss over the aggression and the atrocities committed during that aggression. Chinese sensitivities are further riled by the repeated visits of Japanese Prime Minister Junichiro Koizumi to the Yasukuni Shrine which also keeps the graves of the Second World War criminals. Anti-Japanese demonstrations raged in Chinese cities (in April 2005), the Japanese embassy was attacked and many Japanese business premises stoned by slogan-shouting Chinese demonstrators. The Japanese on their part believe that Beijing uses the pretext of the last world war aggression by Japan to stoke the fires of nationalism within China, thereby helping retain its dominance over the political system. Tokyo also holds China responsible for the loss of property in these riots and demanded a Chinese apology which was not forthcoming.

Japan has for the first time named China, along with North Korea, as a security threat. A decade ago this would have been unthinkable. Quite obviously, the younger generation in Japan as well as a section of the old elite is far more influenced by nationalism than was the case in Japan even five years ago. One major consequence of the Sino-Japanese spat has been a very substantial strengthening of US-Japanese military relationship. With its own military spread thin, Washington appears to be trying to nudge Japan out from under the US security blanket and make Tokyo a more active player in global strategic operations. The United States would like Japan to assume a role very much like the one it has vis-a-vis the British. It may be recalled that the United States has some 50,000 troops based in Japan.[6] The Japanese and the US governments have also agreed to name the commercial airports and harbours that would be made available for US military operations in the event of emergency in areas surrounding Japan.[7] Tokyo has thus become vital for Washington's goals in Asia. It is not accidental that the United States has so far publicly supported only Japan's case for permanent membership of the UN Security Council.

But we may also take account of the duality in this situation: the other side of the picture. Japan has become the largest trading partner of China, momentarily displacing even the United States. Sino-Japanese trade amounted to some $ 150 billion in 2004 and is still rising. China has played more than a marginal role in whatever Japanese economic revival has taken place. China too gains immensely from this economic relationship and, as in the past, enjoyed very liberal Japanese economic aid. It is in this context that Chinese Minister of Commerce, Bo Xilai, appealed to the Chinese people not to boycott Japanese goods. He pointed out that Japanese businesses employ 9.2 million mainland

Chinese workers and contributed 49 billion Yuan in taxes in 2004. He indicated that the chill in political links would not affect the warmth of economic ties.[8] We can see the Chinese dual policy unfolding and a major attempt being made by Beijing to contain the spat with Japan.

All the trends mentioned above, should rule out any armed conflict between either China and USA or China and Japan. The only flash point that this writer sees is Taiwan which is an emotional issue for, not just the Chinese government but even more the Chinese people. Even there Beijing is taking various diplomatic initiatives to enhance its political and economic influence in Taiwan without having to take recourse to actual military conflict. If the Americans prevent a Taiwanese declaration of independence, Beijing might live with the status quo for a number of years.

Some other seminal developments may also be noted before we come to India's foreign policy in this developing international milieu. The US administration is celebrating what it believes to be its victory in Iraq and President George Bush is emphasizing that democracy was on the march with "free" elections held in Iraq. But what is the actual reality? As Naomi Kline wrote in the *Guardian* (12 February 2005): the Americans think that the Iraqi people have finally sent America those long-awaited flowers and sweets, with a large percentage of Shia and Kurd voters having taken part in the elections, but in fact Iraq's voters "just gave them the purple finger". The Iraqis have voted overwhelmingly to throw out the US-installed Ayad Allawi who refused to ask the US to leave, whereas a decisive majority of Shia population voted for the United Iraqi Alliance, which called for a time-table for the withdrawal of the allied forces, something which Mr. Bush had rejected earlier.

In fact religion has come at the head of politics in Iraq. Power has virtually passed into the hands of the clerics. It is Ayattayullah Sistani who has become a final arbiter in the kind of concession that the Shias would make to the Sunnis and in the process USA has succeeded in strengthening Iran's clout as both the Shia and the Kurd top leadership have been very friendly to Iran.

Look at the cost of war: President Bush has recently secured $ 82 billion in emergency spending for Afghanistan and Iraq. The cost of the Iraq war has already hit $ 200 billion and it is a near certainty that it would reach $ 250 billion and a distinct possibility that it would reach $ 400 billion. And there are not too many donors this time. Three years after the US budget ran a surplus of $ 240 billion in 2001-02, in

2003 the deficit rose to $ 400 billion. Instead of the $ 5,000 billion surplus once estimated for the decade ending 2013, the outlook is for a $ 1,800 billion deficit or even $ 4,000 billion deficit. Iraq has in fact become a killer's field. As *The Independent* put it, "Iraq is a bloody no man's land". After the crescendo of violence over the last two years there should be no doubt that the US had not quashed the insurgents. The failure has been in part political, because a large number of Iraqis, both Shia and Sunni, seemed to believe that they had been occupied, rather than liberated. The American massive fire power won them "set-piece battle, but they also accidentally killed so many Iraqi civilians that they were the recruiting sergeants of the resistance."[9]

So, we could say, there is a drift towards a multipolar configuration of world politics in which a number of regional power centres compete for consolidating their position. This drift towards multipolarity has been set off by the severe problems confronted by the United States in its occupation of Iraq and by the decline of the dollar in the international currency markets.

The former has revealed the limitations and vulnerabilities of US military power and the latter has brought forward underlining weaknesses in the US economic system.

In a way the United States has hamstrung itself. It has expended so much political, financial and military capital on Iraq that it is finding it difficult to decisively act elsewhere. As the Pentagon itself has admitted the concentration of American troops and weapons in Iraq and Afghanistan has limited the US military's ability to deal with other potential armed conflicts. This was revealed by no less a person than the Chairman of the Joint Chief of Staff, Gen. Richard B. Myers in a classified report to the US Congress, adding that major combat operations elsewhere in the world would "probably be more protracted and produce higher American and foreign civilian causalities because of the commitment of Pentagon resources in Iraq and Afghanistan."[10]

The fact is that the doctrine of preemption is virtually dead and unilateralism is faltering. USA went into Iraq where there were no weapons of mass destruction. It is chafing at the leash in Iran where at least as yet there are no nuclear weapons. On the other hand, North Korea has defiantly declared that it possesses nuclear weapons and is twitting its thumb at Washington, but the lone superpower is effectively stymied.

Western analysts believe that what Washington has most essentially lost is acquiescence in its leadership in many cases: "It is a game of every power for itself, in which each regional power centre cooperates with others when it shares common interests with them and opposes them when interests conflict. The result is the absence of a single paradigm of world order or even of a coherent pattern of alliances. In their place are coalitions of convenience that taken together have no consistent direction".

Nevertheless, let us not lose sight of the other side of the picture. We need a balanced approach. It would be naïve to ignore or underestimate US power and US economic strength. United States remains by far the most powerful military power as well as the largest economy with the most attractive market in the world. It would be to our advantage to make use of this economic strength without losing our bearings. The basic question for India in the 21st century is whether India can develop multiple relations with multiple countries without being trapped in a web of dependencies. Necessarily dependency is a relative term. In the present day world, no country is really totally independent, as the process of give and take is a continual one. Yet, can India retain its decision-making autonomy in the present day world while enlarging and deepening relations with the United States, Europe, China, Russia and other countries?

United States is our top trading partner. The US, United Arab Emirates, Hong Kong, the UK, Germany, Belgium, Japan and Italy have provided 65 per cent of the share of India's exports to the world between 2000-2004. Of these, the US occupies the top slot, accounting for nearly one-fifth of India's merchandise exports and non-oil imports, according to the National Council for Applied Research."[11]

According to the American Chamber of Commerce, there are nearly 1,000 American companies doing business in India, a 14-fold increase over 1991. The US is also largest accumulative investor in India, both in FDI and portfolio investment currently—at over Rs. 16,500 crore. In 2003, India's exports to US amounted to Rs. 59,800 crore and India's, imports from the US for the same year were Rs. 20,240 crore. The balance of Indo-US trade has remained in India's favour.[12]

There is obvious need to expand and deepen this economic relationship. Our political relations with the United States are equally important. Washington has repeatedly declared its intention to build relationships with India on a long-term basis and often given the impression that it would like India to be a major power, although specifics are still lacking in US pronouncements. It should be the function of our diplomacy to develop further relations with the United States at every level, not just with the administration, but on a broad spectrum with other sections of the US decision-making elites, including intellectuals and public opinion-makers.

Nevertheless, the anxiety about dependency has not disappeared. The fact is that, despite our repeated declarations, the US has been allowed to become the third party in the Indo-Pakistan relationship. It is not the India-China-US triangle that was most talked about, but it is the reality of the India-Pakistan-US triangle, the reality of which we should now be concerned about. As the erstwhile Secretary of State, Colin Powell, has been repeatedly claiming, it was Washington which spurred the Vajpayee-Sharif dialogue and which subsequently pushed Vajpayee-Musharraf into resumption of dialogue. Washington is now experimenting with a new kind of dual policy towards the sub-continent. One end of this dual policy is to assure Pakistan of its stability and security. Principally it has meant underwriting General Musharraf. The chief element of this policy is to ensure that Pakistan does not become a failed state and that its sense of insecurity is adequately defused. Pakistan should therefore be extended whatever economic and military assistance it needs in this regard. Pakistan has also become a non-NATO ally of the United States.

The other end of this dual policy is to strive for a new relationship with India that would not be essentially dependent on relations with Pakistan. Colin Powell while defending accomplishments in foreign affairs during the first Bush administration claimed that "over the last four years Washington has managed the difficult feat of drawing closer both India and Pakistan".[13] To this way of thinking, the United States should recognize India as a major regional power, treated as such and assistance extended to the extent possible without sacrificing the larger objectives of US foreign policy. An essential characteristic of this policy is the continued dependence of the two countries on US good offices. Washington recognizes that India would be a much stronger market than it has been in the past and that US economic interests should be protected by developing better relationship with India.

Some of the phrases used by US foreign policy makers may delight our ego, about America assisting India in emerging as a great power, but it should not be overlooked that so far the United States has given no indication of supporting India's permanent membership of the Security Council, nor has the US promised any assistance in the development of nuclear power at least for the present. What the Americans have so far offered is the sale of F-16 and F-18, which is a commercial proposition in any case, and joint consultations over energy problems of India and the world. It is in this sense that the anxiety about dependency remains. Probing talks have been underway at various levels, the outcome of which is still to be seen.

How does India reduce this dependency or keep it within manageable proportions? Let us not forget what USA is doing to Russia with its steadily creeping advance towards the periphery of Russia and encouragement of "popular revolts" in the countries surrounding Russia as a way of curbing Russian influence as well as securing US presence in this energy-rich area. We can pursue two options simultaneously. One is to expand the dialogue with Pakistan, build more confidence measures, second, strive for a resolution of the disputes within the stated and well-recognized limits, and thus reduce the relevance of USA as a third party. Of course, we all know the constraints in the resolution of Indo-Pakistan divide. So far the maximum we could offer was not the minimum our neighbour was willing to accept. However, if we persist, it is not outside the realm of possibility that light at the end of the tunnel may be seen.

The second course is to be pursued simultaneously is to expand relations with China, Russia, Europe, Japan, Central Asia, Africa and Latin America. That is what I had earlier referred to as the development of multiple relationships with multiple countries in order to expand our political space. Many students of international relations when talking about development of relations with China, Russia and other countries in order to balance the rigours of one power dominance tend to think only in strategic terms often translated into military lexicon. It is time we shed this obsession with military balances. For the foreseeable future there are no military balances available against the United States. The United States would remain the super military power for many years to come and it would be futile on our part to think in military terms in managing relations with the United States nor would it be in our interests. We should concentrate, on the other hand, on political and economic relationships, not excluding the United States, but expanding such relations with a large number of other countries across the continents in order to achieve a healthier political balance in the world.

With China and Japan, we are already moving rapidly, much more with China than with Japan, but still a lot more needs to be done. For the first time, China has talked about "strategic partnership" with India. In the words of the official news agency, *Xinhua*, the two countries were pushing their bilateral relations on to a new stage. They had shown willingness to shoulder more responsibility and play larger roles in the regional and international stages as their regional and international influence surges continuously.[14] Premier Wen Jiabao's visit to India was a major event in this regard.

On the eve of his visit, Premier Wen mentioned three-point expectations from his visit to India. First, to confirm the bilateral relationship from the long-term perspective and strategic height; second, to issue guiding principles to solve the border issue; three, to outline the economic and trade cooperation in the next five years. [15] China and India signed a landmark accord on the guiding principles to be followed in solving the border dispute. Although the Chinese Premier gave the impression that Beijing supported India's bid for permanent membership of the United Nations Security Council, it was somewhat ambiguously couched and could be interpreted in various ways. The joint statement signed by the prime ministers of the two countries on 13 April alluded to the establishment of a strategic and cooperative partnership for peace and prosperity. The two prime ministers agreed that China-India relations had acquired a "global and strategic character."[16]

The two countries have also rightly decided to concentrate on economic ties to push forward their other relationships. The trade with China has risen many times from almost nothing to nearly $ 13 billion in 2004. China has become our second largest trading partner. But it should be recalled that India is not yet a significant factor in China's foreign trade, occupying less than 1 per cent in the total foreign trade of Beijing. If we could achieve a two-way $ 50 billion trade volume and if we could invest in each other's economic growth, we could give long-term stability to our relationship.

Our relations with Russia are even more important. There is so much consensus on the need for a special relationship with Russia in the country that we do not have to dwell on this issue. But it needs recalling that we have absolutely no territorial or other abrasive disputes with Russia and that Russia is one country with whom we can have a real special relationship. Our military muscle has been critically developed by our defence relationship with Russia.[17]

Another area of critical importance in foreign policy in the 21st century is energy security. This is going to be vital to our security as well as to the security of many other countries including China and USA. The US consumes over 20 million barrels of oil per day, while China's appetite amounts to nearly 6 million barrels a day and increasing every year. The world will require some 120 million barrels a day by 2025 for its energy needs to be adequately met. This is a huge challenge that needs to be viewed in a global context. It is apparent that both India and China are now engaged in the race for securing their energy needs around the world, investing in drilling or acquiring oil and gas from countries as far off as Sudan, Brazil, Argentina, Kazakhstan, Uzbekistan, etc. Our energy needs are crucial and must form a critical component of our foreign policy. It would indeed be helpful if both China and India could develop a cooperative relationship in this area, rather than engage in outbidding each other. A similar cooperative relationship is necessary to be developed with the United States.

It is obvious to students of international relations that the centre for economic gravity is shifting from USA and Europe to Asia. Nearly every western commentator and scholar on these matters is writing about the 21st century being the Asian century. There are multiple economic centres arising in Asia, prominent among them being Japan, China, India, South Korea and ASEAN (including particularly Vietnam). This is also the century for economic cooperation. To some extent our foreign policy's success would be defined by our ability to promote wide-ranging cooperation among Asian countries.

All this comes back to not just the Nehruvian vision of a cooperating Asia, but also the determination of India and other Asian countries to maintain their independence in world affairs, as Nehru believed. This has been our goal for the last half century and still remains a prominent goal for the coming 50 years. Developing comprehensive national strength while maintaining our autonomy and promoting cooperation and peace in Asia as well as in the world, as Jawaharlal Nehru had envisioned, are still the polestars for our foreign policy in the 21st century.

References

1. *South China Morning* Post (Hong Kong), 5 February 2005.
2. *China Daily*, 11 May 2005.
3. *Council on Foreign Relations*, 21 December 2004.
4. Keith Bradsher, It's Just Business, Nothing Geopolitical, *New York Times*, 16 January 2005.
5. *Financial Times* (London) 16 February 2005.

6. *Associated Press* dispatched from the Yokota Air Base, Japan, 9 April 2005.

7. *Daily Yomiuri*, 10 April 2005.

8. *South China Morning Post* (electronically), 23 April 2005.

9. The Independent (London), 15 May 2005.

10. Thom Shanker in *New York Times*, 3 May 2005.

11. *Economic Times*, 3 January 2005.

12. Saikat Neogi "Trade Winds", *Financial Express*, 21 February 2005.

13. *The Nation* (Pakistan), 26 December, 2004.

14. *www.chinaview.cn*, 18 February, 2005.

15. *People's Daily* (Elecotronically), 11 April 2005.

16. *Ibid.*, 13 April 2005.

17. For a detailed study of Indo-Russian relations, reader may refer to V.D. Chopra edited, *Global Significance of Indo-Russian Strategic Partnership*, Kalpaz Publications, Delhi, 2005.

3

Global Power Shift: Toward a Polycentric Asian Century

Jasjit Singh

The international situation has been in a state of flux for nearly two decades. Unfortunately there is a tendency to see the future only from the perspectives of the past. New challenges face the world, while the most critical of the old ones—that of peace, human development and prosperity—continue to dominate the situation. To this have been added new challenges like transnational terrorism driven by ethno-religious extremism and political separatism, weakening if not erosion of multilateral approaches to arms control and strategic stability, increased risks of nuclear proliferation along with the existing non-proliferation regimes in a state of crisis, rising demands on energy and the security of its supplies at affordable costs. These and other challenges faced by international community offer China and India unique tasks and opportunities to reshape the international situation toward cooperative peace and human development. These need to be viewed in the context of five major fundamental developments affecting the global strategic landscape which have been under way for more than two decades:

(i) A global power shift from West to East along with a new strategic balance is emerging among Asian powers without necessarily being in conflict with those outside the region;

(ii) The "rise" of China and India, and how they would relate to the world situation in general and to the sole superpower;

(iii) The global centre of gravity of political, economic and military activities and capabilities is shifting to Asia[1]; and

(iv) The response of the United States as the single most powerful state to the emerging geo-strategic realities, especially when seen in the context of its inability or unwillingness to adjust to the above realities, its greater reliance on unilateralism and selective pre-emption with propensity to use military force with or without credible legitimacy, etc.

(v) Future of human development, especially in Asia.

All these developments are interrelated in numerous ways. While most Western observers emphasise the changes taking place with variations essentially in the details, the majority tend to see the shifting equations of capabilities in terms of the classical balance of power that dominated the European scene in the 19th century. But we need to caution that this by no means implies that Asia would have a dominant leave alone hegemonic role in world affairs in the next two-odd decades, or, more important, that this signifies an emerging balance of power within Asia, or between Asian powers and the trans-Atlantic powers like the United States and the European Union.

The international situation as it is emerging is quite different. To begin with, the so-called "unipolar moment" was just that, a moment, and ended long ago. Given the fact that the United States is the sole superpower with unmatched capabilities in military, economic, technological and political-diplomatic fields, this might appear to be a premature and even wrong judgement. But the reality has been that there are finite limits to the use of that power as indeed is clear in the way it has to soft pedal the North Korean issue, or battle it out virtually alone in post-war Iraq. At the same time, the US power has been magnified by the extensive alliance system that it has headed since the Second World War and the rapid collapse of the second pole (the Soviet Union) in what was seen as a "bipolar world." It was inevitable that with the end of Cold War, this alliance would not carry the same importance as it did earlier. But it certainly has continued to harmonise policies and postures among themselves thus providing the perception of the leader being even larger than the reality. The image of "unipolarity," therefore, has come as much from the power of the US itself, as from the collective power and influence of the alliances built around the United States whose members are all the developed industrialised countries.[2] But progressively the US-led alliances have been getting less aligned as the fissures during the lead up to the Iraq War showed, continuing into the aftermath of the war when even a staunch ally like Spain withdrew its troops from Iraq in spite of the critical shortage of forces to manage the post-war situation.

If the world is not bipolar, and unipolarity is more an image than substance, what sort of world are we moving into? The most often described term is that of an emerging multipolarity. Or at least some of the countries, like China, Russia, France etc. have been talking and even working towards that end. India has sought a world in balance and harmony to enable it to pursue its primary interests of what in ancient Indian political thought was termed as the duty of the ruler: prosperity and happiness of its people.

The realities on the ground are that new centres of power have been emerging during the past quarter century or so, while some of the existing centres (like the Soviet Union/Russian Federation) have shrunk though once again showing signs of recovery into a new model. This inevitably would keep altering the global equations of power that many countries seek to define in terms of multipolarity. But multipolarity also implies that each of its poles would exercise influence, if not control, over a set of smaller/weaker powers by attracting them to its fold. Polarisation and hegemonism would be an inevitable development in an international order that is multipolar, as indeed it was when it was bipolar. Multipolarity also requires each of the poles to assume a leadership role in the region around it. For a variety of reasons, such a situation is neither desirable nor is it likely to become a reality in the foreseeable future since the priorities of the major as well as smaller powers essentially are driven by geo-economic realities that necessitate:

- Strong domestic development priorities.
- Need for cooperative peace to ensure uninterrupted human development.
- International order being in transition requires cooperation among major and lesser powers to reshape it toward a more cooperative framework.

For example, China, whose rise to power in the past two decades has been the most dramatic, still carries a great deal of historical handicaps which require it to seek cooperative peace to build its comprehensive national power. Its search for multipolarity, in fact, is a recognition of this limitation and hence its need to work in cooperation with other major centres of power while it pursues its own long-term strategic goals. Japan, the other major power in Asia also carries its own historical baggage that constrains it to move cautiously and almost gingerly in the exercise of independent political role leave alone a military responsibility outside its borders lest it reignite the old images of the Samurai and a resurgent expansionist Japan of the Second World War. Russia is still weak and debilitated from the socio-economic turmoil of the Soviet collapse and the legacies of the Soviet era. India has its own historically inherited baggage in terms of deindustrialisation during the two centuries of colonial rule and the political-psychological scars it left behind, in addition to the current challenges of having to go a long way to ensure the requisite level of domestic peace and human development. The European Union is deeply preoccupied with the processes of integration and historical dependence on the United States to be able to constitute a pole by itself, while some of its individual constituents like France and Germany carry with them legacies of the past and the obvious contradictions of seeking an independent role while resolving the tensions of being part of US-led NATO.

What is clear and empirically valid is the reality of new centres of power rising in the world while many of the old ones are undergoing changes, qualifying the international order to be designated as moving toward an increasingly polycentric world order. Many of the old norms and paradigms of arms control, non-proliferation and strategic stability have undergone fundamental changes. Techno-economic growth is altering the patterns of interaction that marked most of the 20th century, both before the Second World War as well as during the decolonisation of the world and the Cold War. This state of transition would almost inevitably move toward some sort of an end state over time. And this is why the present period may be seen as the foreplay of that end-state. What needs to be recognised is that almost all the new and old centres of power face their own limitations that (severely) constrain their ability to forcefully shape the policies of the 25 member European Union and/or the 45 odd Asian countries. The search for a 'multipolar' world is a recognition of these constraints.

Substantive asymmetry of power, capability, and willingness to exercise that capability among the leading centres of power in today's world is the primary defining characteristic of the evolving international order. This in turn implies that concurrent competition and cooperation would be intrinsic to the situation and the challenge, especially for countries like China and India, is to ensure that this does not translate into conflict. This has to be managed within the context of the information revolution where uncertainty and fluidity in international affairs is accentuated no longer allowing governments the luxury of predictability and long reaction time available earlier. Given the strategic priorities of large emerging powers like China, India and (post-Soviet) Russia, the need for developing cooperative peace is likely to remain the dominant policy choice for them while they deal with other conflicts. The type of consultations between the foreign ministers of these three countries at Almaty (for the third year) is symptomatic of the desire to maintain strategic consultations towards this end. Similarly, India and Japan, after the hiccups of 1998 nuclear tests by India, have rapidly moved to develop closer relations which are being termed as strategic in nature and content. Recently both countries agreed to support each other's candidature for permanent membership of UN Security Council.

It is against this broader backdrop that we need to see the strategic balance in Asia, if it exists, and what shape it would take in the coming years? Asia is too diverse, large and complex for a common political, economic, security and strategic identity to evolve. What is clear however is that the beginning of a strategic balance is noticeable which would have to be nurtured into a factor of strategic stability and cooperative peace if the conflicting goals of the major Asian centres of power are to avoid intra-Asian conflicts with unpredictable results? To be successful, this would have to be built on the basis of cooperative peace. And the trends of international strategic locus (or power as some would describe it) shifting from the trans-Atlantic region to the Asian region places the primary responsibility for reshaping the conceptual and practical basis on inter-state security on the Asian countries.

An Asia-centred Century

Some of the main factors indicating a shift of global power and locus of international relations to Asia can be summed up as follows:

- Asia is the region where the fastest economic growth and social-political changes are taking place with obvious consequences and implications for the future. The South-East Asian economic crisis of the late 1990s is behind us, and economics of the two giants of Asia, China and India, have maintained the upward trajectory at impressive levels. Some of the areas of global techno-economic strength (even if not at the frontier edge) like information technology, services and manufacturing sectors are increasingly centred in Asia. Many high-technology US firms now outsource manufacturing to China, India and other Asian countries, with the trend of major corporate players like Motorola and General Electric shifting R&D and design centres to China and India.[3]
- At the same time, Asia also represents the region which contains the most of the poor of the world and least developing countries and regions. While African countries continue to suffer extremely under the burden of poverty and deprivation, the scale of poverty in Asia is overwhelming. India alone has nearly 300 million people living in extreme poverty.
- The region still has extensive unresolved disputes extending from issues of sovereignty to ideological contradictions and conflict which are often constructed on religious extremism. There are new tentative stirrings of effort to define the contours of security. But with the great diversity of circumstances, cultures and national interests, these are confined to defining principles and seeking better understanding and consultation processes rather than forge any military alliances (except those driven by the strategic imperatives

and culture of European-North American powers).[4] Unlike Europe-North America it has not yet been able to evolve a common paradigm of inter-state security beyond an almost idealistic faith in the United Nations.

• The longest wars since 1940 (World War II, Korean War, Vietnam War, Afghanistan War of 1980s which in a way never ended and spilled over into the 21st century itself, Arab-Israeli Wars, Iran-Iraq War etc.) have all impacted extensively on and/or occurred in Asia.

• Eight out of the nine nuclear weapon states are in Asia and the contiguous oceans.[5] The only time nuclear weapons were used in war was in Asia; and most of the nuclear tests have been conducted on Asian soil. The most extensive nuclear and ballistic missile proliferation ever to have taken place has been experienced in and from Asian countries.[6] New information has been emerging that South Korea, Taiwan, Saudi Arabia have considered and acted to an extent to move toward acquisition of nuclear weapons. Japan, in the opinion of experts, could acquire nuclear weapons at short notice, especially if it is faced with increasing nuclear-missile challenge from North Korea even though its own thinking and the existence of US-Japan alliances would keep it non-nuclear.

• This is the region with the largest concentration of military power. China has been embarked on a massive military modernisation with high-technology acquisitions from Russia after 1993, especially in critical areas like air power and space capabilities.[7]

• Asia and the contiguous oceans represent the area with the last known strategic resource-base in the shape of hydrocarbons with inevitable potential for energy faultlines across the continent. World's energy "demand heartland" composed of Japan, Korea, China and India is in Asia where rapid economic growth and industrialisation has been pushing energy needs sky-high. This is also the heartland of the largest emerging markets. The struggle for control and access to hydrocarbon wealth of Asia and its contiguous oceans has been intensifying for the past two decades in consonance with increasing concerns of impending uncertainties in a key area affecting quality of life across the world.[8] By a curious twist of geography, the energy "resource periphery" extending from Siberia, Central Asia, Persian Gulf, and Northern reaches of the Indian Ocean, South China Sea, and East China Sea surrounds the demand heartland. This is the region containing most of the known reserves of oil and natural gas. Future needs and availability of energy resource base are likely to further emphasise the Asia centred world order while enhancing the role of major centres of power. At the same time, energy faultlines between the heartland-periphery and/or resource periphery and the outer world are already shaping a new 21st century "Great Game" of geopolitics for hydrocarbons.

• Asia is home to sustained terrorism, often driven by ethno-religious ideologies. In fact, Afghanistan-Pakistan has represented the epicentre of religious terrorism in the name of Islamic *jihad* impinging across the world for more than two decades.

• Two of the world's three largest narcotics growing and trafficking areas, that is, the Afghanistan-Pakistan region in South Asia and Myanmar-Thailand-Laos "Golden Triangle" in South-East Asia, are in Asia.

• All three countries that the United States designated as constituting the "Axis of Evil" (Iraq, Iran and North Korea) are in Asia. Out of the four significant wars that the United States has conducted since the end of Cold War, three have been in Asia (Gulf War 1991, Afghanistan War 2001-02, and Iraq 2003). It has expanded its strategic and military presence into Asia (in Pakistan, Afghanistan, Central Asia and Iraq besides the GCC countries) in addition to creating a new naval fleet deployed in the Indian Ocean while reducing its military bases and forces abroad.

It is not without reason that the United States had commenced its strategic shift forward into Asia by the end of 1970s. By 1983 it had established the Central Command with jurisdiction covering the Southwest Asia region from Pakistan in the East to Egypt in the West. It had organised and conducted a proxy war against the Soviet intervention in Afghanistan through "Mujahideen" controlled and supported by Pakistan as the "frontline state."

The United States, as a de-facto Asia power, would obviously remain a major key player in an Asia-centred world. But there is increasing congruence of views that given the rise of new centres of power in the past two decades, "in the long run it cannot succeed in forcing its will on the rest of the world."[9] Paul Kennedy had hypothesised in the late 1980s that the United States and the Soviet Union would succumb to the phenomenon of imperial overstretch and China and Japan would replace them in the hierarchy of leading powers.[10] Four years later the Soviet Union proved the thesis right; and the United States as the sole superpower now seems to be overstretched in its unilateralist imperial mould. John Mearsheimer had cautioned that ascent of new rival to American power would start to alter the global strategic balance in a multipolar multipower world.[11]

Immanuel Wallerstein writing in Foreign Policy before the Iraq War may have been overstating when he concluded that the United States supremacy is a superpower that lacks true power and was declining as indeed the title of his article suggests. But the question really was "Will the United States learn to fade quietly, or will US conservatives resist and thereby transform a gradual decline into a rapid dangerous fall?"[12] Iraq War since the article appeared would tend to confirm some of Wallerstein's hypothesis. But the reality is that global power equations are changing, not the least due to the rise of China and India. The issue is a matter of perspective like whether the glass is half full or half empty. But Wallerstein's point that "The real question is not whether US hegemony is waning but whether the United States can devise a way to descend gracefully with minimum damage to the world, and to itself?" really points to the issue of US ability (or willingness) to recognise the changing dynamics of international geopolitical situation. At the same time, how the US responds to the changes taking place would also depend on the actions and attitudes of other countries in the international community.

More recently Niall Ferguson concluded that the United States suffers from three structural deficits: (i) its dependence on foreign capital, (ii) the deficit of troops level, and (iii) its attention deficit.[13] While it must provide the leadership in the emerging decentralising world where 3-4 mega-states would contest for power, influence and resources, this is where the most notable US deficit is. Other observers are arguing that the "US will not be able to maintain the dominant power and influence that it has enjoyed since the collapse of the Soviet Union."[14] This is less due to the decline of the United States' power and more due to the relative rise of other powers.

But in the nearly two years since the launching of the Iraq War, the United States has faced a serious legitimacy problem. As a consequence of this process, its approval ratings have declined in Europe and the Muslim world. And yet it needs the cooperation of both if it has to win the war against terrorism. Under the circumstances the United States is left with no choice but to seek the cooperation of countries outside of Europe (at least other than "Old Europe") and the Muslim world. That is exactly the region where the new centres of power are rising, where, this would lend strength to the increasing multipolarity favoured by China, India and Russia. For example, Next Steps in Strategic Partnership between the United States and India have received impetus from such developments in spite of India's refusal to send troops to Iraq.

Unfortunately, the current signs point toward US inability to win the peace in Iraq. Here lurks a serious problem. Islamic *jihad* came to believe that it had defeated the Soviet Union in the 1980s. And if the Mujahideen could defeat a superpower, so went the sentiment, countries like India and others would not be able to withstand the onslaught of irregular war waged in the name of religion through non-state actors supported by substate institutions like the intelligence agencies. Islamic jihad erupted across the world from Chechnya to Kashmir and all the way to the Philippines finally coming home to the United States. Here lies another complication. Terrorist organisations do not have to win from legitimate governments; they only need to ensure that they are not defeated and that provides them with the perception of victory especially as long as recruits in the name of religion are forthcoming from impoverished feudal societies. Islamic jihad has taken nearly three decades to get to the stage of "nine-eleven;" and it would take fairly long time for it to be rolled back. And the United States needs to work closely with the Asian powers to reverse global terrorism if not defeat it. This is most visible in the quick shift of the Bush administration's attitude toward China from treating it as a rival competitor to a cooperating power.

Rise of China and India

Various studies now clearly indicate that while the United States remains the largest economy in the world, the next three largest economies in PPP terms are China, India and Japan. In 2000 RAND updated its 1995 study and issued a revised report on Asian economic trends and their implications for security taking data as in September 1999.[15]

Based on the empirical study RAND had concluded that the countries were much more likely to adopt attitudes of "caution" and "restraint" rather than that of any bellicosity. Increasing globalisation of economies would inevitably demand greater cooperation rather than conflict among at least the major players who would remain pre-occupied in building their national comprehensive power for the future. The example of Shanghai Five (Six since 2001) to end "three evil forces" that is, terrorism, separatism and extremism in the region is symptomatic. This also highlights another point. While the Asian powers are increasingly engaged in building cooperative peace in the region (like through CICA), the United States appears to engage Asia unilaterally.

More recently, US National Intelligence Council (NIC) concluded in its report on 2020 Project titled "Mapping the Global Future" based on extensive consultations with experts across the world also concluded that a global power shift is taking place from West to East, and this would have acquired much greater definition and salience in the years leading up to 2020 AD.[16] There is a clear emphasis on the rise of China and India way ahead of other powers like Brazil, South Africa and Indonesia, and how this new constellation of powers would impact world affairs in the coming fifteen years. The debate, therefore, is how the main rising powers—China and India—are likely to act, and how others, especially the sole superpower, would react to them? The NIC report inevitably leaves us with more questions than answers. But if the experience of recent years is any indication, then we may conclude that the United States is already finding difficulty in readjustment to the changes (especially the certainties and their visible consequences) taking place.

For example, the unilateralist war on Iraq two years ago ignored the reality that the international opinion, while nearly united in their unhappiness with Saddam Hussein, were not in favour of the war for the reasons put forward forcefully by the US-UK governments. The consequent war without legitimacy (which was forthcoming in the war against Iraq for liberation of Kuwait a decade earlier) continues to dog US policy and stability in the Persian Gulf region. Continuing inability to succeed in Iraq would inevitably erode US power (to lead) and influence further. As it is, the image of unipolarity rests not merely on US power (which is enormous, and would remain a major factor for decades), but also on the reality that the US sits at the head of a conglomeration of nearly three dozen powers allied to it, and these are all developed industrialised countries that ruled most of the world not so long ago and wield considerable power even in their individual capacity. But as we have seen during the Iraq War and its aftermath, fissures among them are visible.

There is little doubt across the world about the rise of China what with its near ten per cent economic growth for two decades. But it is the rise of India, lagging behind China, that now attracts expert attention worldwide. Even at a somewhat more moderate growth rate, China's economy would overtake today's rich countries (barring the USA) like Japan, Germany and the UK by 2015 or so. And India would do so another 5-10 years later. But what the NIC report does not take into account is that in PPP (Purchasing Power Parity) terms, Indian GDP would overtake that of Japan in another two years, and those of the three richest West European countries combined around 2015, and that of the United States another two decades later! Because of huge populations, per capita incomes in China and India would remain far below those of today's rich countries.

India is one of the countries with a high economic growth and has enormous assets, not the least being a large professional military establishment. While it has around 35 per cent people in middle and higher standards of living, it would continue to have a huge population living in poverty. But, with its 272 universities and nearly 14,000 institutions of higher learning producing on an average 4,000 doctorates and 35,000 postgraduates (besides 75,000 students in USA) annually it would also have the world's largest pool of professional workforce. No wonder that 100 out of Fortune 500 companies have already set up high-technology R&D activities to India. The NIC report concludes that India is well placed to be a leader (along with USA and China) in the expected next technological revolution (through convergence of nano-, bio-, information and materials technology).

The central point of the NIC report is that the locus of world's geo-economics and geo-politics (much of it because of energy resources and consumption) is shifting from the traditional trans-Atlantic to Asia-centred framework. As we have seen in the past two decades, the United States has shifted strategically into Asia. This is concurrently taking place, or because of, the rise of China and India, and their greater engagement in South-East and Central Asia. Historically, major changes in international power equations have been accompanied with wars and armed conflict. It is also clear that there would be increased resentments and realignments all the way across the spectrum of capabilities of nations, especially in the developing countries.

The challenge for countries, especially those at the apex of future equations as well those in Asia is how to ensure a peaceful transition to the emerging world order. This can be built only on the principles of cooperative peace and multilateralism which is networked into regional and sub-regional organisations. Great care would have to be taken in helping the United States adjust to the changes rather than launch itself farther on a unilateralist path. This means enhanced engagement with the United States to nudge and even cajole it into playing by commonly acceptable rules. What we are currently witness to is an increasing strategic balance among the major countries of Asia, including the United States and the European Union (with France and Germany at its core) on the basis what may be termed as "multiple bilateral" cooperation often given the label of "strategic partnership."[17]

References

1. Asia here is taken as the continental Asia extending from the Suez Canal in the West to Japan in the East, and from the Russian Federation in the North to include Indonesia in the South along with contiguous oceans rather than the limited definition of Asia adopted by some people (in East Asia and the United States) that limit the region to East of India.

2. For one explanation of the Western alliance's continuation see Ted Hopf, "Post-Cold War Allies: The Illusion of Unipolarity" in Barry Rubin and Thomas Keaney (eds.), *US Allies in a Changing World*, Frank Cass, London, 2001, pp. 28-46.

3. Nayan Chanda, "Offshoring: Don't Fight It," *Far East Economic Review*, March 18, 2004, p. 29. As of 2004, over 132 multinational companies including 100 in the Fortune 500 list have established high technology research and development centres in India.

4. The earliest attempt in dealing with peace and security issues in their broadest terms was the holding of the Asian Relations Conference in March 1947 on the eve of Indian independence and the India-China *Panchsheel* Agreement of 1954. More recent efforts include the ASEAN Regional Forum, the Shanghai Cooperation Organisation, etc. In its 1994 report titled *Toward a New Asia*, an independent Commission for a New Asia defined the vision and principles of social, political and security dimensions for an emergent Asia.

5. China, India, Israel, Pakistan, Russian Federation are physically located in Asia, while the US is militarily present in all aspects, France regularly deploys nuclear forces in Indian Ocean where it has territories. To these must be added the ninth nuclear weapons state, North Korea, which has withdrawn from the NPT and built nuclear weapons.

6. The recent disclosures about Pakistan's supply of nuclear weapons technology, designs and material to North Korea, Iran, Libya and the efforts to supply it to Iraq, while acquiring missile and nuclear technology from China, North Korea and a worldwide network of clandestine suppliers is now public knowledge.

7. *Annual Report on the Military Power of the People's Republic of China*, Report to Congress by Secretary of Defence, US Government, Washington DC, 2002, p. 11.

8. Nearly 51 per cent of the world's crude oil transportation passes through the choke point of the Straits of Hormuz at the mouth of the Persian Gulf.

9. Brantly Womack, "Asymmetry Theory and China's Concept of Multipolarity", *Journal of Contemporary China*, 13 (39) May 2004, pp. 351-366.

10. Paul Kennedy, *The Rise And Fall of the Great Powers*, Random House Inc. New York, 1987.

11. John J. Mearsheimer, *The Tragedy of Great Power Politics*, University of Chicago, Chicago, 2001.

12. Immanuel Wallerstein, "The Eagle has Crash Landed," *Foreign Policy*, July/August 2002, pp. 60-68.

13. Niall Ferguson, "A World Without Power," *Foreign Policy*, July/August 2004.

14. Jonathan Manthorpe, "Three challengers are hot on the heels of US. influence" *Vancouver Sun*, August 27, 2004, p. A15.

15. Charles Wolf, Jr. *Asian Economic Trends and Their Security Implications*, MR-1143-OSD/A, RAND Corporation, Santa Monica, 2000.

16. *Mapping the Global Future*, Report of the National Intelligence Council's 2020 Project, Washington DC, NIC 2004, 13 December 2004.

17. For example, see Sultan Shahin, "India, Japan eye new axis", *Asia Times*, August 24, 2004.

4

Future Architecture of Security in Asia and the Indian Ocean Region

R.R. Sharma

Indian Ocean is the third largest ocean in the world. It is less than half as large as the Pacific Ocean, and somewhat smaller than the Atlantic. It extends from Africa on the west to Australia and Indonesia on the east. Asia lies to the north and Antarctica to the south. It includes the Red Sea, oil rich Persian Gulf, Arabian Sea, the Andaman Sea and the Bay of Bengal. The Indian Ocean region has 56 countries of Asia and Africa within its ambit, out of which 18 are landlocked. These are largely located in West and Central Asia. The ocean provides the most direct shipping route between Europe and Far East. It thus carries over 70 per cent of the world's mercantile traffic.

The great importance of the Indian Ocean Region (IOR) is clearly reflected in its industrial potential. The natural resources of critical importance found in the IOR are now used by industrial countries worldwide. Huge oil reserves are located in the region. Thus the oil tankers account for high proportion of seagoing traffic. Likewise strategic mineral resources, such as tin, titanium and phosphorus are found in the region. The immense economic importance of these resources can hardly be over-emphasized, particularly in the light of the fact that many Asian countries are now surging ahead in the economic and related fields.

The focus of this paper is Asia, which is viewed from the perspective of security and stability. The geographical spread of Asia is indicative of its importance in global affairs. Asia occupies a little more than one-third of the landmass of world's territorial spread. It is populated by more than half of world's homo sapiens. American analysts Crow and Romberg observe: "The qualities that define Asia are enduring; it is huge, diverse, dynamic and, frequently dangerous."[1]

There is a widespread view that twenty-first century belongs to Asia. In the recent times Asia has grown in importance manifold in the global arena. It now plays more assertive role in both regional and global politics. Its economic and strategic environment has been transformed in a fundamental way. A whole host of indicators pinpoint to the emerging reality that Asia is the most dynamic region in the world in the 21st century. Notwithstanding its vastness and diversity, it is moving forward to, that K. Subramanyam calls "Asian security in strategic unity." Significantly, the traditional rivalries among the Asian nations are increasingly becoming muted, though these have not disappeared. A robust geopolitical framework is in the making in Asia.

I would like to particularly emphasize that the economic, political and security situation has undergone a paradigm shift in Asia. The intense ideological battles have receded into the background. While the ideological conflict domain has narrowed down, the challenges of terrorism and religious fundamentalism have moved into the forefront. The events of September 11 have brought about a vast shift in the security concerns. However, the US agenda of the so-called 'war against terrorism' is much broader than merely eliminating the terrorist groups or states. This, and quite a few other developments, has led Asian affairs to dominate the regional and the global politics in the more recent years. Strategic equations, both global and regional, are fast changing, and consequently the salience of world affairs is shifting to Asia. Evidently, there is a growing international discourse on the evolving Asian security dynamics. The special focus is on the role of India and China in promoting security in the region. Of course, the changing role of US military strategy towards the region, particularly in the Indian Ocean Region, and the role of Asian armed forces is also the focus of heated discussion.

Asian Security

What is the future of Asian security? There are only two possible scenarios, which one could visualize. One way to look at it is in terms of opposing or adversarial alliances or balances. The other approach is to look at the emerging Asia enmeshed in a cooperative security regime or arrangements. For this, obvious reference point is the Helsinki process. There are several hypothetical models of opposing axes, such as US-Japan, India-Australia with Vietnam and Indonesia; China-India, Iran and Malaysia; and Russia-China-India. There are a few other similar speculative visions, which ought to be eschewed. However, in the light of what was discussed earlier, the most pragmatic way to look at future is in terms of cooperative security arrangement. This is the only mechanism, which serves India's optimum interests. In fact it serves the interests of all Asian countries. Obviously, the cooperative framework is complex, time consuming and demanding.

Asia has attracted considerable attention primarily on account of its rapid economic growth over the past decades. Of course, China and India are very convincing examples of this trend. More significantly, Asian Economic Community is in the making. The perception of Asian Economic Community is closely related to the new dynamics in Asia and the already existing synergies. While Prime Minister Manmohan Singh hailed it as "arch of advantage," the Japanese Prime Minister termed it "an arch of prosperity." It is broadly accepted that the eventual formation of such a community would ensure enormous advantage and benefits from closer integration. In addition to China and India, the economies of Singapore, Malaysia, South Korea, Taiwan, Thailand and Indonesia have grown at 5-6 per cent in the recent past. Japan has also finally moved out of a decade long recession. While its economy grew at the rate of 2.7 per cent in 2003, its projected rate of growth in 2004-05 is 3.5 per cent. Some estimates put it even higher at 4.4 per cent. Thus, nearly all the major economies in the Asia-Pacific seem to be quite robust. John Major, former British Prime Minister, recently argued that the "economic success of our age is the rise of Asia." Significantly, economic strength brings in its wake, political, military and cultural affinity and influence. It is evident that political authority is "the child of economic success."

Apparently, there is now widespread realization in several Asian countries, including India and China, on the imperative need of a broad overarching framework to consolidate various regional and bilateral initiatives into viable regional regimes. Regionalism and multilateralism under the umbrella of Asian Economic Community, has the potential to exploit the synergies between several Asian countries. Evidently, the socio-economic bonding would ultimately define and consolidate the identity and the security of Asia. The cooperative security framework is thus already evolving despite several roadblocks.

Now let us look at two major Asian Players. Nehru while addressing the Asian Relations Conference had visualized the prospect of 'closer union' of countries bordering on the Indian Ocean both for "defence and trade purposes, a system of defence stretching from the Middle East to South East Asia." He was conscious of the fact that both India and China were destined to play a key role in Asia in the years to come. In geostrategic terms, China is located at the heart of Asia. Some analysts argue, "China defines Asia, there can be no Asia without China."[2] China has obviously burst into far-reaching economic and military prominence. Its growing pre-eminence as an economic and military power in both Asian and global politics is going to be conclusive. Likewise, India forms the core of South Asia. Its geography imparts a vantage position to her in the geopolitics of Asia. It is growing with impressive determination. It is in the "midst of explosion of ambition." It thus adds huge weight to Asian balance. Both are closely linked with ASEAN, ARF and now SCO. A closer interaction between them could lead to stability, peace and security for all. It could also give an impetus to a multi-layered cooperative dialogue. It is, however, not suggested that there is complete mutuality of national interests between the two countries in all respects. The two countries are bound to compete with each other in quite a few areas. The point being made is that the element of competition could be accommodated within the overarching framework. If the two states work together, it could lead to the creation of a positive and cooperative security arrangement on the Asian Continent.

China has assumed a greater and assertive presence in both Indian Ocean and the East China Seas. Because of its growing energy needs, China is strengthening its presence in South China Sea through which vital oil supplies are navigated. It is thus enhancing its military profile in the South China Seas. Several reports suggest that China is seeking strategic agreements with several South and South East Asian countries. At the same time, it is making all out effort to convince the Asian countries that China's rise is not intended to threaten the region. It has conducted several rounds of strategic dialogue with thirteen countries including Russia, US, France, Britain, Germany, India, etc.

Likewise, India has increased its strategic engagement with several countries in the region. It has also signed military oriented agreements with several countries including Singapore, Indonesia, Thailand, etc. It has conducted joint naval and military exercises with China, US, Japan, Russia, and some other Asian neighbours. Its greater economic, military and naval activism is now accepted as a positive contribution to a stable balance of power in Asia. The implications of this engagement for stability in Asia, and more particularly in the Indian Ocean, are obvious from the standpoint of a new security structure.

However, a major hindrance to cooperative framework in Asia is the preponderance of US power. The US military presence in Asia, particularly in Asia Pacific, is organized around the US Pacific Command and US Central Command. The US is rightsizing its forces in Europe, and diverting some of the resources of US Pacific Command to North Indian Ocean. The Indian Ocean is, in fact, re-emerging as a strategic area of concern. The US Pacific Command has at its disposal a fairly large naval and air force component. The new American grand strategy, particularly after 9/11, based on "muscular dominance" has become a major source of insecurity and instability in Asia. Its strategy of military dominance, 'war on terrorism' and 'preemption' is designed to secure and protect primarily American interests. The presence of a major non-Asian power in Asia's security equations is potentially destabilizing. Significantly, the American policies have transformed the strategic space in Asia. As stated earlier, its security arsenal now includes the doctrines of 'hegemony'; 'preemption,' 'war on terror,' and promoting 'democratic values.' Consequently the US has a huge military presence in several regions of Asia. Guided by the neo-conservative politics, the US strategy, apparently, is to set up a system of global governance and force other nations into compliance.[3] In fact the whole of Eurasia, as Brezezinski points out, has consequently emerged as "the principal arena of future power politics."

However, the major question is what sort of US presence in the region is necessary and desirable. Of course, there are several countries in Asia, which regard US as a stabilizing force. The degree to which nations hold this view vary. This view is put across by Japan, Korea, Philippines, etc. The obvious salient issue is not whether the US should maintain its presence in Asia, but how, at what level, and on what conditions. In the best case, the US role in Asia has to be one of stabilizing presence, more than anything else. While the security of the Asian region essentially depends upon the close cooperation between the Asian nations, major global powers have to be involved. Obviously, the US cannot be excluded. It is, however, in the wider interests of US to help maintain the benign security environment in the region. A new look American presence in Asia undergirded by a stronger commitment to Asian regionalism and multilateralism will serve well for many years to come.

India extended its cooperation to the US by jointly patrolling the Malacca Straits during "'Operation Enduring Freedom." It would be even more productive to undertake similar naval operations with several regional powers. This would enhance not only India's regional profile, but also make a positive contribution to the cooperative regional security framework. These kinds of initiatives on the part of India would strengthen confidence-building measures in Asia.

Internal Challenges to Security

Many countries in Asia as well as in the IOR are in search of domestic tranquility. It is largely because a number of these countries are, by and large, politically dysfunctional.

The people in these countries feel that they are left at the margins and excluded. The missing link is the sense of participation. The failure of the leadership is most marked in the key area of governance. The governance is, of course, poor to very poor. Over and above, the political elites in these countries have opted for a kind of facade (authoritarian) democracies, wherein a systematic effort is made to prevent the expression of popular will through institutionalized pluralism. The facade democracies have been imposed from above, and therefore, do not enjoy any legitimacy. In a variety of cases, cooperation of the people is sought through coercive means. This obviously leads to large-scale popular discontent, which gets channelised into destabilizing radical and underground movements. One of the key problems is the total absence of linkages between the people at large and their governments. This is true of nearly all countries in West and Central Asia, the two most volatile regions in Asia. Consequently, the formation of a healthy civil society has been held in check.

Central Asia

There are several critical questions about Central Asia. The Russian withdrawal from Central Asia after the demise of the Soviet Union gave rise to variety of security problems. The region was left without a security manager. Intra-regional feuds and rivalries eroded the possibility of regionwide cooperation and consolidation. The Central Asian Republics had, therefore, to contend with domestic insurgencies, cross-border terrorism, growth of militant Islam, drug and gunrunning etc. The Republics witnessed the emergence of authoritarian regimes, poor governance and extensive corruption. Because of meaningful political security vacuum, the region has gradually emerged as a hot bed of factional and big power rivalries.

The strategic importance of the region grew manifold after September 11. Central Asia, which was for some American analysts "a strategic quicksand, or a mission too far"[4] became mission immediate and urgent. To begin with, the US decided to be "Central Asia's Security manager". Gradually, the Americans outlined their priorities in the region: "Combating terrorism, reform, the rule of law and Caspian Sea energy resources."[5] Colin Powell, the ex-Secretary of State confirmed that Kazakhastan's oil was of critical importance to the US. Military presence in the region is essential for the US to control Caspian Sea energy resources. The US is not the sole player in Central Asia. Other powers have joined the modern "Great Game," and these include Russia, China, Iran, India, Turkey and Pakistan. India's basic interest in the region is two-fold: To gain benign political and economic presence in the region, and secondly, to gain access to vast oil and gas resources of the region.

Central Asia has thus emerged as one of the most important regions in the world. In a way, it is now the focus of global politics. It is strategically placed between Russia, China and Europe. Moreover, it lives in the tough neighbourhood of Afghanistan. The destabilized

Afghanistan has affected the peace and stability of the adjoining countries not only in Central Asia, but also the whole of Central Eurasia. Geography thus ensures the critical importance of the region. Evidently, it has emerged a major factor in the security scenario, both regional as well as global. It is in this kind of a situation that the Shanghai Cooperation Organisation (SCO) was forged to deal with several issues, including the emerging security issues. Apparently, the major objective of SCO is to deepen the cooperation in the economic and security fields. Russia and China are now pushing the Six-nation grouping towards playing a more proactive role in developing a cooperative security framework for the Eurasian region. They are also seeking to elabourate a strategic vision for the Eurasian landmass. The SCO may also be viewed as a security alternative to US military presence in the region. While the SCO is well perceived, it is, however, yet to effectively counter widely spread fundamentalist militancy in the turbulent region.

To sum up, the security and risk management in Asia, including IOR is closely linked to several developments, which are currently in the making. How do these unfold in the years to come—say till 2017—would largely determine the broader security scenario. Then there is a larger element of global structure of power or the configuration of power in the international system. Within this a lot would depend on bilateral politics based on common interests. For example, India's relations with major powers would be determined by the efforts and investments each side is willing to devote to that relationship. India has before her a variety of challenges and opportunities. These are:

1. India should preserve its primacy in South Asia. This needs to be achieved by addressing various irritants within the SAARC. The SAARC is important to the extent that its effective management enhances India's role in other parts of Asia. The so-called "Gujral Doctrine" could be an effective tool.

2. Countries of East and South East Asia are of critical importance to India. The institutional integration with ASEAN is an imperative. We have registered noteworthy progress in this direction. It is here that the Asian economic community is shaping up. Equally important is to build physical connectivity with the countries of the region through Myanmar and Thailand. All other options should be explored. It is not only close economic cooperation, alone which is of critical importance, but also defence, and Security cooperation, which is on the agenda.

3. India took time to develop relations with Central Asia. It is only now that India's engagement with Central Asia has taken a more productive character. This engagement has to be result-oriented. The

energy resources of Central Asia could become a huge input in the energy security of the country. At the political level, India should make every effort to develop closer ties with SCO. The vast improvement in Sino-Indian relations has opened an opportunity to integrate with SCO, as China is not opposed to India's presence in the Six-nation organization. The trilateral cooperation between Russia, China and India provides a basis for the creation of Asian forum. This forum could be progressively enlarged to include countries of South East Asia. Whether, other countries join the forum or not, the advantage of close tripartite consultations and cooperation between Russia, China and India is huge. They have an important obligation to help forge a system of Asian security and cooperation.

India must continue to make greater effort to improve physical connectivity with both Central Asia and South East Asia. Iran is already lending a helping hand in this direction. More possibilities are gradually emerging, and these must be fully exploited. Developing an energy corridor to Central Asia through Pakistan and Afghanistan is no longer a distant possibility. It is emerging as an open option.

These are the obvious opportunities and challenges. However, in the larger context, the substantial threat for security and stability does not come from without, but from the nature of things, i.e., from within. Poor governance and democracy deficit in IOR countries poses a more substantial danger to the security of the region, because these are greatly destabilizing factors. This needs to be seriously examined and addressed. Non-traditional threats to regional security such as ethnic disputes, sectarian strife and rising terrorism constitute a huge risk. These are potentially dangerous areas, which stoke the embers of conflicts, internal dislocations and social unrest. Their effective management is crucial to the overall security issue. Obviously, this is a complex task, which however, cannot be pushed under the carpet.

Notes and References

1. William J. Crow and Alan D. Romberg, "Rethinking Secuiity in the Pacific," in *Foreign Affairs*, Spring 1992.

2. Varun Sahni, "From Security in Asia to Asian Security," in *International Studies*, Vol. 41, No. 3, September 2004.

3. For a comprehensive discussion of new US policy based on the doctrines of 'Pre-emption,' 'Hegemony," etc., see Ivo H. Daalder and James Lindsay, *America Unbound: Bush Revolution in Foreign Policy*, Washington DC, Brookings, 2003.

4. Eugene B. Rumer, "Feshman's Revenge: Central Asia After September 11," in *Strategic Forum*, No. 195, December 2002.

5. *Ibid.*

5

India's Contribution to the Globalised World Peace

Brig. Chandra B. Khanduri

One of the major developments of the past six decades following the World War was the realisation by most parts of the world, which may be called the eternal *Vedantic* truth that highlights *Vasudev Kutumbakam*, namely, the concept, 'world is one family'. It conveys the human concern for global welfare that transcends regional, national and individualised interests towards common betterment. It involves, inevitably, the security of the world from dangers that continue to haunt our lives, our planet and the human race.

It also involves security from natural disasters. So does it encompass the environmental degradation and ecological imbalance—both caused by the human avarice and greed for exploitation of nature, such as excessive carbon emission and depletion of the Ozone layer, damming the rivers, over-utilization of subsoil level or simply pollution that effects biodiversity. Increase in global population, poverty and wide differences among the 'haves' and 'have nots', have equally contributed to the man-made disasters. Additionally, there have been—and there continue several wars and conflicts, including acts of terrorism, which have larger ramifications for the overall health of the mankind.

Wars, as one analyses, have a cyclic pattern of occurrence. They have been fought in the mythical Satya Yuga—the fabled periods of righteous—and the so-called golden period of human history. In modern times there have been two so-called 'great wars' fought in the twentieth century itself. Then there have been others that could invite global participation as well as reparation but for the useful intervention of the international institutions and able statesmen that somehow keep appearing in the world—somewhere somehow. Korea, the Balkans, the Middle East, the Indian Sub-continent, Asia, besides Africa (with its ever increasing feuds and skirmishes) have been constant battlefields. Territorial disputes, the so-called historical redressals, ethnic cleanising involving genocide such as in the Balkans and Central Africa, exploitations and aberrations of judgments, have all added to the larger cause of these unending conflicts.

Wars—and reflections on their cause and consequence—also often bring in sanity and perhaps wisdom to the erring world. It happened in 1945 immediately after the Second World War that took more than 10 million lives and took the human civilization back to the brink of a precipice, when the right thinking people and institutions agreed to frame the charter of a United Nations Organisation. It could serve as a common forum for resolution of conflicts, disaster management besides alleviating economic degradations, poverty and removal of illiteracy. With the march of time since its inception, the UNO has grown into a truly large body and continues to do so with its membership encompassing some 191 countries from a mere 40 of 1945.

Essential to the UN Charter is the role of peace keeping. It entails the creation of a UN Peace Keeping Organisation with the tasks of Peace Keeping and Peace Making. UN Peace Keeping Operations (UNPKO) are, essentially, provisional measures to prevent a conflict growing into an all out war. It euphemistically prevents a breach in a dam from bursting into a flooding disaster. But the fact of the matter is that while Peace Keeping may stop the hostility through timely intervention, finding suitable and lasting political solution can only be achieved by total resolution of a problem that caused the conflict. Peace Keeping operations, therefore, are designed to promote peace and create adequate climate for goodwill for negotiations to start. This process of creating conditions conducive to political parleys and final settlement of the cause of the conflict is the process of Peace Making that follows Peace Keeping and hence the Peace Keeping and Peace Making are not only intrinsically interrelated but are vital to the overall role of the UN PKO.

The UN PKO takes into account both the minimum military action and the civic action that must follow. The UN PKO, therefore, has both the force level from the volunteer member countries that, as a matter of working principle, is to be selected from countries within the geographical area of the conflict. In practice however, it has not always been followed. The choice invariably falls on the countries, generally neutral (or being non-aligned) to the conflict and with proven ability for effective operations. The civilian component is supportive in logistics and civic actions and is drawn from countries willing to provide experts in logistics.

Learning wisely from the way the world got divided into the two Cold War blocks—the American-led Western countries and the Soviet-led Eastern Block, the Indian Government of the early years moulded its foreign policy on 'Non-Alignment' and the exalted idea of the 'Panchsheel', the five principles that epitomised non-involvement in others' internal affairs while maintaining mutually friendly and cooperative overtures. It forfeited violence and shunned wars and advocated with all sincerity, a policy of peace, non-interference and mutual benefit without aligning with either of the military blocks. India thus made itself an ideal member country to undertake UN PKOs.

Ironically, however, despite its grand charter and noble aspirations, UNO could not keep the world free of wars and conflicts. The Cold War warriors played not only their power games but also skillfully utilised their great secret weapon—the VETO—they had self-awarded at the time of formation of the Security Council. As a result, the world has been witness to 'unilateralism' such as Anglo-French intervention in the Suez, US intervention in Vietnam, (and now in Iraq); Israeli intervention in the Sinai and Gaza; and later in Lebanon; The Russian intervention in Hungary and later in Afghanistan, Vietnamese intervention in Kampuchea; Chinese intervention in Tibet and India and later in Vietnam; Libya's intervention in Chad; Turkey's intervention in Cyprus, Tanzania's intervention in Uganda, and so on.

The Cold War and its nuances also affected India in its formative years very intimately. Until the end of this futile war that ensued an arms race, India had to manage its difficult relations with its hostile neighbours—Pakistan and China—the former having joined a series of Western sponsored military pacts and the latter having invaded and subjugated Tibet began to expand into the Indian borders menacingly. India, restraining itself, still doggedly followed its policy of Non-Alignment. Having proved its credentials through the testing times, now it is in a position to discourage the world from following the doctrine of 'balance of power' and creating 'spheres of influence' that impinge on others' sovereignty and territorial integrity.

India has admirably fulfilled its PKOs obligations throughout these difficult years. Unfortunately in India the degree of awareness of India's role in UN is rather low. According to a UN survey, only 32 per cent of educated Indians are aware of the activities of the UN; this number falls still below 20 per cent when it comes to specifics of Peace Keeping.

India's Contributions to the UN Peace Keeping Operations

Chairman Neutral Nations Repatriation Commission in Korea 1953-54. The Korean War of 1950-53 had resulted not only in a very large number of battlefield casualties in dead and disabled but also over some 400,000 POWs had been captured by both the sides. Of these over 22,000 POWs refused to be repatriated to countries of their own origin. That began to hinder the process of the Armistice. To tide over the imbroglio, India was asked to become the Chairman of a NNRC to help repatriate these unfortunate prisoners. India agreed to act as Chairman of the Commission with four other members—two each from the Communist Block and two from the Western. India also provided a Custodial or Custodian Force of some 10,000 officers and men of the Indian Army to help supervise the repatriation over a period of over 5 to 6 months. Lieutenant General KS Thimayya, the distinguished and eminent General of the Indian Army headed the NNRC and completed, what President Eisenhower called, an 'impossible task'. Korea pioneered the long list of success story of the Indian contribution to the cause of the global peace. Earlier the country had sent a Para Field Ambulance to reinforce the Red Cross medical support during the war, which operated in the battle zones of Korea.

Chairman of the International Supervisory Commission in Indo-China. Following the French defeat at Dien Bien Phu to the Vietnamese guerillas under General Giap in early 1954, and their withdrawal, Indo-China (or precisely Vietnam in particular and Cambodia in general) became a region of unparalleled turmoil. A Geneva Meeting followed and an international supervisory commission was set up under the auspices of the UN. India was again nominated as the Chairman. In this capacity India continued to help the UN to supervise the truce and its violation even during the Vietnamese war of 1966-73 when the US employed its full force. Finally however, the US withdrew its forces abandoning its ally, South Vietnam in a lurch. An eventual reunification of Vietnams (and its independence) followed in 1974. The Commission wound up, but left deep imprints of its impartiality and efficiency.

Congo—The Real Testing Ground of UN's Use of Force to Unite a Country. The Congo (Belgian Congo; sometimes known as Zaire) was reduced to a country where civil war followed its independence in 1960. While its Army Nationale Conglais (ANC) mutinied, its provinces of Kasai and Katanga seceded in next few months. When the UN agreed to intervene in 1961, while Kasai rejoined, Katanga, under a rebel leader, Moise Tsombe, obdurately clung to his decision to break away from the main country. In this design the Belgians and some of the western powers were supporting him surreptitiously. In the circumstance the Security Council authorised the creation of a large military force under the UN that was called Organisation de Nations Unies au Congo (ONUC). As the situation continued to deteriorate, the Security Council authorised use of force by it with a view to "prevent civil war in the Congo". It happened on February 21, 1961, when a brigade group of the Indian Army was ordered to join the 12,000 strong ONUC that included a brigade from Ethiopia, and Sweden besides units from all over the world.

It was a very difficult task from the outset; for, although the ONUC had the mandate to use force, it did not turn out to be straight military operations. The Cold War made ONUC's role extremely hazardous besides being one of 'walking on a tight rope'. Fighting broke out from July but more seriously from September 1961. During the first phase of operations in September, it appeared that the Katangese Gandarmerie fully supported by thousands of mercenaries seemed to have cornered the ill-prepared ONUC. Three months later fighting again broke out with full fury but the Indian Brigade along with the other ONUC troops helped re-establish its authority in the province and made the Katangese authorities see sense to abandon the path of violence and secession. The December war that lasted over two weeks could well be qualified as Peace Making Operations. For, a process of negotiations began between the Governments of Tsombe and the Central Government at Leopoldville. Hopes for reconciliation brightened up although the uncanny ways of Tsombe could hardly be predicted.

Situation, however, remained one of *'comsi-comsa'*, as the French would humorously call a state of confusion and uncertainty. By 1962, the ONUC also reorganised itself. And all the ONUC forces in Katanga came under the operational command of Major General D. Prem Chand of India with full authority to tackle any situation that might emerge.

Tsombe and his supporters chose to ignore the efforts for reconciliation and by end 1962 were again threatening the very presence of the ONUC. Military operations became necessary and a fortnight long operations (operation UNOKAT) in December 1962 saw the end of the Katangese rebellion; and a yearlong consolidation that followed, its demise.

Congo, where the Indian Contingent played a heroic and strategic role as part of the ONUC, has many lessons to offer in Peace Keeping and Peace Making. And it is the only case where the UN applied its ability to the fullest measure to unify a country torn by civil strife and secession. It was also one of the most expensive UNPKOs that not only caused large UN casualties (where the Indian brigade groups that fought full military operations in 1961 and 1962 suffered some 50 casualties), but the death of Dag Hammrskjold, the Secretary General. It was also here, where, true to the tradition of the Indian Army, Captain G.S. Salaria, of the Gorkhas earned posthumously a *Param Vir Chakra*—the highest war gallantry fighting for the cause of peace. The brilliant role the Indian force played won praise and an accolade unparalleled so far.

Cyprus—A Touchstone of Superior Generalship. Cyprus became a member of the UNO at the time of its independence in August 1960. It had a very chequered history as it was, but its story was further compounded by three powers breathing up its neck all the time. Turkey, Greece and UK, which always had something about its past life, continued to keep it in their control and check. They compelled it to sign agreements—which were later embodied into treaties—Treaty of Establishment, Treaty of Guarantee and Treaty of Alliance. These treaties recognised distinction between the Turkish Cypriots and the Greek Cypriots who shared the overall population at a ratio of 18 to 80. In addition both Greece and Turkey maintained their military garrisons there and the UK retained two military bases. And the Greek and the Turkish forces were allowed to maintain a minimum strength of 960 and 600 military establishments on the Island. Additionally, it is often said that Cyprus is the only country that flies more flags than its own. In fact, it flies four flags! And shares equal number of loyalties.

As if this was not sufficient, the Constitution allowed a Greek Cypriot President and a Turkish Vice President, both equipped with veto which ensured that anything that one side thought of implementing was regarded as treading on other's rights and obligations and could be nipped in the bud. Soon, therefore, tension built up that led to the Turkish brigade and the Greek battalion to redeploy. A situation of civil war developed and the treaty members imposed their joint force including creating a "Green Line" that separated the two warring communities. Developments moved fast and by March 1964 the Secretary General created a UN force for Cyprus or UNFICYP with its overall command being vested, as an interim measure, in Lieutenant General P.S. Gyani of India.

The contingents came from Austria, Canada, Finland, Ireland, Sweden and UK. Police detachments opted from Australia, Denmark, Austria, New Zealand and Sweden. By August 1964 the strength of the UNFICYP rose to over 6000. Tension and anxiety grew as both the Greek and Turkish establishments began a free for all campaign and often clashed with the troops of the UNFICYP. That was the position in July 1964 when General Thimayya (Timmy, as he was popularly known all over the world and who had already created history of success in Korea) took over from Gyani as Force Commander. Timmy wanted an unhindered movement of the UN force and returning to barracks of both the Turkish force and the Greek one. It was a battle that carried on until end of his life in December 1965, but the UNFICYP achieved its freedom of movement in the whole of the Island.

Timmy's first task was to redeploy the UN force in accordance with the intensity of the armed confrontation and facilitate ease of UN force to intervene. He also placed his own force in observation role on the 'Green Line'—the earlier ceasefire line with a view to interpose it between the opposing sides. Observation squads with mobile patrols were regularly deployed in the potential troubled areas. He also evolved the Guiding Principles for the UNFICYP, which the Secretary General, U Thant, announced in the Security Council in September 1964. It embodied, 'complete impartiality towards the Greek and Turkish communities', 'maintenance and restoration of law and order', 'that self-defence included the defence of UN posts, vehicles, premises under attack,' 'using minimum force', 'maintenance of close liaison with the Government and other agencies'. It was unambiguous in its final task that enumerated: "If despite its precautionary measures shooting incidents still occur, and the force has to intervene immediately, all endeavours shall be made to end fighting by persuasion and negotiations. In each case thorough investigation will be carried... and frequent patrolling will be carried out for safety on roads and towns and villages in sensitive areas". Constructive Peace Keeping was the new concept that Timmy devised which saw inflammatory situations controlled firmly and expeditiously.

The Indian Force Commander was seeking to achieve the objective of the UN by peaceful means and without resorting to armed force, the use of force only being done in self-defence. But despite these efforts and the appeals, fighting continued. The Secretary General would emphasise that "the UNFICYP was sent to Cyprus to try and save lives by preventing recurrence of fighting. It would be incongruous, even a little insane, for the force to set to killing Cypriots, whether Greek or Turkish; the aim was and remains, to prevent them from killing each other."

Timmy set to control situation so that by beginning 1965 the UN Security Council was eulogizing his "wonderful achievement in situation extraordinary". Timmy had developed the confidence in UNFICYP's capability to enforce peace and generate trust in the UNFICYP of both the feuding communities and the interested countries. Great hopes were being built for the possible detente between the two Cypriots and their mentors. Mediation looked a certainty. It was a return to the normal condition by mid-December 1965. Unfortunately, however, he died on December 18, leaving a void, which could not be filled.

The UN was so thoroughly and deeply impressed with the Indian General's contribution that it began to look for another Indian. And it found it in Major General D Prem Chand who had made good impression in the Congo by presiding over the integration of Katanga with the main country. During his long tenure from 1969 to 1976 he would handle one of the most difficult situations that was thrown up by the *coup d'etat* and the Turkish intervention of July 1974 and the fighting that carried on between the Turkish and Greek forces including by the Cypriots. Prem Chand enforced the UNFICYP positions in and around the Nicosia airport, evacuated the foreign missions of various countries to the British base of Dhekelia and continued to undertake humanitarian missions besides trying to restore peace. He was successful in achieving the conflict control UNFICYP's main task, which he fulfilled for seven years—a record by all counts.

The three Indian Force Commanders—PS Gyani, Timmy and Prem Chand—did yeomen's service to the Peace Keeping in Cyprus. Gyani laid the foundation; Timmy created, what UN Secretary General, U Thant called, "an aura of his strong and forceful personality in maintaining peace and harmony in Cyprus". Prem Chand created a "lasting sincere impression" as his friends and staff termed it. All three added to the cause of global peace and did India proud.

If the Servicemen added laurels to India's efforts at Peace Keeping, so did the civilians. Rajeshwar Dayal, BN Chakraburty,

Chinmaya Gharekhan, Vijay Nambiar were such Indians who became expert mediators in Africa and the Middle East—the real areas of conflicts, as Permanent Member India.

No Full Stop

India continues to contribute to the conflict resolution and global peace. It has provided contingents for the UN PKOs in Palestine, Lebanon and Gaza—the strife torn Middle East—from mid-1950s. Its troops have demined (the mined proverbial 'killing fields') of Kampuchea. It has provided observers in Yemen, Iran-Iraq border. India provided the main component of the UN Transitional Assistance Group (UNTAG) in Namibia from 1977 to 1990. Prem Chand was again there. In Cambodia an advance mission was established in 1991 that was followed by Transitional Authority. In less than three years, democracy set in. It became a big success story to which India's contribution was no less.

Angola (1988) and Mozambique (1993) were two verification missions designed to demobilise foreign troops and internal resistance movements in these two countries. India sent troops to these countries who successfully completed the missions. It was then that Boutros Boutros Ghali, the UN Secretary General acknowledged, the "superior training", "high standard of discipline" that made "Indian contributions more significant".

The Somalian Forays

From early 1990s Somalia became a matter of concern to the UNO. Poor governance culminated in the overthrow of President Barre (pro: Barey) and emergence of warlords Major General Aideed and Ali Mehdi. It led to a civil war and while chaos spread, the country also became an arms bazaar, where arms exporters pumped in more than 5 million rifles and small arms. Famine, internecine fighting, the 1991 Gulf War in Iraq, all led to compounding the Somaliland situation. Efforts were made to send supply reliefs and later by early 1992 as the UN pushed in some 500 troops to open the Mogadishu airport to receive humanitarian aid, UN Operations in Somalia called UNOSOM, began to control the situation.

Interestingly, the American President George Bush (Senior) agreed to send a 37,000 strong US Task Force to Somalia, as did Pakistan make available a battalion of 500 personnel. Some force was also built up from the African countries like Zimbabwe, besides India sending a brigade group. By June 1993, the Americans and the rest of the UN had a bad taste of peace keeping, when in a skirmish, Pakistan lost 24 killed, Americans lost 18 killed and 72 wounded, besides the Zimbabwean losing a post and the Indian casualties rising to 10. Following this action the Americans decided to pull back their contingent leaving others to handle whatever they could. Kofi Annan, the then UN Chief Peace Keeper in Somalia, (and now Secretary General) saw the "most powerful and equipped" Americans as the "weakest link in peace keeping". The Indian brigade, however, continued to complete its role until the end of 1993 and did well.

Rwanda became a case of callous disregard of human rights by the major powers of the world specially USA who turned a deaf ear to the sufferings and the genocide that prevailed in the country in April 1993. This happened during the black one hundred days, when Hutus massacred nearly one million Tutsis.

UNOPROFOR TOO

The 'balkanization' of Yugoslavia resulted in the establishment of UNOPROFOR with the tasks of mediating and maintaining peace. India sent no troops to the UN Protection Force in former Yugoslavia although it did make available Lieutenant General S. Nambiar as Force Commander. In this totally European command, reluctance by the troops to fulfill their basic responsibility led to serious differences. Nambiar admitted their difficulty if not 'failure to forge a sense of solidarity and a sense of dedication'. And finally tendered his resignation. The situation in Kosovo, despite a large NATO force, defied any solution. In fact, violence has resurged in the area and it would be several decades before a lasting solution is found to the problem.

Sierra Leone and Other Experiments

India played a constructive role in Sierra Leone too where it had a reasonable Indian force along with other international force under the force commander, Major General V. Jetley. Here too the Indian contingent became victim of various impediments orchestrated by the interested parties of the majority African force.

In this diamond rich, bitterly divided country which was fully exploited by foreign powers, a part of the Indian contingent had to be rescued by a full mission launched by the Indian Armed Forces from bases in India.

India provided officers to the international force that restored security in East Timor (Timor-Lest) and help the Transitional Government. Missions have been sent to Eritrea, Congo in 1990s and they have done well. In the Democratic Republic of the Congo, as

Zaire rechristened it from 1990s, Indian officers forming part of (the new acronym,) MONUC, UNO Mission in the Democratic Republic of the Congo have been helping the country control its strifetorn Eastern Congo since 1999.

India has thus far contributed nearly 100,000 Armed Forces personnel and civilians for the Peace Keeping Operations and have, more than adequately, done its role, while it continues to show willingness to undertake any other future tasks. It is this policy of the various governments of the day and unhesitating acceptance by its officers and men of the role involved that has kept the 'Peace Keeping' spirit going.

It is this spirit that made Javier Perez de Cuellar, UN Secretary General write in his 1982 report: "Peace Keeping has generally been considered to be the most successful innovation of the United Nations, and certainly their record over the years is one of which to be proud." He added, "They have proved to be most useful instrument of de-escalation and conflict control into the field in a unique way... they (have) traditionally shown an admirable degree of courage, objectivity and impartiality..." To this credit card, the role of the Indian Armed Forces has been pre-eminent.

In India that spirit is now being given shape in the Centre for UN Studies as part of the United Services Institute, New Delhi, and the Army Headquarters' Additional Directorate for Staff Duties, both of which undertake mission analysis, training and help earmarking several units, formation headquarters and individuals for the missions. A marked degree of expertise has thus been developed in the UN operations—their training and preparations. As a result, Indian officers and their training teams have had exchanges with their counterparts all over the world.

What of Future?

Those involved in planning and execution of India's UN missions for Peace Keeping have always felt the need to earmark sufficient force level (one to two brigade groups) for emergency tasks that the Secretary General may be asked by the UN Security Council to undertake in any part of the world. This proposal has its merit, but is yet to be approved although exceptions are being accepted in Africa, where regional brigades are under formation under the 'African Standby Force'. Worked on the initiative of the regional organisations such cooperative arrangements do exist with regional and international security arrangements. These, for example, include ECOWAS (the

Economic Community of West African States) in Sierra Leone, Commonwealth of Independent States in Georgia, UNMIBH in Bosnia and Herzegovina, UNMK in Kosovo working in tandem with NATO, the EU and the Organisation for Cooperation and Security in Europe, and the NATO-led International Security Assistance Force, located in Afghanistan, is closely working with the UN's political support mission. It is quite probable, therefore, that the Indian view may find its acceptance in due course.

By the autumn of 2004 UN Peace Keeping is managing some 15 field operations including one political (Afghanistan) with prospects of half a dozen more awaiting clearance. With this, its uniformed Peace Keepers' strength is expected to shoot up to some 80,000 from the present 51,000, that would include some 25,000 civilians and military observers. It is, therefore, natural that UN's present budget of $ 4 billion would almost double up. It would be interesting to observe how the UNO finds ways and means to raise funds for those inescapable security UNPKOs especially when Anglo-American forces are deeply involved in Iraq, oil prices continue to rise and the major donors find themselves in difficult economic conditions.

In a new study recently completed under the order of UN Secretary General which is themed as "'More Secured World—Our Shared Responsibility", the high power panel of experts have suggested far reaching changes to the structure and functioning of the UN. Primarily these allude to the threats that emanate from situations which cause wars and conflicts and inter-state wars, besides such constant factors as poverty, degradations, including environment, nuclear, biological, chemical and radiological threats. Terrorism, which is identified as the major threat of 21st century has also been given adequate emphasis besides the transnational crimes. Two models have also been suggested for restructuring the United Nations Security Council with a maximum members of 24. Whether all the recommendations of the panel are accepted or not, it is however, a milestone to the future restructuring of 58 year old UNO.

Conclusion

'Constructive Peace' and 'Preventive Diplomacy' are the two new slogans of the UN Peace Keeping—Peace Making operations of the 21st century. But there continue to occur flagrant violations of the UN charter by some of the countries, principally by the Anglo-American block, who are perpetuating what is jocularly called, 'dollar imperialism'. The invasion of Iraq in 2003 is one example. In such a case, the UN has stood as a helpless observer. With the developments in Iraq, it is hoped that these countries would realise, sooner than later, the usefulness of the UN even in settling the differences. In fact, they are now pleading to the Secretary General to do so. There are nonetheless, common grounds and common problems that can only be combated jointedly and unitedly. Alleviation of poverty, control of burgeoning population, a new common enemy in terrorism that often looks like the proverbial clash of civilizations, eco-degradations, nuclear proliferation, continuing conflicts distinctly make the UNO indispensable.

While all other issues listed are, indeed, worthy of priority, international terrorism heads the list. It was with this heightened concern in mind that on October 8, 2004 the UN Security Council unanimously adopted resolution on 'global anti-terrorism' as an enemy of the human kind, and asked every member nation to affirm its full support to its charter both in precepts and principles and, indeed, in practice. It is hoped that all the affected countries, such as India and Pakistan, Israel and Palestine etc. would pool their resources to fight regional and global terrorism. And India would show the way to it.

It will be naïve to conclude that India's Peace Keeping operations have been without problems and glitches. As Chairman NNRC, Korea, General Thimayya faced uphill task that he handled with ever increasing local tensions and the tensions created by the Cold War warriors. But his own principled and unwavering approach to the problem of repatriation of the POWs, the support from the Indian Government and the UN Secretary General saw him wade through the quagmire. It did not stop there. Both Nambiar and Jetley faced almost insurmountable problems in their missions.

In the Congo in 1962, Prem Chand was asked to terminate his offensive against the Katangese Gendarmerie operating in the Kolweizi area when the success of the entire UNOKAT operations hinged on the success of this phase. Under international pressure, the Secretary General dispatched Ralph Bunche, his personal emissary, to stop the offensive, which, if obeyed by him (Prem) would have served the Gendarmerie yet another day and prevented the Katangese reunification with the Congo – the overall aim of ONUC. Prem decided to 'disobey' it. It helped the UN cause, but he was branded as raising a 'General's mutiny'!

Similarly difficulties have been faced by the contingents that have kept the fragile peace in the Middle East, Somalia and indeed, Sierra

Leone. Nonetheless, it is hoped that India would continue to act as vanguard in the globalised peace keeping, as it has always done even at the cost of denuding its own frontiers—as, for instance, happened in 1961 when India provided a brigade group for ONUC.

End Notes

1. It would be fallacious to include the operations of the Indian Peace Keeping Force (IPKF) in Sri Lanka in 1987-1990 as UN Peace Keeping. It was a bilateral arrangement where approximately 70,000 Indian troops and civilians were committed to help control the insurgency in Sri Lanka, begun by the LTTE. That, the mission of the IPKF was akin to that of the UN Peace Keepers is an altogether different issue.

2. For the first time the UNO has been able to define Terrorism. The anti-terror resolution adopted on October 8, 2004 declared "all acts of violence against civilians unjustifiable by any political, ideological, racial, ethnic or religious considerations". It urged all the 191 members to begin a war against terror.

3. The UN Peace Keeping forces are lightly equipped and hence are capable of using force only in self-defence. In dangerous and complex situations, however, UN Security Council has mandated it through Chapter VII "to adopt robust posture with weaponry that creates deterrent effect", "to use all necessary means" to protect civilian lives in their immediate vicinity and prevent violence against the UN personnel. While full use was made of it in the Congo in 1960-64, in Somalia ineffectively; even now the UN missions in the Congo, Liberia, Sierra Leone, Kosovo, Timor-Lest and Cote d'Ivoire operate under Chapter VII. Even the November-December UN deliberations on terrorism attempted to emphasise the need.

4. As to the degree of awareness of the UNO and its activities, despite the fact the UN spends approximately $ 100 million in India and it is one of the ever ready nations to contribute to UNPKOs, is low. Compare Indian's awareness (32 pc) with 61 pc of Brazilians, 71 pc of Kenyans, 91 pc of Austrians and 95 pc of the US citizens. Even among the Services the awareness level is just about 40 pc.

5. The UN has been trying to debate and enlarge the scope and membership of the Security Council. In November-December 2004 it worked on the possibility of increasing the number by nineteen members ironically without the right to Veto.

6

India and the Indian Ocean

Prof. K.R. Singh

India's policy in the Indian Ocean is a reflection of its broader maritime policy both in the field of national development as also in national defence. Following four themes need to be highlighted:

1. National development and maritime policy.
2. National security, maritime dimensions.
3. Projections for the future
4. Policy options.

National Development and Maritime Policy

Constraints of geography and bilateral relations have combined to deny India its land corridors. Sea routes have, therefore, opened the door to its economic development. It is best illustrated by the growth in Indian shipping and related infrastructure as also effort at exploitation of the living and non-living resources of the sea.

Shipping

1951 : 3.72 lakhs gross registered tonnage (GRT); 2004 – 77.40 lakh GRT, with 659 ships of various types. They earned/saved Rs. 7782 crore in foreign exchange in 2004.

Shipyards

2002 : 9 shipyards in public sector and 21 shipyards in private sector. Also, several large dry docks and other repair facilities along the coast.

Port/Harbours

Eve of independence : 3-4 major ports. By 2002, 12 major ports and 184 intermediate and minor ports.

1951 : Ports handled 20 million tons (mt of cargo)

2004-29 mt

Coastal Traffic: 7516 km long coastline, 1985 – tonnage of coastal shipping was 3.12 lakh GRT; 2004 – 8.00 lakh GRT.

Exploitation of Marine Resources

Living/Fishery

1950-51—marine fish catch was 5.34 lakh tons.

2004—28.34 lakh tons.

2002-03—Marine food export worth Rs. 6881.31 crore.

Fishery Harbours

2004—6 major and 33 minor fishery harbours and 130 fish landing sites in operation.

Non-Living Resources

Oil and Gas—About 70 per cent of India's crude oil production is from its offshore oil fields. More offshore oil and gas fields are being found in India's continental-shelf.

Manganese Nodules

India acquired the status of pioneer investor in 1987. It also acquired an area of 75,000 sq km of deep seabed in central Indian Ocean for the exploitation of these nodules in future.

National Security, Maritime Dimension

History of the past 500 years tells us that since India's rulers did not command the high seas, they lost to maritime colonisers from Europe. Today, similar threat is being posed by NATO powers and their allies.

India's efforts to acquire the capability to protect itself from threats across the seas were slow but steady. Its colonial masters were reluctant to pass on their maritime expertise to India. India continued to depend upon Britain for the warships, training and naval experts, Chief of Naval Staff of India till 1957 was a Britisher. Indian Navy was treated as an adjunct of the Commonwealth navy.

Turning Point 1964-65: Three main reasons:

1. British decision to concentrate upon NATO commitment in the Atlantic and the North Sea, and decision to withdraw from east of Suez.

2. Willingness of USSR to transfer modern weapons in large number and at easy financial terms, and

3. Indian Navy's lack luster performance during Indo-Pak conflicts of 1965.

The cumulative effect was that India was forced to develop its Navy by using British and Soviet equipment.

Second Turning Point, 1971

1. 1971 operations vindicated the strategic rule of the Indian Navy.

2. Strategic implications of the dispatch of US taskforce led by USS Enterprise during the Bangladesh operations in December 1971.

3. These developments coincided with the General Assembly's resolution 2832 of December 16, 1971 that declared Indian Ocean as a peace zone. These developments helped India to reorient its maritime/ naval perspective from the narrow focus of Pakistan to Indian Ocean *per se*.

Charges of Hegemonism

Rapid growth of Indian Navy due to the induction of submarines, missile armed destroyers and long-range maritime reconnaissance and anti-submarine warfare aircraft, mostly from USSR, was perceived by some Western powers and their regional allies as capable of posing a threat to their line of communication in the Indian Ocean. It was ironic that the Western powers that were increasing their interventionist capability in Indian Ocean should accuse India of having hegemonic designs in its own waters.

That perception changed after the end of the Cold War; more so after the disintegration of USSR and the removal of the Soviet/Russian Navy from the region. India began to be evaluated by great powers as a major regional power in its own right. That provided the necessary input for improving bilateral ties with great powers and build structures of maritime corporation at regional level.

Projections for the Future

Economic

With globalisation, India's overseas trade and hence its shipping, port facilities etc. will expand. India will also continue to enhance its capability to exploit living and non-living resources from the seas. India's new thrust upon improving its economic cooperation at regional level will lead to better mechanism to encourage intra-regional trade as also related maritime security. Energy security will also continue to be of prime importance for India's maritime policy.

Socio-political

Rising tide of radical Islam as an instrument of confronting local regimes as also great powers in India's neighbourhood will pose ideological challenges to India's own policy of secularism and related liberal democratic values. It will also have broader security implications for India in the Indian Ocean region.

Challenges to India's Maritime Security are posed by two sets of actors: state actors and non-state actors. Threats from non-state actors are best addressed by strengthening maritime dimensions of homeland security and by coordinating the roles of the Navy, the Coast Guard, other central government agencies like the customs and the port authorities, as also the security apparatus at the state level. Proposal to form state-level marine police was long overdue. For more fruitful results India will need to coordinate activities at regional level especially with states in South-East Asia as also island republics like Sri Lanka, Maldives, Mauritius and Seychelles.

Among the state actors three deserve greater attention; Pakistan, China and some NATO members and their allies.

Pakistan is a long-term adversary. The focus has, however, shifted to managing LIC and possible nuclear confrontation. Pakistan unless heavily rearmed by its NATO and non-NATO allies, can pose only a limited naval threat to India.

China is seen by many in India as a potential adversary in the Indian Ocean. It already has close politico-military links with Myanmar, Bangladesh, Sri Lanka, Pakistan and Iran, China has long-term energy security interests in the region. Will China seek strategic cooperation with India or will it confront India? Cooperation with India will help cement relations between China, India and Russia. Policy of antagonism will push India into NATO camp. In all probability, China will prefer cooperative relationship with India in the Indian Ocean.

India's policy in the context of NATO's growing interventionist capability needs to be taken seriously. NATO partners and their allies have already intervened thrice in India's neighbourhood. That has seriously destabilized India's neighbourhood. Can India join NATO without compromising its policy of non-alignment? Such a policy will also undermine its historical friendly ties with regional powers.

Policy Options

1. Multi-lateralist option is preferable. To strengthen that option India needs to reactivise NAM as also General Assembly of the UN where the South can play a meaningful role.

2. Build bridges of bilateral and multilateral cooperation with other littoral states of the Indian Ocean so as to give a maritime dimension to its foreign policy.

3. Seek to evolve coalition based upon interests vis-a-vis great powers, without sacrificing India's basic national interests.

4. Retain and if possible enhance India's overall maritime capabilities both in the field of development and defence so as to enable it to play an autonomous role vis-a-vis great powers.

Pursuing such a policy will enable India to emerge as the center piece of regional cooperation in the Indian Ocean. That will also enable it to play a meaningful role vis-a-vis great powers. Such a vision will also give a sense of direction of India's maritime strategy in the years to come.

7

International Terrorism and India

Ashwini Kumar

Terrorism it appears has found a permanent place on the International political scene—and International terrorism though less in its incidence, than its domestic kind is now being practiced freely in many countries in the world—like in America, Ireland, Spain, Africa, Russia, Afghanistan, Central Asian Republic, Pakistan, India, Indonesia, Colombia and Philippines etc. The pattern is about the same, although the perpetrators have varied motives, ranging from ethnic, religious, drugs territorial and Right Wing fanaticism—blowing up of Airliners in the air, Trade Centers in the US, Oklahoma, and civilians in Kashmir and democratic symbols like houses of Parliament. This variety of International violence appeared on the world stage in the 1960's and continues unabated. There is a loose sort of an inter-nation framework to combat this new violence, globally—though excepting the Islamist Al Qaeda there is no visible link between the other various barbarous outfits. The Shi-hite groups work semi-independently and sometimes with the Hamas but have lately started working with Al Qaeda. The I.R.A. has a weak linkage with E.T.A. (Spain), and the North-East Indian secessionists with the I.S.I. of Pakistan. The Al Qaeda has close ties with the Philippines minority groups and the Indonesian Jamait-e-Isliamiah. Some of the groups are also sponsored by I.S.I. which has often attracted International odium—like the attack on the Indian Parliament in December 2001.

One of the main difficulties in combating Terrorism today particularly in a democratic environment is defining it precisely. Many attempts have been made to define it so that it may not be adjudged as a form of legitimate resistance against tyranny. There is of course the dictionary meaning which puts forth that "Terrorism: The calculated use of violence or the threat of violence to inculcate fear, intended to coerce or to intimidate governments or societies in the pursuit of goals that are generally political, religious or ideological".

Paul Johnson a reputed writer adds, "Terrorism is the cancer of the Modern World. No State is immune to it. Unless treated drastically its growth is inexorable as it poisons the society on which its feeds and drags it down to destruction.

It has been observed that International terrorism is inspired by religious economic, nationalistic and ethnic fervour." Hundreds have died because of it, all over the world—America, Latin America, Lebanon, Peru, India, Afghanistan, Central Asia, Sri Lanka, Philippines, Africa (Rwanda—Liberia etc.), Indonesia and Colombia.

One of the classic arguments against terrorism was advanced by Lenin. In "What is to be done".

"The terrorists bow to the spontaneity of the passionate indignation of the intellectuals, who lack the ability or opportunity to connect the revolutionary struggle and the working-class movement into an integral whole. It is difficult indeed for those who have lost their belief, or have never believed that this is possible, to find some outlet for their indignation and revolutionary energy, other than terror. He also said: "Terrorism is about power. Its purpose is to terrorize, and a means to political power and a way to hold it".

Trotsky developed the case against terrorism as follows:

> "The capitalist State does not base itself on government, ministers, and cannot be eliminated with them. The classes it serves will always find new people; the mechanism remains intact and continues of function. In our eyes, individual terror is inadmissible precisely because it belittles the role of the masses in their own consciousness, reconciles them to their powerlessness, and turns their eyes and hopes towards a great avenger and liberator who some day will come and accomplish his mission."

Another definition, which is more recent, is that of Brig. Malik of the Pakistan army in his writings on "the Quranic Concept of War". He states that "Terrorism is the quintessence of the Islamic strategy for War: Terror struck into the hearts of the enemies is not only a means, it is the end in itself. Once a condition of terror into the opponent's heart is obtained, hardly anything is left to be achieved. It is the point where the means and the end meet and merge. Terror is not a means of imposing decision upon the enemy; it is the decision we wish to impose upon him."

It should, however, be understood that force and state action against terrorists, by itself is not alone sufficient to curb it. The strategy to fight it should be carefully thought of, with the realization that the means of terrorism can never be morally justified, whatever may be stated the perpetrators. The core of the doctrine of terrorism lies in the belief in the snuffing out of innocent civilian life, and by instilling terror in the victims' heart. The crimes that they commit are analogous to war crimes. The beliefs, demands, and grievances, and motivation and the political, social and economic conditions which together constitute the underlying causes of terrorism, should be carefully researched and analyzed lest the terrorist legitimizes his sanguinary quest through terrorism. Surely there are many ways open to a person to attain his goal, and these ways should not use violence and deliberate murder.

International bodies fail in their goals of achievement because of their diversity to attain their goals, independently or jointly. This is the main reason for the UN failure in countering terrorism, A consensus even on the definition of Terrorism has not been reached, and for this reason, in many countries terrorism is an instrument of foreign policy. For liberal democracies, however, terrorism is basically repugnant and against the tenets of constitutional and representative rule. Political violence is abhorred, because change, if it is needed, is also possible through peaceful means. Once political violence establishes itself then it can create its own principles. We know it only too well, because most of our neighbours are a law unto themselves.

Half a century back India was part of a colonial power and was dismembered into two countries – now three. This led to a number of ethno nationalist and territorial disputes, which have had an effect on subsequent terrorist activity – particularly in Kashmir and the growth of the Pak based hydra headed ISI. No matter what official circles may think, this has had a deleterious effect on the stability of India. Three wars with Pakistan, insidious propaganda against the unity of India, the fissiparous activities of the I.S.I. and its continuing operations have affected the peace that India needs for its growth. And now nuclear blackmail has started and the Lord only knows how it will end. It seems that a calm atmosphere is ages away from India. The instability in the NE, the Bombay blasts and the attack on Parliament House by the agents of the I.S.I. have had a destabilizing effect on our country. Local conflicts are with impunity transformed into international issues apart from bringing the two countries on the brink of a bigger conflict. State sponsored Terrorism is a new phenomenon, for it brings into focus a cost-effective means of waging war covertly, through the use of surrogate warriors-terrorists.

Secular India is an eyesore to many of its neighbours. Its booming economic progress, makes many an enemy amongst its envious neighbours. India has never tried to use clandestine methods to achieve its goals—its main goal has been to live at peace with its neighbours. It has been ravaged through the centuries by hegemonistic neighbours who wanted to loot the land of its bounty. It has no evil designs on any of its neighbours, and mounting any terrorist attacks on any country is unimaginable. It has, had, many governments both secular and non-secular but it has never covetously looked at its neighbours. Pakistan our next-door neighbour is now riding the terrorist tiger, and is ruing the day it allowed 'madrasas' to be organized on its soil. It is confronted within its own confines with hundreds of fundamentalists, having their own agenda. Having Washington as its main friend and ally, is not without a price, which it may find it difficult to repay—Al Qaeda now a globally hated institution has its claws deeply entrenched in its vitals of Asia, Africa, Europe and the US. The Taliban once nurtured by the US is now resented everywhere. Where has their terrorism led them? Their President cries hoarse to get rid of these violent-cum-religious bodies as shame is being heaped on his country for having given birth to them.

Kashmir continues to be the centre of terrorist activity. It receives every now and then a dose of Islamic militancy from Pakistan. India has to be careful about its own fundamentalists. Muslims in India should not be made to feel insecure.

Another factor essential for curbing terrorism in India, is the nurturing to health the backward North East—Arunachal Pradesh, Manipur, Meghalaya, Mizoram, Nagaland, Tripura, and Sikkim. We must keep our relations with Bhutan, China, Myanmar, Bangladesh and Nepal warm. In our own heartland the naxalite menace has to be contained by a new humanitarian approach. Already one-sixth of our country is under the shadow of this movement (Jharkhand, Chhattisgarh, Andhra Pradesh, Orissa, parts of Maharashtra, and Madhya Pradesh, West Bengal, Bihar and Uttar Pradesh).

Tracing Terrorism

When tracing terrorism in Asia one has to keep in mind the advent of violence which was brought into the Near East by the continuous Arab Israeli conflict since 1948, the Suez Canal tension in 1956 and the Israeli take over of certain Trans-Jordan area and the Gaza Strip in 1967. The successful retaliation by the Arab force in 1973 and the resurgence of Arab oil prices about the same time, as well as the Iranian revolution under Khomeni in 1979, gave rise to a peculiar belligerence amongst Islamist countries like—a militant Islamic revivalist movement. Some writers in the West, particularly Huntington, in an over-simplification has tried to explain this as an inevitable clash between civilizations. The truth perhaps lies in the fact that it was the legacy of colonialism in the Islamic world, combined with the authoritarian unpopular regimes governing some of them, and also the Muslim perception that the West had a bias against the Arabs in the Arab-Israeli conflict. In the 1950s, 1960s, 1970s, there was an anti-colonial, nationalist sentiment raging all over the globe, and this Islamic revival closely resembled it. Also there was a great urge in most of the Islamic countries in Asia to modernize themselves and not be a victim of a sense of decline and economic dependency. Unfortunately, Muslim nations and societies have been frustrated by a variety of reasons related to their internal social dynamics, in which modernizing 'dictators' have played a significant part.

Adequate attention to the impact of democratic forces with a broader consensus, has been missing, and also emphasis on how to combat any radical forces, as enjoined by Islam. Religious thinking was used as a conservative force as in South Arabia, Syria, and Libya etc. Even the Arab variant of socialism was shunned, and there was no real political participation by the mass of people and less of representative forms of Government. These collective drawbacks made the Governments, more authoritarian and less popular.

Perhaps we can now discuss, briefly the presence of terrorism in some of the Islamic countries, which now seem to be riddled with this curse.

The current resurgence of religious terrorism is mainly within trends observed in today's Islamic world. It is true that the revival of Islamic fundamentalism is universal, and most adherents are not terrorists. Yet it cannot be denied that most of the violent conflicts, both at home or abroad, happen and continue to happen, in Islamist regions. The entire Middle East stretching from Palestine to Afghanistan, till recently was in the grip of violent instability—more than ninety per cent. Most of the violence created by radical Islamists, was against other Arabs or Muslims as in Iraq, Afghanistan and Algeria. There is of course no Islamist monopoly in the field of religious fanaticism—it exists in many other parts of the world—US, Russia, Africa, India and Philippines, Indonesia, etc. United Nations peace forces are without doubt functioning in about 80 per cent of the countries stricken with Arab-inspired violence, where *Jihad* continues to be practiced. Contemporary terrorism poses the greatest danger to Islamic countries and its victims are civilians of Muslim religion.

Algeria

In 1962 Algeria achieved freedom from French colonialism. The new leadership was Islamic but secular in nature. However, global economic forces were not to be denied, and by 1990 there was rampant unemployment, and a feeling amongst the population spread that socialism and Western ideas were responsible for the malaise. In the

1992 elections, the Islamic Salvation Front, won at the hustings, but the Government annulled the elections, and banned the Islamic Salvation which included the terrorist organization—the GIA. The core of GIA consisted of Saudi Arabs and Algerian volunteers, who had fought in Afghanistan. Unlike other Islamist terrorists, they worked in large numbers, and their targets were intellectuals and journalists. Thousands perished before the Al Qaeda led terrorists were bridled. The most inhuman atrocities were perpetrated on women and children, so as to spread the message of terror. More poor were killed in this holocaust, for whom this civil conflict had started.

Israel-Palestine

After the Israel-Arab War of 1948 and the Suez crisis in 1956, the next land war in this area was the six days war in 1967. In-between there had been incidents of assassination, murder, rioting and arson. After 1967, the whole scene changed, when a large number of Arabs in Judaea and Samaria came under Israel. Large groups of Arab terrorist groups came into existence—well financed and fully armed. The main group was Al-Fatah under Yassar Arafat. There were other groups under Marxists and left wing parties.

The operations by these groups are well-known today. Ambushing, hijacking of planes and the attack against Israeli athletes at Munich. The PLO whose military branch was Al-Fatah got a lot of international publicity. In 1980 two new terrorist groups surfaced—the Hizbullah in Lebanon and Hamas in Gaza and in Israeli occupied territories. The Hizbullah was directly connected with Iran under Khomeni, and Hamas under the Egyptian Muslim Brotherhood. Whereas Hizbullah is entirely Shiite, Hamas is overtly Sunni. Thus, terrorism in this part of the world became internationalized. Syria and Iran openly encouraged the Hizbullah—whose membership consisted of poor Shia Muslims from Lebanon, who felt oppressed under the more wealthy Christian Lebanese.

Hamas an offshoot of the Egyptian Brotherhood, is the driving force behind Intifada, and became more popular than Arafat whom the Gaza denizens regarded as a weakling against Israel. It always sabotaged peace talks between Israel and the Arabs and won over many a heart, from amongst the Arabs living in Gaza, and the 'occupied territories' by Israel. It has not lost any opportunity to demonstrate by fighting with the Israeli troops. It has had spectacular success in organizing 'human bombs' to destroy the enemy. Suicide bombing now not so common, was resorted to by them to spread fear amongst the Israeli civilian population and the army. More than a hundred and forty such cases were perpetrated in the Arab-Israeli conflict. It is a 'weapon', which the LTTE also used to kill Rajiv Gandhi, ex-prime minister of India and the Sinhalese President Premdasa. Suicide missions have a tradition in Japan—the Kamikaze tradition. In the Second World War it is learnt that more than 2000 (two thousand), Japanese volunteered for Kamikaze missions.

Radical Islamic groups committed terrorist crimes throughout the Middle East, North Africa and East Africa—Sudan–Somalia and Egypt. In Egypt apart from killing President Sadat, attacks on the police, judges, tourists and hotels were committed to decry the national government and its leaders.

There is a strong fundamentalist movement in Turkey also. Quite a lot of terrorism has emanated from Kurdistan (Turkish) PPK—the Kurdistan Workers Party. The Kurds in Iraq have not been too active for various reasons, but the PKK has protected them from Iraqi forces. The PKK has been active against Turkish workers in Europe—particularly in Germany.

Whilst discussing the global reach of terrorism, it would be worthwhile to examine the state of this activity in this most volatile area of the world—Asia and includes countries which have been savaged by it like Syria, Iraq, Kurdistan, Iran, Afghanistan, erstwhile Asian Central Asian States, Pakistan, India, Nepal, China, Philippines, Indonesia, and Sri Lanka. It feeds on the wretched state of the people which populate it, with all their miseries born of hunger, dispossession, ignorance, squalor, and poverty. The terrorists who function in those countries want to discredit the Governments in power. As a survivor-terrorist of the original band who killed the Olympic Israeli athletes in Munich 1972 said—"Munich put the Palestinian cause in every home".

The fall of the USSR in its struggle with US has been a landmark in the history of the present day world. Although the fears of a war between two evenly balanced superpowers, the USA and USSR disappeared, the world instead of becoming unipolar under the aegis of US, became multipolar under terrorism. The erasure of the USSR brought into view, new nationalistic urges, secessionism, and disputes of horrendous dimensions, between nuclearly armed neighbours. People and thinkers started cogitating about 'clash of civilizations', and the debate has not ended yet. It has given rise to a "terrorism" which has witnessed the destruction of the Twin towers of the World Trade Centre in New York on the 11th of September 2003.

It would also be pertinent to mention here, that the whole process of terrorism got a tremendous kick-start, by the two armed interventions by the superpowers, US and USSR in the closing days of the 20th century—the USSR and USA intervention in Afghanistan. The intervention by the Soviets put an end to its existence, and the US intrusion, gave rise to terrorist violence and the culture of narcotics worldwide, from the Americas to the Philippines. The Kremlin's fatal mistake which was imposed upon by Brezhnev and his advisers, without consulting his top Military Generals and the Politburo, gave the Americans a chance to avenge the happenings in Vietnam. The score was levelled, but at what cost to Asia, and the World. It also laid open the road to oil rich lands of Central Asia, which had remained safe in the 'bear hug' of the Soviets, and where fresh outbreak of terrorist violence lay in the near future. A new Pandora's box had been opened which would have a tremendous impact on events in the 21st century-terrorism. The suicide bombers in Sri Lanka would not only function there, but would have a huge canvas to demonstrate their demoniac fury globally.

Heads of State would fall like nine-pins, and fatal casualties would reach horrendous proportions, leaving surrounding countries in a state of shock. The world will always remember the 20th century as the most brutal, violent and bloody period in human history. As if two world wars were not enough, the nuclear devices with all their devastating power were dropped at Hiroshima and Nagasaki in Japan, horrific pogrammes and massacres of Jews by Nazis, the shameful atrocities of Pol Pot in Cambodia, the decimation of Rwandans in Africa and the ethnic cleansing in Yugoslavia—and now the portals have been opened, for the hard to define terrorism in the beginning of the 21st century. And who are these terrorists who lead and herald this new dance of death—recruits from all over the Islamist world, particularly from Saudi Arabia, and Yemen. The contagion will undoubtedly spread—because "one man's terrorist is another man's freedom fighter".

Traditional terrorism its practiced in Palestine, and other countries in North Africa, is aimed at securing known political ends, in as spectacular a manner as was possible like the assassination of the Israeli athletes in Munich etc. An action like this had a specific aim and was not meant to spread terror like the new horrific procedures of the Taliban, in their own newly wrought concept of Islam, which traumatized all the Islamic neighbours of Afghanistan including the Central Asian Muslim republics, Indian Muslims, even the Muslim rulers and the elite in Pakistan, and Iran. The shock that they generated is still felt all over the world, and is likely to remain so for some time.

Terrorism is becoming increasingly lethal. One has just to peruse figures, to see that from 1960 onwards fatalities have increased from 30 per cent to 100 per cent. Religious terrorism accounts for a disproportionate number in this. Religious beliefs play a major role in this increase. Aum Shrinkyo is a striking example—this Japanese cult whose tentacles had spread into its society deeply, wanted to extinguish all life in Tokyo by spreading a noxious killer gas.

The erasure of the Soviet Union from the comity of Nations has significantly increased the opportunity for terrorists to use nuclear technology for mass destruction. As making a nuclear device is a difficult and complex procedure, obtaining it clandestinely is easier. There is enough proof that "Suitcase nuclear bombs", and fissionable material has been found missing from the erstwhile Soviet arsenals. There is no doubt that the choice of using nuclear devices and weapons has had a tremendous impact on the minds of modern day terrorists. They are not worried about any mass slaying.

(Mao's saying)

> "All men must die, but death can vary in its significance. The ancient Chinese writer Szuma Ebien said "Though death befalls all men alike, it may be heavier than Mount Tai or lighter than a feather". To die for the people is heavier than Mount Tai, but to work for the fascists and die for the oppressors or exploiters, is lighter than a feather"

Mao, glorified a 'heavy' death and absolved the murderer that perpetrated a light death of any moral responsibility or guilt.

The importance of ideology varies from one group to the other. The importance of ideological motivation is that in contrast to groups motivated by other goals, such as emotional separatism, it perpetrates a worldview, and thus lends an international perspective to the cause. The only other alternative in their minds is radiological terrorism, or chemical, biological weapons. Osama is thinking of both. Mass destructive terrorism is now the greatest non-traditional threat to International security. We will ignore it at our peril.

What was once thought in the 1970s, and 1980s, as only the beginnings of an Islamic revival, and loosely called as a "fundamentalist" urge, has now a significant political and economic dimension. The more active Islamist groups now talk of a sweeping change in the economic and social structure of Muslim society, in which an aggressive militant fringe takes over and wants a political change by violent means. The militant components of this movement are very anti-Western, anti-US, anti-Israeli, and anti-Indian. It is essential, though a little late, in particular for the US to understand, through appropriate policies to do whatever is possible to prevent further the radicalization of the militant forces within this revivalist movement. Islam is now being used to express specific social, economic and political grievances and to alter them in a manner so that poverty, injustice and ignorance could be removed. At places it is the support by the West to authoritarian regimes, or a bias in the approach to the

Arab-Israel conflict in the near East area, or an anti-colonial sentiment so rampant in the developing countries about sixty years ago. It is also true that this Islamic revival has also something to do with the Arab victories over the Israelis in 1973, the importance of Arab oil in the economies of the World and the Khomeni revolution in Iran, and the expulsion of the Soviets from Afghanistan in the 1990s.

All these factors made Khomeni declare that the new 'Satan' was the United States, which with its cohorts including Israel were to be destroyed. This cry was taken up by Osama bin Laden, who declared War on the US.

To thoroughly understand the challenge to stability in Asia, posed by terrorism, it is imperative to comprehend the geopolitical issues involved in this extremely sensitive area of the globe. The US and its friends, including Portugal, France, Britain and Iran, waged, proxy wars in Asia and Africa, against possible adversaries they feared were friends of the USSR. These conflicts required no commitment of troops.

The USSR intervention in 1979 in Afghanistan, permitted the US to apply this very strategy of proxy war to this area. These were the true beginnings of a new deep relationship between the USA and Islamism, which initially meant an alliance with the Pakistan military dictator Gen. Zia-ul-Haq, who was more than keen to advance his own interests in Afghanistan by ousting the Soviets and their satellites from there, and further advancing into Islamic Central Asia. According to Pak strategists it also meant a strengthening of their country's position vis-a-vis India and a future expanding for strategic depth into Afghanistan and Central Asia. Help was, therefore, fully extended to the US, who with Saudi finance and Pakistani logistical support, managed to raise and equip and send to war against the USSR a mercenary Islamist Force. The volunteers came from all parts of the Islamic globe, for the plentiful lucre that was being spent on them, and which in turn would give them a chance to fight a 'sacred' war against the communist infidels. A *Jihad* was thus initiated in Asia. The Marxists were finally vanquished in 1989 after almost a nine-year war. This war created problems like four million Afghan refugees, who poured into Pakistan, Iran and Central Asian Republics as penniless refugees, Cities were razed to the ground, and the whole countryside was strewn with mines, which were further to maim a sizeable number of Afghans. A new movement of gigantic size was nurtured to rehabilitate and bring to order their devasted country—the Taliban. The Talibans were the acme of Islamic extremism. The Taliban, consisted of students from 'Madrasas' or religious schools, armed to their teeth, by Pakistan. They exuded the so-called Islamic values, and enslaved Afghanistan for the next few years, but not before giving birth to Al Qaeda-Al-Sulbah (The solid Base), the most demoniac international terrorist group in history. This group is unique in its structure, and no Islamist terrorist group comes anywhere near it—in training, efficiency and secrecy. It is a secret organization and President Bush described it—Al Qaeda is to terror, as Mafia is to crime. It's goal is to broadcast its radical Islamist beliefs globally. Most of present Al Qaeda leadership remains in the tribal areas, which are difficult to access, and straddle the Afghan-Pakistan borders, where even Pak writ does not function. Its modes of attack range from assassination, bombing, ambushes, and use of explosives, to disperse chemicals and biological and radioactive material for mass slaying. It has no reservations against the use of these materials against densely populated regions. It is also reliably learnt that it has a nuclear arsenal.

As every global movement needs a leader—this too was provided by the USSR Afghan War—Osama bin Laden—now called Al Qaeda's Emir General. He is battle scarred and fought at Jalalabad where he was wounded. His father who was in construction business in Saudi Arabia, left him with a lot of wealth, which as an engineer in construction he multiplied. His wealth, influence, and fearlessness made him a natural leader of the Arab Mujahideen.

Within a month of the Soviet invasion of Afghanistan in 1979, Osama left Saudi Arabia for Afghanistan. There he met the leaders and commanders who led the anti-Soviet *Jihad*. He was recommended by the Saudi Government to lead the International Brigade, to which Pakistan acceded. Aid from friendly Islamic countries for their role in Afghanistan started arriving. Osama liberally helped the cause with his own money also. His mentor in this new role of a 'mujahid', was Azzam an Arab, from Jordan—an academician in Islamic studies and its teachings. Together they opened the Afghan Service Bureau in Peshawar in 1984. It catered for foreign Mujahideen particularly the Arabs. It indoctrinated particularly the young in Islamic precepts, and trained them for fighting the Soviets in Afghanistan. Azzam also laboured hard to draw up the parameters of Al Qaeda and instructed Osama in this new terroristic creed. It was Azzam who popularized *Jihad* on the Pak-Afghan border. He conceptualized Al Qaeda in 1987-88. He envisioned an organization that would channelize the energies of the Mujahideen into fighting oppression against the Muslims worldwide. Towards the end of his (Azzam's) life in 1989 the two had differences on tactics for relieving Muslims of persecution by global powers.

To combat Osama's Al Qaeda, liberal democracies have also created an alliance to fight it—these nations apart from many others are North America, Europe, Australia and Japan. The Al Qaeda uses the techniques of Leninism—it is nameless of true identity of its workers, adheres to a cell-structure, follows the idea of a cadre party, maintains strict discipline, and promotes self-sacrifice. With the US building its multinational coalition and deploying its troops in Afghanistan, the Philippines, Yemen and in Georgia and some of the Central Asian Republics in which Al Qaeda is building a strong global network.

Like the Taliban, the anti-Soviet *Jihad* which gave rise to it, was the creation of the Pakistan Inter-services Intelligence Directorate (ISI). As neither America nor Saudis wanted to commit their forces into Afghanistan, they let the ISI do the slogging, dirty role of day-to-day building up of a front against the Soviets. Even arms and ammunition were distributed through it. Only about 30 per cent of the arms reached the Afghans—the rest of them were either 'confiscated' by Pakistan or stored for further use probably in Kashmir.

Nowhere have the locally produced drugs been used to finance war operations except in Afghanistan. This narcotic exercise created havoc, not only in Afghanistan, but also in Pakistan, Russia, England, USA and Europe. The CIA though warned against this danger, by Drug enforcement, did not halt the narcotics trade.

The contagion of Islamic violence has now been spread over the whole of the globe, by the returning Mujahideens. In Algeria alone 100,000 lives were lost to this contagion.

Once the Russians departed from Afghanistan, the weapons sent by US for fighting them started appearing in the hands of the terrorist outfits ranged against India, in the Kashmir theatre. The ultimate target of the Islamist rebels, led by Osama remained the US. In his writings and Fatwas he had already declared war on the US. The semi-successful attack, on the US Trade Centre in 1993, and on CIA Headquarters at Langley were part of this plan. Bin Ladin journeyed to Africa in 1986 and set up bases in Sudan, and organized the attack on the embassies in Nairobi and Dar-es-salam, and the aborted attacks on the US installations in Kampala, Bangkok and Tirana, all these were indications of spreading and globalising of terror. America's fraternal embrace with Islam seemed to have soured somewhere, but it was not clear whether America has paid serious heed to it. Why does it continue to shower its friendship on Pakistan, which on its soil breeds extremist anti-US extremist groups? The US even overlooks Pak coups, the corruption inside the body politic and even nuclear crimes committed by Pakistan scientists.

The core of the problem is that Pakistan's military now courts the 'Mullah'—the Islamist Cleric—a creature who wields a lot of political power in Pakistan. There is not much hope for Pakistan to get any better if it cannot excise the extremist fringe which is baying now for the blood of US. If there is hope, it lies only in a democratic Pakistan—if and when it comes. The youth in extremist schools (Madrasas) have to be provided with a secure future, and the Pakistan-Taliban Al Qaeda combine crushed. General Musharraf is not too certain of the loyalty of his other Generals, who have over time developed their own relations with the Mullahs—even the army men have been affected.

Today the extremist (*Jihadi*) groups are significant in their profile in Pakistan. In 2001-02, Pakistan was host to fifty-eight religious political parties, and twenty-four armed religious militias. The latter are also known as *Jihadi* groups. The mushrooming of the right of the center militant outfits in Pakistan, began with groups like Harkat-Ul-Jihad-I-Islami and Harkatul-Mujahideen in 1980 for action in Afghanistan. As time progressed these 'sacred' warriors attracted many other religious organizations in their country into their fold. Their enemy at that moment was communism—but there in the background of his mind lurked India and the US who were also to be fought. Sectarian rivalries amongst the militant Pakistan groups only sharpened the zeal to serve the 'cause'—anti-Western—anti-Communist anti-Indian anti-US.

Very soon the 'Madrasa' network became the corner stone of the building up of militancy. These groups received considerable attention from Osama bin Laden and his mentor Azzam. When Pakistan came into being there were only 136 'Madrasas'. Today there are over 30,000 such schools—all a barrier to modern scientific knowledge, for they silently breed only monstrous bigotry.

Another feature in Pakistan's drift towards extremism is the phenomenal growth of Sunni and Shia militant groups. These groups have clashed violently a number of times in Pakistan and continue to hold hostage internal peace. Both factions receive financial aid from Saudi Arabia (Sunni) and Iran (Shia), for ultimately fighting the enemies of Islam.

In the meantime Al Qaeda stretched its tentacles all over Asia—the erstwhile Muslim Republics in Central Asia—Sinkiang in China, the Philippines, Malaysia, Indonesia and Muslim migrant populations in Australia and other countries. Its presence in the Philippines has already aroused a lot of notoriety. In 1990 *Jihadi* groups moved into the Philippines and established their presence strongly in this region. A string of events took place in which there were bombings, pillaging and kidnappings. The Muslims are a minority in the Philippines (only 4.6 per cent), whilst the Christian population is about 84.1 per cent of the entire population. The rise of Islam in the Philippines went hand in hand with the cordial economic relations with Arab nations in the Middle East. The main aspect of these relations, centre round the Filipino labour force, which works there consisting of skilled and unskilled workers. They send about 6.5 billion dollars back home, where the GAP is just 82.1 billion dollar! The new Muslim rebels there were led by one Abu Sayyaf and Ramzi Ahmad who held Manila to ransom with their depredations and their aborted plan to down, eleven American planes over the Pacific Ocean in one day in 1994.

Al Qaeda also reached Indonesia and has since taken many steps to heighten terrorism there, including civil strifing, in the Molucca Islands, and in the Bali bombing. The Tsunami which struck Indonesia must have struck a hard blow at the militants, though in Sumatra their hold was not too strong.

Terrorist violence in Sri Lanka (an Island just south of India and formerly known as Ceylon) has been a long affair, between a minority and majority group, but it has no religious overtones. Its underlying cause has not been religious or Islamic revivalism. The LTTE which leads this terrorist movement against the established government in Colombo has been on the warpath since the British granted independence to this Island in 1948. The country is overwhelmingly Sinhalese (Buddhists) and faces a Tamil minority of less than 20 per cent (about 3 million) who are contained in the North and North East of the country—near the Trincomali seaport, one of the finest harbours in the Indian Ocean. The Tamil minority has suffered a lot at the hands of the Sinhalese majority. This suffering has taken them towards terrorism—a militant separatism—The Tamils are originally from India and were brought into Sri Lanka as labourers by the British. Suicide bombings (killing their President Premadasa and the Ex-Prime Minister of India Rajiv Gandhi) had no religious motive. They have had the highest rate of suicide killings, consisting of hundreds of perceived opponents. Conflict between Tamil and Sinhalese continued in the 60s, but in 1976 the LTTE was founded (Liberation Tigers of Tamil Elam). Its gurus have been Balasingham and the undisputed political-military leader Prabhakaran. Growing Tamil militancy brought a backlash from the Sinhalese majority and there were civil riots in Sri Lanka. This bloodshed came to a halt when Indian troops were inducted into the North of the Island per invitation from the Sri Lankan President. The LTTE was forced to retreat into the jungles and lost over 12,000 fighters. After a long respite Indian leadership thought it fit to withdraw its troops, when mutual peace was not being accepted, either by the Sinhalese or the Tamils.

The upshot for India was that they lost to a suicide lady bomber an ex-Prime Minister Rajiv Gandhi and had the State of Tamil Nadu riddled with LTTE safe havens.

The Tamil Tigers who have originally been trained in Lebanon by the PLO, and in military camps in Myanmar, make efficient guerilla fighters. Their approach for a settlement with Colombo has not shown much maturity, and so the fighting goes on. They have an efficient Public Relation groups abroad and have been well served by Tamil propaganda. They use modern IT equipment to maximum use and have developed a small wellrun Navy, and hidden caches of arms and explosives, which they procure from Cambodia, Myanmar, and from Far Eastern sources. Their war effort continues to be paid by Tamil communities living abroad. It is estimated that 50,000 to 100,000 people have been killed in this Sinhalese civil strife, and out of these at least 10,000 are Tamils. At the moment the Tamils are having internal problems of leadership with a breakaway Tamil group.

Drug smuggling has been indulged in by this group, but not extensively. A large number of refugees have fled to India, which is just across the Palk Straits—a short distance of only a few miles. The Colombo Government has made a large number of concessions to placate the LTTE, but it appears that they will not be satisfied with anything short of independence—a prospect which no one in the world will accept. The terrorists are at the crest of a wave fuelled by their own virulent fanaticism. With bated breath everyone awaits a solution, acceptable to all parties—which at the moment is being brokered by Norway.

Central Asia and Terrorism

The picture of Terrorism in the Central Asian Republics is not too rosy, though there is outward semblance of peace, brought about by Big Brother handling by Russia. Radical Islam in this area is monitored by the Islamic Renaissance Party, the Hizb-ul-Tahrir and the Islamic Movement of Uzbekistan. The entire length and breadth of this Central Asian landlocked mass is dominated by the terrorist IMU and the HT (Hizb-ul-Tahrir). These are underground Islamic Movements, and are shadowy and secretive above the surface. There is no doubt, however, that they have the full might of Al Qaeda behind them—apart from the weight of local grievances, in Uzbekistan, Kazakhstan, Krygzstan, Turkmenistan, and Tajikstan. When the Soviet Union disappeared from the map of the world in 1991, the Central Asian Republics were left to fend for themselves. An area which knew only cotton production, and collective farming, it was difficult to be viable. Their borders had been redrawn by Stalin, and because of this they were economically weak, ethnically divided, and forced to practice their religion secretly. The area, however, was the richest in the world in natural resources like oil, gas and minerals. It beckoned to international investors.

The first Muslim Republic to receive Western attention was Kazakhstan, ruled by the iron hand of Nazarbayev. This State has a large population of ethnic Russians, who are always threatening to secede. When Independence came, it had also a large stockpile of nuclear ballistic missiles. Before the dismantlement of these nuclear devices, Nazarbayev was able to negotiate large financial aid from the World Bank and the IMF. He has successfully played the West against Russia, and has also allowed the Chinese to have their finger in the pie of untapped largest oil and mineral resources.

Turkmenistan is also under a flamboyant leader—Niazev. He has almost nominated himself (endorsed by a puppet Parliament) as a leader of the country for the next decade. As in Kazakhstan human rights violations are galore—mainly to stamp at Islamic dissidence. Whereas oil cartels fight over the construction of pipelines (the region is rich in oil and gas), Niazev has a 'neutral' foreign policy. Its borders with Iran are policed by the Russian army, and he awaits a future promising plenty if and when foreign powers decide to let him build a pipeline, which can supply energy to Pakistan, India and US. At the moment it supplies gas only to Iran, which is not at all pleasing to the US. At the moment except for the Hizbul-ul-Tahrir (HT), there is no Al Qaeda presence which comes out boldly. As long as Niazev is there, peace will continue.

Uzbekistan is no better or worse than the other Muslim republics. Its President Karimov is an autocrat and has heavily put down any party, which has embarked on any reforming zeal. His ruthlessness has emboldened the opposing Birlik and the Erlik parties, who have openly asked for Human Rights observance. All this has in turn heightened Islamic militancy, under the IMU, which is a powerful militant Islamic group, and has Al Qaeda protection and guidance. Al Qaeda has now spread its tentacles into Kazakhstan and Tajikistan—particularly in the Ferghana valley. Its leader Juma Namangami (has been reported killed—but this lacks confirmation) has close links with Al Qaeda and Osama bin Laden. Attempts have been made on Karimov's life, but he continues to dominate the scene. The contagion of Islamic violence has, however, entered his State.

Tajikistan was a model State in Central Asia, with a balanced secular and religious leadership. Now it is a haven of extremist Muslim zealots who flee to it from neighbouring Muslim States of Uzbekistan, Afghanistan and Kazakhstan. It has a small population of only 5 million. One million Tajiks live in Uzbekistan and 200 thousand in Sinkiang in China.

The militant fringe of Islamist forces in Central Asia has been provided by the IMU, which is now a pan-Islamic Force.

The threat to Islamize Tajikistan has been aggravated because of its poor economy and hilly terrain. The Pamir mountains cover more than 93 per cent of its territory. Despite all these handicaps, including Stalin's redrawing its map and giving Bokhara and Samarkand to Uzbekistan, it lives its precarious existence austerely. The silk route to China once passed through it, and it has cradled both Persian and Turkic civilizations in it. The National Museum at Dushanbe is a witness to it. The largest sleeping Buddha is in it (40 ft). There has been however Tajik and non-Tajik civil strife—each faction wanting to secede. The Islamic Renaissance Party (IRP) also made its presence felt.

Everything changed after September 2001. The US arrived and after paying huge sums opened bases in some of these Islamic Republics for attacking Afghanistan. Bases were a must for air strikes in Afghanistan, and for the residence of a few combatants. In 2005 this presence has become manifold, and though overtly there is no violence, those who are in the know of it are certain that Tajikistan which was the last Republic to join the USSR, is now in the grip of events which may be much bigger than the Civil War, which ended a few years ago. Ahmad Shah Masood a Tajik who was assassinated just before 9/11 by Osama bin Laden's men is being sorely missed for his leadership. Soviet subsidies on which this State survived have now gone into limbo with its donor. Leadership is everchanging. The popular opposition consists of the newly founded Islamic Renaissance Party—an Islamic fundamentalist organization. President Rakhmonov described the State of his country to be on the road to democracy, but suffering from acute economic problems. Rakhmonov has a lot of detractors in his country, and the State is continually rocked by religious fanaticism by the Islamic Hizb-ul-Tahrir under Namagani. There are continual raids through his country to the Ferghana valley in Uzbekistan. A lot of drugs from Afghanistan are sent to addicts in Russia, and large seizures have taken place by the Russian Border Guards doing duty on the borders of Tajikstan.

Krygstan

Its reputation that it was, perhaps, the nearest Central Asian Republic to democracy, suffered recently due to the authoritarianism of President Askar Akavev. Last month he fled the country for Moscow. It is true that out of all the Central Asian dictators, he was the most well informed, and sophisticated person. His state is situated at a very strategic place—has a long border with China, Afghanistan and Uzbekistan. He was in the top position for more than 15 years. But recently there were large-scale demonstrations against his rule both in the North and the South, and perhaps the virulent HT may have played a part in it. This change has been brought about because US is now on Russian turf and competing with it for influence. The US does not want the fundamentalist groups including Al Qaeda, HT to take from this area. It is now to be seen as to how it stops the eternal splits in this State, and its being a gateway into the Fergana Valley which HT regards as its price for further advancement into Uzbekistan and Kazakhstan, as well as its oil resources which should not go away to China.

Chechnya

It one started a dividing line between patriotism, wars of liberation and organized crime, one will realize that it is not an easy task.

Chechnya declared itself independent in 1991, under General Dudaev. Naturally this was not acceptable to Russia. A bloody conflict in which Muslims globally took part—from Arab countries, Afghanistan, Bosnia, Pakistan, Indonesia, Turkey, Egypt etc. The resistance by Chechens was fierce. They were adept at guerilla tactics and were amply helped by the veterans of the Afghan War and Al Qaeda—in arms and money, despite the fact that the Chechens were not religious bigots. They were also helped by the organized Chechen criminal mafia in Moscow. Radiological substances were also used to demoralize the Russians in Moscow. To begin with, non-Russians abroad thought it was sheer banditry and terrorism by Russia. But now people have realized that there were other factors, like the vicinity of the pipelines from Central Asia and the global Al Qaeda objective that were also involved. The fighting goes on. The breakdown of Russia in between has not helped matters. There has also been conflicts between the Russian and Chechen mafia in Moscow. The Chechen conflict is a classic example of how organized crime, politics and terrorism can get mixed up with each other and interplay interests.

Organized crime has become increasingly politicized. This trend reflects not only an interest in material gain but also in power. The gangsters and the politicians have come to stay, and the difference between the two is a little fainter than before. There is no telling what the future holds—the Al Qaeda is making full use of this interaction.

Narco-Terrorism

This phenomenon came to light in the 1970s. Originally terrorists and guerillas were mortal enemies of the drug cartels and traders in South America (Colombia). Guerilla warfare and terrorism grew in Colombia due to diverse reasons. FARC came into being as the armed wing of the Communist Party. It grew under the active support of

Cuba. As time progressed, it became apparent that Cuba could no longer help it with money and arms. FARC and its associates started narco-trafficking, and got much more money than they envisaged. Narco-trafficking also meant that they indulged in robberies and extortion, and their victims were the producers of the Coca bean, and the paste. Their income today may be anything in the range of a billion pesos. They cooperate with the producers and the owners of laboratories who manufacture this paste. It is said that the communists would have lost their base, if they had not resorted to this practice. There is a constant feud with the producers in some areas, resulting in assassinations and murders.

Elsewhere in South America particularly in Peru the 'Shining Path' has the strongest guerilla terrorist base, but the money harvested is not as much as in Colombia.

Narco-terrorism was also resorted to in Afghanistan and its tribal areas, and certain Central Asian Republics. In Afghanistan and Pakistan border areas in which poppy is grown and heroin manufactured, the money involved is as much as the budget of these countries. The issue finally is, not whether the concept of Narco-terrorism, as claimed by some Al Qaeda workers is non-criminal. The drug producers are not terrorists or viceversa. There is no criminal linkage between every act of violence and the drug trade. But the involvement of the State or Al Qaeda has decisively contributed to their survival, and indeed strengthening their base for the commission of further criminal acts.

ISI

No study of terrorism, particularly in India, would be complete without the mention of ISI (Inter-Services Intelligence Group) of Pakistan. This is a Pak sponsored State Terrorist Unit, which works, under the aegis of the Pakistan Government to create mayhem and instability in the four corners of India. To this end it has harnessed the anti-India sentiment of many Indian Muslims – particularly those who have contacts in Kashmir, the gulf area and in Pakistan itself.

This violent organization which came into existence in 1948, to monitor the work of Pak Military Attaches, and other information – gathering Pak outfits in foreign lands, expanded under President Ayub, and started being trained by the US Military administration. Under General Zia-ul-Haq it grew into monstrous proportions, particularly when the US decided on this agency to run the proxy war in Afghanistan. It created the Taliban, from amongst its ranks and developed close relations with drug-cartels and the Arab volunteers, particularly Osama bin Laden, who moved freely during this period amongst the top Pakistan leadership. At the end of the Russian invasion of Afghanistan, it had a large number of volunteers who had done all the hard fighting there. It diverted a large number of unemployed soldiers to camps in Pakistan-occupied-Kashmir. India again had to bear the brunt of their onslaught on its territory emanating from these camps. A large number of camps are still there, committing atrocities in Indian Kashmir. The ISI is also helping the cause of unrest in North East India and has a base for these operations in Bangladesh. Meghalaya, Assam, Arunachal Pradesh, Manipur, Nagaland and Mizoram are states which are being targeted by their terrorism. In Nepal they have pushed in a large number of Bangladeshis, and Kashmiri Muslims who engage themselves in carpet making. It is one of its resolves to somehow raise the number of Muslims in this Hindu State, to promote instability through them and somehow change the racial ratio. It also organised the Hijacking of IA 814 from Kathmandu (Nepal) December 1999 to Kandahar, for freeing Azhar, the religious terrorist and others of his ilk from Indian jails. This was a great setback for the security setup in India. It also helps in illicit arms deliveries to various terrorist groups in India, which are anti-national in character. Its promotion of disaffection in Punjab and the Bhindranwala cause is well-known. India seems to be the target for this religious terrorism. The world owes a large debt to India for containing this malaise. The US proxy war in Afghanistan and its Taliban fallout, would have been difficult to control, but for India's help in furnishing vital information about the movement of antisocial elements and their capture.

It is today one of the more prominent existing threats to the Indian and the world security, and does everything it can to promote disaffection amongst Muslims in India. Its role in the Gujarat riots is well-known. It insidiously keeps feeding anti-national elements with illicit arms and explosives, and drugs like heroin and fake currency. Its network in India is widespread, and every town in India with more than 200,000 citizens has its agents working in them. They are in reality the agents of Al Qaeda. The Pakistan Government has allotted it a huge budget. The colossal number of arms and explosives it handled during America's proxy war in Afghanistan have given it an elabourate arsenal, which may last for many years. One of its most daring exploits in India was the attack on the Indian Parliament, which nearly brought about a war between India and Pakistan. Today it is the only organization, apart from Osama bin Laden, which knows the plans, location, and future role of the Taliban, the super terrorist setup which is attempting to conquer the world for the Islamists.

The Taliban about whom mention has already been made was the product of the Islamic 'madrasas' which were instituted along the Pak-Afghan border to educate Muslim youth in the refugee camps during the proxy war between the US and Russia. In the period after the war, when Afghanistan, suddenly again became a scene of further civil conflict between Gulbudin Hekmatyar's faction, and the ruling Junta, Taliban moved in from Northern Pakistan into Afghanistan. They consisted of mainly Pashtuns from the border areas of Pakistan, and at first captured Kandahar and Herat. They initially impressed everyone with their honest and austere behaviour. They then moved towards the North and captured Kabul and Mazari-i-Sharif. It was a Pashtun Sunni conquest of the whole of Afghanistan. Unfortunately, Mullah Omar their leader, and Osama bin Laden, encouraged their extremist Islamic philosophy of Sharia (Islamic law). They banned all public appearances of Muslim women and denied them their schools and education. Women were socially degraded to a degree never seen before, and all entertainment, music and recreation was completely stopped. Even the length of the beard on men's faces was laid down. Such draconian measures involving personal conduct had never been enforced before, and there was an international hue and cry against it. The only country which recognized this new Afghanistan was Pakistan. After September 2001 when US suffered an attack on the World Trade Centre, it decided to cleanse Afghanistan of them, and mercilessly bombed their Headquarters in Kandahar and elsewhere. The Taliban leadership disappeared from the scene (the prominent amongst them) and no one knows where—the chief goons have gone. May be they are inside Pakistan, or in inaccessible Afghan border areas, Iran or the Central Asian Muslim Republics. Both Mullah Omar and Osama bin Laden, are also untraceable, perhaps devising ways to wage a new Islamic terrorism on the world and in India. India is high on their agenda for an attack, because *Jihad* is always waged on countries which were once under Islam's sway.

India in its fight against terrorism has arrived at a crucial juncture. Both its Western and Eastern borders are beset with terrorism. In the South the Tamil LTTE makes forays into Karnataka and Tamil Nadu, stretching its security agencies of their limit. In the North West and East violence continues unabated, and in Kashmir cross-border terrorism remains as virulent as ever. The US which dragooned this region into unrest and murderous assaults, continues to encourage Pakistan, which has one of its goals to dismember India and threatening it every now and then with a nuclear holocaust. Osama bin Laden is now no longer been pursued to his death, despite public avowals to the contrary by Bush and his coterie. The emphasis on peace between the two Asian powers based on trade and confidence building measures seems to be given more credence than cross-border terrorism, which has not been stamped out. The militant Islamic parties in

Pakistan have not been reined in or curbed in advancing their designs. Gen. Musharraf to my mind is a hapless onlooker at this tragedy being enacted in his country—his military backing by his Generals is not all that sure, and Balauchistan, Sind and NWFP continue to spew venom against him. Five abortive attacks have been made on his life. The Americans in their heart of hearts are worried at the outcome of the proxy war they ignited in 1980-89, in Afghanistan. They have no other option but to somehow bolster up the sagging image of President Musharraf.

Osama bin Laden is weighing his options for a global strike—nuclear, biological or chemical, so as to bring the US to its knees. It is not realized that blood letting in other countries, and bringing instability by fragmentation of age old Nation, cannot be achieved through their division, and brutalization.

India should strengthen itself against a nuclear attack, and should not succumb to any form of blackmail. If it loosens its hold on internal and external security, it will be a dark day for the world. At the moment it is the only country which stridently condemns terrorism and is keen that Nations should not differentiate between various lethal forms of terrorism. Terrorism by the religious Islamist groups in Kashmir, is no different from the one practiced in New York on the Twin Towers, and America should not bend backwards to give sophisticated arms to those who do only lip service to fight religious violence. Time has now come that just as Al Qaeda and the Islamic Front have threatened penetrating all bodies fighting them, democracies must try to penetrate them. Confusion and dissent should be sown in their ranks. The free world needs to sharpen its psychological warfare plans also.

We should fight both the religious terrorists and the communist PW economically, psychologically and spiritually. Our military weapons should be more powerful and our approach to solve the socio-economic malaise more spirited and pointed. India should draw up long and short term plans, for social regeneration of the affected areas. We should, as soon as it is possible respond quickly, before 'corridors' are built by the terrorists to bridge the projected, Nepal to Cape Comorin route. Our policies should be based on established values. Already one-sixth of the country is under the shadow of Naxals, where their writ in the area cannot be brooked.

Things are never as bad or as good as they may seem. To despair to sins is in core an abandonment of one's belief in existence and in ourselves. Democracy may be an over estimation of human nature, but it is infinitely preferable to the very danger of the opposite. If history teaches us anything, it is that continuation is as powerful as change. We should never abandon what we gained in August 1947.

8

India's Relations with the US: Vision of a Global Partnership

B.K. Shrivastava

Despite differences on specific issues India's relations with the United States have progressively improved since President Clinton's visit to India in the last year of his Administration. During his visit the two countries signed a common vision document, and consolidated improvement on all the three dimensions of relations: security, economic and democratic. When the Bush Administration took office it decided to keep the momentum going. India declared its support for the National Missile Defense when President Bush announced it on 1 May 2001 even before traditional allies of the US endorsed the American announcement, indicating its interest in further improving relations. The then US Ambassador David C. Mulford said that they were "at all time high." He also believed that in the next three-four years relations would "brighten" up. The second Bush Administration would be consistent with the first.[1] This upbeat mood was shared by India. Speaking before the Asia Society in New York in 2003, former Prime Minister Atal Behari Vajpayee had characterized the United States as India's "natural ally." When the new United Progressive Alliance (UPA) government, dependent on the support of the Left, assumed office in May 2004 there were some apprehensions that India's relations with the United States would change. But it soon became apparent that there was not going to be any major shift in the UPA's foreign policy priorities. Indeed, on his way to attend the annual meeting of the UN General Assembly, Prime Minister Manmohan Singh stated in September that improving relations with the United States was among the foremost priorities of his government. The

American analysts see the change as a change from "Estranged Democracies" to "Engaged Democracies". The Bush Administration counts improvement in relations with India as an achievement of its foreign policy. During her confirmation hearings in January 2005 the designated Secretary of State Condoleezza Rice contended before the Senate Foreign Relations Committee: "America's relations with the Asian countries have never been stronger" and went on to cite relations with India as an illustration. "The United States is cooperating with India, the world's largest democracy, across a range of economic and security issues. This, even as we embrace Pakistan as a vital ally in the war on terror, and a state in transition towards a more moderate and democratic future," she said...[2]

India always considered the United States as one of the most important players in international politics. It is the United States perception of India that has changed. The positive assessment gained momentum after the end of the Cold War because the reasons for negative perception, its closeness to the Soviet Union and its support for the Soviet occupation of Afghanistan had disappeared. It was liberalizing its economy and as part of this was opening a new emerging market for trade and investment. American analysts had once called India a "bottom less pit" where American economic assistance could make no difference. It was a "soft state." Now it is seen as the fastest growing economy in the world next only to China and the largest democracy in the world with more than a billion people. It has a rapidly expanding middle class as large as the United States itself. The 1.8 million Asian Indians in the US are visible and important in the professional, economic and political landscape of the US.[3] It is an acknowledged leader in the IT and an important player in pharmaceutical and biotechnology industries. Many in the US regard India as a serious threat to American jobs in the IT and manufacturing sectors.

Although relations have rapidly grown in the last few years in all areas, strategic relations have registered far more progress. There are two aspects of this relationship: the shared interest of the two countries in war on terror and military to military relations. India and the US established a joint working group on counter terrorism in January 2000. After September 11, 2001 terrorist attack on the US, the strategic relationship gathered momentum. In former Deputy Secretary of State Strobe Talbott's view, today India and the United States find themselves on the same side on this issue. He feels that the campaign on behalf of freedom, liberty and democracy and the war on terrorism would go "a long way" to define what might "be a common agenda between the United States and India."[4] The observation is quite valid. But the devil is in the details. Interest of the two has only partially and not totally converged. India has been fighting cross-border terrorism in Jammu and Kashmir since 1989. During the first term of the Clinton Administration, though the US declared that the cross-border terrorism must end it wanted India to address the root cause of terrorism. It suggested that the insurgency in Kashmir was indigenous and could be resolved only through negotiations with Pakistan and with the people of Kashmir and if an agreement was reached on Kashmir bilaterally between India and Pakistan, it should be acceptable to the people of Kashmir. It did not name the representatives of the people with whom India was supposed to negotiate but left no one in doubt whom it considered representing people of Kashmir. It ignored the Indian demand to declare Pakistan as a state supporting terrorism. It emphasized the violations of the human rights in Kashmir by the Indian security forces without taking into consideration that they were fighting secessionist elements. It did not think it necessary to sufficiently pressure Pakistan to end its support for the terrorists' outfits. It was the Al Qaeda attacks that changed American perspective on terrorism. After 9/11 the government of the United States did not hesitate to subordinate the civil rights of its own citizens in the interest of the security of the state. The US Federal courts have declared that holding people without trial is illegal. The government cannot change "due procedure clause of the Constitution."

India backed the US-led war against Al Qaeda and Taliban in Afghanistan because it wanted to see the end of the Taliban rule. India offered fullest cooperation to the US in the war against Taliban including the use of its bases even without being asked to do so. It assumed that its own war against cross-border terrorism would become part of the international war. India and the US entered into agreements to counter terrorist threats. There were agreements on sharing information on terrorist organizations and blocking the transfer of funds to these organizations. The US included some of the terrorist organizations operating from Pakistan in the list of terrorist groups, freezing their assets and banning their activities in the United States. The step did not prove to be very effective for the simple reason that these organizations changed their names and continued to operate as before.

It was due to American pressure that Aftab Ansari, who had allegedly organized the bombing of American Information Center in

Calcutta and was based in UAE, was extradited to India. On the basis of evidence supplied by India, it declared Dawood Ibrahim as the global terrorist. But what showed the limits of this cooperation was that it was not able to persuade Pakistan to hand over Dawood to India, who was responsible for the blasts in Bombay in 1993. The United States succeeded to some extent in reducing the flow of funds to terrorist organizations through hawala transactions. But on the whole India's war against cross-border terrorism did not become part of the global war. By waging the war in Iraq the United States has only strengthened terrorism rather than weakened it. It is attracting Islamic extremists from other countries. In Afghanistan, the Al Qaeda and Taliban have regrouped and are engaging the security forces. If they gain further strength it will pose a serious threat to India's security. In a recently published book on terrorism a well-known political analyst described terrorism as "Endless War". Once the war in Iraq is over and the democratic government in Afghanistan takes root, will the US continue to oppose terrorism. Or it would reverse itself and describe the terrorists as freedom fighters, focus on violation of human rights and ask the victim of terrorism to negotiate a political settlement with the terrorists/secessionist's outfits. Its recent stance on Chechan terrorists does not rule out such a possibility. India should welcome the US cooperation against terrorism, but should be ready to cope up with the problem itself.

After the end of the war in Afghanistan, a sour note of disappointment crept in. India accused the US of having double standards. It repeatedly asked the US to restrain Pakistan. Undoubtedly, the Bush Administration put some pressure on Pakistan. This led to General Musharraf promising that he would not allow Pakistan's territory to be used by terrorist organizations. But India felt that the promise was not being kept and the terrorist bases continued to exist in Pakistan. As late as the first week of August 2004, Congressman Pallone wrote to President George Bush that President Musharraf's support and training of the Taliban has led to increased military insurgency at the line of control in Kashmir. He cited Deputy Secretary of State Richard Armitage's recent admission that Pakistan had not curbed the Taliban and that more must be done to eliminate the training and protection of Taliban in order to reduce terror attacks in Kashmir. Pallone pointed out "a more secure South Asia is in the interest of the United States."[6] The Bush Administration spoke in two voices. It was not willing to go beyond a point in putting pressure on President Musharraf. At the heart of this reluctance was the American assessment so well articulated by Secretary of State Colin Powell: "we couldn't have done what we did in Afghanistan without the assistance of President Musharraf and Pakistan." He stated that the US had entered into a "strategic partnership with India and this had been done in a way that it is US India relations and not US India-Pakistan relations".[7] In January 2005 Indian officials, including the Chief of Army Staff General N.C. Vij acknowledged that "infiltration had almost completely stopped" and the situation in Jammu and Kashmir is progressing towards peace."[8] But the army did not attribute it to the influence of the US or restraint of Pakistan but claimed that it was because of the fencing of the border between India and Pakistan and the effective strategy of the Indian army.

Before the US-led effort in Afghanistan had succeeded in eliminating Al Qaeda and Taliban, the Bush Administration invaded Iraq in March 2003. It declared Iraq to be the new central front in the war against terrorism. The Iraq war emerged as the most important point of discord between the two countries. The Indian Parliament unanimously passed a resolution strongly condemning American invasion and asked for the withdrawal of the coalition troops and restoration of the sovereignty of the Iraqi people. But India was in no position to influence the course of developments in Iraq. It refused to cooperate with the occupation and declined to send troops to Iraq to help the US after the war was officially declared to have ended in May. The two countries differed but that did not result in acrimony and that was the big difference. The force of insurgency in Iraq came as a surprise to the Indians. It silenced those Indian strategy analysts who argued that India should send troops to get a toehold in the new Middle East that was emerging after the war. India expressed its willingness to help in the reconstruction of the country. It offered to train Iraqi security forces in India at the request of the United Nations.

Greater military to military cooperation has been part of the evolving strategic partnership. There were joint exercises, ship-calls, and educational and training programmes, exchange of operational procedures and doctrines and frequent visits of high-level officials. This has established the possibility of easier joint operations. During the Operation Enduring Freedom the Indian Navy escorted the American ships through Malacca Straits. In January 2004, Prime Minister Vajpayee signed an agreement on next step in strategic partnership (NSSP) that included missile defense, cooperation in civilian nuclear and space programme, and high technology trade. Both the governments are engaged in talks on these areas. A Pentagon team arrived in India in February 2005 to hold discussion on missile defense. President Bush gave clearance for a classified technical presentation of PAC 2 (Patriot Advance Capability Missile) system as part of the NSSP. The US has shared this technology only with close allies including Israel, Japan, Germany, Saudi Arabia and Taiwan. Neither China nor Pakistan has presently anti-missile defense capability.[9] Pakistan lost no time in protesting against the possible sale of the missile defense. Its objection was that this would lead to an arms race.[10] Till now the focus of military to military relationship has been on joint exercises. The US is now showing greater interest in obtaining a share in the Indian arms market. Recently the US offered to sell the border management system to India for preventing the illegal and clandestine crossing of border from the neighbouring countries. Attending the Aero show in Bangalore in February 2005 Ambassador Mulford said that the United States would like to have a share of this market. Aware that Indians do not regard the United States as a reliable supplier as it imposes sanctions and suspends arms supply relationship any time it decides to do so, Mulford assured that the US could promise reliability of supply and competitive cost of products. The desire of the US to be an arms supplier reflects not only its commercial interest but enhances its security. Admiral Mark Milliken who was present at the press conference of the Ambassador expressed the hope that there would be more cooperation on naval front. Military to military contacts between the two countries are no longer ad hoc and perfunctory but are becoming institutionalized.

The defense cooperation has transformed the nature of cooperation between the two countries. During the Tsunami relief operations the navies of the two countries were able to cooperate closely. This became possible because of years of joint exercises of the two navies. The experience would be of great use during similar humanitarian crises. On 24 October 2004, the US Congress approved that Administration would have to notify to the Congress sale of equipments to India only above the value of more than $ 14 million. This change puts India on par with such old allies of the United States as Japan and South Korea. One indicator of the progress is that defense related sales to India have jumped from near zero to $ 900 million by 2004. While India is quite content with the progress in strategic relations with the United States, it still reacts strongly when the United States offers to provide/sell weapons to Pakistan. Last year when the US announced one billion dollar arms deal with Pakistan that included Orion P3C, tanks, and planes, India protested. Even former US ambassador Robert Blackwill in Delhi questioned the sale of F-16 to Pakistan since it continued to support cross-border terrorism. These planes are capable of carrying nuclear weapons and even their conventional capacity could undermine India's air superiority." The US now views its relations with India free from its relations with Pakistan. As Rumsfeld put it, US relations should not be seen as a zero sum game. India had been demanding for years that the US should not view relations with India through the prism of Pakistan. Now that is what appears to be happening.

Nuclear non-proliferation has been an important goal of the US foreign policy. India regarded the non-proliferation policy as discriminatory. Its nuclear and missile policy had enormous popular support. No Indian government could agree to give up its options. India's nuclear policy was never Pakistan specific. To counter India's nuclear programme, Pakistan had developed its own capability. Neither of them signed the NPT and in 1996 did not sign the CTBT. In May 1998 first India and then Pakistan carried out their nuclear tests. The Clinton Administration had decided to substantially improve its relations with India. But India's nuclear tests left it with no alternative except to impose sanctions under its Nuclear Proliferation Prevention Act of 1994. Eight rounds of Stobe Talbot Jashwant Singh talks between the two countries took place. Although the talks were inconclusive, an understanding was arrived. The US accepted India's assurance that no further tests would be carried out, it would not be first to use nuclear weapons, there would be no nuclear arms race and India would have only minimum weapons for deterrence, and would not transfer the related technology and material to any country that does not have them. After the US Senate did not ratify the CTBT, the American pressure on India eased. And the issue was placed on the back burner. The Bush Administration was not keen to revive the issue. India's nuclear programme did not stand in the way of development of cooperation in strategic area. Clinton's visit to India and US Administration's stand on the Kargil war to some extent diluted the impression that the United States was hostile to India's strategic concerns.

The UPA government has indicated that there would be no change in its nuclear policy. In a joint press conference with the German Chancellor Gerhard Schroeder in October 2004, Prime Minister Manmohan Singh stated that India would not sign the NPT now. He advanced the same reasons that the NDA government had given before. India is a responsible power, it has the doctrine of "no first use" in place, and has strict control over the transfer of nuclear technology. Without mentioning Pakistan or the affair of Dr. A.Q. Khan he hinted that proliferation was taking place from within the region. During the confirmation hearings of Secretary of State Rice, Senator Kerry asked whether American interests were being served without direct access to Dr. Khan. Rice replied that the Pakistani scientist was now off the market and American interests were very well served." American war against international terrorism is on the top of its foreign policy agenda and non-proliferation in South Asia was still on the back burner.[12] The United States does not consider India to be a security threat either to itself or to its allies. It understands India's position but it does not want India's example to be followed by others. In fact, India is also concerned with nuclear proliferation. In September 2003 the United States launched Proliferation Security Initiative (PSI), which provides for preventing the illegal trafficking of weapons of mass destruction and their delivery system by inspection and raids on suspected consignments. India has indicated its interest in it. However, it has informed the United States that it would consider joining PSI if it would be part of the core group that currently has 11 members including France, Germany and the UK and only if PSI is in conformity with international and maritime law. The United States had raised the issue with India and it is likely to be discussed again.[13]

Larson, US Under Secretary of Commerce, stated recently that in the long run what will define Indo-American relation is its economic dimension. Not too long ago India was a major recipient of economic assistance from the United States and international financial institutions. Now India has graduated from US assistance programme. In the proposed American budget for 2005, India has been provided paltry $ 14 million for education and disaster management programmes.

The United States is India's topmost trading partner. In 1990 India's bilateral trade was $ US 5.6 billion. In 2003 it was $ 18.3 billion, representing a 221 per cent growth in 13 years. It had a favourable balance of approximately 8.4 billion. For more than a decade India consistently had favourable balance of trade with the United States. For nine months, from January to November 2004 the bilateral trade was $ US 19.860 billion. Exports were $ US 14.328 billion and imports were $ 5.632 billion. In nine months it had grown by 18.37 per cent. For India the favourable balance was increasing. But India was way behind much smaller countries as an exporter to the United States. Its export was only slightly more than one per cent, thus pointing vast scope for further expansion.[14] The United States has been pressing India to open its markets so that it could redress this unfavourable balance. Bilateral trade would be boosted considerably if the two countries reach an agreement on high technology trade. There are many contentious issues in trade relations like high tariff, intellectual property rights, and market access which have to be resolved. From 1 January 2005 the Multi-Fiber Trade Agreement has come in to force. The quota system under which India 's textile and garments exports to the United States were governed has been abolished. It is expected that the two countries that would get larger share of the market in the US and EU are China and India. This would further expand the bilateral trade.

Apart from trade what has emerged as a major Indian interest is Foreign Direct Investment (FDI) from the United States. India wants to develop its infrastructure necessary for expansion of manufacturing industries. It has been estimated that India needs nearly US $ 150 billion investment in its infrastructure. However, last year it could receive paltry six billion dollars in FDI. The US is one of the largest FDI investor in India. The US inflow increased from US $ 11.3 million in 1991 to US $ 4132.8 million as in August 2004. This amounts to an increase at the compound rate of 57.5 per cent per annum. The FDI inflow from the US constitutes about 11 per cent of the total actual inflow in to India. There is a wide gap between the approvals and the actuals. While the approval is $ 16853 million actual is only $ 4133 million. The actual thus is only 24.52 per cent of the approval. The FDI from the US has come to power and refineries (3 5.93 %)telecommunications (10.56 %), electrical equipments (9.50%), food processing industries (9.43%) and service sector (8.28%). In Portfolio Investment also the US is a leading investor. Currently there are 234 US based FII (Financial Institutional Investors) and 169 US based subaccounts registered with SEBI. US based FII have made an investment of $ 10.2 billion out of the total of $ 25.3 billion that amounts to 40.5 per cent of the net investment made by the FII since 1993.[15]

Foreign investment has not been a oneway street. India has been making direct investment in the United States. Since 1996 and up to 2004 the total approved Indian investment abroad amounts to 11083.11 million of which 60.9 per cent has been the actual outflow. The US share has been $ 2080.367 million constituting 18.77 per cent of the total approval. Since 1996 US has attracted higher Indian investment (US$ 2080.367 million) followed by Russia (US$ 1751.39 million.) India's outgoing investment has been highest in the field of manufacturing

(54%) followed by non-financial services including software development (35.4%). In the current financial year 2004-2005 (April-August 2004) actual outflows on account of investment was US $ 575.14 million. In the current year the US attracted highest direct investment (US $ 124.4 million.) followed by Australia (US$ 116.35 million).

India is, therefore, keen to see FDI flows to increase several fold. During his visit to the United States in the last week of September 2004, Prime Minister Manmohan Singh assured the meeting of executives of American companies in the boardroom of *The Wall Street Journal* that India is committed to reforms. Finance Minister Chidambram, who followed the Prime Minister next month, told five hundred investors in New York that the Indian government was organized to go even faster. He told them that direct investment in civil aviation would be taken this month and the telecom sector would be taken in near future. He assured that proposal for investment would be cleared in seven days.

A study carried out by the global management consultant firms A.T. Kearney concluded that India and China are aggressively challenging the United States as the world's most favourable destination for foreign investment. The study, based on interviews with the CEOs from the largest companies found that India had risen from the sixth position to third most likely destination just behind the United States. China occupied the top most position. India and China were most preferred offshore investment locations for business processing function and information technology services. The CEOs found in India highly educated workforce, management talent, rule of law, transparency, and regulatory environment as favourable. However, while China currently gets FDI $ 53.4 billion India received meager $ 4.3 billion. India has a long way to catch up with China.[16] Many of Big American corporations in the Fortune's 500 list, like General Electric, Whirl Pool, Ford, IBM, Microsoft, Intel and Wall Mart and others have set up their business in India. However, there are many medium and smaller concerns that are operating in other Asian countries that have to be brought in for further expansion of American investment. The stock of US FDI in India is nearly US $ 20 billion, forming a quarter of the total FDI inflow into the country. The American Chambers of Commerce in India spokesman expressed the hope that this could be boosted to $ 50 billion by 2015.[17]

In the last few years many American corporations have outsourced their business process to India. The reason for this is that business concerns are under pressure to show greater profits. The same job can be done much more cheaply in India than in the United States, almost at one-third of the cost. This resulted in the loss of jobs in the United States. And some politicians raised hue and cry over it in the presidential election year. While some analysts pointed out that while there was job loss at one level more jobs were created at another level with the profit the company earned. It was also pointed out that not all the job losses were due to outsourcing of business. Anyway, the US economy destroys nearly 30,000 jobs every year and then creates new jobs. But these arguments brought no consolation to those who were losing jobs. President Bush defended the outsourcing while his Democratic opponent Senator Kerry opposed it. It was suggested that penalty should be imposed on those companies who get contracts from the government and outsource jobs abroad. The elections are over and outsourcing of business process continues.

From the outset India's relations with the United States have been asymmetric. Yet, during nearly five decades of Cold War it was able to preserve autonomous space for its foreign policy. India was able to do that because the world was bipolar and one pole balanced the other. The end of the Cold War "transformed" the world. And like many other countries India had to formulate its foreign policy in the new post-Cold War environment. Asymmetry remained but India was able to improve its position. The United States could not resent India's close relations with Russia or China when the US-Russian and US-Chinese relations had moved from conflict to accommodation and cooperation. Besides the post-Cold War world witnessed unprecedented integration of world economy. Those countries that had centrally planned economy decided to change over to market economy. India moved from largely regulated economy to a more liberal order opening its markets to foreign investment and technology. India was listed by the United States as one of the ten emerging markets. Opening of the Indian economy resulted in increased cooperation between the two countries.

In June this year India signed the New Framework for US India Defense Relations for ten years. The framework stated that the goal of cooperation between the two countries was to maintain security and stability, defeat terrorism, prevent the spread of weapons of mass destruction, and protect free flow of commerce. It promised to expand defense trade, increase opportunity for technology transfer, collabouration, co-production, and research and development. It set up a Defense Production Group to oversee the defense trade and a Joint Working Group to carry out a mid-year review to be overseen by the Policy Group. More significantly, it provided for collabouration in multinational operations when it was in their common interest. There was no mention of the United Nations in this context. This provision was severely assailed.[18] The critics of the framework ignored the caveat "when it is in their common interest." The assumption was that India would be dragged into joining Iraq like unsavoury American unilateral projects. The United States could not claim to decide what was and what was not in India's interest.

The criticism came from both sides of the political spectrum: the Left and the Right. The Left asserted that the framework was "fraught with serious consequences for the country's strategic and security interest". The CPM Politburo in a statement contented that the framework compromised India's independent foreign policy and its objective of promoting multipolarity in international relations. It would only serve America's strategic goal in Asia. If carried out it would be placing India in the same category as Japan, South Korea and Philippines, the military allies of the United States. The CPI echoed its big brother saying that it offered too much to the United States.[19] The BJP directed its barbs on the presumed loss of independence.

The framework had been in the pipeline for a long time but it was not made public for fear of opposition within the government and outside. It was hidden from the public view while it was being fine-tuned. Before leaving for the United States, Defense Minister Pranab Mukerjee had said that he was going to the United States on an exploratory trip and not with a begging bowl. This secrecy aroused suspicion. The Left wanted the Framework to be discussed with parties and in public. It threatened to stage demonstration against it.

On his return from the United States on July 5, Mukerjee immediately went in a damage control mode... He downplayed its significance by stating that it was just "an expression of intent" to carry forward the 1995 agreed minutes of understanding with the United States. He pointed out that there was no mention of accord, agreement, or treaty anywhere in the document. He assured that specifics would be taken on case-by-case basis and asserted that the government would not deviate from pursuing an independent foreign policy. He also emphasized that closer relations with the United States would in no way mean any parting of the ways with our friends. Foreign Secretary Shyam Saran in the same defensive mode told reporters on July 13 that there was some misunderstanding about the framework. It set out the parameters within which the two countries could "potentially" cooperate if it was in their interest. It could not have adverse impact on India's defense relations with Russia and other countries. The prime minister himself added that the framework was only an innocuous updating of the 1995 agreement. It did not imply any surrender of sovereignty.

Before the controversy over the framework had died down, it was time for Prime Minister Manmohan Singh's four-days visit to the United States. Speaking to the Press on his way to the US after attending the G 8 meeting in the UK, Dr. Singh said that he was not going to the US with any demand. India would never be a supplicant. He pointed out that the bulk of resources for country's development has always been mobilized locally. He wanted to explain to the US Congress India's aspirations. On the issue of the US opposition to the trilateral agreement between India, Iran and Pakistan on gas pipeline from Iran, he said that if the three countries agreed, that should be the end of the matter. In the meanwhile the United States announced its opposition to the G-4 resolution on expansion of UN Security Council. It reiterated its position that the issue of expansion of the UN Security Council should be taken up only after other reforms had been implemented. The only country that it supports for the permanent seat in the Council is Japan. Thus even before Dr. Singh reached the United States, the Bush Administration indicated what it was not going to concede to India.

Dr. Singh subsequently declared that he was worried that India's food production had reached a plateau and during his visit he wanted to emphasize India's need for high technologies to raise the production. During his last visit the prime minister had heavily emphasized India's need of FDI. But during this visit the focus of the discussion was on other areas. However, while addressing the Congress he once again emphasized India's commitment to reforms, justified the pace of reforms by pointing out that being a democracy "we have to assuage and calm the fears that often arise when people face the impact of change." A panel of CEOs of the topmost corporations has been set up to explore further possibilities of trade and investment.[20] He also forcefully presented India's claim for the permanent membership of the UN Security Council.

The most important part of the visit was the meeting between Dr. Singh and President George Bush on July 18. The joint statement issued after the meeting declared the resolve of the two countries to transform their relationship and establish "global partnership". It listed various agreements that had been reached on counter terrorism, agriculture, and control of HIV/AIDs. More impoıtantly, the two leaders expressed their intent to expand their cooperation in space, civilian nuclear energy and dual use technology. It frequently referred to international efforts and reiterated the determination to play a leading part in that effort in such areas as prevention of the proliferation of Weapons of Mass Destruction.[21]

President Bush stated that as "a responsible state with advance nuclear technology, India should acquire the same benefit and advantages as other such states." This was as far as the US would go to indirectly recognize India as a nuclear power. The US promised closer cooperation in space exploration, satellite navigation and launch in the commercial space arena. As India undertook non-proliferation commitments under NSSP, the United States decided to remove certain Indian organizations from Department of Commerce's Entity List. The president told the prime minister "he will work to achieve full civil nuclear energy cooperation and trade with India as it realizes its goal of achieving energy security". He would seek agreement from Congress to adjust US laws and policies and would work with friends and allies to adjust international regimes to enable full civil nuclear cooperation and trade with India, including expeditious supply of fuel to safeguarded nuclear reactors at Tarapore but not limited to it. The president offered to facilitate India's inclusion in the International Thermonuclear Experiment Reactor (ITER) project and in the Generation IV International Forum.

In return India agreed to assume the same responsibilities and practice as other leading countries with advance nuclear technology. It would identify and separate civilian and military nuclear facilities in a phased manner and file a declaration regarding its civilian facilities with International Atomic Energy Administration (IAEA), decide to place its civilian nuclear facilities under IAEA safeguards, sign and adhere to an Additional Protocol with respect to civilian nuclear facilities, continue its unilateral moratorium on nuclear testing. In addition it promised to work with the United States for the conclusion of a multilateral Facile Material Cut Off Treaty (FMCT). It would refrain from transfer of enrichment and reprocessing technologies to states that do not have them. The president and the prime minister agreed to review the progress when the president would visit India in 2006.[22]

The process that culminated in the civil nuclear energy cooperation agreement began when Secretary of State Rice visited India and met Dr. Singh in March 2005. Nicholas Burn, Under Secretary of State, visited India in June. India sent a delegation of officials led by Foreign Secretary Shyam Saran. The acceptance of the agreement was delayed by India for twelve hours while Anil Kakodkar, the Chairman of the Atomic Commission of India carefully scrutinized it. He was virtually given a veto only after he agreed India to sign the agreement. Natwar Singh, India's Foreign Minister explained to Secretary Rice that the Prime Minister was heading a coalition government and he could not accept conditions that he could not sell to other members of the government.[23] Burns in his briefing justified the civil nuclear energy cooperation agreement on the basis of India's exceptional record on non-proliferation, its strong commitment to protection of fissile materials and technology, and its safeguarded reactors. India, he said, committed itself in public to a series of action that it had not committed itself before. He stressed:

> ... It is all about nuclear power and not about nuclear weapons. We are not recognizing India as a nuclear weapons state. We are simply opening up a channel in order to cooperate on a commercial basis and technological basis on nuclear power itself and that is very important distinction."

He went to describe the agreement as "the super structure of new relationship".[24]

The American newspapers only cautiously welcomed the agreement. *The Los Angeles Times* noted that analysts regarded it, as "significant but not ground breaking." The paper however also said that cooperation in nuclear energy marked "a substantial shift in Indo-American relations after the collapse of the Soviet Union." Selig Harrison, a well-known US specialist on South Asia, said that the NPT regime that permitted the United States to sell nuclear technology to China but not to India had become outdated. American nuclear specialists who strongly endorsed non-proliferation of nuclear weapons found the agreement quite disturbing. Some were of the view that by making India an exception the Bush Administration had undermined its own effort to confront Iran and North Korea. Nor were they certain how the accord would be seen in Pakistan.[25] George Perkovitch of the Carnegie Endowment for International Peace felt that the Nuclear Suppliers Groups, comprising forty countries would be reluctant to alter the rules. Although China was nowhere mentioned in the joint statement, a large number of American newspapers believed that one important reason for modifying American nuclear policy was to help India's rise as a global power as a counterweight to the rising influence of China in the region and India would be more valuable as a nuclear power. With strong sentiment in favour of preventing proliferation of nuclear weapons shared by many members of

Congress, President George Bush would have to fight hard to get the Congress change the rules. And convince the forty members Nuclear Suppliers Groups to change the rules. Two factors are in his favour. The Republicans have majority in both the houses of the Congress and there is an India caucus and many influential Democrats are its members.

The civil nuclear energy agreement raised a fierce storm in India. The government had failed to evolve a consensus on it. It had hoped to achieve it after agreement had been concluded, but an acrimonious debate followed. The supporters argued that under the existing laws the United States could not recognize India as a nuclear power. But it had indirectly accepted that India was a nuclear power, without India having to sign the NPT. It ended India's isolation on the nuclear issue and moved the country towards energy security. The agreement was not one-sided and India's security interests were not compromised. The critics on the other hand contended that while India made long-term and specific commitments, the United States made only promises that it may or may not be able to see it through. The former Prime Minister A.B. Vajpayee led the charge. He contended that separating civil and military nuclear facilities would be difficult if not impossible task. Its cost would be prohibitive and would deny flexibility in determining the size of India's nuclear deterrent. He endorsed the view of his National Security Advisor Brajesh Misra that the agreement "amounts to a cap on the size of India's minimum credible nuclear deterrent". India had accepted future provisions of FMCT even before an international treaty has been negotiated. Some nuclear scientists argued that had India's thorium research programme continued, the problem of fuel for the reactors would have been solved giving us freedom from imports for years.

Dr. Manmohan Singh rejected the charge that the nuclear cooperation was one-sided and heavily loaded in terms of obligations. He assured that separation of civil and military nuclear facilities would be national decision that would be on the basis of India's security concerns. The core of his defense was that it was a step forward taken to end India's isolation to meet its energy needs. The agreement would not result in the diminution of India's strategic nuclear capabilities.

Before leaving the United States, in an interview with the *Washington Post*, Dr. Singh responding to a question on Iran gas pipelines said, "I am realist enough to realize that there are many risks, because considering all the uncertainties of the situation in Iran, I don't know if any international consortium of bankers would probably underwrite this." The critics seized upon this statement as evidence of succumbing to American pressure. One analyst declared it "a self goal." India's nuclear reactors generate a meagre 3 per cent of its energy. The mid-term appraisal of the Tenth Five-Year Plan (2002-07) presented a dismal picture of the prospect of the generation of nuclear energy. Of the 15 nuclear reactors India has 11 are operational. Even if India succeeds in enhancing the production of nuclear energy with international assistance, it would still require oil and gas to maintain its economic growth rate to 7-8 per cent. Against this background it becomes highly important the trilateral project for Iranian gas is on. The United States has made known its reservation on the pipeline. It feels that the money Iran would receive from the export of gas would be used for obtaining nuclear weapons and for sustaining terrorist organizations. Mani Shankar Aiyer, the Minister of Petroleum and Natural Gas, has repeatedly stated that though some American officials have expressed their reservations, the Government of the United States has not officially conveyed its opposition. He insists that there is no pressure from the United States. He accepts that the pipeline passing through Pakistan's territory entails risks. But he contends that the risk can be minimized, for instance by keeping the pipeline at least 1.5 metres under the ground and keeping the Pakistan's outlets as near the Indian border as possible. On July 23, he said that the US agreement was not in return for abandoning $ 7.4 billion pipeline. Making a statement in the Lok Sabha on July 28, he called the apprehension of US pressure "misplaced". He again reiterated, "Pipeline issue has not been raised with us." A schedule has been drawn and the process of finalizing the project would be completed by the end of this year. The Prime Minister also indicated that the project is on. Indeed, due to the known opposition of the US to the pipeline, its continuation would be the acid test for the government. India would need nuclear energy as well as gas and oil to sustain its growth rate.

India certainly has accepted conditions that it did not accept before. It has accepted intrusive inspection of its civilian nuclear facilities by IAEA. It would be no longer possible to take the spent fuel generated for the purpose of defense. However, such obligations have been accepted by other nuclear powers. There is a trade off. In the first week of August oil prices have touched an unprecedented $ 62 dollars per barrel. This India cannot afford. It has to minimize its dependence on import of oil. The civil nuclear energy agreement moves the country in that direction. India would implement its part of the bargain only if the United States keeps its promises. Otherwise, the status quo would continue.

Undoubtedly, India and the United States share many foreign policy interests. Our interests have converged in Afghanistan. The two countries support the Karzai government and extend help in the reconstruction of the country. In Nepal the two countries want the defeat of the Maoists and return of the multiparty democracy. In Sri Lanka the United States has declared LTTE to be a terrorist organization and support the peace negotiations. But there are also areas where the interest of the two countries diverges. Iran is one such example. The two countries have common interest in the stability of Asia, a common desire to ensure energy security and preventing the disruption of global energy supply, security of the sea-lanes for commerce, prevention of drug trafficking and controlling HIV. However, there may not always be agreement on the ways to achieve these goals.

The official on both sides has frequently used such words as strategic alliance and strategic partnership. The reality, however, is that India is not yet either a strategic ally or a strategic partner of the United States. The US has not yet supported India's claim for the permanent membership of the UN Security Council. Nor it is likely that India's relations with the United States would ever be like with Japan, South Korea or the Philippines. There are several important differences between the two countries that would pose problems in the relations reaching the level of strategic alliance. India places great emphasis on finding solutions of international problems through the United Nations... and sees no problem in cooperating with the United States as it did in Somalia and other places for peace-keeping operations under the auspices of the UN. India is opposed to unilateral intervention by any country even on humanitarian grounds. If there has to be humanitarian intervention it should be taken by the United Nations that alone represents the will of the international community. Secondly, India and the United States disagree on the issue of nuclear proliferation, India would agree to roll back and terminate its nuclear programme only as part of time-bound programme of denuclearization by all nuclear powers. The United States has rejected the suggestion. It sees itself as a responsible power whose weapons do not constitute a threat to any one. But other countries' weapons are nor secure and pose a threat to others. The US is going in for further development of its own nuclear weapons capability, while wanting others to sign on nuclear non-proliferation treaty. Another important reason that works against India becoming an ally of the US is the long foreign policy tradition of independence. One important aspect of the policy of non-alignment was the ability to judge issues on merit. Being part of an alliance would limit that capacity. Non-alignment was also a democratic movement, as it did not want to concede the right of decision-making on important international issues to a few nations. It was a demand for the democratization of global politics. The Cold War has ended and so has the bloc politics. But the need of democratization of international politics still remains.

To a considerable extent the economic capability of a nation will define its place in world's power structure in this century. The rising clout of China in the world illustrates this point. With 1.3 billion people, 9 per cent annual growth rate, and $ 1.4 trillion economy no country can ignore China. Although the US economy is presently facing a number of problems it would remain the leading economic power in the world for several decades. The challenge that Europe and Japan posed in the seventies to its economic pre-eminence has faded. The massive trade deficit of 617.7 billion, reported by the Commerce Department in February 2005, its fiscal deficit, and the falling value of dollar are matters of great concern. The trade deficit is large but it still accounts for 5 per cent of its economy. Even France and Germany who strongly opposed the United States on the issue of invasion of Iraq do not want to jeopardize their exports to the US. The US is able to use market access as a lever for its influence. Good economic relations with the US serve India's interest. It also serves American interest. India's economic growth in the decades ahead would play an increasing role in the expansion of Indo-US relations. A report by international consultants Goldman and Sachs has said in a recent report that Brazil, Russia, China and India would emerge as significant factors in the world economy. In its report last year, it had said that these countries would emerge as significant factor by 2050. This year's report states that it could be much sooner. Of the present G6 countries only the US and Japan would remain among the six leading economic power in 2050. However, an average individual in India and China would still be poorer than an individual in the G6 countries except in Russia. The continuous industrialization of China and India would push the world growth rate to above 4 per cent. It could remain above 3.7 per cent that is average for the last 20 years. The report forecast was that in India the people with more than $ 3000 annual income could increase to 14 times. These developments would make a deep impact on India's relations with the United States.[26] A US Intelligence Report on 13

January 2005 reached a similar conclusion. It said that the rise of India as global players was heralding an Asian century in place of receding American century. It attributed this to sustained high economic growth, expanding military capabilities and large population.[27]

India's strategic cooperation with the US would move forward. A scholar working at the Henry L. Stimson Center has posed the question whether the growing US-India security relations is a threat to China's security.[28] He is convinced that the United States would not enter into an alliance with a third country against China. Nor is China interested in challenging the United States. Last year China's favourable balance of trade with the United States was $ 162 billion. This was the biggest trade deficit of the US with a single country in its history. There is no plausible reason for China to give up this advantage.

There are quite a few analysts who believe that United States is uncertain about the direction of the future policy of China. They point to China's growing economic relations with the ASEAN countries, its acquisition of weapons at a furious pace and its growing security cooperation with Russia. It is argued that US is viewing India as a counterweight to China. Sometimes pro-India Congressmen have lent weight to this line of argument in order to push the US towards closer relations with India. It has been suggested that economic relations alone are not sufficient for close relations with China. After all India should have an edge over China because it is a functioning democracy with a population that exceeds a billion. This line of argument does not take into consideration that India itself may not be interested in being viewed as counterweight to China. For the last couple of years it has been interested in bridging its differences with China. Its own bilateral trade with it has been growing rapidly. The US wants to use China's influence over North Korea in resolving the issue of its possession of nuclear weapons. The two countries share common interest in containing Islamic militants in Central Asia. India's defense cooperation with the US has to stand on its merit.

As the Cold War ended a new international order came into being. One group of countries is no longer pitted against another, but each country is seeking to maximize its political, strategic, and economic interests. It cooperates with others and also competes with them. India has to play its role in this policy environment. Flexibility and innovation can only result in success. The agreements that Manmohan Singh has concluded have taken the India-US relations to new heights. India has to enhance its relations with other major players like China, Europe and Russia.

References

1. *Times News Network*, 28 January 2005.

2. Text of the address in Official Text (New Delhi: Public Affairs Office, US, Embassy, 19 January 2005).

3. In an interview given to *India Abroad*, Foreign Secretary Shashank said, "The role played by the Indian expatriate community in the United States acted as the lever for the change of perception about India." March 30, 2004. Rediff interviews.

4. Talbott was speaking on "US India relations in the age of Globalisation" in Chennai. Under the auspices of Observer Research Foundation. Report in *The Hindu*, 5 February 2005.

5. Colin Powell designated 39 groups as Foreign Terrorist Organizations on 19 October 2004. Some of the groups operating from Pakistan included in the list were Harkat-ul-Mujahideen, Jaish-e-Mohammed, Lashkar-e-Tayyiba and Lashkar-I-Jhangvi. Fact Sheet, Public Affairs Office, US Embassy, New Delhi, October 20, 2004.

6. *The Hindu*, 7 August 2004.

7. Powell's interview with the USA Today Editorial Board, October 18, 2004. Backgrounder, New Delhi: Public Affairs Office of the Embassy of the United States, October 20, 2004.

8. General Vij was speaking on the annual Army Day. *The Hindu*, 16 January 2005.

9. *The Indian Express*, (Online) 16 February 2005.

10. *The Hindu*, 24 February 2005.

11. For Blackwill's statement see *The Hindustan Times*, 11 January 2005.

12. *The Hindu*, 20 January 2005.

13. *The Hindustan Times*, 19 October 2004.

14. http;///www.www.indiagov/org/trade/trade htm

15. http/www.indiagov/org/Economy.htmlUS%20investment 520on%20india

16. *The Hindu*, 13 October 2004.

17. *Ibid.*, 28 January 2005.

18. *The Hindustan Times*, 30 June 2005.

19. *The Hindu*, 2 July 2005.

20. Full Text of Dr. Singh's address to the joint session of the US Congress see embassy/. Org/India/Review/2005.pdf. The CEO Forum is chaired by Ratan Tata. Some other members are Mukesh Ambani, Deepak Parekh, Nandan Nilakani, and P.C. Reddy. Baba Kalyani and Y.C. Deveshwar. The American group includes the CEOs of City Group, J.P. Morgan chase and Pepisco.

21. For details refer to Official Text: "United States, India Resolve to Establish Global Partnership". Joint statement issued following Bush-Singh meeting in Washington on July 18, New Delhi: Public Affairs Office of the US Embassy, July 19, 2005.

22. *Ibid.*

23. Harish Khare in *The Hindu*, 8 August 2005.

24. Press briefing on the President's Meeting with Prime Minister Singh of India by Burns and Mike Green, Senior Director for Asian Affairs at the NSC on July 18, Official Text, New Delhi: Public Affairs.

Office of the US Embassy, July 19, 2005. Also see Burns on record briefing on the joint statement on the same day.

25. *Washington Post*, 19 July *Los Angles Times*, 19 July, *Christian Science Monitor*, July 20, *The Wall Street Journal*, 19 July, 2005.

Iran responded on the predicted lines. It accused the Bush Administration of practicing double standard and undermining the NPT while agreeing to help India's nuclear civil programme while insisting that Tehran abandon its nuclear ambition or face international sanctions. *The Guardian*, 28 July 2005).

26. *The Hindu*, 24 October 2004.

27. The Report was entitled "Mapping the Global Future", *Times of India*, 14 January 2005.

28. Zhang Guihong, "US India Security Relations: Implications for China," http://www. Satp org/satporg/faultline/volume14/article2.htm.

9

India-Russia Relations

Gulshan Sachdeva

Continuity, mutual trust and confidence are the major pillars of India-Russia relations. On the basis of solid background of Indo-Soviet ties, the bilateral relationship has developed into a strong "strategic partnership" in recent years. This has happened despite weak commercial relationship between the two countries. However, in the coming years, the relationship faces serious challenges. The dynamics of economic and commercial relationship will have serious implications for bilateral ties. In this context, the paper tries to understand present realities of Indo-Russian trade and other economic linkages.

It is argued that economic changes in Russia had adverse impact on bilateral economic ties during the first half of the nineties. Economic relations survived mainly because of Indian defense purchases, a limited protection to its exporters and some public sector investments by India. So far the "special relationship" has been limited only to arms trade and defense technology. Indian private sector is very slow to take advantage from the Russian economic transformation. Similarly, Russian companies, which are not part of the military industrial complex, have not gained much from strong Indian economic growth in the last fifteen years. Things are, however, beginning to change in the last few years, particularly after the signing of "strategic partnership". With a strong economic growth in both the countries, it is time to give a new direction to bilateral economic relations with new initiatives.

Background

One important point of old Indo-Soviet friendship was a special bilateral trade and economic relationship. Although this arrangement had many usual weaknesses like corruption, patronage, transactions in low quality products, it helped many small and medium size private

Indian companies to become exporters. After the disintegration of the Soviet Union, this relationship has been badly damaged. Economic transformation in Russia from a centrally planned economy to a market economy in 1992 coincided with the policies of economic liberalization in India. These developments changed the nature and character of foreign economic relations in both the countries. Therefore, despite having solid economic and trade relations in the past, a large part of the 1990's was a period of difficult adjustments, both for Indian as well as Russian businesses.

The decade of 1990's was a very difficult period for Russian business. It was not only that Russia was transforming its economic system, but this transformation was also taking place in a period, when Russian economy faced one crisis after another. As a result, the Russian economy was already reduced to half of what it was in 1990, when another financial and economic crisis hit the economy in August 1998. In contrast, the Indian economy in the 1990's grew fast, compared to any other time in the recent past. The average annual growth rate between 1990 and 2000 was minus 4.8 per cent for Russia and about 6 per cent for India. So Indo-Russian economic relations also have to be looked within this context.

Bilateral Trade

Since 1953, when the first trade agreement took place, seven long-term agreements were signed between the two countries up to the collapse of the USSR. This bilateral trade as we know was conducted through a specific system of trade and payment, called Rupee Trade System based on annual plans. Important point of the system was payments in non-convertible currency. The trade turnover between the two countries increased from less than Rs. 2 crore in 1953 to about 8,000 crore in 1990-91. In 1990-91 more than 16 per cent of Indian exports went to USSR and about 6 per cent imports came from it.

After the collapse of the Soviet Union, Indian and Russian governments renegotiated the entire trade regime. The 1993 agreement terminated the traditional Rupee trade arrangement and mandated all bilateral trade transactions to be conducted on hard currency basis. But with this agreement, the issue of repayment of civilian and military loans taken by India from the former USSR also came up. Finally, after prolonged negotiations, the Rouble credit was denominated in Rupees and repayment schedule was drawn up. The agreement provided for an annual repayment of about US$ 1 billion equivalent in Rupees to Russia over a period of 12 years starting from 1994, with smaller amounts for a further period of 33 years. The Rupee debt funds were to be used by the Russian side for import of goods and trade related services from India.

As a result of these changes, the bilateral trade, since the early nineties, has been based on payments in freely convertible currencies. All Russian exports to India follow the new system. But in the last decade, about two-thirds of Indian exports were financed through the renegotiated rupee-debt repayment mechanism. As a result of all these economic policy changes, traditional actors in Indo-Russian trade and other economic relations like the public sector units and state trading corporations were no longer as relevant as they used to be in the Soviet era. Sections of Indian private sector, which used to get away with selling many products of questionable quality under the bilateral system, also found it difficult to adjust to radically changed economic and commercial environment in Russia, driven by market forces.

It is evident from the Table 1 that Indo-Russian trade has declined substantially since the early nineties. Last year, some improvement is seen in imports. Although it is too early to conclude, yet it may be beginning of a new era in bilateral trade relations. Already both the governments are talking about US $ 5 to $ 6 billion trade turnover in the next few years. Main items of traditional exports from India are tea, readymade garments, drugs and pharmaceuticals, processed minerals, coffee, plastic and linoleum products, tobacco, wool etc. Recently some non-traditional items have also shown some growth. The Confederation of Indian Industry (CII) expects Indian pharmaceutical exports to Russia to rise steeply in the next few years. Traditional imports from Russia include fertilizer, iron and steel, non-ferrous metals, newsprint, synthetic rubber, chemicals, transport equipment etc. In the last two years, there are some very positive trends in imports from Russia in almost all categories of goods. (For details see appendices 1 and 2).

The agreement on India-Russia transport corridor may also help in reducing transport costs. The present route, which passes through the Suez Canal and enters into the Russian port of St. Petersburg via Kotka (Finland) and Rotterdam (Netherlands), is long and time consuming. The new route would comprise sea and land links across India, Iran and Russia and will shorten travel time by as much as ten days. The new route will be Mumbai-Bandar Abbas (Iran) Astrakhan (Russia).

Table 1: India-Russia Trade, 1993-1994 to 2003-2004

(in US $ million)

Year	*Exports*	*% Share of total Indian exports*	*Imports*	*% Share of total Indian imports*	*Total Trade*	*% Share of total Indian trade*
1993-94	648.60	2.92	256.89	1.10	905.49	1.98
1994-95	807.38	3.07	504.54	1.76	1311.92	2.39
1995-96	1046.55	3.29	857.53	2.33	1904.09	2.78
1996-97	811.84	2.42	628.96	1.61	1440.8	1.98
1997-98	954.12	2.72	679.02	1.63	1633.14	2.13
1998-99	706.26	2.14	545.42	1.29	1254.68	1.66
1999-00	948.99	2.58	623.94	1.25	1572.93	1.82
2000-01	869.93	1.97	517.19	1.03	1387.12	1.47
2001-02	796.83	1.82	538.36	1.05	1332.19	1.41
2002-03	704.00	1.34	592.61	0.96	1296.61	1.14
2003-04	713.76	1.12	959.63	1.23	1673.39	1.18

Source: Centre for Monitoring Indian Economy and Ministry of Commerce, Government of India.

Dominance of Defence and Public Sector

Despite economic policy changes in both the countries, Indo-Russian economic relationship is still dominated by the defence/public sector. Strong economic linkage is still in the military industrial complex. In 1991, 70 per cent of Army armaments, 80 per cent of Air Force armaments and 85 per cent of Navy armaments were of Soviet origin. This is an established fact that India still relies heavily on Russia for its arms. During the Cold War years, the former USSR and India maintained very close defence ties. According to some estimates India has bought some $ 33 billion worth of weapons from Moscow since the 1960s and Russian weapons account for nearly three quarters of India's arsenal. Estimates suggest that India imports US $ 1.5 billion worth of military hardware every year. In the next few years India is going to purchase arms worth $ 10 billion. And a major portion of these imports will come from Russia. In a recent interview the Russian Defence Minister Sergei Ivanov said that "Russia has so far concluded long-term military and technical contracts with India to the sum of $ 5 billion". These contracts, he said will be implemented in the next 5-7 years. Both countries also plan to stage war games of paratroopers at the end of 2005 as part of joint combat training.

Russia's annual military sales to India and China are believed to amount to some 80 per cent of Moscow's overall arms exports, which reached $ 3.7 billion in 2000 and $ 4.5 billion in 2001. According to some estimates, at 1990 constant prices, India imported weapons worth $ 9 billion in the period between 1993 and 2002. And about 75 per cent of these weapons came from Russia. There are also estimates that about 800 Russian defense production facilities are kept in operation by Indian defense contracts.

The major purchases in the last ten years from Russia have been about Su-30MK FGR aircraft, T-72MI and T-90 battle tanks, Ka-31/ helix helicopters and variety of other armaments. Major deals worth billions of dollars are under serious consideration or already signed on variety of SAM and SAM systems.

After nearly a decade of negotiations, India has finally agreed to purchase aircraft carrier Admiral Gorshkov. The modernization of the carrier will cost India around $ 700 million, and the remainder of the billion dollar deal will include up to 30 MiG-29K fighters and six Kamov-31 anti-submarine helicopters. According to Russian Defence Ministry sources already three stages of the Admiral Gorshkov contract have been implemented.

In the area of investment cooperation a few deals are worth mentioning. These include ONGC Videsh's investment in Sakhalin-1 ($ 1.7 billion), the SUN group's contribution to Russian brewing, Doctor Reddy's Lab's and Lupin's in pharmaceuticals. ONGC has also shown interest in developing the Vankor field in Krasnoyarsk territory in East Siberia, with recoverable reserves estimated at 125 million tons of oil and 79 billion cubic metres of natural gas. Both countries also signed a deal in 2001 for the construction of two large reactors for nuclear power station at Kudankulam in Tamil Nadu, expected to generate 2,000 MW of power (total cost 2.6 billion dollars). Another joint venture which has been in the news lately is BrahMos. This venture has been set up between Federal State Unitary Enterprise NPO Mashinostroyeniya of Russia and Defence Research and Development Organisation (DRDO) of India to design, develop, produce and market a multi-role supersonic cruise missile named BrahMos (stands for Brahmaputra and Moscow rivers). Russian company has invested about $ 72 million in the venture. The BrahMos is essentially an anti-ship missile that can be launched from ships, submarines and silos on land. President Putin during his 2004 visit called the missile "a real joint venture between Russia and India, which showcases strengths of both the countries". According to some market estimates, BrahMos can capture about 20 per cent of the international market for such missiles. Out of about 10,000 such missiles sold worldwide everywhere its share could be about 2,000 missiles. In these circumstances, Indian President, A.P.J. Abdul Kalam stressed recently that thrust should now be on the marketing of the product. If not marketed in time, it could face competition from other missiles in the next 5 to 10 years.

Five Indian public sector undertakings are active in Russia. These are: State Bank of India, Canara Bank, India Trade Promotion Organisation (ITPO), Tea Board of India, and Oil and Natural Gas Commission (ONGC). As mentioned earlier, the most important in all these is ONGC investment in Russia. Under an agreement signed on February 10, 2001, between Rosneft-Sakhalin (Rosneft-S) and Sakhalinmorneftegaz-Shelf (SMNG-S), subsidiaries of Rosneft, the Russian oil company, and ONGC Videsh Limited (OVL), a subsidiary of the Oil and Natural Gas Corporation (ONGC), OVL acquired a combined 20 per cent interest in the Sakhalin-1 project from Rosneft-S. ONGC *Videsh's* initial investment in the Sakhalin-1 project is expected to be about US $ 1.7 billion.

Most of these initiatives, however, are co-operations at the public sector level. Along with these companies, the presence of some big Indian business houses in the Russian market is very important. Indian industry has already identified areas of mutual interest viz. information technology, pharmaceuticals, telecommunications, financial services, hydrocarbons, energy and power, oil and gas, food processing, financial consultancy, management services, textiles and diamond processing. In the last few years major Indian private company to invest in Russia has been "Sun Group of Companies" in the areas of beverage and food processing. According to company sources, the commutative amount of its direct and portfolio investments into various industrial units in Russia is about $ 500 million since 1991. Some other Indian companies like Videocon Ltd. etc. have also signed MOU with Russian companies.

State Linkages

Since 1992, eleven summit level meetings have taken place and about 110 agreements have been signed between the two countries. In addition, Indian President Mr. Kalam and Congress President Mrs. Sonia Gandhi have also visited Russia recently. To improve economic relationship, an Indo-Russian Inter-Governmental Commission on Trade, Economic, Scientific, Technological and Cultural Cooperation has been working towards promoting bilateral cooperation. The Commission covers 11 joint working groups viz., Trade and Economic Cooperation; Pharmaceutical; Petroleum; Coal Industry; Metallurgy; Science and Technology; Cultural Cooperation; Information Technology; Power and Energy; Environment and Natural Resources and Cooperation with the Regions.

After few ups and downs, a major turning point in bilateral relationship has been the signing of "strategic Partnership" between the two countries during the visit of Russian President Putin's to India in October 2000. Broadly this agreement means enhanced cooperation in the political, economic, defence and cultural fields. The agreement talks of "deepening and diversifying cooperation in sectors such as metallurgy, fuel and energy, information technology, communications and transport, including merchant shipping and civil aviation". To promote bilateral trade it also talks of "further development of cooperation in banking and finance, and improving credit and insurance facilities". There was also mention of simplifying rules and procedures for travel by entrepreneurs and businessmen of both countries. It was also agreed to jointly explore the possibilities of regional trading arrangements with third countries. Altogether 16 agreements were signed during that visit including an agreement on establishing an Inter-governmental Commission on Military-Technical Cooperation. As per this agreement, two heads of States are also meeting regularly every year, either in India or in Russia.

In 2001 during Indian Prime Minister Vajpayee's visit to Moscow another 16 documents were signed including Moscow declaration on international terrorism; line of credit agreement between EXIM Bank of India and Vnesheconombank of Russia; and MOU between Confederation of Indian Industry (CII) and Russian Union of Industrialists and Entrepreneurs (Employers) (RUIE) for opening representative offices in Moscow and Delhi. Another six documents were signed during President Putin's visit to India in 2002. Further ten documents were concluded during Indian Prime Minister's visit to Russia in October 2003. The crux of all these summit meetings has been common positions on major global issues international terrorism and desire for a multipolar world and bilateral relations. These summits have been very useful platform for formulating common positions and responses to emerging global political and economic issues. However, in pure commercial terms very little was achieved from Indian point of view despite very long nicely worded declarations.

Although it can be argued that under new circumstances, business in both the countries is no more the business of the governments. Therefore, it is up to the private sector to take advantage of conditions and atmosphere created by these agreements and meetings. Despite this, these high level visits could have been used more effectively to promote Indian economic interests in Russia. Compared to India, Russian companies have done good business during these visits. Russia has comparative advantage in arms industry, and India has purchased arms worth billions of dollars during these visits. These annual summit meetings were good opportunities where some special bilateral economic relationship could have been created, even under entirely different circumstances.

President Putin's Visit in 2004

Russian President Putin's visit (3-5 December 2004) to India tried to further strengthen the "strategic partnership" between the two countries. During the visit, altogether ten agreements were signed. These include agreements on long-term cooperation in joint development and use of the Russian global navigation satellite system (GLONASS) and cooperation in the study and use of space. Gas Authority of India Limited (GAIL) signed agreements with Gasprom and Stroitansgaz. For direct banking relations, agreements were signed between the State Bank of India, Canara Bank and Russian Sberbank. Another agreement on cooperation was reached between Vnesheconombank, Roseximbank and the Indian Export Credit Guarantee Corporation. On academic cooperation, an agreement was also signed between the Jawaharlal Nehru University and Russian Centre for National Glory. India has also agreed that it would recognize Russia as a market economy in anti-dumping negotiations, it would support its efforts to join the World Trade Organisation (WTO), and also finalize an intellectual property rights (IPR) agreement to protect defence technology in the next four months. In the joint declaration both the countries have agreed on most global and regional issues including the reform in the UN system, need for multipolar world, fight against terrorism, situation in Iraq and Afghanistan, stability in Central Asia and cooperation in the energy sector.

But what does it mean in real terms? There are many ways of looking at these developments. The diehard proponents of old Indo-Soviet/Russian friendship will certainly emphasize the need to look at these agreements and declarations as a testimony of a time tested mutually beneficial friendship. They can even go one step further and suggest that along with Russia, we should forge solid friendships with other like-minded countries including China, to counter some of the negative trends of a unipolar world, dominated by a single economic and military power.

However, many people in the new generation of Indians, who have entered the business or academic professions since the early 1990s, have somewhat different impressions about these summit meetings and declarations. They argue that since 1992, eleven summit meetings have taken place and more than 110 agreements have been signed between the two countries. Various inter-governmental Commissions and Committees are working to improve bilateral relations. We also have a "strategic partnership" with Russia. Still our exports to Russia are lower than even to countries like Bangladesh, South Korea and Israel. In recent years, bilateral trade with Russia is less than 1.5 per cent of total Indian trade. Only about 1.5 per cent Indian exports enter Russia and only about 1 per cent imports come from Russia. In today's Russia, about seventy per cent of the economy is in the private sector. Still we have not moved beyond the public sector and government declarations. So we need to strengthen the commercial component of our relationship through the linkages between the dynamic sectors of the Indian industry, commerce and services and the newly emerging Russian private sector. In the absence of this relationship, "strategic partnership" will start losing its charm soon.

Realistically speaking, there is truth in both the arguments. Even after more than a decade of the Soviet collapse, our relationship, particularly in the economic field, is still in transition. After some disruption, we have been able to restore and improve our political linkages. In the economic and academic fields, however, most old linkages have broken and we have not been able to develop new ones. Now both the governments have recognised this fact. Still these summit meetings have been able to tackle the issue only partially.

Conclusion

In the last fourteen years, the relative economic position of India and Russia has changed dramatically. Military-technical cooperation seems to be the only solid pillar of the "strategic partnership". Future bilateral economic relations will depend on Russia's importance to India's developmental needs and vice versa. In the past, USSR played an important role in India's industrialization process. It had a comparative advantage in sectors like steel and coal etc., which were central to India's needs. India has to assess now where Russia has a comparative advantage. So far India is able to identify only defense production and oil and gas sector. It is one of the top buyers of the Russian arms and has made one of the biggest public sector investments in Sakhalin-1. With BrahMos complex, the relationship has grown from the simple buyer-seller to joint defense production. President Putin mentioned during his recent visit that he admires achievements of the Indian economy and Russia plans to participate in Indian projects in civil aviation, road and railway construction, and transportation of hydrocarbons. Along with Indian partners, already a Russian oil and gas construction company OAO Stroytransgaz has built Baroda-Ahmedabad-Khalol gas pipeline. This year the company has signed another contract with Essar to construct a 688 km Chennai-Trichi-Madurai product pipeline.

Indian companies could also help Russian restructuring and modernization through its expertise in information technology, management and financial services. While addressing the members of Confederation of Indian Industry (CII) and Federation of Chambers of Commerce and Industry (FICCI) in Bangalore, President Putin said that India's cooperation would be useful in areas such as ongoing research and development of super computers in Russia. He called for bold steps in joint projects in basic electronics, information technology, telecommunications, biotechnology, pharmaceuticals, space, atomic energy, machine and technical production for the coal industry, and metallurgy. While realizing the potential, the CII has already reopened its office in Moscow.

In the immediate future, the sustained growth of the Russian economy and competitiveness of Indian industry, commerce and services will determine the future of bilateral relations. The strong political will in both the countries to improve bilateral economic relations could be converted into real economic gains through imaginative initiatives. There is a lot of merit in studying a bilateral preferential or free trade agreement. This kind of initiative has the potential to give new direction to bilateral relations. The "strategic partnership" document also says that both the countries will jointly explore the possibilities of regional trading arrangements with the third countries. So far nothing has happened on this front. Some kind of regional economic initiative is possible in the CIS region, particularly in Central Asia. Some reports suggest that CII and FICCI are also examining a trilateral arrangement involving Russia, China and India. Both Indian and Russian economies are expected to grow at about 6-7 per cent this year. This is the right time to give a new direction to Indo-Russian economic relations. But both the countries need to improve business environment. And the beginning will be made if they start removing basic obstacles like providing market information to business communities, removing cargo problems and improving visa regimes. These steps will go a long way in realizing the real meaning of "strategic partnership".

Appendix 1 : Composition of Indian Imports from Russia 1995-96 to 2003-04

(US$ million)

	1995-96	*1996-97*	*1997-98*	*1998-99*	*1999-00*	*2000-01*	*2001-02*	*2002-03*	*2003-04*
All commodities	**857.53**	**628.96**	**679.02**	**545.42**	**623.94**	**517.19**	**537.33**	**594.15**	**962.05**
Fertilizer Manufactured	168.33	29.52	77.17	149.44	200.96	86.31	137.76	96.76	141.06
Newsprint	85.38	74.13	82.26	60.93	53.01	64.04	63.92	63.32	71.03
Non-ferrous metal	179.1	164.33	136.17	55.57	60.7	61.38	59.35	68.61	144.49
Iron and steel	130.66	77.17	157.42	75.16	60.91	101.27	51.43	102.53	189.41
Synthetic and reclaimed rubber	4.42	4.83	8.1	12.41	17.1	16.76	30.83	37.60	54.93
Non-electrical machinery	47.57	27.83	39.09	21.88	30.81	16.78	17.59	28.71	33.45
Other crude mineral	2.86	3.66	4.13	3.08	5.71	6.85	15.01	15.11	21.94
Coal, coke and briquettes				5.71	43.41	6.27	12.01	16.04	49.62
Printed books, newspaper etc.	1.98	0.84	0.05	0.08	4.39	14.91	10.92	18.14	25.20
Organic Chemicals	45.72	29.19	34.73	19.19	15.33	5.09	6.89	12.09	21.99
Silver					8.38	1.12	6.83	7.13	15.38
Transport Equipment	12.9	37.58	16.82	5.9	7.44	30.28	6.32	9.72	60.27
Electronic goods	2	1.52	1.51	1.34	6.51	11.06	5.87	17.25	27.34
Manufactures of metals	2.49	1.4	1.56	2.36	3.04	3.17	5.34	6.63	11.67
Medicinal and Pharm. Products	2.57	5.22	5.78	5.56	5.08	5.01	5.09	3.13	2.12
Inorganic Chemicals	1.88	14.43	17.89	13.11	3.2	10.49	4.85	19.27	16.29
Metalliferous ores and metal scrap	9.97	10.89	17.21	13.4	21.91	7.26	4.05	6.74	7.93
Primary steel pig iron based items	28.68	8.51	10.46	4.15	23.42	13.99	3.65	4.11	8.84
Pearls precious/semiprecious stones			0.99	0.01	0.49	0.83	0.38	1.00	1.44

(Contd.)

(Contd. Appendix 1)

	1995-96	1996-97	1997-98	1998-99	1999-00	2000-01	2001-02	2002-03	2003-04
Project goods	16.3	9.27	1.18	18.32	17.82	4.45	3.10	2.06	6.78
Professional Inst. Optical goods etc.	1.29	1.64	1.09	0.94	2.14	1.27	2.57	1.16	3.87
Pulp and waste paper	23.23	6.44	10.73	0.7	0.96	1.08	2.39	2.10	3.42
Chemical material and products	1.08	0.15	0.1	0.24	0.13	0.83	2.32	0.74	1.99
Pulses		0.06					1.98	9.03	2.72
Artificial resins, plastic materials etc.	4.65	1.98	1.73	0.29	1.12	1.21	1.66	1.63	3.14
Electronic machinery	0.86	0.47	1.36	1.27	2.7	0.51	0.72	0.41	1.15
Wood and wood products	0.03	0.55	0.73	0.09	0.05	0.08			
Cotton raw and waste	5.36			1.51	15.35	9.45			
Machine Tools			2.24	0.11	0.06	0.17	0.15	0.05	0.51

Source: Centre for Monitoring Indian Economy.

Appendix 2 : Composition of Indian Exports to Russia 1995-96 to 2003-04

(US$ million)

	1995-96	1996-97	1997-98	1998-99	1999-00	2000-01	2001-02	2002-03	2003-04
All commodities	**1046.56**	**811.84**	**954.12**	**709.26**	**948.99**	**869.93**	**800.90**	**705.83**	**710.55**
RMG of cotton incl. accessories	39.66	30.47	52.92	93.13	152.37	208.23	216.80	219.72	157.14
Drug, pharm and fine chemicals	90.92	108.99	106.07	47.65	122.89	108.95	101.22	107.24	136.38
Tea	142.69	75.04	198.49	197.89	162.07	105.01	84.78	59.48	55.37
Coffee	102.1	85.78	93.97	59.17	56.77	63.19	67.02	46.33	45.63
RMG of man-made fibres	12.26	12.22	16. 6	26. 01	44.56	44.95	50.78	18.68	8.74
RMG wool	33.23	33.52	25.76	15. 74	38.14	33.12	40.92	12.32	14.12
Cotton yarn fab. madeups etc.	35.52	61.78	76.61	51.23	69.18	66.78	26.71	15.61	18.09
RMG of other textile materials	8.07	5	6.59	3.5 8	10.61	23.1	22.07	14.34	10.47
Electronic goods	18.2	4.75	20.1	5.84	33.63	15.16	18.64	9.61	8.25
Tobacco unmanufactured	21.63	30.35	59.27	25.12	46.6	27.49	21.62	24.15	20.92
Machinery and instrument	20.39	20.92	14.15	18.84	24.27	10.09	16.96	12.56	14.53
Plastic and Linoleum products	27.94	32.82	30.8	12.64	25.48	21.35	16.46	13.62	22.61
Castor oil	13.54	2.2	1.83	1.06	11.57	10.91	11.97	7.39	12.41
Cosmetics/Toiletries	34.88	19.09	20.26	7.86	8.12	6.73	9.06	5.19	7.11
Leather goods	5.61	6.41	8.28	5.37	13.2	18.77	7.91	5.96	5.32
Transport equipments	10.07	3.82	4.25	3.93	3.48	2.22	5.69	14.31	6.01
Non-basmati rice	31.61	89.51	41.37	33.51	36.09	0.45	5.34	5.60	12.20

(Contd.)

(Contd. Appendix 2)

	1995-96	1996-97	1997-98	1998-99	1999-00	2000-01	2001-02	2002-03	2003-04
Finished Leather	13.95	2.61	3.55	1.72	1.19	2.58	5.41	3.19	4.64
Man-made yarn fab. made-ups	6.77	6.72	5.02	2.65	5.72	6.22			
Inorg/org/agro-chemicals	15.11	4.3	6.97	5.88	1.41	4.14	3.58	2.57	4.24
RMG of silk	2.05	2.52	0.35	0.91	0.18	1.52	3.18	0.24	5.38
Manufactures of metals	2.37	2.16	2.26	2.91	2.88	3.32	3.08	3.04	9.17
Glass/glassware/ceramics/cement	1.16	0.71	2.5	0.04	0.49	0.54			
Rubber manufactured products	4.78	2.34	3.77	3.81	5.78	4.00	2.48	1.90	3.48
Dye, intermediates	0.81	2.06	1.85	0.67	1.19	2.03	2.27	3.73	5.32
Marine products	3.6	1.72	0.94	0.05	0.1	0.24			
Cashew			4.31	1.14	1.71	1.27	1.30	1.44	4.04
Paperwood products			0.55	1.64	1.82	1.95	1.81	2.06	3.41
Ferro Alloys								0.02	3.30

10

Sino-Indian Relations in the 21st Century

V.D. Chopra

Recent developments have once again underlined that regional relations have begun to exercise considerable weight in the international politics. It is in this context that an objective estimate should be made of new trends in Sino-Indian relations, which have their own peculiarity, commonality of economic interests and divergence on geopolitical perceptions. At the moment, what is important is that Sino-Indian relations are being more and more influenced by commonality of their economic interests.

Let us examine the evolution of Sino-Indian relations in the recent years. It has to be taken into account that China and India are the largest and the most populated countries on our planet, which are described as the Asian giants.

Sino-Indian relations remained at a low level after 1962 conflict till Indira Gandhi took the first step to upgrade the diplomatic relations between the two countries. Rajiv Gandhi's visit to Beijing in December 1988 marked a turning point in the evolution of the relations between the two countries. This was followed by the visit to India in 1991 by Chinese Premier Li Peng and by P.V. Narasimha Rao to China in 1993. These visits brought in a large measure of political and military stability to a completely normalised pattern of India-China relationship. After that, several important visits have been exchanged. K.R. Narayanan's visit to China in June 2000 and the visit of Jiang Zemin to India are events of great significance. This reflects how the two countries have put the past aside and are now constructing their relations in mutual interests of both the nations. Let us leave this at that and examine the content of the new relationship.

China is facing Islamic militancy, which is fuelling separatism in the Xinjiang province inhabited by Uighur Muslims. The same problems are being faced by Russia in Chechnya. A similar scenario exists in Kazakhstan, Kyrghyzstan, Tajikistan and Uzbekistan and in Jammu and Kashmir in India. This situation has led to the formation of the "Shanghai Co-op Organisation" (SCO). The six nations have joined hands to fight the "three forces"—terrorism, separatism and extremism. This in turn has begun to influence positively Sino-Indian relations on the crucial issue of terrorism.

China and India are engaged in economic development and modernisation. China is keen to participate in various projects for development of infrastructure in India. Indian goods and services have entered the Chinese market. There are more than one dozen Indian companies operating in the eastern part of China. It should be kept in mind that the Chinese economy is the second largest economy in the world, next only to the US in terms of purchasing power parity as estimated by the World Bank's criterion.

Serious efforts are being made by both the countries to resolve the border disputes. This is confirmed by the fact that after recording their perceptions of the Line of Actual Control (LAC) along a 345 km "middle sector" stretch, India and China are gearing up for a similar exercise along their frontier in the Ladakh area. Both sides have defined their individual perceptions of the LAC along their border in Uttaranchal and recorded it on maps. There is a convergence of views on the LAC alignment along large portions in this sector. However, they differ on the lay of LAC in some segments. This confirms how efforts are being made to resolve this dispute.

This does not mean that Sino-Indian relations are developing on the same model as Indo-Russian and Sino-Russian relations. India has serious reservations about supply of nuclear capable missiles by China to Pakistan. If Sino-Indian border dispute is resolved, it will open new vistas of economic and political cooperation.

Within a short span of time after the brief chill that descended on Sino-Indian relations following the nuclear tests of May 1998, New Delhi and Beijing have rapidly transformed their bilateral relationship. Underlying this transformation has been a new Indian pragmatism that has evolved over the years in approaching the relationship with China. That realism began with the visit of Atal Behari Vajpayee to China in 1979. It broke a big taboo in Indian thinking about the relationship with China after 1962. Nearly a decade later, Rajiv Gandhi travelled to China to produce that elusive political breakthrough—the simultaneous pursuit of a solution to the boundary problem as well as a rapid normalisation of bilateral relations. Both Vajpayee and

Rajiv Gandhi had to face intense opposition from their own parties and the foreign policy establishment against what was seen as "adventurism" in the diplomacy towards China. This institutional resistance, however, succeeded during the 1990s in slowing down the pace of Sino-Indian rapprochement. Vajpayee did pick up the threads again during his visit in 2003 and opened the doors for a more purposeful negotiation on the boundary dispute and a more imaginative approach to future economic cooperation. More fundamentally, Rajiv Gandhi and Vajpayee were instrumental in burying the victim mentality that India carried since the 1962 war with China. A new generation in India with greater self-confidence about its own future is now capable of thinking about the difficult issues with China in a more relaxed manner. That the initiative for recasting the relationship with China has come from both Indian National Congress (INC) and the Bharatiya Janata Party (BJP) is an important guarantor of national consensus, which is so necessary to deal with the emotive boundary question with China. The talks on the boundary dispute have demonstrated the commitment of the Congress Government to pursue the process initiated by its predecessor with equal vigour. This has provided the much needed assurances to the Chinese on the continuity in India's approach to the boundary question. There is no reason to believe that the Manmohan Singh Government will not keep the BJP leadership fully in the picture on the boundary negotiations with China and preserve the current valuable national consensus. India and China are negotiating their boundary dispute in a radically different manner. In the past they argued on the basis of historical precedent and legal claims. While both sides have inherited what seemed inflexible positions, they have agreed to resolve the question within the overall political perspective of the evolving bilateral relationship. In short the current negotiation is a political one rooted in their calculus of national interest. Beijing and New Delhi have agreed that there has to be "give and take" in resolving the boundary dispute. Those mutual concessions will have to be worked out—on the basis of a broad set of principles—in the future rounds of boundary talks. The second factor transforming the relationship is an economic one. The dramatic expansion of bilateral trade in recent years has provided a stabilising element that did not exist before. Coupled with India's commerce with Hong Kong and Taiwan, Greater China today is already India's third largest trading partner. While the Sino-Indian trade has many structural limitations, it has not showed any signs of slowing down and continues to grow rapidly.[1]

Until recently, China was a worthy rival to India, not only in the political domain but also in the business arena, as Beijing aggressively pushed global trade. This was a cause for concern to New Delhi, as the trade patterns of the two countries are complementary. However, till two years ago, no one would have imagined that China would emerge the engine for India's export growth. In 2004-05 China was India's second biggest trade partner and the second biggest destination for India's exports. In 2002-03, it was ranked the sixth export destination. Interestingly, during these three years, India's exports logged highest growth. In 2002-03 and 2003-04, India's exports grew at over 20 per cent and in the first nine months of the current year they soared to 29 per cent, though the global trade was dismal. China had become the catalyst for India's peak export growth, as evident from its contribution reaching 2.3 per cent during 2002-03 to 2004-05 compared to the US 1.4 per cent. What has made China the major destination for Indian exports? It was China's hunger for raw materials, intermediates and components. Exports of iron ore to China more than doubled this year, pushing Japan to the second place. Iron ore constitutes around 40 per cent of India's exports to China. The other major exports were plastic materials, steel, chemicals and soyabean oil. The sudden predominance of China in India's exports has, however, raised two crucial issues: Whether the exports to China will sustain and whether they will exceed that to the US. It is not unrealistic to forecast that if its economy continues to be as robust, China will, in the near future, overtake the US. Which means, the demand for imports of raw materials, intermediates and components and parts will continue to rise. According to a forecast by *The Economist* of London, China's imports are expected to surge at the rate of 17-18 per cent a year till 2008. China and the US are the two engines of world economy, which grew by 3 per cent in 2002, 3.9 per cent in 2003 and is projected to grow by 4.6 per cent in 2004, according to the International Monitary Fund (IMF). China contributed 27.7 per cent to the global economic growth in 2003, the highest among all nations. The global trade increased by 16.1 per cent in 2003 and China was the top contributor. In 2003, China contributed 10.9 per cent to the global export growth and 11.2 per cent to the world import growth. In 2003, China's exports increased by 34.6 per cent and imports by 39.9 per cent. China's imports are likely to remain high, considering its growing GDP. *The Economist* forecast China's GDP to grow between 7.7 per cent and 8.7 per cent from 2004 to 2008. Alongside, exports are expected to surge 14-20 per cent during this period. Then, China has the advantage of a huge domestic demand. So the country is well insulated from any overheating. *The Economist* has forecast that the upward in Foreign

Direct Investment (FDI) flows to China will be sustained and help in gearing up the economy this decade. It estimated that FDI would touch $ 79 billion by 2008, up 44 per cent from $ 55 billion in 2003. The cheap labour and good infrastructure are the main attractions for foreign investors. China has been attractive enough for Multi-National Companies (MNCs) to shift their manufacturing there. A number of Japanese firms relocated their factories to China to produce goods cheap. Interestingly, a large part of the goods produced in these relocated factories went to meet the domestic demand of Japan and expand the exports of the Japanese MNCs. Thus, China's potential as world's biggest manufacturing hub is unlikely to be affected in the near future. Not just for India, China has turned friendlier towards a number of South-East Asian countries. For instance, for ASEAN-4 (Thailand, Malaysia, Indonesia and the Philippines), China has emerged the next generation export market after Beijing entered the World Trade Organisation. The combined exports of ASEAN-4 to China soared by 196 per cent from 2001 to 2003. In fact, for these four, China has emerged the engine for export growth, replacing the US as their biggest export market. China's ubiquitous growth in trade and economy and its predominance in global trade turn it into a springboard for several developing and developed countries. The air is taken out of the fears of a Chinese bubble as the country rests on the strong pillars of large domestic demand and cheap labour. Its saving ratio is as high as 40 per cent, which insulates it from any fears of foreign investments flying away. And, China's entry into the World Trade Organisation (WTO) has opened up numerous areas with huge investment potential. In this perspective, India should create an atmosphere to foster closer trade and economic ties with China. The difference between China and Pakistan is that while for Islamabad politics dictates business, for Beijing it is business that takes the precedence. Also, China appears quite eager to partner India to conquer Asia Inc. Boundary disputes can wait.[2]

According to some researchers, China is emerging as the world's manufacturing bases for low cost goods, like clothing and shoes, and India as the global Information Technology (IT) exporter. However, the western scholars have so far failed to recognise the new reality of growing economic cooperation between the two Asian giants. In fact in India too there is a school of thought, which is grossly underestimating this new trend of 21st century. According to Wang Dehua, Director of the Institute of South and Central Asian Studies, Western China has been especially eager to promote regional cooperation. In early August 2004, a trade delegation from Yunnan province visited India and signed a Joint Declaration with the

Confederation of Indian Industry (CII). This development will strengthen economic ties and further facilitate cross-border trade and investment between the two countries. The complementary nature of their economies and the size of their markets (nearly 2.2 billion people in total), the economic cooperation between the two countries, if it grows it will dramatically change the world trade balance. The international significance of this development in the beginning of the 21st century has far reaching significance than what appears on the surface.

A perusal of the Shanghai technology corridor reveals a hint of the countries' industrial interconnectedness. Walk through one of the main complexes in Shanghai's Pudong Software Park, and you will see a prominently displayed sign for Infosys, one of India's most respected IT firms. The same complex also holds Satyam, the first of India's software service companies to set up offices in Shanghai. Nearby are the headquarters of the largest software services company in Asia, Tata Consultancy Services (TCS), which currently runs an outsourcing centre for GE in the town of Hangzhou. TCS is owned by the Tatas, one of India's most prominent business families. Across the river is NIIT, the principal software-training centre in India's private sector. NIIT, operating in China since 1998, now runs an extensive two year course in 25 provinces, training around 20,000 students to be software professionals. There is widespread speculation that Wipro, India's only giant IT firm without a presence in the city, will establish a Shanghai office very soon. It is no surprise that Indian software companies are setting up in China. They, like everyone else, sense great opportunity in one of the largest, fastest growing economies in the world. What makes the activities of Indian companies particularly interesting is that they are helping to create links between these giant neighbours—two countries that have been estranged since the 1960s. For thousands of years, the Sino-Indian "border" was crisscrossed with trade routes. The flow of goods and ideas, particularly Buddhism, had a profound influence on shaping the entire culture of Asia. As India's first ambassador to China, K.M. Panikkar writes in "*India and China: A Study of Cultural Relations*," the prolonged contact between the neighbours "has been the major factor in the shaping of the Asian mind, for, from China, its influence radiated to Korea, Japan, Mongolia, and other more distant lands".[3]

These new trends in the economic, cultural and political relations between the two biggest nations in the world in the 21st century will become a key geo-strategic factor.

This analysis shows that Sino-Indian relations are reviving and deepening. What is more important is that if one goes by statistics and policy statements of the ruling elites of the two countries, these relations have begun to reveal stability.

Though it will be simplistic to over emphasise this aspect, the fact of the matter is that in the triangle of relations between China and Pakistan, India and Pakistan and India and China, there are indicators which show that Beijing is exhibiting changes in its assessment about geopolitical strategy of India. This is illustrated by these facts.

In May 1999, Kashmiri militants, with the support of the Pakistani military, crossed the Line of Control into the Kargil area in Jammu and Kashmir. The Indian army launched military operations seeking to repel the intrusion. As the conflict escalated, threatening a major military confrontation between the two nuclear states, both New Delhi and Islamabad were seeking international support. Pakistani Prime Minister Nawaz Sharif and Foreign Minister Sartaj Aziz went to Beijing soon after the crisis broke out and sought to secure Chinese support; however, their requests were turned down. Instead, the Chinese leaders advised the Pakistani visitors to seek a peaceful settlement with India. This stand of China had its own impact on the Indian foreign policy makers.

It is significant to mention here that Sino-Indian relations continued to register an improvement. This is confirmed by the then Indian President K.R. Narayanan's visit to China in May 2000 to mark the 50th anniversary of the establishment of Sino-Indian diplomatic relations. Chinese parliamentary head Li Peng and Premier Zhu Rongji visited India in January 2001 and 2002, respectively, further consolidating the bilateral relationship. Of all the key events over the past few years, perhaps the most important would be the then Indian Defence Minister George Fernandes' week-long visit to China in April 2003 and then the Prime Minister Atal Behari Vajpayee's June 2003 visit.

This stabilising and maturing relationship is clearly marked by the two countries' converging interests in developing a fair, equitable, international political and economic order, the role for the United Nations, and support of global disarmament, including efforts to prevent the weaponisation of outer space. Beijing and New Delhi are seeking to promote greater equality and fair distribution of wealth between the rich and poor by working to improve the current international economic system. As developing countries, both China and India are interested in gradually integrating their economies into the global trading system in ways that provide the necessary protection and transition time for their industries to adjust. In addition, Beijing and New Delhi are also calling for greater economic assistance from the northern industrialised countries to the vast majority of developing countries in the South.

It is significant to mention here that New Delhi has shown greater appreciation of Beijing's sensitivity over the Tibetan issue by affirming for the first time that the Tibetan Autonomous Region is part of the territory of China. Beijing, on the other hand, has extended *de facto* recognition of Sikkim being a state of India, something that Beijing had refused to do ever since the small Himalayan kingdom acceded to India in 1975. During the visit of Chinese Premier Wen Jiabao in New Delhi from April 9-12, 2005, he stated that China regarded Sikkim as an 'inalienable part of India' and that Sikkim was no longer an issue in India-China relations. The Joint Statement signed between India and China on this occasion explicitly refers to 'Sikkim State of the Republic of India'. The Chinese side has officially handed over to India a revised map showing Sikkim as within the international boundaries of India. While Chinese diplomats continue to characterise the issue as a historical legacy that takes time to resolve, the fact that official Chinese maps are showing Sikkim as part of India suggests that Beijing considers the issue closed. Indeed, New Delhi is confident that *de jure* recognition will not be long in forthcoming.

Above all, the most significant development for any study of Sino-Indian relations in the beginning of the present century is a marked change in their economic relations. A Sino-Indian Joint Study Group on Trade and Economic Cooperation was formed in March 2004. In addition to growing bilateral economic ties, the two countries are also active in exploring potentials for regional economic cooperation, including the sub-regional "Kunming Initiative. "During Wen Jiabao's visit, the understandings reached about economic relations assumed a new dimension. It was for instance pointed out that Sino-Indian bilateral trade has been growing rapidly and crossed the US $ 13 billion in 2004. The bilateral trade will grow to $ 15 billion by 2007. A target of US $ 20 billion by 2008 is envisaged.

To say all this does not mean that Sino-Indian relations have no constraints and reservations. This relates to a large number of issues including resolution of border dispute. However, the harsh reality is that in the 21st century the Sino-Indian relationship is bound to be one of the most important bilateral relationships in the global order. How they manage their relationship will have a tremendous impact on peace and stability in the regional and, increasingly, global context.

It will be relevant to mention here that the visit of Chinese Premier, Wen Jiabao marks yet another face of improvement of Sino-Indian relations. This visit perhaps is of far-reaching importance than in more than one sense. The visit was substantive in its outcome. Wen Jiabao himself has described this visit as 'historic'.

It is for the first time that a series of agreements, covering almost all aspects of bilateral relations between the two countries were signed. These agreements include:

(i) Agreement on Political Parameters and Guiding Principles for the Settlement of the India-China Boundary Question.

(ii) Report of India-China Joint Study Group on Comprehen-sive Trade and Economic Cooperation.

(iii) Protocol on Modalities for the Implementation of CBMs in the Military Field along the Line of Actual Control in the India-China Border Areas.

(iv) Agreement on mutual Administrative Assistance and Cooperation in Customs Matters.

(v) Memorandum of Understanding (MOU) on the Launch of the India-China Financial Dialogue.

(vi) MOU on Civil Aviation.

(vii) Protocol of Phytosanitary Requirement for Exporting Grapes from India to China.

(viii) Protocol of Phytosanitary Requirement for Exporting Bitter Gourds from India to China.

(ix) MOU on Provision of Hydrological Information of the Sutlej/ Langqen Zangbo River in Flood season by China to India.

(x) Protocol on India-China Film Cooperation Commission.

(xi) MOU on Cooperation between the Indian Council of World Affairs and the Chinese People's of Foreign Affairs.

(xii) Memorandum on the Construction of an Indian style Buddhist Temple on the Western side of the White Horse Temple in Luoyang, China.

These agreements show that for the first time Sino-Indian relations have not only assumed a multidimensional character but also begun to touch a new height. In fact it will not be incorrect to say that sponsors of Panchsheel, India and China are setting a new model of bilateral relations between two countries with different social systems. In this sense, this visit by the Chinese Premier and these agreements mark the beginning of a new phase in Sino-Indian relations.

The most significant part of this historic document is the Agreement on the Political Parameters and Guiding Principles for the Settlement of the India-China boundary question. Though it is too early to assess how fast India and China will be able to resolve their border dispute, one thing is certain that the leadership of India and China have taken a major step forward to resolve their border dispute through dialogue and negotiations. Prime Minister Dr. Manmohan Singh underlined that this "Agreement is truly a major milestone on the way to the settlement of the boundary question. It provides for a 'political settlement' of the boundary question in the context of the 'overall and long-term interests' of the two countries. Both sides have agreed that an early boundary settlement should be pursued as a 'strategic objective'". He did not leave at that. He emphasised that the Agreement sets out for the first time ever principles for an overall settlement of the India-China boundary question. "While this understanding is of great significance, we do acknowledge that we are still quite some distance away from a final boundary settlement. We have agreed that in the meantime, the two sides will strictly respect and observe the Line of Actual Control (LAC), maintain peace and tranquillity in the border areas and expedite the work of clarification and confirmation of the LAC. The Protocol on the modalities for the implementation of Confidence Building Measures in the Military Field in the Border Areas signed during the Chinese Premier's visit will help in maintaining peace along the LAC".

This shows how a wind of change is blowing over Asia and if China and India resolve their differences, strengthen and consolidate their economic and political relations, Asia would once again play a historic role in the global affairs for peace, tranquillity and equality.

Notes and References

1. C. Raja Mohan, Professor of South Asian Studies, Jawaharlal Nehru University, Now Delhi, *India and China: A Shifting Paradigm.*
2. S. Majumdar, Senior Researcher with a Japanese MNC in New Delhi, *Business Defines Sino-Indian Relations.*
3. Anna Greenspan, Independent Scholar working in the areas of digital culture and globalisation, *The Great Reverse* Part III, Yale Global.

11

India-China Friendship and the Trilateral Dimension

Dr. Jagdish P. Sharma

The infusion of a new warmth in India-China relations resulted from the successful four-day state visit of Chinese Premier Wen Jiabao to India. It gave a new dimension to the trilateral India-China-Russia informal grouping, which had three meetings so far at the level of Foreign Ministers. Chinese Premier Wen Jiabao, when asked about an India-Russia-China strategic partnership and the issue of multipolarity vis-a-vis the sole superpower, said the partnership must in no way be seen as an "alliance" targeting another country. "China, India and Russia are all influential countries. The cooperation among these three countries will help democratize international relations and achieve world peace, coordination and cooperation for peace and stability in the world," Wen said, adding in a postscript, "It is by no means an alliance targeting any other country," while none of the three countries may consider playing the "alliance" card against the US, Wen's articulation of a "democratized" international world order is an obvious criticism of the American unilateralism currently on display across the globe.[1]

The laying of political parameters and guiding principles to solve the India-China border problem announced during Mr. Wen's visit will vastly enhance the friendly ties between the two countries. With Russia, India's relations have been traditionally cordial. The three-power grouping is interested in the development of multipolarity in world relations. In the post-Cold War world dominated by one superpower—the United States, the international equations have been changing. One approaches the US with caution, even while friendly relations are maintained. India, China and Russia have all friendly relations with the US. They have their problems too with the US. They do not share the strategic and military perceptions of the superpower. They see the need for working towards a multi-polar world. The nature of global geo-politics, mutually complementaries in trade, techno-economic cooperation, extensive convergence of national interests and other factors had provided the foundations of that relationship. Much of that remains. The India, China and Russia consultative group of foreign ministers, holds regular annual meetings to exchange views on issues of common concern. The first meeting of their Foreign Ministers was on the sidelines of the conference on Interaction and Confidence Building Measures in Asia held in Kazakhstan in October 2004. The three countries preferred to take a positive and inclusive approach by projecting their interaction as a process that would "strengthen a collective approach to world affairs." While this approach seems low key, there is apparently a new seriousness in thinking and application. The three rounds of trilateral discussions to-date have been held on the sidelines of international conferences. None of them has endorsed the policies that Washington unilaterally sought to implement in Iraq and post-Yasser Arafat Palestine. The three countries have now agreed to hold the first standalone meeting in Russia this year and to focus on a few selected issues. During his visit to New Delhi, Russian President Vladmir Putin backed India for full veto power in the enlarged UN Security Council, and found no reason why New Delhi should be relegated to second rung in the international body. Russia also sought to transform its defence ties with India and suggested that New Delhi and Moscow should venture into joint development of frontier technology. The power of Russia and China is currently in the process of being contained by the West. The new policy of containment is what Moscow calls "the geopolitical encirclement" of Russia—extension of NATO to include Ukraine, Moldova, Georgia, Uzbekistan and other Central Asian countries. Both are facing threat to their national unity and integrity by cross-border terrorists and secessionists. They are handling this problem in the context of their won specific situation. If India is facing this challenge in Jammu and Kashmir and North Eastern States, Russia is confronted with the same problem in Chechnya. In such a situation, India as much as China, seems a natural Asian partner for Russia. With all the three countries agreed on multipolar world vision, strategic partnership comes naturally to India, China and Russia.

It is noteworthy that on the question of combating terrorism, India's joint declarations with both Russia and recently China emphasizes the need to give substance and credibility to global fight against the threat, avoiding selective approaches. On the question of Iraq, all sides have called for a wider degree of international consultation. It would be in the interest of the international community to restore the efficacy of the multilateral approaches in addressing the situations such as in Iraq. New Delhi can take heart from signs that this nascent move towards trilateral cooperation will boost its chances of securing a permanent seat in the UN Security Council. While China has not in clear terms declared that it would support this bid, it has agreed to examine jointly with Russia and India the report of a high-level panel on UN reforms. If the three countries can sustain this cooperation spirit, they can bring a measure of corrective balance in international affairs.

The changing contemporary international situation is helping the three countries to exert their influence on developments concerning their security and economic prosperity.[2] This leads to their coordinating their policies at the United Nations, WTO and other international and regional fora. The first strategic dialogue of India with China recently came in the context of greater bonhomie between the three nations. When Foreign Secretary Shyam Saran received Chinese Vice-Foreign Minister Wu Dawei at Hyderabad House, on 24 January 2005 the bilateral Security dialogue was raised to a strategic level. Both sides reported a "broad convergence" on important regional and global issues.[3] The extensive discussions, which were held in New Delhi (24th January 2005) covered important regional and global issues like democratization of international relations, UN reforms, nuclear non-proliferation and terrorism. For the first time both were looking at each other's concerns.

The subsequent meeting between Chinese Premier Wen Jiabao and Prime Minister Manmohan Singh had committed both nations to an early settlement of the boundary question:[4] which has for the first time been recognized and upgraded to a political and strategic level. They agreed on a set of 11 political parameters and guiding principles for resolving the issue. The two have also worked out several safeguards to ensure that bilateral relations and peace and tranquility are not affected by delays on this front. Mr. Wen's visit saw a total of 11 agreements being signed on political, economic and cultural fields. The report of a joint study group on trade and economic cooperation was made public. The discussions between Prime Minister Manmohan Singh, and the Chinese Premier were truly trailblazing.

The two countries reached agreement on the "modalities" to implement the confidence building measure along the Line of Actual Control (LAC) by enhancing contacts between the two militaries giving previous information of planned exercises, adding border meeting points in the eastern and middle sectors of the LAC and eschewing the use of force in any "face to face" situation. The joint statement on the visit said that India and China agreed that their relations had now acquired a "global and strategic Character."[5] Manmohan Singh and Wen Jiabao are reported to have agreed on a roadmap to settle the border dispute involving Arunachal Pradesh and Aksai Chin which is now in China. The two leaders signed several agreements that will allow more passenger flights between the two countries strengthen the efforts to boost trade and expand military cooperation.

Till now, India and China had confined themselves to a "cooperative" partnership. Now the word "strategic" has been profixed to the relationship. Keen not to cause too much concern among the other big powers and allay suspicions of a new axis in the region, India later clarified its position on the "strategic" partnership. "It is not a military alliance and not directed against this or that region. The main aim of this partnership was for peace and prosperity," Foreign Secretary Shyam Saran said.

Emphasis has been given to the economic front and the countries have decided to start a financial dialogue. The trade volume between the two has already reached over $ 13.6 billion. They want to achieve the $ 20 billion mark by 2008 and start negotiations on setting up an India-China Regional Free Trade Arrangement.[6] Winding up his "historic" visit to India and South Asia, the Chinese Premier said that he backed a "bigger role for India," but did not explicitly support India's candidature for permanent membership of the UN Security Council with veto power. Speaking to newspersons Mr. Wen Jiabao said, "China reiterates that we attach great importance to the important role of India in international affairs. India is a very populous country and is also a very important developing country... We fully understand

and support India's aspirations to play an even bigger role in international affairs, including in the United Nations."

Stating that his visit had taken bilateral relations to a new level Mr. Jiabao said that three major results were achieved. First was the upgradation of relations to establish an India-China strategic and cooperative partnership for peace and prosperity. Secondly, the two sides agreed on a plan for comprehensive cooperation in economy and trade. Thirdly, the two sides agreed on the guiding principles and political parameters for settling the boundary dispute, he said.[7] Jiabao's recent visit saw India and China cross the bridge of peace over a border festering since 1962. The agreements signed by them are yet another indication that the leaderships in New Delhi and Beijing are determined to put the past behind and start a new unique chapter in bilateral relations. In the discussions, both sides underlined the need to improve the relationship at "all levels and in all areas while addressing the outstanding differences including the boundary question, in a fair, reasonable and mutually satisfactory manner." The year 2006 has been designated as the year of India-China friendship.

"Both sides agreed that the current international situation characterized by globalisation presented an opportunity as well as posed a challenge. The two sides emphasized the need for making international relations democratic in order to face this challenge. In the bilateral talks, the two sides shared the view that terrorism, particularly the possibility of weapons of mass destruction (WMD), and sensitive technologies falling into the hands of terrorists, presented a grave threat and recognized the importance of international cooperation in meeting this threat. They agreed that these dangers could not be tackled unilaterally. It is learnt that the issues such as Iraq, North Korea, Afghanistan, non-proliferation and counter-terrorism were also discussed.

Both India and China had been invited to attend a meeting of the G-7 finance ministers on February 4, 2005. China is already edging towards inclusion in the group, having attended an October meeting in 2004. India's presence is an acknowledgement of its growing economic clout as well as a greater international role. The G-7 comprises the world's leading industrial nations—US, UK, France, Germany, Japan, Italy, Canada and recently Russia was added to the group. Apart from India and China, finance ministers from Brazil and South Africa have attended the Group meetings recently. It was in

June 2003 that India was first invited to be part of a G-8 Summit in Evian, France. The discussions were a heady mix of strategic politics and economy. As the Indian economy is poised to post growth of over 7 per cent this year, strategic projections post India and China as being the drivers of growth in the coming decades.

"In the same way that commentators refer to the 1990s as the "American Century" the 21st century may be seen as the time when Asia, led by China and India, comes into its own", a recent CIA report titled, 'Mapping the Global Future' observed. "A combination of sustained high economic growth, expanding military capabilities and large populations will be at the root of the expected rapid rise in economic and political power for both counties". The CIA report has compared the rise of the two Asian giants to the advent of a United Germany in the 19th century and a powerful US in the 20th century.

At the meeting with Prime Minister Manmohan Singh had with Mr. Wen Jiabao on the sidelines of the ASEAN summit in Vientiane in November 2004, the Chinese Premier said expensively. "The handshake between you and me will catch the attention of the whole world". Going back to history, the India-China and India-Russia relationships dating back to dawn of history is sustained by common traditions and struggles, ideas and values. These relationships, forged by commercial and cultural contacts over centuries are today a major factor in the stability of the fluid political situation of the Asian and Afro-Arab World. Jawaharlal Nehru foresaw that Asia and Africa, having suffered the worse indignities of the earlier or European forms of colonialism would modify their own ideas to create a new nationalism. Consequently these emergent countries would eschew "narrow" national interests, would seek instead to cooperate, to avoid dispute and war, to resolve differences through peaceful negotiations–all from the perspective of new enlightened self interest." This was a criterion he applied to China as well and his policy towards that country was really a dual purpose policy. On one hand, it was designed to emphasis China's Asianism and thus to wean it way from communism. On the other hand, it was intended to channelise China's vast potential energies towards the methods and purposes of the new nationalism and away from past patterns of being self-centred.

The latest developments have to be seen in the contemporary context. India, China and Russia are multiracial, multi-cultural and multi-religious societies. They have a collective commitment to intensify political and economic dialogue and enhance mutual trust.

India, China and Russia will hold their first "stand alone" high-level trilateral meeting, Foreign Secretary Shyam Saran said.

"The meeting will be held on its own merit and not on the sidelines of a particular event. This adds certain significance to it," he added.

Mr. Saran stated that as part of their economic and commercial cooperation, the three countries could jointly work in the development of Central Asian energy resources. All three — India, China and Russia– have demonstrated "Convergence of views" on various issues. Prime Minister Manmohan Singh visited Russia in May 2005 for the celebrations marking victory in Europe Day, the 60th anniversary of the defeat of Nazi Germany and the end of World War II in the European Theatre. The large number of foreign dignitaries present on the occasion included President Hu Jintao of China. Russian President Vladimir Putin's advocacy of an India-China-Russia alliance, has earned some critical comments from the Western media. At Almaty on the sidelines of conference on Interaction and Confidence Building Measures in Asia (CICA) in October 2004, the three countries had decided to intensify their fight against terrorism and drug trafficking.

External Affairs Minister K. Natwar Singh during a meeting with his Russian counterpart Sergei Lavrov and–Chinese Foreign Minister Li Zhaoxing at Almaty proposed establishment of a trilateral forum for business communities of the three countries. The three Foreign Ministers would be meeting for the fifth time, sometime later this year.[8]

India's foreign policy of following the Nehruvian tradition sees the three countries coming together to promote world peace and to democratize international relations in the 21st century. The concept of trilateral cooperation is gaining strength and popularity with each meeting of the group which has become a permanent feature in the international calender.

References

1. *The Hindu* (Delhi) 13 April 2005 (For detailed framework on Trilateral cooperation, see Mikhail Titarenko, Vishnu Bhagwat and XIA Yishan, "China-India-Russia trilateral cooperation" in *World Affairs* (New Delhi) Vol. 8, No. 4, October-December 2004, pp. 68-76.

2. Stanley A. Weies, "Estranged democracies or engaged partners", *Daily Times* (Lahore) 9 March 2005.

3. *National Herald* (New Delhi), 25th January 2005.

4. Pramit Mitra and Drew Thompson, "China and India: Rivals or partners? *Far Eastern Economic Review* Vol. 168, No. 4, April 2005, p. 30.

5. *The Hindu* (Delhi) 12 April 2005.

6. *The Telegraph*, 12 April 2005.

7. *The Statesman* (New Delhi) 13 April 2005.

8. Quoted in *National Herald* 18 March 2005.

12

India-Pakistan Relations

Kalim Bahadur

There has been a flurry of movements in the relations between India and Pakistan in the recent past. Some kind of euphoria is building up. This has no precedence in the history of the two neighbours. India's relations with Pakistan have always been full of tensions and conflicts ever since the two countries became independent in 1947. The relations between the two countries have been influenced by three groups of factors; the first; the history of the last one century of the political developments in the subcontinent, the rise of India's anti-imperialist and anti-colonial movement, emergence of the Muslims in politics, and the origin and the growth of Muslim separatist movement called the Pakistan movement. The second; the bitter controversies surrounding the partition of the country and the way it was implemented and the third; the aftermath of the partition and disputes arising out of the division of assets, etc.

The British rule in the wake of the 1857 uprising followed a policy of divide and rule, directly and indirectly encouraged Muslim communalism by introducing separate electorate, division of Bengal etc. The rise of the national consciousness and identity provoked controversies like Hindi versus Urdu, Sir Syed Ahmad Khan's opposition to the Indian National Congress, etc. The Khilafat movement in the early 20s was followed by the 1937 election in which the Muslim League suffered a sweeping defeat. The League leaders responded by projecting the two nation theory, which led to the Lahore Resolution of 1940, also-called the Pakistan Resolution and this further widened the gulf between the two communities. In the post-Second World War period when it became clear that the British would have to withdraw from India, bitter controversies for and against Pakistan erupted which also led to the outbreak of communal riots in Bihar, Bengal, Punjab and elsewhere. The partition of India in 1947 satisfied no one. The Muslim League did not get what it had wanted as it was a 'moth eaten Pakistan'. In the post-partition period the division of India proved very difficult and left behind complaints and rancour on all sides. India over the centuries of the Mughal and the British rule had evolved into one integrated economic, political and social unit. The demarcation of boundaries of the two countries, the division of assets and the question of the princely states left indelible scars on the psyche and mindset of the people of the two countries.

Another dimension of India-Pakistan relations was the failure of the Pakistan leaders in nation building after they took over in the new country. Throughout the Pakistan movement during the forties, the movement was carried on slogans that Pakistan would be an Islamic state. However, there never was any discussion or awareness about what political system would be built up in the new country. The Muslim League leader Jinnah was a bright politician, but he was neither a political thinker nor a visionary. The immense task of nation building in a brand new country was beyond the intellectual capacities of the leaders of the new state. The result is apparent in the more than fifty-eight years of Pakistan's history. The country had four constitutions and almost thirty years of direct military rule. For Pakistan's ruling elite the only plank to mobilize the people was to project India as the main threat to Pakistan's sovereignty and territorial integrity. The publicly stated belief of the Indian leaders that Pakistan would not last and one day they would be again reunited was taken as the refusal by Indian leaders to accept Pakistan and their determination to undo Pakistan. Therefore, every controversy and problem caused by the complexity of partitioning the country was held out as motivated to hurt and harm Pakistan.

Pakistanis have been taught a highly biased history in which India is held out as the villain of every thing that has gone wrong in Pakistan. The controversy about Kashmir is a typical of this mindset. It is argued by Pakistan that Kashmir should have gone to Pakistan as it was Muslim majority state in accordance with the principle on which India had been partitioned, i.e., the two nation theory. This argument ignores the fact that Kashmir was not a part of British India but a princely state and it was at the instance of Jinnah that it had been provided that for the option on their accession to either India or Pakistan, the decision of the rulers would be final. Accepting Pakistan does not mean that the ideology of the two nation theory should also be accepted by India. Indian leaders had accepted the reality of Pakistan which was reflected in the visit of Indian Prime Minister Atal Behari Vajpayee to the Minar-i-Pakistan in Lahore. Accepting the existence of a state is one thing but accepting the ideology behind it is a different thing in international relations. Pakistan has accepted the existence of North Korea and has developed good relations with that country, but has it accepted the ideology of its founder Kim II Sung? The Kashmir issue has played another role in Pakistan's history. It has over the years become hostage to the military establishment in Pakistan. The successive military rulers have justified and legitimized their regimes using the Kashmir plank to mobilize public opinion in their favour. As far back as 1948 some military officers were caught planning a military coup because they were not satisfied with the government's Kashmir policy which culminated in the famous Rawalpindi conspiracy case. Pakistan's military establishment over the years has developed a vested interest in what has been called the unfinished agenda of partition. It is even said that if there would be no Kashmir dispute, Pakistan's military would lose its dominant position in that country's political system. General Zia-ul-Haq began to call Kashmir as the "Core dispute" and all other relations with India would be dependent on the solution of the core issue.

Another determinant of India-Pakistan relations has been the disparity in the size and resources of the two countries. India is larger in territory, population, natural resources, economic strength and scientific and technical assets. Pakistan's policy toward India has been to seek equality and parity with India. In fact India is larger than all its South Asian neighbours combined. Wherever two neighbours have such disparity the smaller neighbour is always suspicious of the bigger neighbour. Whatever the bigger country does it cannot allay the suspicions and doubts of the neighbour. Pakistan is also too conscious of this inequality. It projects itself as one country in the region which is standing in the way of India imposing its domination or hegemony. This is one reason of the inability of the South Asian Association Regional Cooperation (SAARC) to take off. Many of the problems between India and its neighbours are the inheritance of the common colonial past. India's size is the reality of life and it cannot cut itself down to please the recalcitrant neighbours.

India-Pakistan relations have to be seen in this context. Pakistan has gone to war with India three times believing that it would be able to achieve its objective of forcibly seizing Kashmir. Most Pakistani foreign policy moves have been India centric. In the early eighties Pakistan supported, armed and trained the Mujahideen for fighting in Afghanistan against regime and later of the Soviet army. Pakistan's patronage of the Taliban was barely concealed as an attempt to acquire strategic depth in case of a possible confrontation with India. Pakistan's nuclear programme was also India centric as that country faced no threat from any other side. Pakistan has been using the Organisation of Islamic Conference (OIC) for carrying on propaganda against India.

A new situation has been created in the wake of the events of 9/11 in 2001. Pakistan had realized that its policy of sponsoring terrorism in Jammu and Kashmir had not paid off. Pakistan had been isolated in the world community because of its support to Taliban. During more than a decade of war in Afghanistan and sponsoring of terrorism in Kashmir, Pakistan had become the centre of International terrorism. All kinds of terrorists from all around the Muslim world had made the country their home base in the name of participating in the holy *Jihad*. Most of them stayed put in Pakistan after the end of the withdrawal of the Soviet army from Afghanistan. They settled down in the Afghan-Pakistan border. Many of the Afghan veterans were redirected to fight in Kashmir. Those foreign terrorists were co-opted by the Pakistani fundamentalist parties. Many of them had settled in the Waziristan area and are now fighting against the Pakistan army inflicting heavy casualties on it. It is in this context that Pakistan's military rulers have been compelled to set on the present phase of diplomatic manoeuvering. They carry on relentless barrage of propaganda about urgency of the solution of the Kashmir issue.

The current phase of India-Pakistan relations began with the April 2003 initiative by the then Indian Prime Minister Atal Behari Vajpayee for breaking the deadlock in India-Pakistan relations provoked by the terrorist attack on the Indian Parliament on 13 December 2001. In response to the terrorist attack both India and Pakistan had mobilised their armed forces in eye ball to eye ball confrontation. The April initiative restarted the composite dialogue which had been broken in the late nineties. There have been many rounds of talks at many levels on the different items of the composite dialogue agenda though there is little to show by way of progress on some of the basic issues. As the first steps it was decided to restore the relations which had been broken as the direct consequence of the attack on the Parliament. The diplomatic relations were restored, overflights of the air services, the Delhi-Lahore bus and train services were resumed. Some small steps have been taken more for the purpose of showing that both the countries are moving forward. There were no indications that the basic determinants of Pakistan's India policy have undergone any change. There have been talks for improvement of trade but the MFN status would not still be granted. Frequently Pakistani leaders denounce and denigrate the CBMs and claim that unless Kashmir issue is resolved nothing else would happen. Gen. Musharraf is on record having said that even if the Kashmir issue is resolved, conflicts and tension would be there in India and Pakistan relations. He has gone on to announce several times that unless the Kashmir issue is resolved many more Kargils would happen. Pakistan claims that it would not sponsor terrorism from its territory, and this assurance was repeated by Gen. Musharraf in the joint statement with the Indian Prime Minister in January 2004, at the time of the SAARC Summit in Islamabad. However, most of the terrorist camps are still in business in the POK, and most of the leaders of the terrorist groups are free, some of them are organizing sectarian attacks within Pakistan.

It must be understood that the problems that bedevil India-Pakistan relations are complex. Their roots go back into history and politics of the last more than hundred years particularly the issue of the state of Jammu and Kashmir. These problems would need patient and continuous dialogue over a period of time. They do not admit of quick fix solutions. What is needed at present is that the engagement with Pakistan must continue.

In order to resolve problems of decades which have to be settled both sides have to avoid an overambitious attempt to settle everything at once. Here is the major hurdle. The idea of the composite dialogue was adopted at the insistence of Pakistan as they wanted the Kashmir issue to be settled before any other problem is resolved. There have been outbursts in Pakistan against any hint of any alleged attempt to put the Kashmir issue on the back burner.

One analyst has remarked that there is still a possibility that this phase of India-Pakistan talks may end in a stalemate. India's domestic compulsions regarding the Kashmir issue would preclude it from satisfying Islamabad's basic demand for 'progress' on that dispute in order to permit the dialogue to continue. General Musharraf, even while he was preparing to take off for New Delhi to watch the India-Pakistan cricket match asserted that Kashmir issue has to be resolved otherwise many more Kargils will happen. He went on to assert that flexibility could not be one sided. The only flexibility he himself showed was that he did not specify the date when the next Kargil will be launched. As things stand Pakistan will resurrect militancy. Attempt should be made to build something positive out of the present atmosphere even much of it may be just euphoria.

A new phase in the India-Pakistan relations could be seen to have begun with the coming to office of the Manmohan Singh government in New Delhi in summer 2004. The thread of the composite dialogue initiated by the outgoing NDA government was restarted. The Manmohan Singh-Musharraf talks at the sidelines of the United Nations General Assembly in September 2004 reiterated the mutual desire to continue the composite dialogue stated in the joint statement of Prime Minister Atal Behari Vajpayee and President Musharraf at the time of the Islamabad Summit on January 4, 2004. Since then several rounds of talks on the various components of the composite dialogue have been held. Many confidence building measures have been floated around which include the release of the fishermen arrested by both the countries, the preparation have been made to start the Munabao-Khokrapar rail link, ceasefire across the Line of Control in Jammu and Kashmir etc., have been initiated.

In spite of all the hype about the composite dialogue General Musharraf had been constantly fretting about the Kashmir issue. He at first wanted some timeframe for the solution of the Kashmir problem and denigrated the confidence building measures (CBMs) that were being proposed by India. In fact during the last two years people to people contacts in social, cultural and economic fields have been increasing at a faster pace and have been transforming the entire atmosphere of the India-Pakistan relations. Yet there was no progress on the most contentious issue that comprises the agenda of the composite dialogue. They are the issues viz., the Kashmir, Siachin, the Sir Creek, the Wuller Dam, the nuclear issue, terrorism, trade etc.

It was in this background that Gen. Musharraf expressed a desire to watch one of the India-Pakistan cricket matches which were going on in India, in the month of March and April. Naturally India immediately extended him an invitation to watch any of the matches according to his convenience. It was reminiscent of eighties when General Zia-ul-Haq had visited this country to watch the India-Pakistan cricket match at Jaipur. President Musharraf eventually decided to watch the one day cricket match at New Delhi on 17th April 2005. The whole thing snowballed into a full-fledged India-Pakistan Summit. Probably that was also the intention and design of President Musharraf.

There have been many India-Pakistan Summits in the past but this Summit was somewhat different from all others held earlier. The contrast was with the Summit held in Agra in 2001. At Agra the atmosphere around the Summit was full of tension and rancour. The two leaders that is the Prime Minister of India Atal Behari Vajpayee and the President of Pakistan General Parvez Musharraf did not agree to issue a joint statement and they did not even decide to meet again. General Musharraf left in a huff in the night without fanfare and farewell. But at the New Delhi Summit in April 2005 the General claimed he has come with a new heart. In a significant departure from Pakistan's traditional stand he recognized that borders cannot be redrawn though the *LoC* could not become the permanent border between the two countries. The joint statement issued at the conclusion of the Summit did not exactly reflect the emotional content of the declarations of the General, but it did signify one big step forward in the peace process in India-Pakistan relations. To quote the statement they assessed positively the progress that had been made so far through confidence building, people to people contacts and enhancing areas of interactions and determined to build on the momentum already achieved. They declared that the peace process was now irreversible.

The leaders decided to continue the dialogue on the issue of Jammu and Kashmir in the spirit generated so far till a final settlement. They decided to further enhance interaction and cooperation across the *LoC* by providing additional meeting points for the divided families, trade and pilgrimages, etc. The two leaders welcomed the Srinagar-Muzzafarabad Bus service and that terrorism would not be allowed to impede the peace process. They proposed additional provision of bus services between important cities in the two countries. The much discussed Khokrapar-Munabao, train link, it was agreed, would be opened by 1st January 2006. The two countries would reopen their respective consulates in Mumbai and Karachi by the end of the current year. They endorsed the decision already taken by the officials to schedule meetings to discuss other issues of the composite dialogue. They instructed officials to further the existing international mechanisms to begin discussions immediately on the issues of Sir Creek and Siachin glacier. It was decided to enhance cooperation in the fields of trade and commerce and in this connection it was decided to reactivate the Joint Economic Commission and the Joint Business Council.

The decisions of the Delhi Summit were widely welcomed both in India and Pakistan barring some fringe hardline groups. The rightwing parties in Pakistan like the Jama'at-i-Islami and other groups immediately condemned the joint statement and called it a sell out as in their view the issue of Jammu and Kashmir had not been resolved to their satisfaction. There were others who said there was nothing new in the statement which had not been said already. Some others pointed out that none of the issues contained in the composite dialogue had even been touched in the statement. There were reservations in some circles in India also given the past record of General Musharraf. Some of the statements soon after the Delhi Summit by General Musharraf and the Pakistan Foreign Minister Kasuri lent strength to Indian suspicions. Both the leaders have harped on the Kashmir issue deriding the confidence building measures taken during the last two years. The Prime Minister of Pakistan Shaukat Aziz declared in Bangkok that until the Kashmir issue is resolved, economic relations with India could not be fully restored. It cannot be denied that the Delhi Summit was a milestone in the process of peace building between India and Pakistan.

The problems between the two countries are not confined to the contentious issues, but they are heavily influenced by history and the mindset of hostility and animosity. It will require patient and prolonged efforts by the leadership of both the countries to build mutual trust and normalize the relations between the two neighbours in South Asia.

13

Indo-Pak Relations: A Historical Perspective

V.D. Chopra

No objective study of Indo Pak relations is complete without an assessment of the role of imperialism in this subcontinent; both before and after the two countries became independent and sovereign states.

For centuries this subcontinent has been the main base of imperialist expansion and domination. The area of united India on the eve of independence was fifteen times the area of the British Isles and twenty times the area of Great Britain. Its population was nearly one-fifth of the human race. The 400 million people of this subcontinent constituted three quarters of the total population of the British Empire and nearly nine-tenth of its subject colonial population.

If we compare the total population of India in the late thirties with the eight leading colonial empires of the world, it will not be difficult to see that every other person in the colonial population of the world was an Indian.[1] Thus, pre-partition India was the largest and the biggest colonial possession of imperialism. It was also the oldest, the longest exploited colony of the world. Colonial India was not only the central region of imperialist domination but was also the main focus of attention of all European colonising powers.

I

India was the lifeblood of British imperialism. It was a great market for its consumer goods as well as for the products of heavy industry, for owning the means of production and a haven for export of capital. Tens of millions of pounds were siphoned off from India every year. India became the centre and keystone of the whole economic and financial fabric of the British Empire.[2]

If we examine the geopolitical aspect, we will find that India occupies an important strategic position. Around the vast expanse of the Indian Ocean, with India as the commanding centre, stretches the Persian Gulf, the Middle East on the west; the Red Sea and Egypt and Africa to the southwest; to the east Myanmar and the Malay; to the South-East, Australia and through the straits of Singapore, as well as through the new Myanmar-Yunnan Road, the route to China.

The conquest of India, therefore, became an essential element in the capitalist development of Europe and in particular of Great Britain. For two centuries European capitalism was nourished to a large extent on the spoils gathered from India. As early as 1898, Lord Curzon made a revealing admission that "India is the 'pivot' of our empire... If the Empire loses any other part of its dominion we can survive, but if we lose India, the sun of our Empire will have set". To British imperialism, equally important was the strategic significance in many ways, a launching pad for the further expansion of the empire, main contributor to the exchequer and supplier of manpower for wars and expeditions against other countries.

Thus whenever there was a challenge to British authority, and it was challenged at every step, the rulers came out with new political and administrative measures to further tighten their grip over India.

The popular uprising of 1857-59—the first war of India's Independence was an important landmark in its history. It brought to light the relative weakness of the social basis of British rule and the deep seated hatred of the masses for their oppressor. Jawaharlal Nehru in his book *The Discovery of India* rightly remarked: "Though the revolt had directly affected only certain parts of the country it had shaken up the whole of India and, particularly, the British administration".

After this uprising, the British rulers subsequently changed the system of colonial administration with a view to consolidating their base and refurbishing their apparatus on the one hand and creating their own social base among the Indian vested interests, on the other.

History tells us that the Muslims were most active participants in the various revolts against the British rulers. Consequently, a number of their officers serving in India became exasperated with continued Muslim uprisings, which lasted over half a century. In 1843, for instance, Viceroy Lord Ellenborough wrote to the Duke of Wellington: "I cannot close my eyes to the belief that the Muhammedan race is fundamentally hostile to us and our true policy is to reconciliate the Hindus". Many British officers held the Muslims solely responsible for 1857 uprising.[3]

As a matter of fact, it was on the basis of this estimate that the British rulers drew up a twofold strategy to divide the Indian people.

On the one hand, they started appeasing the Muslim landlords and on the other, planting a sense of 'independent entity' among the Muslims. It is significant that in the last two decades of the 19th century, a number of communal riots rocked the country. Some of them were triggered off by the agitation for cow protection and the opposition to it. Parallel to the intensification of our national movement, the British rulers too accelerated their drive to divide the country on communal lines.

The policy of division of the Indian people through the instrument of princely states was closely matched by the policy of creating gulf between the Hindus and Muslims.

Before the advent of British rule, there was no trace of the type of Hindu-Muslim conflicts that followed it. There were wars between states which might have had Hindu or Muslim rulers; but these wars at no time took on a Hindu-Muslim complexion. Muslim rulers employed Hindus freely in the highest positions and vice versa. It will not be incorrect to say that Hindu-Muslim division and conflicts were the direct product of the British policy of 'divide and rule'. Facts are unassailable, both in the testimony of witnesses and in historical records to strengthen such a conclusion.

In the earlier period, the weapon of 'divide and rule' was more openly employed than in the last phase of the British rule. More than one and a half centuries ago, a British officer writing under the name of 'Carnaticus' in the Asiatic Review of May 1821 declared that "*divide et impera* should be the motto of our Indian administration, whether political, civil or military". Towards the concluding decade of the nineteenth century, in 1888, Sir John Strachey was more outspoken when he said : "The truth plainly is that the existence side by side of these hostile creeds is one of the strong points in our political position in India".

Again as late as 1941, the influential British daily, *The Times* wrote: "The divisions exist and British rule is certain as long as they do".

In this connection, still another important fact may be mentioned. With the installation of popular ministries in the thirties and the initiation of constitutional discussions in the face of rising revolutionary upsurge, the princely states became the storm centres of the Indian political situation. The states witnessed spontaneous struggles against feudal autocracy, which were suppressed by the princes backed up naturally by the British political department. The high watermark of such agitations was reached in Kashmir where the slogan 'Quit Kashmir' gripped the minds of the people. This development completely upset British calculations since the colonial rulers wanted to balkanise India and the state of Jammu and Kashmir occupied a key position in their nefarious plan.

Nonetheless the truth remains that till the goal of physically splitting India into India and Pakistan was achieved, the British rulers used every instrument to drive a wedge between the Hindus and Muslims. After 1947, the same policy acquired the new garb of fomenting Indo-Pak tensions—an extension of the old policy in the new situation.

II

So far we have examined briefly the British policy of keeping India under subjugation. The compulsions, both economic and geopolitical, continue to operate even now, though the United States has assumed the major role for itself. Whenever these compulsions become acutely pressing either concurrently, as whole, or in part the stage is set for Indo-Pak tensions, which on occasions escalates into open confrontation such as in 1947, 1965, 1971 and in 1999.

In every escalation, there was a specific scale of importance of the 'stimulating factors' such as the dispute over Kashmir in 1947 and in 1965 and liberation of Bangladesh in 1971 and Kargil War in 1999. But the range of the confrontation did not go beyond the framework of Indo-Pak conflicts. However, the situation has changed now. Indo-Pak tensions have international ramifications, an entirely new development dominating Indo-Pak relations at present.

Before we go into reasons for this, a peep into the recent past is necessary. Soon after India became an independent state, US imperialism started restructuring its policies towards it on the basis of the rich experience of British imperialism.

"The key to Asia is now India. If India is lost, then all of Asia is lost. The smaller nations would not have the capacity to survive..." "America would then stand alone without allies. It might then be too late to win even a war". This is what Justice O. Douglas said on 14 August 1951.

At the same time George C. McGee, assistant secretary of State stated in the House of Representatives: "If one turns to the individual countries in this area, India, of course, looms the largest, both in terms of size and population.... It is the largest country of the free world... India is extremely important from the standpoint of its people and its mineral and other material resources".

These two quotations from high US officials are not only revealing but they continue to be valid even today.

Friction with Pakistan on the Kashmir issue, the role of British-American bloc to create destabilisation with the help of the United Nations Commission on Kashmir and later through the UN mediator made the intentions of the Anglo-American axis clear to India in regard to this strategic region of the world. India not only repeatedly rejected UN proposals to hold a plebiscite in Kashmir but also foiled several military interventions—1947 Pakistan aggression, 1962 Chinese aggression, 1965 and 1971 Indo-Pak conflicts and subsequent attacks such as 1999 Kargil war—aiming to transform Kashmir into a military bridgehead to subserve their geopolitical ambitions.

It had become increasingly clear even in the fifties that Pakistan had been 'assigned' a key role in realising Washington's global plans in the subcontinent.

American Vice-President Nixon's visit to Pakistan in 1953 was a curtain raiser of this grand design. These were formative years for the newly born state of Pakistan. Its hate singing, fanatic leaders in their frenzied search for an ally landed in the lap of that notorious brinksman, John Foster Dulles. He was frantically looking for satellites to contain India which had already embarked on the path of independent economic development internally and a policy of non-alignment externally. This visit formalised mutual defence pacts and agreements between America and Pakistan. Pakistani rulers allowed a number of American bases to be set up on Pakistani soil. The Peshawar base, in the extreme west of Pakistan, equipped with the most sophisticated spying radar equipment, became a vantage point to mount a watch over the vast Central Asian territory of the Soviet Union. The notorious 'U-2 episode' is now part of history.

The advent of US-Pak alliance marked a 'qualitative' change in Indo-Pak relations. The 1955 Pact constituted a threat to India's independence and in collaboration with SEATO, it posed a danger to peace in Asia as well. This threat could evidently be met with by building Asian unity. India, under the leadership of Jawaharlal Nehru, undertook this task boldly and without any reservation. This exacerbated American hostility towards India and quickened the process of arming Pakistan. The Americans confirmed this when they withdrew restrictions on the transfer of US arms to Pakistan by third countries, thus regularising the clandestine sale of arms and grant of loans by SEATO and NATO powers and other US allies to Pakistan. Natural enough, Pakistan was able to repair its military machine severely mauled in the 1965 conflict. This process continued through the late sixties till the early seventies.

Another fact needs to be mentioned here. Washington had become very bitter about the foreign policy of India under the leadership of Prime Minister Indira Gandhi, particularly after its firm stand on the US invasion of Cambodia and its open opposition to the supporting of Israel, both politically and militarily.

It appears that after the myth of American invisibility was exploded in the countries of Indo-China, Pentagon had conceived what could be described as a policy of 'Vietnamisation' of the Indian subcontinent. As early as May 1970, a decision was taken to resume arms supply to Pakistan, though Assistant Secretary of State, Sisco had then tried to soften its effect by maintaining that the "decision was subject to congressional consultations".

Even when the US administration had conceded that US F-86 aircraft and tanks and other deadly weapons were being used to crush the liberation movement in Bangladesh, arms continued to be placed in the hands of the military dictator of Pakistan. In a testimony before the Senate subcommittee on refugees, the general accounting office, watchdog of US Congress conceded that the US air force was airlifting arms to Pakistan on a priority basis. According to one estimate, 5 lakhs dollars worth of aviation spare parts were rushed to Pakistan in July 1971.

Another report published at that time showed that the Pakistani ship SS Padma was preparing to sail on 22 June 1971 from New York harbour to Karachi. It was carrying aircraft, parachutes, tonnes of spare parts and accessories for aircraft and military vehicles.

These facts indicate beyond any doubt that behind the scene, the Pentagon was doing everything to fuel the tension and thereby create conditions for an armed conflict between India and Pakistan. And this is precisely what happened towards the end of 1971. The events consequent to this need no repetition, particularly the diabolic act when American President Nixon despatched a taskforce of the US Seventh Fleet into the Bay of Bengal.

It is against this backdrop that the recent military buildup of Pakistan by America and tilt in its pro-Pakistan policy should be seen. It had till recently its own impact on Indo-Pak relations.

The crux of the matter is that Pakistan has grown since its inception in a manner that it becomes easily 'vulnerable' to American pressures and policies. Pakistan's history shows that the US has been instrumental in deposing governments and installing new ones with a view to turning the country into a springboard against those countries which follow an independent course, the chief among them being India. If in the fifties it drew Pakistan into a military alliance and forced it to expand its scarce resources for military buildup, in the seventies Z.A. Bhutto was overthrown from power because he was becoming much too independent to be tolerated by the US.

This raises another question: Why have the ruling classes of Pakistan become a willing tool of American imperialism? A study of the reasons for this is directly related to the internal socio-economic structure of Pakistan.

III

Pakistan, it must be emphasised, functions within the structural framework of peripheral capitalism and its imperatives and constraints. It is subject to the collective interests of three economically dominant classes, which together constitute the ruling block—the metropolitan bourgeoisie, the new emerging bourgeoisie and landowning classes. Awareness of this background is important for an understanding of the full implications and future functioning of the present military regime in Pakistan, its avowed claim to be laying the foundations of an 'Islamic economy and polity' and, above all, its relations with India.

A relevant factor in these developments is the great stake of American imperialism in keeping in power a military regime. "It was evident from the record that the US did not want restoration of democracy in the country for fear of an opposition party coming into power and upsetting US policies in the region", Khan Abdul Ghaffar Khan made it known in a comment in seventies. Apart from the strategic interests of the Pentagon, there are several other objective reasons for this.

It is well-known that at the time of independence in 1947, industrial capital in Pakistan had hardly developed. All the major industrial units were owned by the Hindus who migrated to India. The class that controlled the largest sector of Pakistan's economy was the landlords. It was mainly from among the landowners that the new class of traders and industrialists started emerging from a few who had migrated from India.

It appears that in the initial stages, the Pakistani leadership led by Mohammad Ali Jinnah, did make efforts to follow the path of independent economic development. This view is supported by a number of indicators—incentives by the government for investment in industries, setting up of an investment enquiry committee and of the Pakistan Industrial Development Bank. But this was a temporary phase. Again when Bhutto rose to power, he too took a series of measures including nationalisation of some industries with the objective of building an independent capitalist economy. While Liaqat Ali Khan was murdered, Bhutto was ousted from power and hanged. This does not seem to be accidental, though future historians of Pakistan might be able to throw more light on it. Nonetheless, except for these two short periods, the growing tendency in Pakistan has been to be content with a dependent economy.

It is not necessary to go into details regarding this. The lack of proper data also discourages such an exercise. Nonetheless, it is obvious, that foreign capital operates in Pakistan extensively, rather freely, either directly or in partnership with local capital.

Dependence of Pakistan on metropolitan states, particularly America, has taken the country on a zigzag course, mostly influenced by the geopolitical strategy of Washington. However, Pakistan has accumulated a vast burden of foreign debt, which (including Bangladesh) amounted to 0.2 billion dollars in 1960. At the end of 1979, it stood at 8 billion dollars for Pakistan alone. In 1979-80, debt servicing absorbed 38 per cent of Pakistan's export earnings.

While it is difficult to assess with any precision the operative strength of the landowning classes, it is clear that even half-hearted land reforms have not been implemented in that country. There is a particular class of affluent farmers, who dominate the agricultural economy. On the other hand, there are 24 lakhs landowners who own less than 5 acres of land, that is, nearly 50 per cent of the landowners. Those who own less than 12.5 acres of land number 37.43 lakhs. They constitute 77 per cent of landowners and own 32 per cent of the area under cultivation. Small landowners who work on the land of others, besides cultivating their own small plots, number 8,34,257. The number of landless tenants comes to 20.27 lakhs. Almost every second cultivator in Pakistan is a tenant farmer.

In contrast, the number of agricultural workers working on big farms is around 12 lakhs. According to the 1972 census of agriculture, 2 per cent of agricultural holdings (those over 100 acres) accounted for 28 per cent of land. This obviously is a gross underestimation of the degree of the concentration of land because owners of large holdings always conceal the size of their actual landholding.

At the other end of the scale stand those who have meagre holdings or are landless. This shows that the middle peasant strata in Pakistan is virtually on the way out or is already non-existent.

What has happened in Pakistan is that big landlords have become capitalist farmers. According to one figure, 86.5 per cent of the cultivated area of the mechanised farms is in the hands of owners with holdings above 100 acres; of this, no less than 43 per cent are with holdings of 500 acres and over.

There is yet another aspect, which needs to be analysed. The development of vested interests by the civil bureaucracy and military officers in the economy of the country is easily noticeable. In this connection two important elements in Pakistan's state structure need to be underlined.

The policy of granting land to army officers and senior civil servants has been followed with vigour. As a result, army officers and senior civil servants have acquired landed interests and have a corresponding class commitment.

From the sixties of the last century onwards, many army officers have established a deep liaison with the business community. Consequently, some retired generals and civil servants have become big businessmen. In fact, there is a growing trend in Pakistan of retired officers grabbing key positions in the economy, and those who are still in service build their influence with an eye on the future. In this process, military officers have also forged economic ties with multinationals operating in Pakistan.

Under the present military regime, this trend has assumed an alarming magnitude and has thus acquired a qualitatively different character. Army officers, both retired and those in service are now using state power to consolidate their position in the state corporations. Consequently, almost all the state corporations are manned by army officers.

Another relevant factor, which needs to be mentioned, is that economically backward regions of Pakistan—northwest Punjab and the northwest Frontier Province—are the main recruiting centres for the army. Ideological indoctrination of these recruits is easier because they have no experience of political education or links with political movements. Since the army in Pakistan is generally deployed for internal repression, role of Islamic ideology make its deepest impact. The Pakistani army is being politically equipped to fight the 'enemies of Islam', both internal and external.

While Islamic ideology is being liberally employed to fan revivalist passions in the army rank and file, in the higher echelons it is US influence, which has become pervasive. As an upshot of all these developments, the military bureaucratic oligarchy has gained a key position in the evolution of peripheral capitalism in Pakistan.

What is equally significant is that the military regime is distributing patronage to defence personnel and their relatives in every conceivable manner with a view to expanding its social base. It is not unusual for martial law officers exercise arbitrary powers for personal advantage. Their relatives are appointed in influential positions in bureaucracy and the numerous state corporations. Businessmen find that they cannot get permits for various ventures unless they accept military officers or their relatives as partners. Army men on martial law duties share this loot with civilian officials and function to each other's advantage.

It will not to be incorrect to say that the military itself has become General Zia's main constituency and now that of General Parvez Musharaff.

This shows that the corrupt landlord-capitalist leadership of Pakistan, which has secured a stranglehold over the new Pakistan state, would continue to manipulate internal and external political game they have been playing for decades. This brings into sharp focus the consequences of building a dependent capitalist economy, which stands in complete contrast to the socio-economic structure, which India has been building.

Just as Indo-Pak relations cannot be delinked from Pak-US relations, the socio-economic structure of Pakistan too has a direct and determining influence on these relations.

To say all this should not mean that one should throw up one's hands and completely rule out the possibility of bringing Indo-Pak relations on an even keel. Fortunately, the main thrust of India's policy has been and continues in the larger interests of the people of this subcontinent, in spite of the internal and external constraints weakening these efforts. The aim has to be to wean Pakistan away from imperialist pressures and influence through the validity of its own experiences. And evidently, there are no short cuts or easy paths in the realisation of this goal!

This survey will be incomplete, if we do not take into account socio-economic changes, which have begun to unfold in Pakistan in the beginning of the 21st century. The emerging new middle class, rise of local capitalists who want to build their country and above all the new generation of Pakistani people have begun to outgrow the influence of the feudalists and fundamentalists, that Muslim League and Pakistan's Peoples Party have united to demand democratisation of their country is a welcome development. It is in this background that current trends in Pakistan's polity have begun to unfold. Therefore, historically it will be incorrect to base India's Pakistan policy on the basis of past history alone. A balanced view of the past, the influence of American imperialism and new trends should be taken. That precisely seems to be the driving force of India's Pakistan policy in the beginning of the 21st century.

References

1. R. Palme Dutt, *India Today*, Bombay, 1947, p. 8.
2. A.L. Morton, *A Peoples' History of England*, London, 1945, p. 454.
3. See V.V. Nagarkar, *Genesis of Pakistan*.

14

India-Pakistan Relations in the Twenty-First Century

Manohar Singh Batra

India and Pakistan attained freedom from the colonial rule in 1947 and ever since have been embroiled in an adversarial relationship. Within two months of their independence, they entered into a ferocious war and in-between periods of hostile tension crossed swords twice again in the battlefield. Just before the end of the last century, their skirmishes on the heights of Kargil in Jammu and Kashmir wrote another acrimonious chapter in their strained relations. The widespread anger and loathing generated by the terrorist attack on India's Parliament by five Pakistani militants exacerbated the feelings of animosity and antagonism in the Indian masses against the rulers of Pakistan.

The Pakistani politicians have been bending all their energies to project Kashmir as a core issue and have been striving hard to convince the world community that their ideological survival depends upon this. They also call Kashmir as the unfinished agenda of partition and have been trying every possible method to achieve this goal. These methods have included open wars, attempts to involve other nations in pressurising India to implement the UN resolutions, albeit without Pakistan carrying out the provisions contained in those resolutions, occasional bilateral talks with India while at the same time endeavouring to internationalize the issue and lastly a low-intensity conflict to bleed India with an intent to coerce it to strike a deal gratifying Pakistan. The current leadership has added the nuclear dimension, which most people consider a blackmail, though some credulous quarters may tend to take it seriously as a possible flashpoint.

The main reasoning of the Pakistani demagogues has been that Jammu and Kashmir being a Muslim majority State should have been a part of that country as a logical culmination of the idea of Pakistan based on the two-nation theory. The endowment of J&K with natural resources like forests and river waters has also been nibbling at their hearts, apart from the fact that an all—weather road from Rawalpindi to Srinagar provides them with the shortest link to the valley.

Pakistanis also feel concerned about their military security, with J&K being a part of the Indian Union. Akbar Khan in his "Raiders in Kashmir" has argued that "In peace-time, the situation could be just unacceptable because we would remain permanently exposed to the threat of such magnitude that our independence would never be a reality. Surely this is not the type of Pakistan we had wanted." Irrespective of the fact that the water sharing agreement between India and Pakistan has been in force to the mutual benefit of the two countries, some Pakistani leaders have been raising the bogey of India controlling these waters with unfriendly intentions of harming the interests of Pakistan at some stage. Pakistani leaders of various hues have been obsessed with Kashmir; they have been claiming this piece of territory as lifeline of Pakistan. In the words of Sardar Abdul Qayyum Khan, a former President of the Pakistan-occupied Kashmir: "Pakistan cannot exist as an independent entity by withdrawing its claim on Kashmir. It will be turned into a virtual hostage to India, and its lease of life will depend upon the period which India will allow it to exist."

Quite a few Pakistani leaders have been proclaiming their love for the people of Kashmir as their kith and kin. Zulfikar Ali Bhutto addressing the UN Security Council had said: "The people of Jammu and Kashmir are part of the people of Pakistan, in blood, in flesh, in life, in culture, in geography, in history and in every way and in every form. They are part of the people of Pakistan." He conveniently forgot that the initial invasion of Kashmir by the tribals and the Pakistan army irregulars was engineered by the Pakistani politicians resulting in huge losses of life and property to the Kashmiris. Their refusal to withdraw Pakistani troops from the territory they had occupied by aggression was another factor working against the implementation of the UN resolutions on Kashmir. In fact the United Nations Commission for India and Pakistan (UNCIP) rejected the Pakistani demand to equate the presence of its troops in the areas it had occupied by force at par with the Indian Army presence in Kashmir. In December 1949 the UNCIP in its report to the Security Council had said that the deployment of the Pakistani army on the side of the invaders and the constitution of an "Azad force" which grew to 32 well-equipped battalions had changed the military situation. Owen Dixon, who had taken over as the UN representative in 1950, had said that the roles of both the tribes and the Pakistan army in the Kashmir conflict were contrary to international law.

Major powers like the USA and UK have been helping Pakistan to keep the Kashmir issue alive in the UN as was evident during 1957, 1962 and 1964. Encouraged by such support, Pakistani leaders have been exhorting the Kashmiris to wage a relentless struggle against India. In the 1990s just after assuming power in her country, Benazir Bhutto said, "We support self-determination for Kashmir, to be exercised through a plebiscite, and no one must be left in any doubt about that." Pakistan has been playing a proactive role in raising the Kashmir issue at all international fora ignoring the Shimla Agreement, under which they were supposed to solve the issue by bilateral negotiations. Khan Abdul Wali Khan, the Awami National Party leader said, "The Shimla Agreement was ratified by the National Assembly. It does not provide for any military offensive or plebiscite in Kashmir. Until it is annulled, both Pakistan and India are obliged to resolve the dispute through negotiations under the Shimla Agreement."

Pakistan has also been trying to enlist the support of the Islamic countries on the Kashmir issue. The OIC set up a Kashmir Contact Group in 1994 in Casablanca under pressure from Pakistan. The group has been trotting the issue of implementing the UN resolutions on Kashmir, though some members of the OIC have been increasingly emphasizing the need for a bilateral resolution of the Kashmir issue. Some OIC member states have shown little interest in Pakistan rhetorics and the blame games played by it. Pakistan's admission of offering political, moral and diplomatic support to the people of Kashmir in 'their just struggle' against the occupation by India has also not engendered much credibility among the nations. The slogan of *Jihad* and any support for bloodshed and subversion are repugnant to the spirit of the UN charter. Innumerable attacks on the security force and peaceful civilian population in the state of Jammu and Kashmir mounted incessantly by infiltrators trained, armed and supported by the Inter-Services Intelligence and the arrests, confiscation of arms and ammunition and confessions by those involved in depredations reveal active support by the Pakistani authorities. At recent stages, several countries including friends of Pakistan have asked her to check infiltrations.

Zulfikar Ali Bhutto had advocated a people's war against India. In a communication to General Tikka Khan, he had said: "In the new war, the enemies around us will be depending largely upon material superiority and not the human factor, upon technique and not force of an ideal. In this can lie their weakness and our strength... Recent history has amply proved, in China, in Korea, in Israel and in Vietnam that a people's war can withstand innumeranle ups and downs but that no force can succeed in altering its general march towards inevitable triumph...And we ourselves have ruled them for eight centuries. All these are not ancient history."

Pakistan never believed in resolution of the Kashmir tangle by bilateral negotiations. According to Stanley Wolpert, Bhutto's commitment to Shimla Agreement was not above suspicion. Bhutto never doubted that Pakistan would rise again some day to reclaim Kashmir, for it was a Muslim state and thus 'belonged' by definition to Pakistan. No agreement could change that 'reality', which according to Stanley Wolpert, "was firmly rooted in the labyrinth of Zulfi Bhutto's brain."

Pakistan never left any stone unturned to antagonize India. It eagerly walked into the US sponsored alliances in the early fifties. Pakistan had asked for US military assistance under the Mutual Security Act in February 1954. Almost immediately President Eisenhower announced that USA had acceded to that request. The same year South East Asia Collective Treaty was signed in Manila on September 8, 1954 which came to be known as SEATO. The Baghdad Pact was signed by Turkey and Iran on February 24, 1955 to which Pakistan acceded on September 23, 1955. This pact was rechristened CENTO, which in fact was directed only against communist aggression.

Pakistan has also been under a misapprehension of India's dominance in South Asia. According to the late General A.I. Akram, India had an increasing ambition to become a global power and Pakistan was determined not to let India establish its hegemony over the subcontinent. There were many fallacies in Akram's statement, which only leads one to believe that it was consistent effort on the part of influential Pakistanis to mislead their own people on the one hand and to malign India among the smaller countries in India's periphery on the other. As regards General Zia-ul-Haq, he relentlessly kept up anti-India campaign and siphoned off large quantities of arms and ammunition acquired from USA and Saudi Arabia for anti-Soviet operations in Afghanistan, to terrorist training and use in Jammu and Kashmir.

Some problems arose after independence not directlyy related to the partition. One of them is Tulbul Navigation Project. The Baglihar 450 MW hydrogen power project and the Sir Creek demarcation are some of the other issues, which have come up for resolution during the course of composite dialogue initiated in 1997. Baglihar appears to have proved intractable so far in view of a rigid stand taken by Pakistan. The World Bank neutral expert, Raymond Laffitte from the Swiss Federal Institute of Technology, who has inspected the project, is likely to complete his adjudication work by early 2006.

Before Pakistan went nuclear in May 1998, following India's experiments, nuclear capability was debated openly in that country Various political leaders delighted in flexing the potential nuclear muscle as an appendage to the Kashmir issue. They seemed to be convinced of the usefulness of a nuclear umbrella while lending support for violence in Kashmir. Many a defence analyst has relied on the hypothesis that nuclear deterrence worked in Pakistan's favour. Shireen Mazari of the Institute of Strategic Studies, Islamabad veciferously argued that the nuclear option would restrain India from expanding the conflict to a full scale war. Qazi Hussain Ahmed, a religio-political firebrand leader in Pakistan exhorted the Bhutto government in 1994 to develop nuclear weapons to deter India from a wider conflict. The same year, Nawaz Sharif warned India that "an attack on Pakistan could trigger a nuclear war." He also said that "an escalation of the crisis over Kashmir because of New Delhi's refusal to surrender Kashmir to Islamabad was inevitable." Pakistan has thus amalgamated its nuclear capacity to its operational position in Kashmir. India, according to Pakistan strategists, feels itself hamstrung, while Pakistan continues with its low intensity operations.

Many Pakistani thinkers believe that Pakistan could successfully stymie India's superior strength in conventional war with a combination of nuclear threat and unconventional combat. Pakistani agencies also revel in the hope of igniting *Jihadi* terrorism in other parts of India, while at the same time believing that India could be deterred from launching a counter attack on Pakistan. While doves in Pakistan have been occupying a back seat, the hawks have been thriving on extending threats projecting Kashmir as a highly emotive religious issue linking it to Islam. They have often invoked Islam as a means of promoting their strategic goals in the region.

General Parvez Musharraf, like his predecessors, has tried to aggregate power by using *Jihadi* organizations as means of achieving foreign policy goals. He has been attempting to differentiate between terrorism and *Jihad* to hoodwink the western countries. General Musharraf's gestures to clamp down on militant outfits proved to be illusory. According to the report of the International Crisis Group of July 2002 entitled "Pakistani Madrassas, Extremism and the Military", those gestures were aimed more at curbing inter-sectarian terrorism within the country rather than beyond the borders of Pakistan. Pakistan's military links with the Al Qaeda have given credence to the view that Pakistan has been continuing with its policy to support militancy.

On June 24, 2002, Parvez Musharraf reiterated that he would end infiltration from POK to the Indian side, but he denied this subsequently. In an interview to *Newsweek*, the General flatly denied having given such an assurance to the US. "I have told President Bush, nothing is happening across the Line of Control. This is the assurance I have given," he said. He further added, "I am not going to give you an assurance that for years nothing will happen." The State Department, however, issued a categorical contradiction on June 25 to the effect that "Deputy Secretary Armitage was given assurances by President Musharraf on June 6 that ending of infiltration across the Line of Control would be permanent. These assurances were given to the Secretary of State, to the President of the United States in their conversations as well as repeatedly to our representatives, our charge and Ambassador in Islamabad." A well-known Pakistani columnist described Pakistan's relationship with the US as "one of dependency and subservience on the one hand and deceit on the other."

In the meantime, Pakistan, by all accounts has become a US protectorate. The 9/11 Commission Report prompted the US Congress to enact a legislation to implement the recommendations of the commission to help Pakistan develop a promising, stable and secure future. Assistance is sought to be provided to Pakistan to continue and improve upon its commitments to combating terrorism, to seek to resolve any outstanding difficulties with its neighbours and other countries in its region, to continue making efforts to fully control its territory and borders, to progress towards becoming a more effective and participatory democracy, to participate more vigorously in the global market place and to continue to modernize its economy, to take all necessary steps to halt the spread of weapons of mass destruction, to continue to reform the education system and to implement a general strategy of moderation.

The third phase of arms transfer to Pakistan from US has already begun. She is getting more P3Cs and TOW 2 missiles, some Phalanx antiship missile systems and C-130 transporters. Pakistan has been given the Major Non-NATO Ally status, which means it can pick up other military stuff as well. Pranab Mukherjee, India's Defence Minister, reacting to the Report said on December 12, 2004 that the supply of sophisticated weapons-F-16 aircraft, lethal missile arrangements and naval surveillance reconnaissance aircraft-to Pakistan by the United States would jeopardize the peace process between the two countries. These weapons are for big wars and not to fight terrorism. Nobody uses F-16s to fight terrorism. Pranab Mukherjee further said that US Secretary of Defence, Donald Rumsfeld was impressed upon on the issue by the Indian government.

General Musharraf has been repeatedly saying that Pakistan would never give up Kashmir. This problem needs to be resolved, as peace and prosperity of this whole region hinges on this. A large number of analysts in India are of the view that Pakistan is not really interested in a solution of the Kashmir issue, as it can sustain a low cost proxy war indefinitely causing India to be weakened economically and in human lives. Most of the sensible people in this country have come to accept the idea of turning the Line of Control into some kind of a permanent border. Perhaps, this is the only possible solution. The leader of the Muttahida Quami Movement (MQM) of Pakistan, Altaf Hussain reinforced this idea in an interview in London on November 4, 2004. This assertion came at a time when Musharraf floated the idea of dividing the territory into zones and then deciding who should control what, and that added a new dimension.

The Indian Prime Minister, Dr. Manmohan Singh said on November 14, 2004 that the people of Jammu and Kashmir had suffered a great deal due to militancy during the past decade and a half and it was time to heal their wounds. India and Pakistan were capable of dealing with all issues bilaterally and there was no scope for third-party intervention. Dr. Singh informed the Parliament on December 21 that he had told the Pakistani President in New York that while we are willing to look at various options for a negotiated settlement of the issue of Jammu and Kashmir, we would not agree to any redrawing of boundaries, or another partition of the country. Spelling out his government's approach to foreign policy, Dr. Singh said, "Our objective is to focus on the centrality of national interests in the conduct of our external relations and the pursuit of our economic interests. We have taken important initiatives, keeping in mind the imperative of retaining our freedom of options, remaining alive to our concerns." He categorically stated that the country would not agree to the redrawing of our boundaries under any pressure.

In J.N. Dixit's view, adversarial relations with Pakistan (and China) have resulted in India having to divert its scarce financial, material and trained manpower resources for defence purposes, thereby reducing its capacities to formulate and implement social and economic policies for national consolidation and reconstruction. India's territorial integrity remains under threat from Pakistan and India will have to remain vigilant until some agreement is concluded. There are some misconceptions about India's foreign policy in this region. One is that India, with its large resources and larger technological and economic capacities, desires to capture and dominate the economies of other South Asian countries. Another is that the growing population of India will generate demographic pressures leading to Indian migration to neighbouring countries backed up by Indian political and military power. Still another idea prevailing among India's neighbours is that India should show more willingness to grant concessions on matters of dispute between them and India. India, they feel, should not only be fair but should also be generous in responding to their demands, whether it is Kashmir or any other point of difference. But it is not realized that vital territorial or economic interests can never be sacrificed by any nation.

It may be recalled that in January 1994 India had made a very important suggestion to Pakistan that both sides should sign a bilateral agreement not to attack each other's economic and populous centres and not to use their respective nuclear capacities against each other under the 'no first use' doctrine, but Pakistan had rejected this suggestion. India has never shown any hegemonic intention or made any move in this direction. It is Pakistan who inflicted wounds on India by attacking it repeatedly in efforts to grab its territory and at one time gifting a huge chunk of land seized by it in J&K to China.

Almost all initiatives to improve Indo-Pak relations have been taken by India. Apart form the confidence building measures set in motion by the I.K. Gujral government, Mr. Atal Behari Vajpayee's concrete gesture of undertaking a bus journey to Lahore and signing a Declaration of Peace kindled some kind of hope of breaking the gridlock, but it was sabotaged by the Kargil incursion. Immediately after 9/11 in USA, an abominal attack on India's Parliament was mounted on the 13th December by the Pakistan based terrorists. The Vajpayee-Musharraf talks in Agra too fizzled out because of undiplomatic postures of the Pakistani leader. Pakistan's agreement to talk with India on all outstanding issues (instead of focusing mainly on Kashmir) in response to Mr. Vajpayee's offer in April 2003 also hinged on India's desire to restore normalcy with Pakistan. But contradictions inherent in Pakistan's policy towards India surface time and again, for instance harping only on Kashmir being the core issue. It casts a doubt whether a real rapprochement would ever occur between the two countries in view of General Musharraf's formulation that hostility between India and Pakistan is bound to exist even if the Kashmir problem is solved. This doubt is further strengthened by a statement of General Muhammad Aziz Khan on June 23, 2003 to the effect that "India's religious and economic values are such that Muslims cannot adhere to these. So even if the Kashmir issue is resolved, we cannot become intimate friends." This bent of mind creates an impression that the General is using talks with India to gain legitimacy in his own country and abroad. It is also known that Islamisation of the Pakistani army was introduced by General Zia-ul-Haq, but it is not known exactly to what extent this element exists at the present moment.

Another point attracting attention is that whereas India's strategic doctrine is not Pakistan centric and its sweep is much wider in view of its environment and geography, Pakistan's defence doctrine is entirely India centric. Its aspirations and desperate attempts to acquire lethal weapons with its focus on India do not demonstrate its propensities to have an ambience of peace, cooperation and prosperity in the sub-continent.

Democracy has sill to take roots in Pakistan. At regular intervals it gets fractured and bed-ridden. No sooner does it start feeling the hard ground under its feet than it receives a mortal blow again. An independent judiciary and rule of law are also Pakistan's necessities. Its mindset is still feudal. Its people are awaiting a new dawn, when no Army General or a military junta would be able to break into the citadel of democracy and deprive the people to be governed by a truly elected government. Greater people to people contacts between India and Pakistan would, perhaps, be helpful in strengthening the resolve in that country to nurture democratic institutions and not to be cowed down by jackboots. In the resent circumstances, however, it seems that the Army in Pakistan would keep its stranglehold over the semi-democratic government put in place by its chief.

Perhaps, General Musharraf has come to realize that there cannot be a quick fix solution to a waxed problem like Kashmir. The State enjoys a special position within the Indian Union, as defined by the Constitution. There being a special clause forming the basic structure of the Constitution, it cannot be amended. J&K is a pluralistic territory and its partitioning, as suggested by General Musharraf, would throw up a plethora of problems. Any vivisection of the State would generate further tensions and that might trigger a chain reaction in the whole sub-continent. Free and fair general elections held recently in the State have given a chance to the populace to choose their representatives under a multi-party system and, apart from some ill-conceived measures erroneously adopted, the whole State has almost remained a secular society without communal and fundamentalist undertones. Only extremist pressures from across the border vitiated the air along with some wanton militant and terrorist activities. Despite such extraneous influences, new political formations have come up with their political manifestoes and they have their own mandates. In order to encourage people to people contacts, a right move has been made to open the Srinagar-Muzaffarabad bus route, which would enable citizens on both sides of the Line of Control to meet and intermingle with one another to understand their situation better and to come closer culturally, emotionally and ideologically. It might also encourage economic cooperation between them leading to prosperity.

Among the positive measures to bring a thaw in relations between India and Pakistan is an understanding between Iran, Pakistan and India to set up a gas pipeline that would be profitable to all the three countries. That would enable Iran to sell an abundant quantity of gas to India, while Pakistan would earn millions of dollars as transit fees and royalty. Since Pakistan has serious reservations in improving its trade and commercial relations with India and has suggested delinking the gas pipeline project from other economic proposals, India has conveyed to Iran that we should pay for the gas received at this end and the safety of the pipeline should be a matter between Iran and Pakistan. The unwillingness on the part of Pakistan to grant the Most Favoured Nation status to India in the matter of trade is another unfortunate aspect of the Indo-Pak relations, which has delayed and dampened the spirit of cooperation that could have benefited millions of our people. Free trade and transit facilities to other countries could be a factor of immense value to India and Pakistan, which along with other measures has remained hostage to the deep-rooted prejudices.

India has already reduced its armed strength in Jammu and Kashmir and the process is likely to continue. This is in spite of unceasing infiltrations, though to a lesser degree than before, from across the border and mindless terrorist attacks on security forces in J&K as well as the civilian population. Terrorist training camps in POK and Pakistan are still active and there has been little abatement in infiltrations by the cadres of terrorist outfits like Lashkar-e-Toiba not only into J&K, but other parts of India as well. The collusion between ISI and fundamentalists in Bangladesh and Nepal working against the interests of this country is too well-known. Leaders of the All Party Hurriyat Conference have been freely meeting the Pakistani diplomats in New Delhi and the visiting leaders of Pakistan. Recently a Hurriyat delegation was allowed to travel to POK by the Srinagar-Muzaffarabad bus, but they spilled over to Islamabad for a hearty meeting with Musharraf and his associates.

In the long history of discussions on Kashmir, the first ever interaction of a delegation of the All Party Hurriyat Conference with India's Prime Minister took place in New Delhi in the first week of September 2005. Dr. Manmohan Singh emphasized on those delegates the need for cessation of violence in Kashmir and an end to infiltration, which could well be a precursor to the reduction in the presence of the armed forces in the valley. The Kashmiri separatists have been putting this as a major demand, along with review of cases of detenues under the Public Safety Act and the already abrogated POTA. The Prime Minister reiterated his resolve to protect human rights in J&K and to ensure for them a life of peace, self respect and dignity. Both the Central government and the Hurriyat representatives agreed to carry forward the talks by bringing on board all regions and shades of political opinion.

In addition, Pakistan has dithered on the question of opening its airspace for India's civil aviation. Its insistence on India giving an undertaking that it would never stop its overflights in its airspace in future is considered to be highly unreasonable and misplaced. In any case the April 2004 initiative by Atal Behari Vajpayee was embraced delightfully by the people of Pakistan and since then a deluge of delegations of journalists, writers, legislators, lawyers, women and businessmen have crossed the Wagah border to reach each other's country. Earlier, the 12 point confidence building measures floated by India were eagerly clutched at by the common man in Pakistan, as the successful outcome of some of those promised to conform to their long cherished objectives of forging closer bonds with the people on this side of the border.

The Indian proposals concerned the technical level talks on the resumption of civil aviation and train journeys, resumption of sporting events, easier visa regime, crossing the Wagah checkpoint by senior citizens on foot, augmentation of the capacity of the Delhi-Lahore bus service, establishing links between the coast guards of the two countries, non-arrest of the fishermen of either side within certain limits at sea, India's offer of free medical treatment to more Pakistani children, augmentation of the strength of the respective diplomatic missions of the two countries, a ferry service between Mumbai and Karachi and a new bus link between the two sides of Kashmir and a road or rail link between Khokrapar and Munabao.

The big package of confidence building measures has been welcomed by a large number of Pakistanis and a new era of hope and warmth seems to have been ushered, unless cold water is poured over their joy by the whims of hardboiled politicians. The latter have already shown resistance to some of the Indian proposals, reminiscent of their past intransigence. They are fully aware that denying opportunities to people for ferry travel between Mumbai and Karachi and rail journey between Khokrapar and Munabao would prolong the hardships of the people living in the border areas of both the countries. The Pakistani response to India's offer for free medical treatment to some Pakistani children was so vexatious.

In spite of Pakistani claims of a ceasefire on the Line of Control, its personnel have been resorting to sporadic firing, causing damage to life and property on the Indian side. There have been examples of feigning ignorance of such violations on the part of their military commanders. In some instances they have been providing artillery cover to their infiltrators and 'suicide squads.'

The political situation in Pakistan continues to be in a flux. When the President has reneged on his promise to give up his military uniform by the end of 2004 and has manoeuvred to continue to play the dual role as the President of Pakistan and the Chief of the Army Staff, the Alliance for Restoration of Democracy (ARD) and the

Mutahidda Majlis-e-Ammal (MMA) have reached an accord on March 8, 2005 for launching a joint struggle to force the General to quit the presidency and the Army Chief's post. The MMA and ARD leaders have agreed on the objectives of ousting General Musharraf from both the jobs he is holding at present, pressing for the restoration of the 1973 Constitution as it stood on October 12, 1999 and the setting up of an independent and autonomous election commission. The leaders of the two alliances have reached an agreement that they would work for a system in which no army general would ever be accepted as future ruler after Musharraf quits his offices.

On the sidelines of a cricket match played in New Delhi in April 2005. Manmohan Singh and Musharraf had a hearty talk between themselves on various Indo-Pak issues. Soon after their conversation, Musharraf told a close aid, "We have the gravest responsibility to ensure that the peace process does not go off-track. I got a clear sense that we both understand this very well and that is our hope." Manmohan Singh, on his part, said of Musharraf, "He was frank, forthright and forward looking. We have a leader we can do business with." Musharraf talked of Pakistan's willingness to look at permitting trade between the two parts of Kashmir. He agreed to designate meeting points on the Line of Control for divided Kashmiri families apart from allowing cultural interaction and people going for pilgrimages. But Pakistan's hardliners kept up the refrain of Kashmir in their country and underlined the futility of any dialogue that does not resolve the real bone of contention, as they called it. A hawkish newspaper *The Nation* described the summit in New Delhi as a "national humiliation". Musharraf has started believing that "military option is not an option any more. Now is the time for conflict resolution."

The Pakistani delegation insisted that it was not necessary to spellout the details of the January 6, 2004 joint press statement issued in Islamabad, in which Musharraf had committed to the then Prime Minister of India, Atal Behari Vajpayee that Pakistani territory would not be permitted to be used for any terrorist activity against India. India had to be content with just a mention of the January 6 statement at this round of talks and a pledge that "the two leaders would not allow terrorism to impede the peace process". It is an irony that in spite of the high decibel of peaceful solution to the Kashmir problem, Pakistan kept the option of militancy intact.

Contrary to general perception that Pakistan is keen on augmenting people to people contacts across Indian borders, the authorities have been less than generous in granting visas to artists and other cultural performers from this country. Pakistan's ambivalence is clear from its reluctance to increase the frequency of the Srinagar-Muzaffarabad bus service, though she has agreed to introduce a Lahore-Amritsar bus service from November 2005.

Pakistan has been vacillating between confrontation with India punctuated with short spells of rapprochement, and seeking extra-regional partnerships that could provide her with relative strength to counter its traditional adversary. Pakistan has been trying to enlist all support from the People's Republic of China in procuring all sorts of lethal weapons and has also been wooing USA for moral and material assistance to counter India's natural superiority in men and resources. Pakistan's vision has mostly been narrowed to India to the extent of an obsession. The world, in its view, is divided in two parts–one which can provide it with help to strengthen itself against this country and the other which is not willing or not interested in doing so, and that part is irrelevant to Pakistan.

According to some renowned economists, the granting of the MFN status to India would bring substantial gains to Pakistan. It would be better off with legalized trade that would generate tax revenues instead of losing the same to smuggling. Agricultural and industrial products would gain much larger access to the vast Indian market. A soft border in Kashmir would also create another growth centre and herald peace in the region so badly needed.

It has also been suggested that Pakistan's improved relations with India could produce economic opportunities for her in the sector of information and communications technology. The six Indian Institutes of Technology have earned high reputation of producing world class engineers and scientists. USA has started depending more and more on Indian experts in the matter of information technology. Pakistan can learn from the Indian experience. Fundamentalism and *Jihadi* mentality have become a stumbling block in Pakistan's progress. The two assassination attempts on General Musharraf must have convinced him to eliminate this menace, which would also bring peace with India.

As a part of the composite talks between the two countries, their delegations held discussions on Sir Creek, the disputed coastal strip off the Gujarat coast, at the end of May 2005. Five months earlier, both sides had deployed eight teams each for the survey of the horizontal segment of the creek. The demarcation of boundary along a 96 km long strip of water between the Rann of Kutch in India and Sindh in

Pakistan has been under dispute. There are naval installations on the Indian side and the other side of the creek has been under Pakistan's control. India's stand has been that the boundary line would be defined by "mid-channel" of the creek as indicated in the map of 1925, when the final demarcation was completed, but Pakistan's view has been that the notion of mid-channel is applicable only to the navigable channels. India has proposed that pending formalization of the boundary, delimitation of the maritime boundary from seawards may be considered, which would be according to the internationally accepted principles and would be to the advantage of either country.

Pursuing his agenda of peace, Prime Minister Dr. Manmohan Singh has suggested to turn Siachen, the world's highest battleground into a "mountain of peace", but there is a clear apprehension among the army brass that after India pulls back from Siachen, Pakistani forces might eventually move up the Saltoro range to posts vacated by India. The Indian army insists on "authentication" of the location of present posts held by both sides. The sole purpose of authentication is to ensure that after a withdrawal has taken place, Pakistan will not move back to its old positions or up Gyong La, Bilafond La and Sia La–the three passes along the Saltoro range–to positions currently held by India. It is a view within the Indian establishment that if Pakistan reneges on any Siachen deal, it would lead the bilateral relations towards deep freeze.

As both India and Pakistan have high stakes in energy security, it has been heartening for the region that both have been seriously considering to give shape to the project of a gas pipeline from Iran to India via Pakistan. With the project materializing both countries would stand to gain enormously, which is likely to contribute to the subcontinent's economic prosperity. In addition, India and Pakistan announced the setting up of a joint working group for energy cooperation with focus on gas pipelines, in the beginning of June 2005. The proposed 2600 km Iran-Pakistan-India pipeline is one of the major options the Joint Working Group would consider. During his September 2005 visit to Afghanistan, Prime Minister Manmohan Singh also mentioned the Turkmenistan-Afghanistan-Pakistan pipeline, for which India has already asked Pakistan to facilitate its entry into this ADB sponsored project. India has offered to sell diesel to Pakistan and it is quite possible that Pakistan, instead of incurring high costs on diesel imports from distant sources, would be more pragmatic in getting it nearer home.

Though Pakistan has always been trying to manipulate third party intervention in the Kashmir issue, India's stand against this and its firm posture of its being a purely bilateral affair to be negotiated only by peaceful means has recently shown some chinks. Now both sides have been allowing USA to have a toehold in a matter which is primarily of their bilateral concern. Pakistan has been using all possible opportunities and every conceivable forum to raise the Kashmir issue, which India has been resisting on the plea of J&K being entirely an internal issue of this country, the State being an integral constituent of the Indian Union. But now the Indian leadership is not totally averse to responding to the US promptings. On September 13, 2005, Dr. Manmohan Singh told President Bush that India's belief is that Pakistan still controlled the flow of terror in J&K and this must stop for any realistic progress. Musharraf too pleaded with Bush seeking reduction of Indian troops in J&K. Obviously in Pakistan's reckoning USA's pressure on India would work. Any acquiescence on the part of India to give in to a third party prodding could subject it to external pressures at a later stage, which, of course, would not be to India's liking. At New York, US Secretary of State Condoleeza Rice asked Manmohan Singh to give some concessions to Musharraf on Kashmir, which he could carry back home. Both countries should avoid creating such scenarios when third parties start meddling in their purely bilateral problems. And General Musharraf should give thought to his penchant for equating Kashmir to Palestine, while touring US or Europe, because people there know that there is hardly any similarity between the two issues.

The future of Indo-Pak relations in the twenty-first century rests on the mindset of the leaders of the two countries. Even though the people of the two nations are generally in favour of shedding the old prejudices rooted in hostility born out of bigotry spawned by the self-centred leaders at the time of the Partition, the successive leaders of Pakistan kept the cauldron boiling in a desperate attempt to extract greater advantage from the 'weak' India. The same mentality has been evident in the almost constant acts of sabotage and terrorism resulting in an endless blood-letting and the building up of hysteria on the so-called human rights violations and the suppression of Kashmiris. Everyone who cares to know the truth is aware that the highly imaginary human rights violations spill out of security operations against the infiltrators and mercenaries emerging from across the border with the help of the intelligence agencies, and as the hostiles mingle so well with the locals, it becomes well nigh impossible to distinguish between them.

There is no case of justifying violence from any quarter, but one has to see what the supreme leadership in Pakistan feels about the long-term relations .between our two countries. Though the irreversibility of the current confidence building measures is acknowledged, there are hidden threats of further conflicts unless the 'core issue' is resolved entirely to Pakistan's satisfaction. The General has also warned that if the solution is not found early, Pakistan would again raise the demand for a plebiscite.

India's steadfast stand has been that for any meaningful dialogue, violence must stop and the terrorist infrastructure on the Pakistani soil as well as in the POK territory must be dismantled. As far as J&K is concerned, any solution can be discussed without effecting any change in the borders of the State. India is ready to put its stake on peace and tranquility along the Line of Control. This country is for evolving a mechanism for allowing interaction between people on both sides of the LOC, and permitting border/*LoC* trade at some points. As for terror, both countries should jointly fight it with all their resources. If Pakistan is not going to accept *LoC* as border, then what are the other plausible steps that can be taken to resolve the issue and to establish durable peace. In this context, one is reminded of an observation made by an enlightened Pakistani academic, Dr. Ayesha Agha Siddiqa that in the eyes of her country's armed forces "New Delhi still remains the top enemy that will have to be fought or vanquished." According to Siddiqa, the Pakistani army's connections with *Jihadi* groups are intact and Musharraf would find it difficult to deal with the situation.

There is a palpable feeling among political observers that the charm offensive by Musharraf may be a tactical retreat and he has been trying to win on the negotiation table what he could not on the battlefield. And those who think he has turned into a dove are probably dwelling in a fool's paradise. He has been trying to acquire highly lethal and deadly weapons from his friends in China and USA. The latter is more than willing to equip Musharraf with whatever arms he fancies as a reward for his cooperation in fighting the Al Qaeda and the Taliban, though without tangible results. Because he has not been able to nab Osama bin Laden and his close associates and the Taliban are reported to be regrouping to put a spoke in the wheel of the burgeoning liberalism in Afghanistan.

Even if someone may believe that "soft border" has emerged as common vocabulary, what it would boil down to, one wonders. According to Prime Minister Manmohan Singh "short of secession, short of redrawing boundaries, the Indian establishment can live with anything." But Musharraf categorically stated that Pakistan would not accept the proposal that the *LoC* be converted into a permanent border. Both sides have been talking of making the *LoC* irrelevant.

Though Pakistan has been overly worried about the future of the Jammu and Kashmir State of India, its leaders have not been earnest in addressing India's concerns about the continuous support being provided by that country to infiltrators and terrorists, who have been busy blowing up security men and civilians alike in the name of *jehad*. Speaking at the Carnegie Endowment for International Peace, a Washington think tank, on June 29, 2005, India's Defence Minister Pranab Mukherjee said that while there have been some positive developments in India's relations with Pakistan, the infrastructure for terrorism in Pakistan and Pakistan-controlled territory of Kashmir still exists. "We do not hear of operations like the ones being conducted by Pakistan in cooperation with the USA against the war on terrorism at its western frontiers towards its eastern borders with India," he elaborated.

Though Prime Minister Manmohan Singh lavished praise on President Musharraf for proposing demilitarization of a part of Kashmir, the disturbing reports regarding revival of terrorist groups and seizure of huge quantities of explosives in the valley, the capability of the terrorists' penetrating the fencing along the Line of Control and the reinforcement of the largest terrorist group, Hizb-ul-Mujahideen in the valley have been a source of much concern and anxiety to those who have been hoping for a peaceful solution. Manmohan Singh, however, continued to be optimistic and hoped for a movement forward in the relationship between the two countries.

Manmohan Singh and Musharraf at their meeting on the sidelines of the UN General Assembly session in New York in September 2005 held forth their commitment to the search for a pragmatic solution to all outstanding issues. The Indian Prime Minister was, however, surprised at the General's invocation of the Security Council resolutions on Kashmir and at a divergence with the tone and tenor of his speech at the United Nations last year, when he had made no such mention. The maverick Musharraf, however, tried to allay the apprehensions of the miffed Manmohan Singh at a dinner saying that he had no intention of muddying the waters of the peace process. Despite Musharraf's petulance, the Indian leader brushed off his barbs and remained firm on keeping the talks on track in the future.

If all the hardliners on both sides accept it as a reality and the only means of peaceful settlement of the chronic problem, that would be a great miracle. Let both countries divert their attention from strife and convert all the past bitterness into cooperative effort to alleviate poverty, illiteracy and disease and allow the people to mingle with one another to share the common cultural heritage, including both the Kashmirs, that could usher a new dawn on the subcontinent and Asia. That would mean a new life for one-fifth of the humanity. For this, Pakistan would have to banish terrorism and India would have to be more earnest. Pakistan must also adopt the policy of no-first-use of nuclear weapons, as India has done. Let both countries retain their respective nuclear stock for deterrence as long as distrust persists, but both should disavow their use or threat to use against each other or any other State for settling disputes or resolving differences. That would be real pragmatism and statesmanship.

To wash off its rancour, Pakistan ought to stop opposing India in its quest for occupying its rightful place in the world community. She should support rather oppose India's campaign for permanent membership of the UN Security Council. She should also grant the Most Favoured Nation status to India, its closest neighbour in trade and should also provide transit facilities to this country for sending economic aid and essential goods to the war ravaged Afghanistan. In case she allows India a trade route to the Central Asian countries, that would be of enormous gain not only to India, but also to Pakistan herself.

Now that Musharraf has been taking part in the dialogue process with India, he must for sure eschew his old thinking and carry it to a logical conclusion. Let there be peace and tranquility rather than conflict and violence. India is not a Hindu country, as religious and political leaders have been trying to project it. It is a secular country having more Muslims in its fold than the entire population of Pakistan and these Muslims are loyal to their Motherland. They enjoy equal rights under the Constitution and are full partners in the democratic polity of the country. At least three illustrious sons of this land have been the Heads of State and other Muslims have been occupying important positions in the judiciary and other organs of the State. Once the Pakistani leadership understands these realities, the 21st century can be an epoch of peace rather than being an era of conflicts and confrontations.

References

1. *South Asian Journal*, January-March 2004; April-June 2004; July-September 2004; January-March 2005.

2. *World Focus*, June-July 1998; October-December 1998; October-December 2001; September 2002; October-December 2003; August 2004; October-December 2004.

3. Indian Council of World Affairs–Foreign Affairs Reports July-September 2004; October-December 2004.

4. Pakistan in a Changing Strategic Context: The Evolving Strategic Environment: Advantage Pakistan by Jasjit Singh, Pakistan Squanders a Strategic Advantage by Pran Chopra, The Army in the Power Struggle by Sumita Kumar, Changing Dynamics of Pakistan's Kashmir Policy by Smruti, S. Pattanaik, A Multi-layered Policy for India-Pakistan Relations by Balraj Puri, Post 9/11 World: Implications for Kashmir Issue by S.D. Muni.

5. International Studies 35, 1 (1998), Sage Publications by M.S. Rajan.

6. World Affairs January-March 1999–Foreign Policy in a Changing World by J.N. Dixit.

7. Strategic Analysis July 1999–The Gujral Doctrine and Beyond by Padmaja Murty.

8. Pakistan Pendulam by Vikram Sood; *Hindustan Times*, May 2, 2005.

9. Peace Initiative is Fine by G. Parthasarathy; *The Tribune*, December 4, 2003.

10. CEMs not enough by M.B. Naqvi, November 3, 2004.

11. World Bank recommends neutral expert on Baglihar dam issue by Amit Baruah; *The Hindu*, April 29, 2005.

12. Mission Kashmir by Manoj Joshi; *The Hindustan Times*, April 29, 2005.

13. Baglihar: Pak fears unfounded by R.N. Malik; *The Sunday Tribune*, May 15, 2005.

14. In the deep freeze by Ajai Shukla; *The Indian Express*, May 23, 2005.

15. Beyond the zone drone by K. Subrahmanyam; *The Hindustan Times*, May 24, 2005.

16. The heights of contention by B.G. Verghese; *The Tribune*, June 15, 2005.

15

India's Relation with Pakistan: A Critical Estimate

Afsir Karim

Preamble

The state of hostility between India and Pakistan for the last fifty years has been a fact of life. The roots for this state of affairs lie in the bitter confrontation between Indian Muslim League which wanted partition of India on communal lines and the nationalist parties who opposed it. Pakistan was eventually formed amid much bloodshed and the bitter legacy of communal holocaust has been the main cause of mistrust and hostility and frequent military confrontations between the two countries. The basis of the two-nation theory was finally laid to rest after the birth of Bangladesh. Pakistan suffered a humiliating military defeat in the process and this led to further bitterness and created a new crisis of confidence in Pakistan. After the partition of the country and military defeat in 1971 Pakistan realised that it can no longer match India's military might in a conventional war; it therefore adopted other methods to confront India. It also acquired nuclear capability though it kept it hidden till India's nuclear tests in 1998. Pakistan's proxy war and sponsoring of terrorism under its nuclear shield, and attacks on high value targets like the Indian Parliament brought the relationship between the two countries to the brink of another war.

Pakistan had embarked on a plan to destabilise India with the ultimate aim to balkanise it so that the balance of powers shifts in its favour in South Asia. Annexation of J&K was a pivotal part of this scheme, although the target areas included Punjab, Assam, Nagaland and other states of Northeast India. The industrial hubs and the Northern Indian heartland were also targets of subversion and destabilisation. The modus operandi adopted was to encourage communal and caste strife, promote general disorder and internal strife through subversion and terrorism. Terrorism was used as the cutting edge of this confrontation, and through it communal strife, retardation of economic progress and destabilisation of Kashmir, Punjab and the Northeastern India was to be achieved.

Till 2003 the prospects of peace between India and Pakistan were rather bleak. Pakistan sponsored terrorist attacks in Kashmir and threat of terrorist strikes in various high value targets persisted. Pakistan maintained that violence in Kashmir was domestic and related to the actions of freedom fighters. The hostile environment continued till Atal Behari Vajpayee came forward with a peace offer in April 2003, which mainly focused on increasing people to people contact and implementation of several confidence building measures. India proposed a bus service from Delhi to Lahore, rail/bus service from Munabao to Khokropar in Sindh and across the Line of Control from Srinagar to Muzaffarabad to facilitate trade and people to people contacts. Pakistan wavered for a while but eventually accepted these proposals. Later Pakistan declared ceasefire on the LoC where firing had continued in and out of season. It provided great relief to the people as artillery duels across the LoC mainly killed civilians on both sides and disrupted day-today life of the border villages. The problem of both countries has been that the hardliners were not ready to budge an inch on the Kashmir issue. The extremists in Pakistan and Al Qaeda supported *Jihadi* terrorist groups always tried to thwart the peace initiatives. They had already made it clear to Musharraf that they would not accept any comprise on Kashmir.

Indian Initiative

A major breakthrough was signing of a joint statement by Atal Behari Vajpayee and Musharraf during the SAARC summit at Islamabad in January 2004. The joint statement set a positive trend because it was highly conciliatory and contained the following agreements:

- An agreement to start a composite dialogue on all subjects including Kashmir.
- A commitment that no territory under Pakistan's control will be allowed to be used by terrorists against India.
- Confidence building measures to continue.
- Talks to be held some time in February that year.

Hopes for peace rose as the joint statement opened a new era of dialogue instead of confrontation between the two countries. India preferred a step by step approach, while Pakistan wanted fast progress for resolving the Kashmir issue. The people both in India and Pakistan generally welcomed the dialogue and the peace process initiated by

India and the response by Pakistan to peace gestures. It remains to be seen if the process of reconciliation will be allowed to proceed smoothly or peace be derailed by terrorist attacks on high-value Indian targets. There is also a possibility that segments of Pakistan army may violate the ceasefire on one pretext or the other and vitiate the atmosphere. But the military situation, unlike the terrorism can be brought under control and cannot derail the process of dialogue for long because both India and Pakistan are now mentally prepared to take such eventualities in their stride and ensure that the peace process is not affected by small infringements of rules of the ceasefire or some terrorist activities.

The dialogue process may bog down on the Kashmir issue as Pakistan is likely to demand a good part of the Kashmir valley if nothing more as the price of peace, but India would not accept a second partition on communal lines. This may result in postponement of the peace process or confrontation on the Kashmir issue. The conditions in Kashmir have improved lately and the people are keen that peace and tranquillity should be maintained; in these circumstances it may not be possible for Pakistani hardliners to carry out large scale terrorist activities in J&K.

Dialogue with All Party Hurriyat Conference, a motley crowd of Kashmiri hardliners has remained a non-starter. These leaders stand to lose their status if the peace process succeeds and hence are not ready to cooperate with the government of India. If Musharraf is assassinated or deposed the situation may change rapidly as in such circumstances Pakistan is likely to be taken over by hardliners from the army in collabouration with the radical religious groups.

The Current Situation

Much progress has been made and India and Pakistan seem to be inching towards a peaceful resolution of various problems between the two countries but Kashmir remains a tough nut to crack. Pakistan has realized that it is better to find a peaceful solution to the problem but has not given up its ambition to wrest Kashmir from India. Pakistan continues to support Kashmiri and *Jihadi* terrorist operations in J&K, but at present attacks on other parts of India have been put on hold perhaps under international pressure.

General Parvez Musharraf's declaration that he will not allow acts of terrorism against India from any territory controlled by Pakistan was the first positive signal India received from Pakistan after the SAARC summit in January 2004. After this declaration there has been no major *Jihadi* operation in India, except in J&K, since Lashkar-e-Tayyaba (LeT) carried out two bomb attacks in Mumbai that killed several innocent bystanders on August 25, 2003.

In the recent past Pakistan has been blowing hot and cold and both positive and negative signals are being received. Amongst the positive indicators, was the ceasefire declared on the Line of Control (LOC). In J&K which held, besides rather muted protests regarding fencing segments of the LOC/international border by India to curb infiltration from Pakistan/PoK.

Reliable reports and statistics of the Ministry of Home Affairs India, indicate that there has been '21 per cent' decline in acts of terrorism in J&K, nevertheless in the recent past a number of terrorist related incidents have resulted in more than 500 fatal casualties. The pattern of the terrorist operations in J&K indicates that the small terrorist groups are now generally attacking the security forces, government establishments and political leaders. Despite India's gesture of reduction in troop deployment in sensitive areas of J&K, Pakistan shows no inclination to demolish the infrastructure that supports cross-border terrorism, obviously it is keeping its options open to restart large scale attacks should the peace process and talks fail.

A significant confidence building measure has been the final agreement on running a bus service between Srinagar and Muzaffarabad from April 2005. This step, that mainly relates to reestablishing contacts between the people J&K and POK, will have a favourable impact in India-Pakistan relations.

In various discussions on J&K the focus remains on those parts of J&K which are under India's control, little has been said so far on the present and future status of Pakistan Occupied Areas.

General Musharraf's Solution

General Musharraf suggested a possible solution of the Kashmir problem on October 25, 2004 that he claimed was based on geography and not on the religious entities. The formula was based on the tehsil as the determining administrative unit for future of J&K. Pakistani officials termed it as loud thinking on the part of General Musharraf while sharing his thoughts with the media, but it was more likely that he wanted to send a feeler to India and to test domestic waters on the possible options he had in mind. Musharraf has stated that this was an indication of his flexible approach in a bid to find a solution, and his willingness not to stick to the demand of plebiscite. This idea may have been suggested to him by a thinktank in the US, that has been projecting such options in the past.

Musharraf proposed that the peace process should proceed as follows:

- Agreement on the level of decision-making.
- Agreement on demilitarization of J&K.

• Determination of future status of J&K, areas that could be under India or Pakistan or the UN or even joint administration.

Musharraf suggests determination of the areas that should form part of Pakistan at Tehsil level rather the existing divisional boundaries, because if count is taken at district or Tehsil-wise the Muslim majority areas of the Jammu and Ladakh division will go to Pakistan. Presently Muslims are in an overwhelming majority in the Kashmir valley, the Hindus constitute a majority in the Jammu Division while the Buddhists are in majority in the Ladakh. This kind of partition on communal lines will, however, never be acceptable to India.

Concluding Remarks

The situation in J&K is delicately balanced, infiltration from Pakistan continues despite various goodwill measures from both sides and a definite improvement in the security environment in J&K.

Bilateral dialogue is well underway without many problems. The popular mood in J&K has changed greatly and people are yearning for peace, but despite a measure of success in bringing people back to the mainstream restoration of complete normalcy in the state is still far away.

The sponsored and domestic terrorist groups are still receiving support from the domestic fundamentalist organisations whose radical leadership continues to foment trouble and facilitate attacks by Fidayeen groups.

There is lack of cooperation between political parties to combat terrorism within J&K and this makes the situation politically favourable for the fundamentalist groups to operate with impunity and create an environment in which violence thrives. The national parties have also been unable to reach a consensus on methods of bringing peace to J&K; they seem to be ignoring national interests for political gains.

Pakistan is following a dual policy of continuing the dialogue and supporting terrorist groups. Pakistani still seems to believe that pressure must be maintained on India so that it does not ignore Pakistani point of view. Many in Pakistan seem convinced that terrorist pressure will ultimately become unbearable and force India to accept the demands of the separatist groups and agree to change in the status quo in favour of Pakistan.

Pakistan as well as India is under considerable pressure from the US and the international community to reach an amicable solution of the J&K problem soon since the acquisition of nuclear weapons by India and Pakistan, and after 9/11 the issue has received greater international attention because of the danger posed by the growing influence of the fundamentalist groups in Pakistan and their potential of stirring trouble in the region and creating a situation in which India and Pakistan may go to war in which nuclear weapons come into play.

The J&K problem was first internationalized in 1948 when India lodged a complaint against Pakistan in the UN for disturbing peace in the region. Later in the Cold War environment in which Pakistan was an ally of US it gained strategic advantages and India lost ground. However, India held its ground and in 1972, under the Shimla Agreement, Pakistan accepted that J&K problem was a bilateral issue to be dealt with exclusively between the two countries.

The status quo continued till 1989 when Pakistan launched a proxy war in J&K. After 1998 when India and Pakistan acquired nuclear weapons, Pakistan successfully played on the apprehensions of the western world by repeatedly declaring that a nuclear war may erupt between India and Pakistan during a conventional war over Kashmir, if a solution of J&K problem is not found expeditiously.

J&K problem became a serious concern of the international community after the terrorist attack on Indian Parliament and subsequent deployment of the Indian army on Pakistan borders poised for an offensive. However, whether we accept it or not Pakistan has been successful in internationalizing the J&K issue to its advantage. This does not mean that international intervention is now a possibility; but international community is keen to find an early solution of the problem, and may intervene if a nuclear confrontation between India and Pakistan becomes imminent.

Terrorism is likely to continue in J&K in its present form regardless of the peace process. Indigenous terrorists and *Jihadi* infiltrators would continue their depredations to terrorise both the people and the government of Kashmir.

It should be obvious that no solution of Kashmir issue is likely to emerge in a short time frame. If the process of negotiations and the confidence building measures continues and the ceasefire holds on the LoC, peace may eventually return to the subcontinent. A realization, both in India and Pakistan, that if economic cooperation were given greater importance, political problems may eventually wither away due to economic compulsions.

On balance it can said that the relationship between India and Pakistan has improved in the recent past and there is a possibility of peaceful settlement being reached on most issues except for the final solution of the J&K problem. It will not be easy to find a solution of the J&K problem in the medium time frame, which is acceptable to all parties. Efforts to find a peaceful solution must continue, as there is no military solution to this problem.

16

Geostrategic Importance of Jammu and Kashmir

V.D. Chopra

Pakistan's President General Parvez Musharraf has been again and again reiterating that Kashmir dispute between India and Pakistan is the 'pivot' around which the process of normalisation of relations between the two countries will begin. This assertion by him conceals more than what it reveals. It brings into sharp focus that after the disintegration of the Soviet Union, Jammu and Kashmir has assumed a new geostrategic importance, an aspect, which the Indian political elite seems to be minimising. It is relevant to recapitulate the various factors, which have led to the new importance of Jammu and Kashmir in geostrategic politics. This alone will enable us to analyse the American and the British policy on the status of Jammu and Kashmir, which is an integral part of India.

First, the Jammu and Kashmir state, to give it its full name, is the northern most part of India and has an area of over 84,471 sq miles. Much of the suffering of its people is due to its extremely strategic location. The Kashmir valley is surrounded by hilly and mountainous terrain. The areas Jammu, Poonch, Muzaffarabad, Gilgit, Baltistan and Ladakh constitute the ring of highland that stands sentinel over the valley. They border on Pakistan, Afghanistan, and the Xinjiang and Tibet parts of China. Only a few miles separate it from the former USSR, the Central Asian Republics of Tajikistan, Turkmenistan and Uzbekistan being nearest. This geostrategic location of Jammu and Kashmir has assumed its own importance with the changing balance of forces in the region.

Second, it is vital to note that the Taliban régime was dislodged from power in December 2001 from almost the whole of Afghanistan.

The virtual disappearance of the Durand Line, the 'tying' of Taliban infrastructure into Pakistan's border areas, especially Peshawar and its environs, and most of all the so-called 'Talibanisation' of these bordering areas under Taliban regime were indeed dangerous developments. This process has been partly reversed after the installation of a new regime in Afghanistan. This is a welcome development for the region including Pakistan, which is already witnessing ethnic and sectarian conflicts. Notwithstanding this development, Pakistan's ambition to destabilise Jammu and Kashmir and reverse the wheels of history are still valid as before. This facet of Pakistan's policy is being minimised both by the western countries and United States of America. In this sense what happens in Afghanistan after the recent developments will have a direct bearing on this strategic part of India. This will have a chain reaction on the entire region. How Pakistan will be able to readjust itself to the new realities is anybody's guess? It clearly stands out that General Musharraf is under heavy pressure from the extremists in his own country, though in the recent period he has begun to take some measures to contain extremism and religious fundamentalism. Playing up Indo-Pak conflict on future of Kashmir is the only escape route he has. His strategy therefore is to focus the attention of his people on Kashmir on one hand and to internationalise this issue on the other with a view to paving the way for third party intervention. The situation may take an ugly turn if Pakistan does not reverse its policy of cross-border terrorism in this strategic area of India. The political atmosphere is uncertain in the subcontinent. The possibility of unpredictable developments including armed conflicts between India and Pakistan cannot be completely ruled out.

Third, the global arms business is on the upswing again and the US, as has been the case many times in the past, accounts for nearly 50 per cent of the sales to developing countries. A Congressional Research Service Report highlighted in *The New York Times* shows that international arms sales grew by 8 per cent in 2000 to nearly $ 40 billion and the US contracted for about $ 18.6 billion of it. Between 1999 and 2000, the US sales increased by about $ 6 billion thanks to a large extent by the contract to sell 80 F-16 jets to the United Arab Emirates, a deal that is put at around $ 6.4 billions. Saudi Arabia is another big buyer of arms from the US. Moreover, Pakistan is a major buyer of arms from China. This arms race has its own implications for the geopolitics of the region.

Fourth, it is now a well-known fact that oil resources of the Gulf region are decreasing. With this development, oil wealth of the Central

Asian Republics will play a key role in geopolitical interest of Pakistan and its mentors in the Central Asian Republics. Seen in this context the entire belt from Jammu and Kashmir, Pakistan, Afghanistan to Central Asian Republics has assumed a new geostrategic importance. Pakistan wants to become a key player in this region. Let us not make any bones about it and see the harsh reality.

These are some factors, which have been shaping the geostrategic policy of Pakistan in this entire belt.

Historically speaking, geopolitical and economic interests of British imperialism in Jammu and Kashmir surfaced themselves in the 19th century and assumed a new dimension after the First War of Independence of 1857. In 1866, the Survey General of India started a systematic survey of the frontier areas. The famous Kohala Bridge over the Jhelum was built in 1870, connecting Murree with the Valley. Murree is a cantonment near Islamabad.

Again Mortimer Durand negotiated a border agreement with the Amir of Afghanistan in 1893. Under this agreement, the Amir was allowed to keep under his occupation Wakhan, Asmer and the valley above it, Kairistan, Mohamand and a portion of Waziristan. The Amir, in his turn, undertook not to interfere in Swat, Bajour and also relinquished his claim over the rest of the territories under British occupation including Darwaj, Kurrum Valley, Chegeh and New Chaman, the tribal areas around Gomel Pass including those occupied by Ghilzai and Lohani tribes. This clearly establishes that long before the Russian Revolution, the British rulers viewed Jammu and Kashmir and Afghanistan as an integral part of what they called their 'forward policy'. Let us leave this at that for the time being and not go into further details.

The fact of life is that during the British regime, Kashmir ruled by the dynasty of Maharaja Gulab Singh was one of the most despotic, backward and poverty ridden feudal states in India. What is more important is that the British rulers always kept it under their grip because of its contiguity with Central Asia against which British imperialism always harboured expansionist designs. After the Russian Revolution and the formation of the USSR, Kashmir assumed still greater strategic importance in imperialist eyes.

From the end of the Second World War, the US also started taking a keen interest in Kashmir. Papers like *The New York Times* and *The New York Herald Tribune* started writing about the strategic importance of the state because of its proximity to the Soviet Union and its new industrial centres. American newspaper correspondents in India sent despatches on the US interest in Kashmir. *The New York Times* published a map captioned the West's programme for containment and 'gaps'. Kashmir was shown as one of the 'gaps'. Top American military experts were sent. Montgomery and Mountbatten also visited Kashmir to discuss 'the future British defence of North India'. The Royal Air Force brought in bombers and planes and carried out air manoeuvres in Kashmir. American interest in Kashmir had thus begun much before January 1948 when the Kashmir case was brought to the United Nations Security Council.

The American press reported in February 1948 that an American, Haight had served for some months in the Azad Kashmir forces as a Brigadier General and that he had boasted of killing many Kashmiri people with his own hands. This fact was mentioned in the Security Council by Sir B.N. Rao in February 1950.[1]

It should be clear from these facts that the US were for several years interested in Kashmir because of its strategic location. As Rosinger indicated "the interest of the United States presumably arose in part from Kashmir's strategic location, close to the USSR and bordering on Afghanistan, Chinese Turkistan (Xinjiang), Tibet, India and Pakistan."[2] American policy therefore on Jammu and Kashmir has deeper ramifications than what appears on the surface.

The Indian government was not unaware of American interest in Kashmir as a base for operations against China and the Soviet Union. Reporting the views of Indian officials, Robert Trumbull said that there was sentiment in Ladakh for independence and that "such fragmentation of Kashmir is what India wishes to avoid in this strategic state next door to Russia."[3] In the new historical conditions, the strategic interests of the US in Jammu and Kashmir should not be minimised in the context of its proximity to China and Central Asian Republics.

It is pertinent to recall that before the merger of Jammu and Kashmir with India, the Anglo-Americans were counting without their host. And that host was the upsurge for freedom in India and Kashmir. This spread like a wildfire in Jammu and Kashmir in 1946. Linked with the freedom movement in India by the closest bonds, it demanded complete abolition of feudal despotic rule in the state, abolition of landlordism without compensation, land to the tiller, and a genuinely popular government. Alarmed at the tidal sweep and power of the movement, Kak, the notorious stooge of the British political department and the Prime Minister of the state, unleashed unbridled repression against it. The state was handed over to the army, which gave bloodbath to the people with all the frightful and humiliating accompaniments of martial law.

Even this terror, it must be noted, was planned and executed by British officers and Kak together. The plans were prepared by the British Commandant of the Kashmir state army, Brig. Scoff, Inspector General Powell and Kak, who openly boasted that "we have been preparing them for eleven months". *The Kashmir Times* wrote of "moving in British troops from Rawalpindi and Sialkot in the name of India's defence". India's defence, indeed! The only thing Kak was defending was his British masters and their stooge, the autocratic ruler of Kashmir, from the popular upsurge for freedom. Of course, he was executing the British plan of giving them full military power in the 'strategic' state of Kashmir.

Events moved in rapid succession. Confronted with the irresistible national upsurge, the British were preparing to divide the country and transfer power to the Congress and the Muslim League in India and the proposed state of Pakistan respectively. What were their plans for the future status of Kashmir when on partition, the rulers of the Indian states would be free either to accede to India or Pakistan or to remain 'independent'.

For Kashmir, the status proposed by the British was 'independence'. Lord Mountbatten visited Kashmir in June 1947 and had long talks with the Maharaja and Kak. Immediately a campaign was launched by Kak, the Kashmir Muslim Conference and the Jammu Prajya Sabha demanding 'independence' for Kashmir from the prospective states of India and Pakistan. Telegrams were showered on the viceroy. Both the above-mentioned organisations, be it noted, had opposed the Quit Kashmir Movement and supported the princely rule. Both represented feudal reaction in Kashmir. In addition, one represented Muslim communalism and the other Hindu communalism.

The British plot of an 'independent' Kashmir stands revealed in a letter addressed by the Maharaja to Mountbatten when the former finally decided on accession to India. Wrote the Maharaja in his letter, dated 26 October 1947:

> As Your Excellency is aware, the state of Jammu and Kashmir has not acceded to either the dominion of India or Pakistan. Geographically my state is contiguous to both... Besides, it has a common boundary with the Soviet Republic and China... In international relations the dominions of India and Pakistan cannot ignore this fact... I wanted to take time

> to decide whether it is not in the best interest of both dominions and my state to stand independent.

The only 'independence' of which this tool of the British could speak of was unfettered freedom for the British power to treat the whole state as an occupied territory and position; to utilise it for keeping India and Pakistan eternally at loggerheads; and of course, use it as an imperialist strategic military base. The Maharaja was incapable of talking about 'independence' except on British instigation.

While pressuring the Maharaja to declare 'independence' the shrewd and calculating British rulers were conscious of the immense strength of the National Conference, its close ties with the Indian National Congress, which was in sympathy with the popular movement in Kashmir, as also its opposition to the Muslim League, which was supporting the Maharaja against the popular movement. In this situation, the Kashmir ruler was compelled to accede to India and the dream of 'independent Kashmir' died a miserable death. This is a fact of history, which cannot be erased from the consciousness of the people of the state.

These facts are being recapitulated to make out that the strategy of making Jammu and Kashmir an 'independent' state is still alive, though at the moment it has been put on the back burner. The American and the British policy on Jammu and Kashmir and an Indo-Pak conflict on this issue should not be seen in isolation from this factor. This is the crux of the problem.

However, it will be naïve to ignore that in the midst of confidence building measures between India and Pakistan, once again attempts are being made to raise the shrill cry of making Jammu and Kashmir an independent state. The Indian policy makers in the 21st century will be sooner or later confronted with this problem.

References

1. *The Hindu*, 14 February 1950.
2. Rosinger Lawrence K., *India and the United States*, p. 105.
3. Robert Trumbull, *The New York Times*, 28 October 1947.

17

Right of Self-Determination and Kashmir

V.D. Chopra

It is intriguing that a curious combination of forces—some western scholars and politicians, Muslim fundamentalists and above all, the rulers of Pakistan—are demanding self-determination for Kashmir with growing insistence. It is an irony of history that the forces, which have been suppressing the liberation struggles for decades, some of them even today, such as in Pakistan, should be crying out for self-determination for Kashmiri people.

Certain historical facts cannot be forgotten from memory; however, unpalatable they might be for the ruling elite of one country or the other. It must be remembered, for instance, that the boundaries of Pakistan, Iran and Afghanistan were drawn by the colonialists without taking the wishes of the people or even the geographical, cultural or historical factors into account. The international boundaries of these countries run through territories inhabited by indivisible peoples, cutting them into several parts. The boundaries of Pakistan had to be redrawn in 1971 because the Bengali speaking people of Pakistan, who constituted the majority of the population of undivided Pakistan, were not willing to live as 'second class' citizens. Pakistan even today is witnessing conflicts, the most important characteristic feature of which is the conflict between the Punjabis and the non-Punjabis—Baluchis, Sindhis, Pushtoons and Mohajirs (those who migrated from India). Again, in Punjab new sub—nationalities have emerged such as Pothwaris and Saraikis.

Baluchistan's borders were demarcated during the middle of the 19th century without consulting the Baluch people, who objected and revolted against the colonial decisions. In the 1930s Baluch nationalists protested against the division of Baluchistan. In 1947 the Khanate of Baluchistan became independent and announced as its goal the unification of the Baluch areas, and in consequence had to face brutal repression. This raises the question: Will the ruling elite of Pakistan give this right of self-determination to the Baluch people, for instance?

The word nationality is acquiring increasing usage in the context of the grievances of Sind and other smaller provinces of Pakistan. While it may be gaining acceptance in some quarters, it still remains a buzzword in many circles particularly, those belonging to Punjab and the Urdu speaking people. In Pakistan, many people support the demand for autonomy and greater share of the various nationalities both in the economy and administration. Notwithstanding the fact that the democratic and secular movements in Pakistan are still weak, non-Punjabi nationalities have again and again expressed their protest over the domination of the Punjabi nationality over the power structure and economy. The demand for a democratic and federal structure raises its head periodically.

The perception of the Punjabi, Sindhi, Pushtoon and Baluch peoples to be distinct nationalities is not based on the mischief of 'anti-state' elements, as Pakistan's rulers would want us to believe. Its roots lie in the thousands of years of history of these peoples. Each of these peoples evolved into distinct ethno-linguistic communities, which in political terms should legitimately be called nationalities.

It is pertinent to recall here that Pakistani scholars refer to the All India Muslim League session of 1940 at Lahore, where the resolution for the creation of a separate Muslim state in the subcontinent was passed. It is interesting to mention here that just at the time when the Muslim League passed the resolution for the creation of a Pakistan, known as the Lahore Resolution of 1940, the President of the Muslim League, Mohammad Ali Jinnah, as the legal adviser to the Khan of Kalat, was fighting a constitutional battle for an independent sovereign state of Baluchistan. What is more revealing is that Baluchistan was not represented in the Lahore session of the Muslim League. This important fact of history has been forgotten by the present rulers of Pakistan for obvious reasons.

The concept of self-determination is of recent origin and has been given divergent and conflicting interpretations. Even the Marxist concept of the right of self-determination has come under critical scrutiny in recent years, particularly the Stalinist interpretation. Some of the western scholars, such as Selassie have interpreted it as "the principle" which lays down that "the government must rest on the consent of the people". The dominant interpretation of the concept of self-determination is that it is the connotation of 'national self-determination'. In the developing countries, the right of self-determination is defined with political independence and the right of the people to mould their own destiny. Scientifically, therefore, to equate right of self-determination with the 'secessionist self-determination' or 'separatism' will not only be incorrect but historically wrong also. In fact, this—a fine sounding and highly ambiguous—concept is now being purposely wielded by religious fundamentalists and revivalists in whole of Eurasia.

In multiethnic and multicultural societies, which are engaged in modern state building, a synthesis has to take place between the aspirations of the nationalities and sub-nationalities and the unity of the respective countries. This is the real content of the concept of 'unity and diversity'. This concept was concretely evolved in India during the freedom struggle. The Congress, for instance, organised its state units on the linguistic basis. After the independence, the various states were organised on the basis of language formulae and this too was a product of this concept. It is this concept, which is the bedrock of the unity of India and this process is still going on in the sense that Indian states are demanding more and more powers while maintaining and consolidating the unity of the country. As against this in Pakistan, this process has shaped itself in the opposite direction. It has become a highly centralised state with the entire power structure controlled by the army. The installation of the military dictatorship in Pakistan including the recent referendum clearly confirms this conclusion. The evolution of Pakistan as a highly centralised and militarised state with one nationality that is Punjabi dominating over it cannot make it a stable state in the long run. Such a state has to again and again drive its strength from religious revivalism and theology. The shrill cry of Pakistani rulers that Kashmir should be merged with it because it is a Muslim majority area should be seen in this context, notwithstanding the fact that Kashmiri people have a distinct nationality, history and culture. Above all, Pakistani rulers forget that next to Indonesia, India has the largest Muslim population in the world, which hold a balance in at least 25 per cent to 30 per cent of the parliamentary seats of the Lok Sabha. That multilinguistic and multiethnic countries like Pakistan should be vociferously supporting the so-called demand of the Kashmiri people for self-determination conceals more than what it reveals.

In the context of a new emerging pattern of interdependence, interconnected world, and globalisation to push the so-called right of self-determination and promote forces of secessionism by organising insurgency will prove to be disastrous both for those who are organising it and those who are its victims. For Pakistan itself it will be like opening the 'Pandora's box'. The tragic events of Afghanistan highlight the dangerous consequences of this policy both for the people of this country and regional peace.

To say all this does not mean that one should not objectively assess the significance of the concept of the right of self-determination in a fast changing international situation, in which restructuring of democratic relations have queued up to get on passions and the emotions and above all by organising armed insurgency in other countries. Notwithstanding the fact that the concept of right of self-determination is still vague and is being given conflicting interpretations, it does have a core of reason about it. The core lies in the right of a community, which has a distinct character to have that character reflected in the apparatus of the government and the state machinery under which it operates. This is precisely what is not happening in Pakistan. Unlike India, for instance, Mohajirs have not been absorbed in the social fabric of Pakistan even after 55 years. They are treated as second-class citizens.

The other nationalities such as Sindhis and Baluchis are facing discrimination. No lessons were learnt from the experience of liberation struggle of Bangladesh. The Baluch people were subjected to armed suppression from 1973 to 1977, resulting in almost total alienation of Baluchis from Pakistan in the recent past. When the Sindhi people staged a national uprising against the Pakistan army, even those who cared to analyse the roots of their discontent went little further than blaming the army for its exceptionally harsh treatment of Sindhis since 1977 and pointing out a few socio-economic indicators of 'disparity' suffered by the Sindhis. No one mentioned that the national oppression of Sindhis is even more severe than that of the Bengalis and that the degree of their dispossession is comparable to that of the Palestinians and American Indians.

It was the prophetic mind of Jawaharlal Nehru who grasped this content of the right of self-determination and boldly undertook the reorganisation of the states on linguistic basis as mentioned earlier. He went beyond that. He paid special attention to the development of language and culture of the people in different parts of India. He evolved a language policy, which unified the people. This is how people in different parts of India began to develop a distinct identity of their own and along with it also the identity of oneness.

The rulers of Pakistan, the British and American ruling elite and some others have been demanding self-determination for Kashmir. This combine also accuses India of suppressing the democratic rights of the people of Kashmir. The heroic, though also tragic, history of Kashmir has itself thrown light on the true meaning of self-determination for the Kashmiri people. A summing up of the question would be useful since it is being raised once again in the context of the present conflict between India and Pakistan and in view of the consistent efforts to misguide honest opinion outside India, that are being assiduously made.

The demand for a plebiscite in Kashmir can only be treated with contempt it deserves. The imperialists, who have always attempted to crush national liberation movements by force, and who have never given freedom to any of their colonies or dependencies before they have been thrown out by national liberation struggles, have no right to talk of self-determination for Kashmir. Besides, so far as Kashmir specifically is concerned, they have thoroughly exposed themselves by their intrigues to get a hold over it for strategic military purposes under the clandestine garb of supporting an 'independent' Kashmir.

For many years, and in reality till now, the Pakistani demand for a plebiscite in Kashmir was based openly on the 'two—nation' theory, in accordance with which all the Hindus of the Indian subcontinent formed one nation, and all the Muslims another. Having equated nationality with religion, the Muslim League leaders just could not understand, at least claimed not to understand, why the people of Kashmir considered themselves an integral part of India and not of Pakistan. Naturally, the rulers of Pakistan will never agree that the people of Kashmir have become free or have been liberated until and unless they join Pakistan just because they are Muslims. The theory of Muslims being a nation is fast cracking up in Pakistan itself with the growing struggle for autonomy by Baluchis, Pushtoons and Sindhis. The ruling elite of Pakistan, in recent years, seems to have learnt the 'language' of anti-colonialism, self-determination, people's rights and so on. So now, they speak of the right of the people of Kashmir to self-determination against India's colonial domination' over Kashmir. They also call upon the people of Kashmir to revolt against India, as they are Muslims. There are others in Pakistan, who invoke the people in the country to liberate their Muslim brethren in Kashmir in the name of Allah and *jihad*.

No democrat can ever accept that the principle of self-determination can or should be applied to a community based on religion. Self-determination is a right of nationhood, not of religious groups. If it is attempted to be applied to the latter, it can only lead to communal bloodshed and violence on a mass scale, as proved by experience, overpowering the most elementary human values, not to speak of democracy and freedom.

It must also be pointed out that the rulers of Pakistan from the very beginning, and far more so after the establishment of the military dictatorship, have never nursed even the semblance of democracy in Pakistan, or for that matter in occupied Kashmir, while championing the cause of freedom and self-determination for that part of Kashmir which they failed to grab by force. Both democracy and national movements in Pakistan are being suppressed even today. And how now the democratic institutions are being destroyed, elected prime ministers are arrested and exiled. How the nascent democracy of Pakistan depends on the army is a well-known fact and needs no elaboration.

The demand for giving the right of self-determination to the people of Kashmir is therefore malafide. Geopolitical importance of Kashmir has always attracted the attention of western powers. And they certainly are not so ignorant of the problem as not to know that the demand has been raised on a blatantly religious basis and has nothing to do with national self-determination. Their support for the demand can have only one meaning, which in recent years has been playing enough havoc for all honest and impartial people. Therein lies the design to disintegrate and dismember India. Whatever be the aims and motives of the western powers and the rulers of Pakistan, all honest democrats in and outside India, must clearly understand the true purpose of the demand for self-determination in Kashmir.

Prior to the attainment of national independence in 1947, the people of India were under British rule and domination. This was true not only of the great majority, which was under direct British rule. This was essentially true also of the people in the India princely states. The only difference was that British imperialism, while firmly holding in its hands the essence of political power had additionally imposed its servile puppets, the feudal princes on the people in the princely states. The British power never made a secret of the fact that the princes had to serve as their subservient instruments. This was stated in the very 'treaties' in accordance with which they were enthroned as rulers by the British power. Many viceroys reminded these princes of this status whenever they thought it necessary to do so.

The objective of the national movement in India, 'British' as also 'princely' was the ending of British rule and domination, the ending of feudal princely rule, and the unification of the whole of India as a free, democratic, sovereign state. This and this alone was the meaning of the exercise of the right of self-determination as understood by the Indian people, by the millions who fought and suffered for it, by the thousands of martyrs who laid down their lives for its realisation in 'British' and 'princely' India alike.

Seen in this context, it was precisely in this sense that the heroic people of Kashmir, having abolished the princely rule in Kashmir, and having fought and defeated the desperate British effort to reimpose its hold over Kashmir through the barbarous tribal invasion, decided to exercise their right of self-determination, their urge to merge, to unite with India in 1947. The accession of Kashmir to India in October 1947 was signed and sealed in law and united voluntarily the people of India and Kashmir because they wanted to do so. They had been separated by brute force, by the British power in 1846 when their territory was gifted to Gulab Singh, formerly an army general of Maharaja Ranjit Singh as a reward for the services rendered by him to the British for crushing the patriotic, independent and anti-British Sikh state in the Punjab ruled over by the illustrious Ranjit Singh. This is stated so in black and white in the *Kharita* given by the British to Gulab Singh in 1848. The separation of Kashmir from India was thus the result of the price of treachery paid by Singh. All that the people of Kashmir did in 1947 was to wipe out this crime of the British and their hireling.

Here another fact of history needs to be recapitulated. It was the people's freedom movement of Kashmir led by the National Conference that once again confirmed Kashmir's accession to India, through its Constituent Assembly, elected in 1951 on the basis of adult suffrage.

Was the Constituent Assembly a free and independent body? This question has been again and again raised. What is the content of freedom and independence? Historically speaking, Kashmir was a part of India and they were the British rulers who handed it over to their stooge in 1848. In 1947, Kashmir again became a part of the sovereign and independent state of India and its accession was confirmed by the Constituent Assembly of Kashmir. Thus, a final and irrevocable seal was put on the accession by the people of Kashmir under the leadership of the National Conference. The Constituent Assembly of Kashmir, in fact, gave freedom a deeper and richer content by abolishing feudal ownership of land without compensation.

Kashmir's accession to India stands in complete contrast to Baluchistan's accession to Pakistan. In 1947, the Khanate of Baluchistan became an independent state and was recognised as such by Pakistan. It was in 1948 that with the collaboration of the British government, Pakistan managed the accession of the Khanate without the consent of the Baluch people. But the exponents of the right of 'self-determination for Kashmir' conveniently forget this fact and have never raised this issue in any international forum. This in itself graphically illustrates how two different norms are being used, one for India and another for Pakistan. Behind this demand is concealed a deeper conspiracy to dominate this strategically important region and unleash a process for complete disintegration of India. In this way, ever since the accession of Kashmir to India, one attempt after another has been made to destabilise Kashmir. The attempt by Pakistani ruling elite, Inter-Services Intelligence (ISI) in particular in collusion with Taliban should be seen in this context.

There is yet another aspect of this problem which, however, needs to be analysed. The so-called 'Kashmir question' was first raised in the Security Council of the United Nations after Pakistan's invasion of 1947. At that time, it was raised as a question of protecting the population of Kashmir from subversive activities of Pakistan sponsored tribals.

The reference by India pointed out:

(i) that the invaders are allowed transit across Pakistan territory;

(ii) that they are allowed to use Pakistan territory as a base of operations;

(iii) that they include Pakistan nationals;

(iv) that they draw much of their military equipment, transport and supplies including petrol from Pakistan;

(v) that Pakistan officers are training, guiding and otherwise helping them.

India, therefore, requested to ask the Government of Pakistan:

(i) to prevent Pakistan Government personnel, military and civil, participating in or assisting the invasion of Jammu and Kashmir state;

(ii) to call upon other Pakistan nationals to desist from taking any part in fighting in Jammu and Kashmir state;

(iii) to deny the invaders;

(a) access to and use of its territory for operations against Kashmir;

(b) military and other supplies;

(c) all other kinds of aid that might tend to prolong the subversion.

This shows that this reference to the Security Council was limited to certain specific issues involving Pakistan in the invasion of Kashmir.

In effect, Pakistan not only admitted that they were aiding the raiders but made it clear that they would continue to do so till certain political objectives of theirs were achieved. Subsequently, in the course of the discussion of that question in the Security Council, its original meaning was changed and the Security Council focused its attention not on assistance in solving the question of Kashmir but on the preparation of a plebiscite with no interference from outside.

Such a move was in complete contradiction to the real interests of the Kashmiri people, who were attempting to carry out a peaceful and creative life and who had no desire to become the objective of imperialist designs.

In an attempt to put an end to this controversy in the United Nations Organisation and to establish political stability, the Kashmiri people in 1951 elected a Constituent Assembly. This Constituent Assembly passed a number of important laws including a law, which confirmed the accession of the state of Jammu and Kashmir to India. In 1956, the Constituent Assembly of Kashmir adopted the Constitution of the state, according to which the state would enjoy rights of autonomy within the Republic of India.

Thus, the question of Kashmir was settled by the people of Kashmir themselves. They decided that Kashmir is an integral part of the Republic of India. The people of Kashmir themselves have finally and irrevocably decided the question of their right of self-determination. The people of Kashmir and India have decided that they will remain united and free, that their destiny and future are indivisible.

Nevertheless, since the early 1950s an altogether new proposition was advanced by the UK and the US delegations in the Security Council, a fact which Jawaharlal Nehru himself underlined in his speech in Parliament on 28 March 1951. This is what Jawaharlal Nehru had to say: This is "an entirely new and fantastic theory that Kashmir is a kind of no-man's land where sovereignty is yet undetermined. Neither the United Nations Commission nor the Security Council have ever advanced such a theory before and indeed they could not because the facts were indisputably clear. Kashmir is juridically and politically an integral part of India and at no time have the United Nations Commission of the Security Council challenged this fact. The fact that Pakistan is guilty of aggression in Kashmir and that, as a result of this, a certain portion of it has been removed from our factual control cannot and does not detract from our status and our rights in Kashmir".

This clearly shows that the accession of Kashmir to India is entirely in conformity with the Indian Independence Act and the negotiations that preceded it; it is also fully in accord with all that has happened in the case of other princely states, which acceded to India. What India's detractors fail to recall is that Kashmir acceded to India when she was still a dominion of the Commonwealth and the accession was accepted on behalf of the Crown by the then governor general.

India had never asked the United Nations, for that matter any outside power, to adjudge the validity of Kashmir's accession or to determine where the sovereignty lay. India did not ask for any arbitration. It only went to the United Nations with a complaint about aggression. But both Washington and London had different designs. Have their designs changed in the new situation needs to be examined in the context of the role, which has been assigned to Pakistan in Asia, in the Southwest Asia in particular.

This historical survey clearly establishes that Jammu and Kashmir is an integral part of India and no attempts can be made to reorganise the boundaries of the country. This has been abundantly made clear by all the political parties in India including the Indian Parliament. However, once again attempts have been made to revive this controversy notwithstanding the fact that recent elections to the State Assembly of the Jammu and Kashmir have clearly demonstrated that this State is part of India. These attempts should not be underestimated if one goes by the recent history of Soviet Union. The Soviet Union was disintegrated by secessionist forces and Russian President, Vladimir V. Putin rightly said the disintegration was the biggest tragedy of the last century. The Indian political elite should draw appropriate lessons from the multiethnic, multi-religious, multi-cultural state of Soviet Union and even today Russian Federation is facing the problem of secessionism.

18

India's Foreign Policy: An Afro-Arab Perspective

Dr. Jagdish P. Sharma

India and the Arab and African World have been travelling alongside since historical times. Geographical proximity and close historical and trade links have given India and the Arab and African States a special sense of neighbourliness. The economies of India and many countries of this continent are by and large complementary. Indo-Arab-African cooperation in the political, economic and cultural fields was in focus at a conference of diplomats held in New Delhi recently. The meeting attended by Indian diplomats stationed in Africa, Arab and African diplomats hosted in New Delhi discussed problems varying from support for India's candidature for permanent membership of the United Nations Security Council to cooperation in economic, scientific and technological spheres. The question of agricultural cooperation also figured in the exchanges. In a major economic initiative recently India offered an ambitious $ 50 million programme to connect all the 54 nations of the African Union by a satellite fibre optic network. The offer of a "connectivity mission" for the African Nations was made by the President, Dr. A.P.J. Abdul Kalam, in his landmark address, the first by a non-African head of state to the second session of the Pan-African Parliament in Johannesburg. After rounding off his four-day visit to Tanzania and Zanzibar, the President was in South Africa for five days. It was the first visit by an Indian President to South Africa. "We have prepared for this visit a long, long time and coming at this time, it is a pilgrimage for any Indian leader", said Indian High Commissioner to South Africa, Shiv Shankar Mukherjee.

Dr. Kalam's African visit was significant as it took place in the year in which South Africa was celebrating a historic decade of democracy and freedom after shedding the rule by a white minority.

The visit was aimed at taking India's Afro-Arab Policy forward. It was a boost to India's Developing World Policy. "This is in continuation of our Africa policy. The visit is not ceremonial but a substantial one with huge content", Secretary (West) in the External Affairs Ministry, Shashi Kant Tripathy said. A few months after the President's visit a novel programme for agricultural development was launched for the African countries. The first batch of 500 farmers from Andhra Pradesh State, who have expertise in water-deficient crop cultivation were chosen to help African farmers improve their harvests under the agreement signed by representatives of Andhra Pradesh Government and the Governments of Kenya and Uganda.

The MOUs on information communication and technology and another on a waiver of a loan of Rs. 40 crore were signed during the President's visit to Tanzania. India and Tanzania have decided to set up a task force to identify and implement projects to utilize the $ 200 million credit line extended by New Delhi. A suggestion to form the task force was mooted by President Kalam during a one-to-one meeting with his Tanzanian counterpart Benjamin William Mkapa. The largest and most political stable among the East African Troika–with Uganda and Kenya–Tanzania has shared common goals and aspiration with India ever since its late President Julius Nyerere bonded with Jawaharlal Nehru and his non-aligned vision. Nyerere was conferred the Jawaharlal Nehru Award for International Understanding in 1974 and the Indira Gandhi peace prize in 1995. Both countries have had regular exchange of visits at the highest levels since the 1950s. Indian dignitaries who have visited Africa include Dr. S. Radhakrishnan in 1956, President Venkataraman in 1989 and Prime Ministers Indira Gandhi, Rajiv Gandhi, I.K. Gujral, and Atal Behari Vajpayee. President of Ghana, John A. Kufuor and the Tanzanian President Mkapa visited India in 2002, followed by visits of President Thabei Mbeki in 2003 and the Zanibar President in 2004.[1]

These visits underline the importance accorded by India to the development of friendship and socio-political, economic and diplomatic ties with the wider comity of Arab and African nations with many of whom a common bond existed during the independence struggles. India values its close historical ties and traditional cultural affinities with the countries of the region. The trade and cultural links between India and the Afro-Arab region go back to ancient times. For thousands of years, the Indian Ocean has served as a great highway for commercial and cultural interaction between them. The Afro-Arab region continues to occupy a special place in India's post-independence diplomacy and foreign policy. The countries in the region have become a main source for energy imports and amongst the most important trade, investment and joint venture partners for India. One of the main goals of India's foreign policy under Jawaharlal Nehru was to secure for the newly independent Afro-Arab and Asian countries the voice and influence to which they were entitled in the councils of the world. Nehru was critical of all forms of domination and exploitation of the country by another on the ground that it was contrary to the national interest of all states. He held that freedom and world peace were indivisible and elimination of colonialism and imperialism was an essential precondition for the realization of world peace.[2] India is vitally interested in the peace, prosperity and stability of the region, India's core strength of a vibrant democracy, steady economic growth, a large pool of scientific, technical and academic manpower and a diversified experience in development, provide a functional frameworks for a sustained partnership with individual Arab and African countries, as well as with regional groupings in the continent.

Algeria

A look at the interaction with individual nations gives the following picture.

Algeria is one country in Arab Africa with which India has had cordial relations all through. Algeria along with Egypt acted as the bastion of revolutionary nationalist movements in Africa.[3] India-Algeria relations date back to the days of the Algerian liberation struggle (1954-62) when India advocated the cause of Algerian independence at the United Nations and other international fora. Following Algerian independence, the ruling party Front de Liberation Nationale (FLN) favoured a radical, socialist ideology and an active foreign policy based on third world solidarity and the creation of a new international economic order. This policy orientation brought India and Algeria closer. India-Algeria relations have been characterized by a convergence of approach on major issues of international concern. Active partnership within the Non-Aligned Movement and agreement on issues of basic importance to developing countries have been cementing factors over the years in this relationship. The year 2001 witnessed a high point of Indo-Algerian relations. The then Indian President K.R. Narayanan and Algerian President Abdulaziz Bouteflika together called for increased cooperation between the two countries for mutual economic benefit and for restoration of peace in the region torn by conflicts, when the Algerian President made a state visit to India in January 2001. President Bouteflika was the first Arab-African leader to be invited as chief guest to witness the Republic Day Parade.[4]

It has been noticed that there is a strong political will on the part of India and Algeria to grow and develop relations in a holistic manner.

Many Indian companies are actively involved in the developmental process in Algeria. Companies like Videocon, Ispat and ONGC Videsh are already reaping the rewards of their investment in Algeria. A Cyber Park on the lines of the ones set-up by India in Nepal and Mauritius is in the offing in Algeria.[5] The 8th session of the Indo-Algerian Joint Commission for Economy and Trade took place in Delhi from 8-10 October 2003. The Algerian delegation was led by Minister of Transport Mr. Abdelmalek Sellal. Issues relating to trade, finance, energy, mining, fertilizers, small and medium scale enterprises, railways and shipping, culture and information and consular matters were also discussed. An MOU on cooperation in the field of small and medium enterprises, the Cultural Exchange Programme (CEP) and an agreement between the news agencies of the two countries, viz. PTI and APS, were signed. The third joint Business Council meeting between the two countries' business organizations also took place simultaneously.[6] The continuing process towards political pluralism and full democracy, along with Government's efforts to contain violence and terrorism in Algeria were noted with interest and encouragement.

Egypt

The Indo-Egyptian relationship dating back to the dawn of history is sustained by common traditions and struggles, ideals and values. This relationship forged by commercial, cultural and civilization contacts over centuries[7] is today a major factor in the stability of the fluid political situation of the Afro-Arab and Asian world. Bilateral ties of friendship, mutual understanding and cooperation with Egypt have been strengthened in recent times by building upon the momentum imparted by the Indian Prime Minister's visit to Egypt in October 1995. The meetings between the Indian Prime Minister and President Hosni Mubarak at the G-15 Summit at Harare, and between the Minister of External Affairs and Egypt's Foreign Minister at the UN General Assembly in New York, sustained the ongoing high level dialogue. The Grand Sheikh of Al Azhar (Cairo) visited India in October 1996. The visit served to add a new dimension of mutual understanding at intellectual, academic and cultural levels. The visit of Minister of State for Planning and Science and Technology to Cairo, to the Middle East and North Africa Economic Conference in November 1996 afforded opportunities to explore additional measures of cooperation in economic and technology fields. A high level inter-ministerial delegation led by Dr. Hamdy Al Sayed, Chairman of the Health Committee of People's Assembly (Parliament) visited India in August 2003. They studied meat exports' facilities throughout the country. A Ministerial delegation led by Dr. Hassan Al-Khedr, Minister of Supply and Internal Trade and including Mr. Fayza Abou El-Naga, Minister of State for Foreign Affairs visited New Delhi in October 2003. Talks were held with the Ministry of Consumer Affairs, Food and Public Distribution and other concerned Ministries and agencies with a view to concluding an inter-governmental agreement to enable supply of Indian wheat to Egypt and import of various Egyption commodities by India, through a buyback arrangement. A delegation from the Egyption Ministry of Foreign Trade, led by First Under Secretary Mr. El-Said Kassem visited India in April 2003 for the third round of discussions on a Preferential Trade Agreement (PTA) and the Joint Working Group on Bilateral Trade.

Secretary, Small Scale Industries, Mr. S.K. Tuteja visited Cairo in October 2003 with 4 member delegation to review the implementation of the Joint Action Plan concluded between the Egyption Social Fund for development and the Indian Ministry of Small Scale Industries. The Third Round of Talks on the Preferential Tariff Agreement (PTA) with Egypt, under the auspices of the Indo-Egyption Joint Committee on Trade, was held from 8th to 10 December, 2003 in Cairo. Indo-Egyption Trade and Economic interchanges continued to expand. Similarly, India continues to be one of the major investors in Egypt with investments of about US $ 350 million. In September 2003, the Aditya Birla Group decided to set up a plant for manufacturing acrylic fibre near Alexandria. More Indian investments are in the pipeline. Egypt is a trading partner in Africa and occupies a prime place in so far as India's exports are concerned. India shares with Egypt a common desire for peace, stability and security in the region and for safeguarding the independence, sovereignty and territorial integrity of the Arab-African nations.[8]

Libya

Compared to its potential and in the context of friendly political relations that India and Libya have developed over the years, economic cooperation and trade between them are still far too limited. Even though there has been pressing realization on both sides that political amity and cooperation should be strengthened by dynamic and growing trade relations and economic collaboration between the two sides, this has not come about to the necessary extent and on the scale desirable. India's relations with Libya were characterized by efforts to strengthen economic cooperation in recent times. Secretary (North Africa) visited Libya from 20-22 March 2004 and held talks with Foreign Minister Mr. Abderrahman Mohd. Shalgam, Energy and Trade Minister, Dr. Fatehi Oman Ben-Shatwan, and a number of senior government officials in Oil, Energy and Foreign Affairs Ministries.

Various areas of cooperation were identified during the visit. He also called on Mr. Suleiman Sassi Al-Shahoume, Chairman of Foreign Relations Committee of the Libyan Parliament and Mr. Salem Ben Amer, Special Envoy of President Col. Gaddafi for South Asia. Libya has invited participation from Indian companies for cooperation in the field of road construction, maintenance and repair of airports, maintenance of hospitals and management of hotels. During the visit of Libyan Minister of Industry and Minerals Dr. Muftah Azzouzah in November 1997, the two sides identified petroleum, steel and power generation as new areas of bilateral cooperation.[9] Indo-Libyan economic relations registered progress with BHEL and ONGC Videsh Ltd. bagging fresh contacts. BHEL secured a contract for the US$ 215 million Western Mountain Gas Turbine Power Project in Libya. This was followed by ONGC Videsh Ltd. (OLV) securing oil and gas exploration contract worth US$ 30 million in Libya in collabouration with the Turkish Petroleum Oil Co. (TPOC) in August 2003. In the cultural field, a 12 member Bhangra Group visited Libya from 1-11 April 2003 in connection with Tripoli International Trade Fair.[10] The lifting of economic sanctions on Libya by the US and the UN have vastly increased the importance of the Libyan market for trade and business ties.

Morocco

The organization of an exclusive "Indian Trade Expo" in Casablanca, Morocco, in April 1996, was a major initiative to promote bilateral commercial exchanges. Deputy Chairperson of Rajya Sabha, Dr. Najma Heptullah visited Morocco on this occasion. The visit to Morocco's External Commerce Minister to India in December 1996 ensured that the momentum of growing bilateral trade would be maintained. Minister of Textiles, Mr. Syed Shahnawaz Hussain visited Morocco on 23-24 June 2003 to inaugurate the Textile Festival in Casablanca. King Mohammed VI paid a private visit to India in October 2003. The Second Indo-Moroccan Foreign Office consultations took place on 8-9 January 2004 in New Delhi. Mr. Mohammed Rachad Bouhlal, Secretary General, Ministry of Foreign Affairs, Morocco led the Moroccan delegation while the Indian delegation was led by Secretary, North Africa. Bilateral and regional issues were discussed during the consultations. An MOU for interaction between the two Foreign Service Institutes was signed during the visit.[11] Morocco along with other Arab African countries looks to India as an important leader of the Developing World.

Sudan

In the current context in addition to bilateral economic activity, India has offered humanitarian assistance to the people of Darfur region in Sudan. Sudan is keen that the Darfur refugee problem should not be politicized and exploited to whip up anti-Sudanese sentiments. During my visit to Khartoum recently, officials and intellectuals explained to me that the problems of the region were being exploited by interested powers. They wanted to stir trouble for the government with an eye to securing a foothold in the region, which is rich in oil and other mineral resources. Indo-Sudanese relations had never a high profile earlier. But of late the situation has been changing. President Abdul Kalam's October 20-22, 2003 visit to Sudan was a major landmark in the strengthening of Indo-Sudan ties.[12]

President Kalam held talks with the Sudanese President Mr. Oman Hassan Ahmed Al-Bashir and addressed the Sudanese Parliament. He also interacted with academicians and students at the University of Khartoum and held a meeting with the Sudanese alumni of Indian Universities. During the visit of the President of Sudan, the Bilateral Investment Promotion and Protection Agreement (BIPPA), the Double Taxation Avoidance Agreement (DTAA), and the MoU on Cooperation in the field of Information Technology were signed.[13] Sudan came out strongly in support of a permanent seat for India in the United Nations Security Council and both sides agreed to closely coordinate positions in the international fora. The two nations shared the view that there was an imperative need for comprehensive reform of the UN system including an expanded Security Council to make it more representative and responsible to the needs and aspirations of the developing countries.

Following the historic State visit to Sudan by the President in October 2003, there was an upward momentum in bilateral interaction. Several Ministers, in different fields, paid separate visits to India during December 2003. Mr. Al-Jaz, Energy and Mining Minister visited India from 5-9 December 2003. Similarly, Minister of National Defence Lt. Gen. Bakri Hassan Salih, accompanied by Defence Secretary, DGs for Training and Military Industry and other senior officials visited India from 12-15 December 2003. Towards the end of the month, Transportation Minister Mohd. Elsamani Elwasile, accompanied by State Minister of Finance Dr. Hassan Ahmed Taha, visited India from 22-29 December 2003. Sudanese Minister of State for Defence Mr. Ahmed Mohammed Ali led a five-member delegation to the DEFEXPO INDIA 2004 from 3-6 February 2004. The above visits indicated appreciation of our sensitivity and interest in Sudan.[14]

Tunisia

India and Tunisia have had contacts with each other since the pre-independence period. Tunisia has consistently pursued a balanced policy of openness and moderation in its international relations.[15]

Delegations were exchanged with Tunisia in several fields, including trade, agriculture, science and technology, and environment. An Indian textiles exhibition was organized in Tunisia in June 2003, which was attended by Textiles Minister, Mr. Syed Shahnawaz Hussain. Tunisian Industry Minister, Moncef ben Abdellah visited India in April and the Minister of State for Foreign Affairs Madame Saida Chtioui visited India for bilateral consultations in October 2003. Minister of State for Information Technology and Internet Mr. Montassar Ouaili visited India from 8 to 14 February 2004. An MoU on Cooperation in Communications and IT was signed during the visit. A new $ 10 million credit provision has been made by EXIM Bank of India to promote investments. Tunisians have invested in the Godavari Fertilizers and Chemicals Ltd. Bilateral trade between India and Tunisia is now touching US $ 200 million.[16]

Western Sahara

It is sad and surprising that the government of India withdrew the recognition it gave during the Rajiv Gandhi period to the Sahrawi Arab Democratic Republic (SADR). It goes against the spirit of our 55 years of foreign policy of supporting genuine liberation struggles in the Afro-Arab-Asian continent. By derecognizing SADR India has undone its decision to recognize it in 1985.[17] It is attributed to the pressure from Morocco. The Congress-led United Progressive Alliance Government headed by Dr. Manmohan Singh would do well to reexamine the policy towards Western Sahara in the light of the policy decision taken by Rajiv Gandhi.

Conclusion

When India got independence in 1947, there were only four independent countries in Africa (Ethiopia, Liberia, South Africa and Egypt). By 1957 Libya, Morocco, Sudan, Tunisia and Ghana had gained independence swelling the number of independent nations to nine. Between 1957 and 1966 another 31 countries (17 in 1960 alone) became free. With the independence of Namibia in 1990 and Eritrea in 1993 the number of independent countries in Africa increased to the present 54. The historic dismantling of the brutal system of apartheid in South Africa and the inauguration of the Nelson Mandela government there in May 1994 marked the full liberation of the Afro-Arab world, with the sole exceptions of Palestine and Western Sahara.

India's trade and economic ties and technological collaboration with Arab and African nations have widened to a great extent in recent years. From oil exploration in Sudan and Libya, to defence cooperation with South Africa and supply of Indian wheat to Egypt to collaboration in information technology, health, medicine and agricultural research ties with many countries, it is a wide canvas. All along, India has enjoyed warm relations with the struggling and independent countries of the Afro-Arab region. During his African visit Dr. Kalam has offered technical and financial help to meet one of the continent's gravest health problem, that is HIV/Aids. This is a new area of cooperation. In the international fora India and the Arab and African states have pledged to keep up the unity displayed by developing countries at the recent World Trade Organization talks. They have reaffirmed their commitment to promote the formation of an equitable multi-polar world order based on equality of states, principle of rule of law, territorial integrity of both Iraq and Sudan and non-interference in the domestic affairs of states with a view to removing threats to stability and international security. Both feel that the United Nations should be "equitable" and "represent a just order". They have expressed grave concern over the expansion of international terrorism, religious intolerance, international crime, drugs and arms trafficking. On the West Asian peace, India and the Arab and African states have reiterated their support to the existence of two states, a Palestinian and Israeli state, living side by side in secure and internationally recognized borders. The traumatic passing away of the father figure of Palestine Liberation Organization (PLO), President Yasser Arafat has given a new impetus to the international efforts to resolve the Palestinian—Israeli conflict and hasten the liberation of Palestine. The lingering crisis in Iraq has implications for the whole world, particularly the Afro-Arab and Asian world. The transition from occupation to the installation of a new Iraqi government by the US have not broken the long cycle of violence and instability. A new initiative is called for to bring peace and stability to Iraq and in this the Afro-Arab and Asian world should play an important role. Both India and Arab-African states have much to offer to each other for their mutual benefit. Conditions must be created to achieve the full potential of the interaction. With efforts and commitments from both sides, their cooperation will be strengthened for mutual benefit and lead to the social-economic development, progress, peace and stability of the peoples of India and the Arab and African region. The historic ties of India with this region should logically lead to expanding interaction in economic and political fields in keeping with the rapid changes taking place in the world in various spheres particularly in science, technology and economic cooperation.

References

1. Jagdish P. Sharma, "Kalam's Africa Pilgrimage" in *National Herald* (New Delhi) 23 September 2004.

2. Jagdish P. Sharma, "Nehru, Nasser and the Afro-Asian People's movement" in *Nehru and the People's Movement* (ed.) (New Delhi: Manak Publishers, 1997) p. 255.

3. Jagdish P. Sharma, *Foreign Policy Challenges: India and the Afro-Arab World* (New Delhi: Anamika Publishers, 2003) p. 30.

4. Jagdish P. Sharma, "Great Potential for India-Algeria Trade" in *Algeria-2001*. (New Delhi, Embassy of Algeria, 2001), p. 21.

5. Abdelkrim Belarbi, Ambassador of Algeria to India and Benchikh Mohamed, Former Councellor, Embassy of Algeria, quoted in *"Algeria-47th National Day"*, *The Indian Express* (New Delhi, Mumbai), 1st November 2001.

6. *News from Algeria* (Embassy of the Democratic and People's Republic of Algeria in New Delhi), No. 11, November 2003, p. 6.

7. For details see Jagdish P. Sharma, *Peace Policy of Nations: Egypt, Palestine and India* (New Delhi, Manak Publishers, 1995) and *Afro-Asia and Contemporary Politics* (New Delhi, Anamika Publishers, 2003).

8. *Egypt in Focus* (New Delhi, Embassy of Egypt, 23 July 2004), pp. 20-29.

9. "India-Libya Socio-Economic Relations" Resort of Embassy of Libya quoted in *Kayadat* (New Delhi) 16-30 September 2004, p. 30.

10. Ministry of External Affairs *Annual Report (1st January 2003-31 March 2004)*, Government of India, p. 59.

11. *Ibid.*, p. 59.

12. Quoted in *Press Trust of India* report (Khartoum) October 21, 2003.

13. Ministry of External Affairs, *Annual Report 1st January 2003–31 March 2004* (Government of India), p. 60.

14. Ministry of External Affairs, *Annual Report 1st January 2003–31 March 2004*, p. 60.

15. *Tunisia Today* (New Delhi, India–Tunisia Friendship Association, 2004), p. 12.

16. Ministry of External Affairs, *Annual Report (1st January 2003–31 March 2004)*, p. 60.

17. For details see, Jagdish P. Sharma, *Foreign Policy Challenges: India and the Afro-Arab World*, New Delhi, Anamika Publishers, 2003.

19

India's Policy Towards the Arab World in the 21st Century

Prof. A.K. Pasha

India's historical ties with the Arabs are well-known. The commercial, cultural and other relations enabled both the peoples to interact quite vigorously. With the rise of Islam in seventh century A.D. Arab traders spread Islam to coastal areas of India especially in Kerala. Many Arabs married with local women in the Malabar area and their offsprings are called Mappillas. Despite the destruction of the Abbasid Empire and its capital, Baghdad in 1258 A.D. by the Mongols and the subsequent Ottoman domination of the region, it did not substantially disrupt the links between India and the Arabs. Indian intellectuals' contribution at Baghdad was widely appreciated by the Abbasid Caliphs. The discovery of direct sea route to India from Europe by the Portuguese sailor Vasco da Gamma (with the assistance of Ibn Majid – a famous Arab captain and navigator) to Calicut in 1498 and the subsequent European colonialism disrupted the close interaction India had with the Arabs. The British after consolidating their rule in India (especially after defeating Tipu Sultan of Mysore in 1799) and with the assistance of Indian soldiers dominated the Persian Gulf region, Yemen, Sudan, Egypt and encroached on the Arab lands under Ottoman control. Even though some Arabs saw Indians as collaborators with British imperialism, Indians continued to trade with Arabs although the volume was shrinking. It must also be pointed out that Indians played a vital role in the expulsion of Portuguese from Oman and elsewhere in the Gulf region.[1]

In order to defeat the Ottoman Empire, the British during the First World War signed many treaties, made many promises and too many pledges to countries and peoples. The Sykes Picot Treaty (1917) with France and Russia is by far the most notorious. The Jews were promised a homeland in Palestine through the Balfour Declaration. The Sheriff Hussein of Mecca was promised a United Arab Kingdom over the liberated Arab lands from Ottoman rule. The contradictory pledges and duplicitous policy of the British lay exposed after the war as League of Nations mandate's rule was established in Iraq and Palestine by Britain and over Syria and Lebanon by France. The Sheriff's two sons were installed as Kings of Jordan and Iraq much against the wishes of the local Arab people. The Mufti of Jerusalem accused the British of having a design to settle in Iraq "many million Hindus from British India". Hundreds and thousands of Indian soldiers died suppressing the Iraqi Arab nationalists (Shias especially in southern Iraq) who were opposed to imposition of the Hashemite monarchy under British mandate rule. Elsewhere in the Arab world many more thousands of Indian soldiers died fighting for the British during and after the war suppressing the Arabs.[2]

The Palestine Issue and India

Britain the mandatory power in Palestine allowed large-scale immigration of Jews into Palestine with a view to colonizing and dominating the country at the cost of the native Palestinian Arabs. Soon after the First World War, due to Jawaharlal Nehru's abiding conviction that India's freedom struggle is closely linked with the struggle of other colonies, he felt the need to maintain close contacts with the Arab nationalist movements. Jawaharlal Nehru was put in charge of developing contacts with Arab leaders. In this connection the Indian National Congress [INC] passed a resolution as early as in 1927 demanding the withdrawal of Indian troops from Palestine, Mesopotamia, Egypt and other Arab lands. In the following year assurance of sympathy and support were conveyed to the peoples of Egypt, Syria, Iraq and Palestine in their struggle for freedom. Nehru maintained close ties with the Egyptian Wafd party and invited them to attend INC annual sessions. He also extended support to freedom movements in Sudan, Morocco, Algeria, Tunisia and South Arabia (Yemen). His approach against colonialism rested on two cardinal tenets: support for freedom; and strict adherence to peaceful method.[3]

In April 1926, the Palestinian Arabs opposed the take over of their lands by the Jews under British protection and declared a general strike, which lasted for nearly six months in spite of every attempt by the British authorities, through massive military force and reprisals to crush it. Nehru accused the British of pursuing a "ruthless policy of destruction and killing thereby seeking to crush the Palestinian national struggle for freedom". The Palestinian Arab uprising during 1936-39 to oppose Jewish settler colonialism and the ruthless and brutal measures adopted by the British to suppress Palestinian Arabs were condemned by Nehru. Even through he sympathized with the sad plight of the Jews in Europe and especially their persecution by the Christians of Europe but Nehru believed strongly that "we must remember that Palestine is essentially an Arab country and must retain so and the Arabs must not be crushed and suppressed in their own homelands". In subsequent years the INC during its annual sessions supported through its numerous resolutions the just and legitimate cause of the Palestinian Arabs. As a mark of respect the INC observed 27 September 1936 as Palestine Day by holding meetings and demonstrations throughout the country as an indication of support for the Palestinian Arab cause. Mahatma Gandhi had similar ideas in 1938 in the background of mounting persecution of Jews in Europe especially by Hitler. Gandhi's attitude is best reflected in his famous statement in *Harijan,* "Palestine belongs to Arabs..." Since Gandhi's influence on Nehru was deep, the latter shared Gandhi's concern of the sad plight of the Palestinian Arabs and maintained that within the framework of a pluralistic though Arab state both Jews and Arabs should peacefully work for the upliftment of the country in a cooperative manner.[4]

The British came under tremendous pressure from the US for allowing immigration of Jews from Europe into Palestine which was opposed by the Arabs. More and more Jewish groups in Palestine were using violence against the British and the Arabs. Unable to control the deteriorating law and order, the British referred the Palestine issue to the UN in 1947. As a member of the UN Special Committee on Palestine (UNSCOP) India vehemently opposed the Partition Plan for Palestine as a solution and strongly urged that the independence of Palestinians should be the primary goal of any plan for the future stability of the country. India favoured a federal state in Palestine which would enable full participation of all citizens—Jews and Palestinian Arabs in the political system. The Indian delegation head to UN told the General Assembly that partition would merely be a temporary solution for the problem and warned that it would increase instability in the region for several decades to come. India consistently challenged the view that remote historical connection of the Jews to Palestine was not a sufficient argument for the creation of a separate Jewish State. Ultimately the UNGA accepted the majority plan and Palestine was partitioned in November 1947 by the UNGA Resolution 181. Israel was unilaterally declared by the Zionists as a Jewish State on May 14,

1948 and in the war with the Arabs that followed Israel increased her territory by military conquest over and above the area allocated to it by the UN. Soon a very large number of Palestinians were expelled by Isreal who became refugees in the neighbouring Arab states. It is interesting to note that on May 23, 1948 Nehru received request from Dr. Chain Weizmann, President of Israel, to recognize the Jewish state. Meanwhile the UN in May 1949 admitted Israel as the 59th member. India voted against Israel's membership because it "could not recognize an Israel which had been achieved through the force of arms and not through negotiations". Nehru continued to resist the idea of according recognition to Israel but after great reluctance finally decided to recognize the Jewish State on September 17, 1950. However India assured the Arab states that it would continue to support the cause of Palestinians and that its stand on the status of Jerusalem remained unchanged and that recognition did not mean endorsement of Israeli position on its borders. It was pointed out that India's "continuing natural non-recognition is not only inconsistent with overall relationships but limits effectiveness of India's role as a possible intermediary between Israel and the Arab states". Around this time one should also keep in mind Pakistan's role in working for a Pan-Islamic bloc with the help of UK-USA especially in the Arab world, along with the Kashmir issue, and advocacy of rights of Indian Muslims. Israel continued to urge India to establish diplomatic ties without response from Nehru. He finally relented partially when in 1953 an Israeli Consulate was allowed to function in Bombay. The Israelis in subsequent years kept up their pressure on Nehru for an Indian embassy in Israel through numerous ways but nothing concrete emerged out of these Israeli endeavours.[5]

India and Egypt

In July 1952 a fundamental change took place in Egypt with the overthrow of King Farook and the emergence of Jamal Abdel Nasser as the new leader. This was an event of momentous significance for Egypt and a landmark in the history of the Arab world. Nasser decided to follow non-aligned policy and opposed the UK-US backed Baghdad Pact in 1955. Nehru had also criticized the Baghdad Pact and said it "has in fact created in West Asia far greater tension and conflict than ever before. It has certainly put one country against another among countries that were friendly to one another". Both the countries signed a treaty of friendship and cooperation of April 5, 1955. It must be stressed here that Nehru urged Nasser and other Arabs not to rule out negotiations as a means of settling the Palestine issue with Israel. He also took care not to involve India too deeply in the Arab-Israeli dispute. India also did not endorse the irrational demands of some Arab leaders in the Arab-Israeli dispute.[6]

Nehru supported Nasser during the Suez crisis in 1956 when UK, France and Israel attacked Egypt to regain the Canal and overthrow the Nasser regime. Nehru publicly branded Israeli aggression as a case of "clear, naked aggression". Through his support to Nasser in the Suez Crises a much closer rapport between the two leaders was established. Whatever little sympathy was left for Israel in Nehru's heart vanished due to its aggression on Egypt and its alignment with Anglo-France military attack. Nehru concurred with Nasser on Israel, which was seen as an outpost of western imperial interests and as a country that did not have any links in the West Asian area. India's close ties with Egypt to some extent neutralized the Pakistani campaign against India in the Arab world, especially over the Kashmir issue. Egypt went to the extent of declaring that Kashmir was an integral part of India and that "Suez is as dear to Egypt as Kashmir is to India". Pakistan was branded as the "number one enemy of Cairo and Arabs". Pakistan's membership in the Baghdad Pact led to its isolation in the Arab world with even Saudi Arabia clearly denouncing the Pakistani decision. King Saud was astonished to find that the "Islamic state of Pakistan should accede to those who have joined hands with the Zionist Jews" and called the "Baghdad Pact as a stab in the heart of the Arab and Muslim states", and urged it "to return to the right path", by withdrawing from the widely unpopular Western military pact. Egypt's support to India during the 1961 Goa liberation from Portuguese rule was significant: Nasser did not allow the Portuguese ships [on their way to Goa] to cross the Suez Canal. The secession of Syria from the UAR in 1961, Egypt's intervention in North Yemen after the 1962 revolution, US decision to supply offensive weapons to Israel under President Johnson, emergence of Feisal as Saudi King and his emphasis on Pan-Islamism to counter Nasser's Arab nationalism, all these were major issues which impacted India's Arab Policy which had come to be identified as Cairo-centric. In order to contain Nasser, the US encouraged a Saudi-Iranian-Pak-Turkish alliance since 1964. Soon Riyadh termed India as an aggressor in the 1965 Indo-Pak war and warned New Delhi not to take undue advantage of its close ties with the Arabs.[7]

India and the Arab-Israeli Conflicts

Egypt's defeat in the 1967 war with Israel and Nasser's death in September 1970 pushed Riyadh as the leading Arab State influencing the politics and foreign policies of several Arab states. Soon Riyadh took interest in the establishment of the OIC in May 1971. For India the 1969 Rabat Islamic conference over Al Aqsa mosque (in Jerusalem) gave a jolt to Indian diplomacy in the Arab-Islamic world. After having been officially invited to participate in the conference at Saudi intervention, Pakistan staged a walk out from the conference due to the presence of Indian delegation. This event evoked sharp criticism from several political parties in India. For India it had become obvious that Pakistan would use the Islamic gatherings to denounce India and raise the issue of Kashmir, along with its declaration of world Islamic solidarity.[8]

By 1970 India had come to establish close ties with secular nationalist Arab states like Egypt, Algeria, Syria, Iraq, Libya and the Palestinians. In the light of new regional developments, India had to reorient its policy from one of heavy reliance on Cairo to other power centres which had emerged especially in the Gulf area. Israel's refusal to withdraw from occupied Arab lands pushed Egypt and Syria to launch the 1973 October war. India supported the Arab military initiative and declared that the cause of tension in the area is due to Israeli aggression and its refusal to vacate lands occupied by armed force. India joined other countries in demanding immediate implementation by Israel of UNSCR 242 and 338. Israel's refusal to withdraw from Arab lands made several of Israel's supporters to abandon it just before and after the 1973 Arab-Israeli war and the subsequent oil embargo by the Arabs against USA and other supporters of Israel. India did not have to make such opportunistic changes in its policy towards the Arabs for the sake of oil. The Arab states due to India's unequivocal support for the Arab and Palestinian causes assured New Delhi uninterrupted supply of oil and treated India as a "friend". Thus, India due to its consistent support to the Arab causes was assured oil supply. Moreover, India's policy opened significant possibilities for Indian exports. It soon led to a large presence of Indian workers in the Gulf area. So far India's economic ties were mainly with Egypt, Iraq and Sudan and at a low key with other Arab States. But after 1973 India's economic and political contacts widened with the oil rich Arab Gulf States. This partly alleviated India's balance of payment situation caused due to increase in oil prices.[9]

The outcome of the 1973 war convinced Egypt's President Anwar Sadat that in the prevailing international situation a limited success in the war was the maximum that the Arabs could achieve and he visualized that only through diplomacy the AIC could be solved. He calculated that the US alone could compel Israel to vacate Arab lands, hence his famous saying that 99 per cent of the cards in the AIC are with the US. This led to peace treaty between Egypt and Israel in March

1979 ending thirty years of armed confrontation. India's response to the Camp David accords was "uncritical but guarded". In fact, New Delhi did not openly endorse or condemn the accords. One reason for incoherent Indian response was the Egyptian factor. Although India wanted to steer clear out of any intra-Arab disputes, yet New Delhi valued friendship with Cairo and all efforts were directed towards preventing Egypt's suspension from NAM at the Havana NAM Summit in 1979. Earlier the emergence of Janata Party in 1977 raised the question of a review in India's Arab Policy. This was mainly due to A.B. Vajpayee of the Jana Sangh becoming India's new Minister of External Affairs, who had been a vocal critic of India's support to the "Arabs" and who had advocated close ties with Israel. It was during this period that Israeli leader Moshe Dayan paid a secret visit to India in August 1977. Unfortunately, for Israel, Dayan achieved nothing concrete as Prime Minister Morarji Desai refused to establish diplomatic ties with Israel unless Israel withdrew from all Arab lands. He told Dayan that if he establishes ties with Israel at this moment, his government would collapse. To the surprise of Israelis, A.B. Vajpayee reiterated India's traditional policy towards Arabs when he said "there is no change in India's stand, Israel must vacate all occupied Arab territories and the legitimate rights of the Palestinian people must be restored". Since then up to 1992 successive Indian governments highlighted the absence of diplomatic ties with Israel as an indication of support to the Arabs.[10]

The Iran-Iraq War

The outbreak of war between two major NAM members Iran-Iraq (in September 1980) was a cause for deep concern to India. Of particular significance to India was the fact that both were New Delhi's major suppliers of crude oil supplying bulk of Indian oil imports. In addition many Indians were working in several projects in both the countries sending valuable remittances. Indian policy makers feared major powers involvement in yet another conflict in the Gulf area where developments related to security and instability had a direct bearing on India. India as Chairman of NAM did try hard to find a solution of the Iran-Iraq war but without success.

Non-involvement in internal or intra-regional disputes has been an integral part of India's Arab policy and it applied to Iran-Iraq war as well, though in fact both sought India's support against the adversary, which India found hard to provide. On surface, India was strictly neutral but friendly ties with Iraq gave a certain tilt towards Baghdad. India's inability to mediate in the war exposed the inadequacy of Indian diplomacy in the region. Much to the dismay of

India towards the end of the Gulf war, great power naval presence substantially increased in the Gulf area and in seas surrounding India which assumed large dimensions in the wake of the 1990-91 Iraq-Kuwait crisis. The Soviet withdrawal from Afghanistan and the disintegration of USSR together with the end of the Cold War and the emergence of Pax Americana in the Arab world initiated a gradual but necessary change in India's policy towards the Arab world while at the same time continuing its basic policy. It can be said that it is now much more realistic as well as practical in terms of its objectives.

The 70's and 80's saw India's ties growing with gulf states as India began to import its oil requirements from them, started getting growing remittances from Indian workers, exports to the region and investments from the region became important. All these issues brought India and the Arab Gulf states closer.[11]

India and the GCC States

The Gulf crisis over Kuwait when Iraq marched into the oil rich Emirate on 2 August 1990 posed India a major challenge. Due to India's close political and economic ties with Iraq, an impression was created in the initial stages of the crisis that New Delhi tended to support Baghdad. This led to misunderstanding between Kuwait [and other GCC states] with India. To be correct, India strongly disapproved the Iraqi invasion of Kuwait and called it illegal and should be vacated but stopped short of condemning the invasion. Since India did not openly take sides, Kuwait and other GCC states assumed India's sympathics lay with Iraq. The Kuwaiti crisis affected India in many ways. New Delhi mainly due to domestic turmoil displayed no apparent enthusiasm to resolve the crisis. The minority government of V.P. Singh appeared to be primarily concerned with the evacuation of more than one lakh Indian citizens from Kuwait and 25,000 in Iraq. Public pressure and also the decision of MPs from Kerala to sit on a day long fast at the Parliament House on 16 August 1990 to protest against the "inaction of the government regarding the plight of Indians" in both the Gulf states forced the government to accord the safe evacuation of Indians top priority. This partly explains India decision not to condemn the Iraqi action as it could have jeopardized the repatriation of Indians from the Gulf. India was also faced with the loss of crude oil supplies from both Kuwait and Iraq, which compelled New Delhi to look for alternative supplies. During 1990, Kuwait had agreed to sell India about 1.5 million tonnes of oil and Iraq 6.25 million tonnes, which included about 4.5 million tonnes that Iraq was transferring to India on behalf of the USSR against rupee payment. Before the crisis began, India had received only half the oil from the total of about 7.75 million tonnes and it was difficult for India to procure the rest. Moreover, increase in oil prices in the spot market from about $ 16-17 per barrel in July 1990 to $ 35 per barrel upset India's budget and economy. According to one conservative estimate, India lost nearly $ 3 billion [US] in foreign exchange alone. This includes $ 2.36 billion for extra import of oil; $ 200 million to evacuate Indians from Gulf; and $ 200 million as loss of exports to these two states; and also about $ 200 million as loss of remittances sent by Indian workers from both the countries. All of these economic compulsions pushed India to seek IMF loan where US support was crucial. The Indian government partly shared the fear of the West, in particular the US, that Iraqi leader Saddam Hussein would control fifty per cent of the world's oil reserves, if he were not pushed out of Kuwait. No wonder India allowed [initially] the refueling of US military planes and went along with the sole superpower at the UN. According to K.P. Fabian, who was Joint Secretary, Gulf, Ministry of External Affairs [MEA], "we did not join the US-led coalition as we were engaged in finding a non-military resolution. The US resented this. Its friends outside India told us that we were getting isolated. Since our principled position conveyed the impression of a pro-Iraq tilt, the decision was taken at the highest level under pressure to agree to US request for refueling facilities". In reality, India isolated due to acute domestic, regional and global factors, had no worthwhile role to play in most of the UN resolutions, which were passed before it became a non-permanent member of the UNSC. Under the leadership of Yugoslavia, NAM went along with the West and UN Resolutions and India's role was marginal. Many have attacked India's approach to the Iraq-Kuwait crisis as "malleable", "deliberate ambiguity", "wait and see" and "opportunism" and so on. Undoubtedly, getting back Indian workers and their welfare and safety in other Gulf States was uppermost in the minds of the Indian policy makers, besides securing oil supplies, but New Delhi was equally concerned over the escalation of the crisis and its probable spillover effects. On the other hand, India was committed to adhere to the UN resolutions on Iraq, but at the same time, took care not to openly condemn Iraq's aggression. This was in line with India's policy to seek friendly ties with all states in the Arab world. India by neither condoning nor condemning the Iraqi takeover of Kuwait justified its position by saying that "condemnation is not part of the Indian nature". India, of course by simply "regretting" the invasion did not win the gratitude of either party. It was in fact misunderstood by both the parties and by others also. Room for India to manoeuver in the Gulf crisis was rather limited, given the resolve of the West [US] and the GCC States to contain Iraq. India on its own could not take peace initiatives to resolve the crisis, because as seen earlier, the Indian government was beset with serious domestic problems, but as a leading member of NAM, it did take some feeble initiatives but these came too late, partly because of deep differences within the movement, especially Yugoslavia's one-sided stance. India's economic linkages with the GCC States had increased during 1970's and 80's especially due to growth in oil imports. Also the oil rich GCC States with their massive oil revenues embarked on ambitious economic development, which led to demand in GCC States for labour. India with its surplus labour became a major source of supply. The rapid modernization of GCC States generated demands for goods and services for which India seized the opportunity. The four million plus Indians send about $ 10-12 billion [US] dollars as remittances. Gulf Indians helped recently Resurgent India Bonds for raising foreign exchange. Indian banks have also mobilized deposits and investments from the Gulf Indians.[12]

GCC and the Babri Masjid Issue

The GCC on 6 December 1992 at the summit in Abu Dhabi [UAE] described the Babri Mosque destruction by the BJP and its ideological allies as "sacrilege and unpardonable act". The Council adopted a resolution titled "Aggression against the Babri Mosque" in which it expressed its "deep condemnation of the Babri Mosque demolition" which was described as a "crime against Muslim holy places". The resolution called upon the Indian government to uphold its responsibilities and to take further measures to protect the Indian Muslims, their religious rights and places of worship. It urged the Indian government to rebuild the mosque as promised. Clearly the GCC had gone beyond the expected condemnation of the demolition already voiced by some of the members, the severest of course, from Saudi Arabia and the most moderate stance from the UAE. India reacted sharply to the GCC resolution on the Barbri Masjid demolition and voiced its unhappiness. An Indian government spokesman said: "These matters pertain to internal affairs of India and concerns expressed from abroad in this context however well meaning they may be, are not helpful in meeting the challenge posed by communal elements". What upset India over the GCC stand was that it had expected the summit merely to deliberate on the Babri events and in view of the earlier condemnation by individual members, it would not mention the issue in the final communiqué. In view of Iran's tough stand on the Babri Mosque, even moderate members of the GCC like UAE had to fall in line because no GCC member wanted to be charged with being soft on India. The UAE deplored the Babri event as a "shameful act". In a statement it said actions causing damage to places of worship were against the spirit of harmony and coexistence among various sections of society. Further, the UAE called upon India to "take urgent steps to end such acts and protect the sanctity of places of worship". In the UAE, hundreds took out several protest processions in various parts, expressing anger and outrage over the Babri Masjid demolition. In Dubai the protesters stoned an Indian temple and surrounded the Indian consulate and raised slogans against the Indian government and some resorted to looting and stone pelting. The worst affected area was Al-Ain, 250 kms east of the capital Abu Dhabi, where angry protesters set fire to the girls' wing of an Indian school and a church which was attacked and ransacked. Several policemen were killed in violence who tried to control the riots, "without use of force". Of all the GCC States, it was only in UAE [may be due to the large presence of immigrants from the Indian subcontinent] that riots broke out over the Babri Masjid, especially after the call for a protest day was given by Pakistan. The Pakistanis, who attacked a Hindu temple and some Indian business houses, were deported by the UAE. Many Indians were also deported. The UAE acted with unusual firmness against those who indulged in violence. The Commander-in-Chief of Dubai Police, Brigadier Dhahi Khalfan said: "Those who want to create unrest here should go back to their countries and launch protest against what annoys them. Our country should not be used as a place to settle the differences that exist between different communities, groups and faiths."[13]

India and the UAE

Among all the GCC states, India enjoys the strongest economic and political relationship with the UAE since the latter became independent on December 2, 1971. India's trade [exports] and import of oil and the presence of Indian workers in UAE is economically very significant. India's first Ambassador to UAE Mr. Said E.H. Rizvi was appointed on March 1, 1973. External Affairs Minister Sardar Swaran Singh visited UAE in February 1973. The UAE Foreign Minister Ahmed Khalfia al Suwaidi visited New Delhi in February 1974. Al Suwaidi came to India after the Lahore Islamic summit, which Pakistan used to strengthen its ties with the Islamic states. Both India and UAE exchanged letters for the establishment of an Indo-UAE Joint Commission during the visit of UAE Petroleum Minister Mr. Manna Saeed al Otaiba to India during 1974. India's new External Affairs Minister Y.B. Chavan visited UAE in November 1974. The Ruler of Dubai and UAE Vice-President Sheikh Rashid bin Saeed al Maktoum paid an official visit to India from 15-22 June 1974. The UAE President Sheikh Zayed Bin Sultan al Nahayan visited India in January 1975. India's President Fakhruddin Ali Ahmed paid a return visit to the UAE in October 1976. The then Minister of External Affairs A.B. Vajpayee visited UAE in June 1977. Sheikh Tahnoun bin Mohammed al Nahayan, Governor of the Eastern Province and Chairman of the Abu Dhabi National Oil Company visited India in October 1977. Morarji Desai, India's Prime Minister under the Janata Government sent Mr. Sikander Bakht, Union Minister of Works and Housing as special envoy in September-October 1977. In early 1979 India's Labour Minister Ravindra Varma visited Abu Dhabi with a four member official delegation to study the conditions of Indian workers in UAE. The Secretary in India's Ministry of External Affairs Romesh Bhandari visited UAE in February 1980, and the visit of UAE Health Minister Mohammed Abdul Rahman in November 1980 improved ties further between India and UAE. In 1981 Mrs. Indira Gandhi, Prime Minister of India visited UAE. The ruler of Sharjah, Dr. Sheikh Sultan bin Mohammed al-Qasimi visited India in May 1982. A FICCI delegation visited the UAE in December 1982. The Commerce Minister of India, P. Chidambaram visited UAE in 1991. The UAE President again visited India from April 26-30, 1992 along with the ministers for foreign affairs, finance, industry, information and culture. India's Minister of State for Petroleum and Defense Mr. S. Krishna Kumar visited the UAE in October 1992.[14]

India—GCC Trade Ties

The GCC states provide good market for India's exports. During 1999-2000, India's exports to GCC were nearly $ 5 billion [US] and imports from GCC of $ 7 billion. The bilateral two-way trade exceeded $ 12 billion. Information Technology exports to GCC currently are at $ 170 million and are poised for a significant upswing. India's exports to UAE in 1976-79 stood at 167 crore [Rs 1670 million] and imports at about Rs 77.5 crore. In 1979-80 it was Rs 130.77 crore and Rs 208.8 crore. With a trade turnover of $ 4.4 billion in 1999-2000, the UAE was India's biggest trade partner in the GCC. India's exports to UAE in the same year were $ 2 billion and its imports were $ 2.3 billion. In 2003-04 India-UAE trade was $ 7.2 billion [US] of which Indian exports were $ 5.1 billion and UAE exports to India were $ 2.1 billion making it the second largest trading partner of India after the USA. Some of it is for and from third states and Pakistan imports via Dubai some Indian products.

UAE was the first GCC State to provide aid to India through *Abu Dhabi Fund for Economic Development [ADFAED]*. During 1974-75 it gave Rs 37.5 crore and in 1975-76 Rs 15 crore. Since 1976-77 ADFAED started directly giving aid instead of UAE government. In 1976-77 it gave Rs 12.9 crore, in 1977-78 it was Rs 5.25 crore, in 1979-80 Rs 5.94 crore, in 1980-81 Rs 1.73 crore. The aid has been given to Garhwal Rishikesh Chila Hydro Electric Project in Uttar Pradesh and other projects.

A large number of India's public and private companies have taken active part in the industrialization of the UAE. They are either contracts or joint ventures. Some of them are the refinery in the Ruwais area in Abu Dhabi by Engineering Projects [India] Limited [EPI], a tube blending plant and a turnkey project by the Balmer Lawrie group, consultancy works for the Abu Dhabi National Oil Co. by ONGC, the laying of a multi-purpose pipeline by Engineers India Limited [EIL] and, civil construction work for the Airport at Abu Dhabi by Engineering Construction Corporation [ECC]. Dubai now allows ownership of real estate to foreigners. Reputed Indian companies like the Tatas, Kamanis, Dastur and others have taken part in the industrial development of UAE. In the Jabel Ali free trade zone about 160 Indian companies—the largest number from anyone country have taken part. 56 are joint ventures. The Sadiyat free trade zone is attracting many Indian companies. Software is the new field in bilateral trade with firms like Satyam and Infosys active in business. The UAE has about 20 joint ventures mostly in private sector, in India especially in Gujarat and Maharashtra. The offshore and onshore oil drilling platforms plant in Maharashtra is the most significant. Towards the end of 2003 the UAE organized its first trade exhibition in Mumbai where it secured contracts worth $ 140 million. Dubai and Sharjah in March 2004 signed two MOUs between Chambers of Commerce and industry. This opens possibility for UAE investments in India in the fields of infrastructure where projects worth $ 20 billion are being considered. IT has emerged as a major area of exports. Many Indian IT firms are trying to capture the software market in the Gulf region through the UAE.

The stand adopted by the UAE on Kashmir at all meetings until recently had been remarkably restrained. But since the Babri Masjid event and Bombay bomb blasts, the UAE appears to have shifted from its earlier position. At the OIC foreign ministers at Karachi in 1994 the UAE minister of state for foreign affairs in his speech expressed concern over the situation in Kashmir and called for settlement of the problem. He said: "The situation in Kashmir is still tense and could flare up unless tension is defused, before it is too late". He further added: "We appeal to all parties concerned to work for resolving this problem through wisdom and objectivity and we hope to see a peaceful solution that is acceptable to all parties within the framework of international resolutions and bilateral agreements that will guarantee the national rights and the Islamic identity of people there [Kashmir]". A change that too a significant one, had taken place in UAE's position towards India and this was obvious since the demolition of the Babri Masjid when it took series of steps to express its displeasure, including its disagreement to immediately receive India's Minister of state for external affairs R.L. Bhatia, its attempts to cold shoulder goodwill Indian naval visit and its lack of enthusiasm to specify dates for a visit by Prime Minister P. V. Narashima Rao. Some have linked the UAE's attitude with the extradition related issues. R.L. Bhatia finally visited the UAE on 25 May 1993 where he rejected any mediation bid by any country to resolve the Kashmir issue. He said, "people can advise on friendly basis, but we cannot accept any mediation". He also said that the Kashmir issue is a bilateral matter and we do not want any outside interference. But the UAE gave every possible support to India in connection with the Bombay bomb blasts. It condemned all sorts of terrorism and violence which resulted in the killing of innocent people. It agreed to work with India to curb terrorism and step up cooperation in security measures. The former Indian Ambassador to UAE Ranjit Sethi said: "There has been no adverse impact on our relations in any manner. We have been given every assistance by the UAE authorities, at every level". Moreover, he added that the UAE is ready to help in every possible way in matters vital to the security of India. The refuge given by UAE to Indian nationals whom the "government of India wants them for crimes committed" in India has become an issue in bilateral relations. In this connection L.K. Advani, India's Home Minister visited UAE from 13 July 2001 for issues related to extradition treaty. He called on the President of UAE and discussed with him regional and international issues of mutual interest. Some in the government bureaucracy and mass media of India continue to portray UAE as a country, especially Dubai as a haven for Indian terrorists. The UAE also gets negative publicity in India. This image needs to be corrected as this might lead to unpleasant problems in future.[15]

India and Kuwait

India's External Affairs Minister Madhavsinh Solanki visited Kuwait in mid-February 1992, the first ministerial visit to Kuwait since the 1990-91 Iraq-Kuwait war. The visit was primarily aimed at building bridges with Kuwait after India's ambivalent attitude during its occupation by Iraq. As seen earlier, relations between the two had deteriorated and Kuwaiti leaders publicly expressed anguish and surprise at India's stand during the Kuwait crisis. After the talks with the Kuwaiti leaders, Solanki said, Kuwait wanted India and Pakistan to resolve the Kashmir issue through peaceful negotiations in accordance with international norms. L.L. Mehrotra, Secretary in the MEA who accompanied the minister claimed that the visit was a "diplomatic triumph". Apparently both were impressed by Kuwait's support to the Shimla agreement and India was also satisfied with Kuwait's explanation about its criticism of India at the OIC meeting. Kuwait's Foreign Minister expressed the hope that India would rebuild the Babri Masjid and hand it over to the Indian Muslims. He said: "we hope that the Prime Minister Narasimha Rao who had earlier promised to rebuild the structure will stick to his resolve". In an interesting development, the Kuwaiti government blocked a decision by a community run supermarket to dismiss Hindu employees from India in protest against the Babri Masjid demolition. The Kuwaiti Minister of Social Affairs and Labour. Mr. Jassem Mohammed al Qun ordered the *al Sabaahiya al Ahmadi Cooperative Society* supermarket to rescind its 15 December 1992 decision. In a related development in a letter to the editor of Kuwait's *Arab Times*, writers requested GCC States not to recruit Indian Hindu workers and send back those who were already in the country. It was also reported that many in Kuwait were very keen to organize demonstrations and close shops in protest against India, but apparently this could not materialize in view of the Kuwaiti government's tough opposition to such activities.[16]

In protest against the demolition of the Babri Masjid, a proposal was tabled by two Kuwaiti independent MPs, Khalid al Adwah [an Islamist] and Mohammed Sharar, in the Kuwaiti National Assembly, in January 1994 for boycott of Indian Hindu workers and a ban on their entry and recruitment into Kuwait. The Kuwaiti government on 15 August 1994 rejected the proposal saying such a move would worsen Kuwait's relations with "friendly India" and stressed that the proposal violated political and religious norms. The state minister for cabinet affairs Abdul Aziz al Dakheel said Kuwait was not solely responsible for Muslim affairs around the world. "Defence of Muslims should be made in a collective way through Islamic organizations concerned especially the OIC," he said. Dhakeel also said "only a small group of Hindus were terrorizing Muslims in India and this should not be generalized. By taking a decision to ban Hindus such relations will worsen and India may take a decision to ban Kuwaitis from visiting India", he added. Dhakeel stressed that Muslim countries like Pakistan, Bangladesh and Indonesia had not even thought of taking such a measure. He felt the proposal was likely to give the impression that Islam was a racial religion and thus harm the cause of Muslims rather than serving them. He felt that the adoption of the proposal would spoil Kuwait's image and its human rights record. Moreover, Kuwait is still subject to criticism on several issues, including that of human rights, Dhakeel said. Acceptance of the MP's demand would also have encouraged the Islamic fundamentalists groups in Kuwait, the Minister pointed out. The Kuwaiti government's firm position in rejecting the call by the two MPs to punish the whole Indian Hindu community for the mistake of a fraction of the community is commendable and demonstrates the progressive character of the Al Sabah regime in Kuwait. Moreover any acceptance of the MP's demand would have weakened Kuwait's struggle against Iraq as several groups in India would have publicly called for an end to the UN sanctions against Iraq from which India had been suffering in terms of lost export opportunities, stop in remittances, the need to find alternative sources to offset loss of oil supplies from Iraq. Kuwait-India total trade turnover during 1999-2000 was $ 2.07 [US] billion. India's exports to Kuwait were $ 154 million while imports were $ 1.91 billion. The volume of bilateral trade in 2001-02 was $ 279.94 million and in 2002-03 it was $ 430.07 million. This excludes crude oil and petroleum products.[17]

Kuwait Fund for Arab Economic Development [KFAED] has been giving economic aid to India on low interest rate since it started in 1975-76 when it gave Rs 31.5 crore. In 1975-79 it was Rs 19.74 crore and in 1980-81 Rs 6.12 crore. The Fund has tried to limit the impact of political considerations on its lending operations. Most of the studies regarding operations offered have noted lack of discrimination on political grounds in loan disbursements. In 1981-82 it gave Rs 52.50 cr, in 1982-83 Rs 30.03; 1985-86 Rs 14.70 crore; 1988-89 Rs 36 crore; 1990-91 Rs 1 crore; 1992-93 Rs 6 crore 1993-94 Rs 9 crore; 1994-95 Rs 4 crore; 1995-96 Rs 17 crore; and in 1996 Rs 134 crore. Kuwait has given aid to the following projects in India: Kalindi hydro electric project, power projects I, II [Rs 29, and Rs 31.5 crore]; Kopli hydro electric project [Rs 20 crore]; Anpara thermal power projects and coal handling and transport [Rs 3.3 cr, and 19 crore]; Kerala fisheries development project [Rs 36 crore]; and Thal Fertilizer project [Rs 36 crore].[18]

Despite Kuwait's unhappiness over India's ambiguous position during Iraq's invasion, a number of Indian firms were given contracts in the rebuilding of Kuwait. India has shown interest in Kuwait's downstream petrochemical sector whereas Kuwait has evinced interest in Indian petrochemical complexes. India has also shown interest in a gas based fertilizer plant in view of huge quantities of gas in Kuwait and a refinery on the west coast of India. There is also a one billion US dollar joint venture proposal between Indian Oil and Kuwait Petroleum

Corporation [KPC] to build a refinery in Orissa. A 14-member delegation from Power Loom Development and Export Promotion Council visited Kuwait from 23-27 May 2001 and organized a Buyer-Seller Meet. An Indian Jewellery and Gold exhibition was held in Kuwait from 2-6 June 2001. Lt. General R.K. Sawhney DCIOS-[T&C] MOD paid an official visit to Kuwait on 29-30 April 2001 and met senior Kuwaiti defense officials to discuss defense related issues. A Bilateral Investment Protection Agreement [BIPA] was signed between India and Kuwait on 27 November 2001. During the visit of Kuwaiti Foreign Minister Sheikh Mohammed Sabah al Salem al Sabah in 2004 three agreements were signed—on extradition, mutual legal assistance in criminal matters and another to boost bilateral trade and economic links. The kidnapping of Indian truck drivers in Iraq [2004] employed by a Kuwaiti company was amicably resolved.[19]

India and Saudi Arabia

Soon after independence, Pakistan tried hard to mobilize Arab and Islamic states to its side on the Kashmir and other issues. In this, Pakistan's relations with Saudi Arabia were to prove most rewarding. But soon India established close ties with Egypt's Nasser. Many Arab states resented Pakistan's attempt to raise the Kashmir issue in Islamic meetings. Pakistan's membership in western sponsored military pacts was also denounced. Saudis attacked Pakistan's decision to join the Baghdad Pact. In fact, Riyadh was astonished to find that the "Islamic state of Pakistan should accede to those who have joined hands with the Zionist Jews" and spoke of the Pact as a "stab in the heart of the Arab and Muslim states" and urged it "to return, to the right path", by withdrawing from the widely unpopular western military pact. Pakistan, which had launched a campaign against India on the issue of treatment of Indian Muslims, also got a setback when Riyadh publicly sided with India on the issue. In a now famous public statement, the Saudi King Ibn Saud during his visit to India in November-December 1955 said: "I desire to say to my Muslim brethren all over the world with satisfaction that the fate of the Indian Muslims is in safe hands". When Nehru returned the visit in September 1956 he was given a rousing welcome with slogans of "Welcome Prophet of Peace" which obviously angered Pakistan.[20]

In the aftermath of the 1956 Suez crisis, Riyadh-Pakistan ties became closer with the result a Saudi-Pakistan alliance virtually came to be established in mid-1960s with Riyadh terming India as an aggressor in the Indo-Pak war of 1965 and warned India not to take advantage of its close ties with the Arab and Islamic states. Saudi criticism of India was due to close Indo-Egyptian friendship and

Nasser's support to Indian position at several forums. An Islamic Conference to discuss the Al Aqsa mosque was held in Rabat on September 22-25, 1969. India was officially invited to participate in the conference at Saudi request, but Pakistan staged a walk out from the conference against the presence of Indian delegation, which was led by Fakhruddin Ali Ahmed. The Bangladesh crisis and the Indo-Pak war of 1971 had a major impact on Indo-Saudi ties. Riyadh's position on the crisis at the UN was that the developments in East Pakistan were Islamabad's internal affair and that no other country had any right to interfere in the same. However, India managed to convince the Saudi rulers of New Delhi's sincere desire to live in peace with Pakistan and respect its territorial integrity. The 1972 Shimla Pact and the release of Pakistani prisoners by India helped the atmosphere, as Saudi concerns for Pakistani territorial integrity had become an issue in India's bilateral ties. The 1979 Iranian revolution, Soviet intervention in Afghanistan and the Iran-Iraq War [1980-88] brought about closer Saudi-Pak ties, which the US supported. This made General Zia ul Haq, Pakistani ruler say, "if Saudi Arabia's security was threatened and help was sought from Pakistan he would personally lead Pakistani forces in the defense of Saudi Arabia". Saudi military aid to Pakistan became a major irritant in relations between New Delhi and Riyadh. It is in this backdrop one should see Mrs. Indira Gandhi's visit to Riyadh in April 1982 which ended the 26 years long communication gap between two states. Her visit paved the way for better relations and heralded a new era. It must be mentioned that despite lack of better political understanding Indo-Saudi economic ties have flourished. Mrs. Gandhi's visit to the kingdom paved the way for a new chapter in economic cooperation. The most tangible gain was the setting up of an Indo-Saudi joint commission to promote economic and technical collabouration. It was inspired by the assumption that a combination of Indian technology, skilled manpower and Saudi money could work to strengthen South-South Cooperation. The Joint Commission was established under an economic and technical cooperation agreement in April 1981. The commission first met in 1983 in Riyadh, then in New Delhi in 1986, in New Delhi from November 13-15, 1991 and again in 1996-2002.[21]

India's trade with Riyadh has increased since Nehru's visit and risen steadily especially since 1973. The two-way trade in 1963-64 was a mere Rs 24.3 crore India's exports to Riyadh have always been less than its imports. In 1990-91 imports were valued at Rs 2897.73 crore and exports at Rs 418.42 crore. The trade turnover during 1999-2000 was $ 3.75 billion. India's exports were $ 741 million and imports $ 3 billion. Saudi-Indian bilateral trade in 2002-03 was estimated at $ 5 billion with Saudi exports being $ 3.65 billion and India's exports were at one billion US $. IT products were a major component of Indian exports. Saudi-Indian trade during 2001-02 stood at $ 1290.42 million [US] and in 2002-03 at $ 1445.47 million [US] excluding crude oil and petroleum products. Saudi Arabia at the moment is the 13th largest market for Indian exports and a source for 5.5 per cent of India's total imports. India is the 4th largest market for Saudi goods and ranks 10th in the Saudi imports market list. By exporting half a million barrels of crude oil per day and a total of 23.55 million tonnes [annually] which comes to about 23 per cent of India's total crude oil requirements, the Kingdom has become the largest sources of oil for India. These figures are among the highest between India and an Islamic country. However, much of this adverse balance is made up by the flow of remittances by the over 1.7 million Indian workers in the kingdom. Moreover, Indian companies both public and private have taken and completed numerous lucrative projects in the Kingdom and earned huge profits.

The Saudis have given loans to India through the *Saudi Development Fund* as follows: 1977-78 Rs 75 crore; 1981-82 Rs 17.70 crore; 1983-84 Rs 17.23 crore; 1985-86, Rs 28.72, crore; 1987-88 Rs 50 cr, 1988-89 Rs 6 crore; 1989-90 Rs 43 crore; 1990-91 Rs 30 crore; 1991-92 Rs 27 crore; 1992-93 Rs 2 crore; and in 1996 Rs 152 crore. These loans given at low interest rates were for the following projects: Srisailam and Nagarjunasagar power projects in Andhra Pradesh [1977 Rs 75 crore]; to the Rajasthan Canal Project; Koel Karo power project in Bihar [1981 Rs 17.70, crore]; Koraput Rayagad Railway project [1983 Rs 17.23 crore]; Ramagundan Thermal Power Project II [1985 Rs 50 crore]; Nhawa Shiva Project [T&C, 1987 Rs 50 crore].

Saudi Arabia's position on Kashmir now emphasizes the bilateral process with a dialogue with Pakistan on the basis of existing agreements like Shimla and Lahore. It condemned all forms of extremism and made a fervent appeal for peace, between India and Pakistan. The appeal was made during Crown Prince Abdullah's meeting with Najma Heptullah, Deputy Chairperson of Rajya Sabha in Jeddah. It also sent aid to the victims of Gujarat earthquake [2001] and it condemned the attack on India's Parliament as an act of terrorism. Despite growing Indo-Saudi economic ties, the political ties have not progressed. Except for the visit of Mr. Jaswant Singh, India's Foreign Minister to the Kingdom in January 2001, no high level visit has taken place so far. Saudi Arabia is not only a major economic partner of India, it is also a major power in the Gulf region, with substantial influence on other GCC states, major producer of oil, Saudi financial power, which gives them enormous ability to influence many groups, parties and states worldwide, location of Islamic holy places [Mecca and Medina] in the Kingdom as also Riyadh wields considerable influence in the OIC being the leading state in its establishment, giver of a major portion of the OIC budget and with the headquarters being located in Jeddah. Mr. Omar Abdullah, India's Minister of State for External Affairs led a delegation to the Kingdom to sign the hajj agreement in Jeddah on 22 August 2001. A five-member delegation led by the Chairman of Indian Oil Corporation visited Saudi Arabia from 6-8 April 2001 to renew a term contract with Saudi Arabia for the supply of crude oil and other petroleum products to India for 2001-2002. A 12-member team from the National Defense College paid a 5-day visit to the Kingdom from 21 May 2001. This was the first visit of an NDC team after a gap of ten years. The team visited major defense and economic institutes and held discussions with Saudi officials in Riyadh, Dammam and Jeddah. The Saudi ministry of Labour has launched [2005] a major campaign to achieve full Saudiization in the sectors of gold and tourism [travel agency]. The Saudi Arabian General Investment Authority has given licenses to Indian companies to set up 62 joint ventures in different areas. Many Indian companies have also taken advantage of 100 per cent foreign ownership of companies in the Kingdom and are establishing themselves in designing, financial services, software and so on.[22]

In a smaller or larger measure, Bahrain, Qatar and Oman have either expressed disinterest or toned down their earlier stance on Kashmir. Bahrain is now allowing Indians with more than 15 years experience and a healthy bank balance to reside in the country even without work permits. Bahrain which takes a balanced view of "UN resolutions and framework of Shimla" position, has removed UN resolutions and kept the Shimla framework from its published text in the context of Indo-Pak relations for a number of reasons. Indo-Bahrain trade turnover in 1999-2000 was $ 435 million. India's exports to Bahrain were $ 60 million and imports $ 375 million. The Electronic and Computer Software Export Promotion Council of India sent a 15-member delegation to Bahrain in May 2001. They signed an MOU with Bahrain Economic Development Board for Development of IT sector. Bilateral trade at the end of 2003 stood at $ 186.8 million. During the first ever official visit by a Bahrain PM Sheikh Khalifa bin Salman Al Khalifa in January 2004 an extradition treaty was signed. Agreements on mutual legal assistance and judicial cooperation were also signed. ICICI and SBI were given an offshore banking unit license and a restricted full commercial bank license in Bahrain in 2004.[23]

Indo-Qatar trade turnover in 1989 was $ 38 million and in 1995 $ 130 million. India's exports to Qatar increased from $ 22 million in 1989 to $ 32 million in 1995. In 1999-2000 the trade turnover was $ 245 million. Indian exports were $ 35 million and imports $ 209 million. The total trade between Qatar and India during April 2001 and March 2002 was $ 140.07 million and during 2002-03 was $ 209.17 million. This excludes crude oil and petroleum products. There is a wide gap in Indo-Qatari trade and is reflected in adverse and growing deficit in balance of trade of India. Qatar's Rasgas has tied up with Petronet LNG for supply of 7.5 m tonnes per annum of LNG for Petronet's plants at Dabhol, Maharashtra and at Cochin, Kerala. There are about 2 lakh Indian workers in Qatar who send valuable foreign exchange, which is quite helpful in reducing the balance of trade deficit faced by India in its trade with Qatar. The Qatar Minister of Energy met with the Indian Petroleum and Natural Gas Secretary on 16 May 2001 at Seoul and discussed import of LNG by India from Qatar. A two member delegation from Indian Oil Corporation visited Qatar from 23-25 June 2001 to discuss cooperation in the areas of technical consultancy and training manpower. M/s Bharti Shipyard of Mumbai signed a contract worth $ 4.6 million with Halal offshore services company of Qatar in July 2001. An Indian ship builder ABG Shipyard entered into a $ 100 million contract with a Qatari company for four identical supply vessels. India's first LNG venture, Petronet LNG's venture with a capacity of 5 million tonnes [mt] received its first gas shipment from Rasgas of Qatar as part of 25 years deal estimated at $ 859 million annually. For the last 4 years the necessary infrastructure was being built in this connection. India imported 2.5 mt of gas in 2004 and in 2005 it will be getting 5 mt gas from Qatar. Gas supplied by Qatar is likely to cover 25 per cent of India's requirements.[24]

India's relation with Oman are very old and historic. Among the Indian rulers Haider Ali and Tipu Sultan of Mysore maintained good political and thriving economic ties. These came to an end with the British assassination of Tipu Sultan in May 1799 and the subsequent domination of India and through it the Gulf region by the British. It is only since 1970 Oman has been following an independent foreign policy under Sultan Qaboos. During the 1971 Bangladesh crisis, Oman was the only Arab and Muslim country that did not completely side with Pakistan. In recent times high level visits have taken place between the two states. Prime Minister P. V. Narashima Rao visited Oman in June 1993. Oman has decided to participate in two oil refineries in

India. Oman-India Fertilizer Company (Omifco) is $ 1 billion project and is expected to produce 1.65 million tonnes of granulated urea and 0.25 m tonnes of surplus ammonia per year. President Shankar Dayal Sharma visited Oman in October 1996, the Omani Sultan came to India in April 1997 and in August 1998 Prime Minister A.B. Vajpayee visited Oman. There is modest military-security cooperation between the two states. Indo-Oman trade improved from $ 96 million in 1990 to $ 134 million in 1996. India's exports to Oman increased from $ 56 million to $ 114 million in 1996. India's imports from Oman declined from $ 40 million in 1990 to $ 20 million in 1996. In 1999-2000 Indo-Oman trade turnover was $ 194 million. India's exports to Oman were $ 132 million and imports $ 62 million. The total bilateral trade during 2001-02 was $ 157.47 million and during 2002-03 was $ 212.44 million. This excludes crude oil and petroleum products. Among all the six GCC states Oman is the only state in the GCC with which India has balance of trade surplus. India and Oman are working to establish a fertilizer plant in Oman. The Indian Minister of Chemicals and Fertilizers visited Muscat on 4-5 December 2001 and signed key agreements relating to the Oman-India Fertilizer project in Qalhat, south of Muscat during the visit. There are a number of joint ventures which Indian companies have taken up in Oman. A delegation from National Defence College visited Oman from 20-25 May 2001. The delegation called on the Ministers of Defense and Foreign Affairs and interacted with the Omani defense officials and visited defense institutes in Oman. Also, an Indian military delegation led by Vice Admiral M J Singh visited Oman from 27-31 October 2001 to observe the Oman-British Joint exercises at the invitation of Oman and had extensive interaction with their Omani and British counterparts. George Fernandez, Indian Defense Minister visited Muscat in September 2002 and both are exploring the possibility of joint ventures related to the defence production. Both countries celebrated 50 years of diplomatic ties with a number of programmes and visits by a number of ministers like Natwar Singh, E. Ahamed, Jagdish Tytler and others. Both signed an extradition treaty. Both have agreed to study further cooperation in IT, tourism, HRD, healthcare and small and medium scale industries.[25]

India's old historical ties with GCC states coupled with the current presence of over four million Indian workers in the region, increasing imports of oil [over 70%] and gas, growing trade [16% of exports], aid and investments opportunities are vital interests of India. From the strategic point of view both India and GCC States share the need for political stability and the need to reduce the role of non-regional states whose policies are undermining peace, security and stability leading to the periodic threats of military intervention. The common political and strategic concerns of India and the GCC States and the desire to work for peace, security, and stability in the Gulf region and South Asia and the emerging common threat perceptions will create opportunities in future. The past two decades have seen the reassertion of regional and local identities in the face of outside interference. The GCC States are going through important changes and the process of reconciliation and understanding is maturing relatively fast. The critical space is widening and it is in this context that India and GCC States can create opportunities for mutual benefit not only in the oil gas-sector, trade and commerce, sharing and development of human resources, but also for mutual security and jointly prepare to meet the emerging domestic and regional challenges. Pakistan's attempt to use the crisis in Kashmir to put pressure on India and isolate in the Gulf region is nothing new. India's growing ties with Israel were also sought to be used to undermine our linkages with the GCC countries, but it has not worked as the GCC states led by Saudi Arabia are themselves willing to normalize relations with Israel as made clear by the Saudi peace plan of Crown Prince Abdullah at the Beirut Arab summit in March 2002. India by continuing to support the just causes of the Palestinians and other Arabs and also to work for closer ties with Israel and the US has shown the unique balance one can maintain by having good ties with both the parties. Although critics have said that India's ardor for the Arab causes has waned and become muted, but is it not a fact that most Arab states including the GCC states despite having very close ties with the US and EU have been unable to restrain the US and others in their blind support to Israel in the latter's continued defiance of UN Resolutions, violation of international law, contempt of world public opinion and opposition to the establishment of an independent Palestinian state. Not only due to the collapse of USSR and the Kashmir issue, but also due to a variety of other factors India has been working hard to improve relations with the US. If the US has become India's largest investment and trading partner and cooperation in military and security matters is increasing it is due to the desire of both the states to achieve it, which is helped by the growing role of private sector in this relationship. Despite overwhelming opposition from the public in the GCC states, the US is looked upon by the leaderships [GCC] as a security and defence partner. India has been striving hard to remove the factors creating instability in the Gulf region. It is with this objective India had been urging Iraq [before its invasion and occupation by the

USA] to implement the UN resolutions and at the same time calling for the lifting of UN sanctions imposed on Iraq for more than 12 years.

Both the GCC States and India face the menace of terrorism and religious extremism and the need to combat such forces. A modest beginning has been made for cooperation in the field of security with the GCC states which has a rich potential field ahead. Many also emphasize the need to fulfill the growing aspirations of the Gulf people to play a greater role in the sphere of political participation and decision making process. Political systems which allow more space for civil society, and work for enhancing their legitimacy would prove to be more enduring as also develop stake in peace and stability. Of course, outside support will continue to be a major factor in Gulf politics, but it is internal support, which will eventually decide the final outcome especially major issues concerning peace, security and stability.

Important developments in India's domestic affairs like the Rath Yatra of BJP leader L.K. Advani from Somnath to Ayodhya and the destruction of the Babri Masjid [1992] which followed as also the communal hatred directed at Muslims especially have shaken the confidence of the religious minorities in India. There is need to show greater tolerance towards them. The inept handling of the Kashmir issue, soft attitude towards some religious [Hindu] groups which are spreading hatred and crackdown on other groups, the partisan role of the state government in the infamous Gujarat riots [2002] and the killings directed at one community, need for early resolution of the Babri Masjid issue, and the unsettled conditions in Kashmir and on Indo-Pakistan border, call for greater care and caution as such domestic issues invite adverse global reactions. The reach of present day mass and electronic media is far and swift inviting instant reactions and complications. Unlike our food security the issue of energy security makes us vulnerable to outside pressure. As PM A.B. Vajpayee said: "A situation should not be created at home which forces us to bow our heads in shame before others [abroad]". So far Indian diplomacy has been fairly successful in containing the negative impact flowing from domestic issues on India's relations with the GCC States, but things are rapidly changing in the region. Lest we become complacent, there is urgent need to do hard thinking how best to keep our house in order and not give to others the chance and opportunity to harm India's interests. It would be foolhardy to assume that things would remain the same despite serious developments domestically and that any disturbance of status quo would hurt the GCC States more than India. We must be vigilant and not allow domestic developments to get out of hand due to the electoral politics and posturing and allow outsiders to interfere in our domestic affairs.[26]

The Palestine-Israeli Peace Process

In the wake of the 1990-91 Kuwait crisis and the Madrid Peace Conference which was held in October 1991, India decided to establish diplomatic ties with Israel on 29 January 1992 under the Congress government led by Prime Minister P.V. Narasimha Rao. Things changed dramatically after 1991 when both the Arabs and the Israelis decided to sit down and negotiate their problems. With this new development India was encouraged to break the ice with Israel, as the Jewish State was no more a pariah as before. There were also major changes as far as PLO was concerned. Since Yasser Arafat appeared before the UN in 1974 and PLO was recognized by Arab States at Rabat, the PLO went on a peace offensive [under Egyptian influence] after it moved to Tunis in 1982-83 when Israel invaded Lebanon. In 1988 Arafat accepted UNSC Resolution 242 and renounced violence and recognized Israel. After the 1991 Madrid conference and the Oslo Peace Accords of September 1993 many expected Israel to withdraw from Arab lands leading to final peace between Israel and its neighbours and the establishment of an independent Palestinian state. But the assassination of Israeli PM Yitzhak Rabin on November 4, 1995 and the emergence of Benjamin Netanyahu and Ariel Sharon as Likud leaders and as Prime Ministers led to the collapse of peace between the Palestinians and the Israelis. Many have accused Arafat of rejecting Israeli peace offers in Camp David (July 2000) talks with President Clinton and PM Barak. To be true Arafat was willing to concede 77 per cent of historic Palestine provided Israel withdrew from the 23 per cent of Palestine, i.e., Gaza, West Bank and East Jerusalem. Of course, Israel offered to withdraw from Gaza and parts of West Bank, but refused to remove the Jewish settlements from West Bank and Jerusalem and rejected the right to return of the Palestinian refugees and reiterated its stand that Jerusalem will remain the eternal and undivided capital of Israel. Moreover it continued the building of its security wall in West Bank on the Palestinian land in clear violation of international law and against the ruling of the World Court and said its control over water resources in West Bank will remain absolute. Meanwhile Ariel Sharon reoccupied Palestinian land in March 2002 and carried out indiscriminate arrests, killings, curfew, house demolitions, humiliating check points and so on. The result has been that deprivation, destruction and death rained on the Palestinians. Palestinian suicide bombings against Israelis and the Jewish state's excessive use of force continued. Arafat was seen as an obstacle to peace and Israel painted him in the darkest colours since the Al Aqsa intifada in September 2000. The result was US President Bush and his neo-condominated team refused to meet and deal with Arafat whom he described as an obstacle to peace. If Arafat had accepted US-Israeli proposal at Camp David he would perhaps have become the hero eligible for another Nobel Prize. But Arafat avoided violent end to his life by rejecting the US-Israeli proposals which fell far short of the UN resolutions and hence he remained largely popular among the Palestinians.[27]

More significantly Ariel Sharon now projected Yasser Arafat as a terrorist. Under the circumstances the US and UK were telling others that the road to peace in Palestine runs through Baghdad. Iraqi WMD's and the toppling of Saddam Hussein regime became priority for the US President Bush. The result was US invasion of Iraq in March 2003. One must recall that Menachem Begin Prime Minister of Israel had bombed Iraqi nuclear reactor in May 1981 and since then Israeli policy had been to destroy Baathist Iraq which was perceived as a mortal threat to Israeli security. Soon after the US invasion and occupation of Iraq the Quartet—the US, EU, UN and Russia announced the Road Map for Peace between Israel and Palestine, calling for a "viable and independent Palestine". Sharon had raised 14 objections to the plan and the US insisted on political reforms in the Palestinian National Authority. Arafat appointed Mahmoud Abbas and subsequently Ahmed Qoreai as PM, but Israel continued its policy of relentless killings of Palestinians in the Gaza and West Bank, demolition of houses, confiscation of land and construction of Jewish settlements on Palestinian land. Hamas and Islamic *Jihad* and young Palestinians took to violence in the aftermath of such a hostile Israeli attitude. The death of Yasser Arafat in November 2004 and the election of Mahmoud Abbas as PA President on 9 January 2005, together with heavy resistance in Iraq to US occupation, growing anti-Americanism sweeping the Arab-Muslim world, made the US put pressure on Israeli Prime Minister Ariel Sharon to implement the Road Map for peace. The Sharam el Sheikh summit in Egypt involving Mahmoud Abbas, PM Ariel Sharon, President Hosni Mubarak of Egypt and King Abdullah of Jordan has produced a ceasefire between Israel and Palestine. Sharon has promised to withdraw from Gaza and a few settlements in West Bank and ease the living conditions for Palestinians. But the recent statement by Sharon's advisor Dor Weisglass that there will be no Palestinian state and no full withdrawal from West Bank are negative developments. What we may come to see in future is partial peace and perhaps less harsher treatment of Palestinians by

Israel. Sustained international pressure on Israel and the US has to be maintained so as to get justice to the Palestinians. In the 9 January 2005 elections to the post of President of the PNA, Mahmoud Abbas was elected with 62 per cent votes. Most Palestinians believe Abbas is the leader who can put the peace process back on track and end the cycle of violence (Al Aqsa Intifadah) which has taken the lives of nearly 5000 Palestinians. Many more thousands have been injured on both sides especially more among the Palestinians. From the very beginning Abbas expressed his determination to end the violence. He has already effected substantial changes in the police and security structures. Some of Arafat's cronies who were seen as corrupt have been removed. He has engaged the Hamas in a dialogue and persuaded them to support his cease-fire efforts. Egypt also helped him in the Gaza. He has had two meetings with Sharon, Condoleezza Rice, and Vladimir Putin of Russia and with President Bush in Washington in May 2003. Abbas has made it clear that achieving peace remains his priority and in this connection he has been visiting not only Arab states to heal the rift but has also visited China, Japan, India and others. Recently Hamas has won 24 municipal councils and made strong inroads in key urban centres in West Bank and consolidated its influence in Gaza. Abbas has so far shown that he is capable of controlling the security situation but the real crux is how far Israel and US will be honest in implementing their part of the promises. Until mid-2005 Israel has withdrawn its forces from some key towns in West Bank and released a few hundred Palestinian detainees.[28]

Mahmoud Abbas visited India on 19-20 May 2005 and met India's PM Manmohan Singh who promised Rs. 65 crore in aid for infrastructure projects in West Bank and Gaza. Although India reiterated its support to the Palestinian struggle for self-determination, it also-called for an end to violence. Fully aware that the UPA government is as keen as the NDA government to consolidate ties with Israel, Abbas confirmed that India's ties with Israel were its own internal affairs. The visit of Abbas could have been used to expose Israeli brutality against the Palestinians and to call for an end to Israeli occupation of Arab lands in a time bound schedule. The continuing violence in Palestine is basically due to Israeli occupation and refusal to end it and also due to the harsh and inhuman treatment of the Palestinians. But India is toying with the idea of mediating in the Arab-Israeli conflict. Many in the Islamic world thought that the Congress-led UPA government would resotre the balance it had pursued in its policy towards West Asia earlier compared to the marked tilt shown by NDA government towards Israel during its period. Any contention that Israel is a major arms supplier to India and hence the UPA government should soft pedal any firm stand against Israel will affect India's credibility in the Arab world where bulk of our interests lie.

That India reiterated its support to Palestinian self-determination and also-called for an end to violence is clearly aimed at finding a fine balance between the two parties. Abbas is aware of the previous NDA government's tilt towards Israel and also the fact that Israel has emerged as one of India's leading arms suppliers. That Abbas had to confirm that India's ties with Israel are its domain without making any visible adverse remarks on them suggests that he got less than he expected from his visit. Although the MEA is cautious in dealing with Isreal, the Defense Ministry is keen not only to host visits by Israeli delegations to India but also to send delegations to Israel. Two way trades with Israel have crossed $ 3 billion mark, bulk of it being for defense products. But any continued close identification with Israel especially in the field of security cooperation is not in the larger interest of India. Wherever Israel has managed to have close ties especially in the security field it has tried to influence the military, security structures to the detriment of the host country. The ties with Israel should not compromise India's security interests. There was no doubt about the BJP led NDA government under A. B. Vajpayee giving primacy to the US and Israel in its foreign policy. But it was expected that the UPA government under Manmohan Singh led by the Congress would be mature in its policy towards the Arab world, but unfortunately it appears to be keen to continue with the previous government's pro-Israeli policy. The ties remain the same more or less as warm with India continuing to maintaining its strategic cooperation with Israel in the name of combating terrorism. All this is being done without giving wide publicity as was done previously by the NDA. Undoubtedly, India's core interests are in the Arab and Islamic world and it should have used Mahmoud Abbas's visit to signal its displeasure to Israel over its continued occupation of Arab lands and mistreatment of the Palestinians. Even though the Left parties have called for a review of India's ties with Israel in view of continued occupation of Palestinian lands and harsh treatment of the Arabs, the Congress appears to continue the ties started by the former Prime Minister P.V. Narasimha Rao in 1992. That UPA government wants no such change in its policy towards Israel clearly suggests the continuity in the old policy of less emphasis on the Arabs. It must be emphasized that the Palestinians need India's support at this critical juncture in their history, if they are to find justice after their long suffering at the hands of Israel but the Israelis remain as adamant as before except for some minor concessions. The Palestine-Israel issue remains an important flashpoint and if repeated violence is not contained, it could adversely affect India's national interests. It is shocking to hear that some in the MEA have become so bold as to argue that non-resolution of the Palestine-Israeli conflict might be in India's interest.[29]

India and Iraq

Since 1991 the USA despite its best efforts failed to dislodge Saddam Hussein. In October 1988 the US Congress enacted the Iraq Liberation Act to replace Saddam Hussein and a sum of $ 97 million was allocated for carrying out the task through covert operations. The emergence of George W. Bush as US President in 2001, and the 9/11 attacks on US have enabled the Bush administration to launch its war on terrorism. Under this garb it is working to play a more permanent role in the oil rich Gulf region. The unresolved conflict with Iraq made the US to become more strident in its demands especially due to huge Iraqi oil reserves. Since Iraqi oil was outside the US influence so the aim was to make Iraq conform to the dominant requirements of the capitalist exploitation. US invasion and occupation of Iraq was over oil and also for the continued control of the global oil economy through the US dollar. The issue of WMD, democracy and human rights were mere pretexts. The fall of Baghdad to US forces on April 9, 2003 had led to toal chaos in Iraq. The Iraqi resistance to US occupation has not only intensified but the US has confirmed that from being sporadic attacks by the remnants of the old Baathist elements, a full scale guerilla warfare and now a well organized resistance is going on against the US forces. US had hoped to achieve quick victory over Iraq and then to reorder the map in the strategically important Gulf region, but due to mounting resistance in Iraq, the US is now facing new and entirely unexpected challenges to its objectives.

India under the leadership of A.B. Vajpayee of the BJP-led NDA government under US pressure was initially considering the idea of sending Indian troops to Iraq for stabilization work, [to crush the Iraqi resistance] but due to mounting opposition from the Congress and the left parties, it had to drop the idea as also due to the Parliament resolution opposing US invasion of Iraq and calling on Washington to end its occupation of a non-aligned country. Due to the anarchy and chaos, suicide attacks, kidnappings and indiscriminate killings of civilians, all due to US invasion has led to unprecedented hardships to the Iraqis. Some Indian truck drivers working for a Kuwaiti company were kidnapped in Iraq and later released due to the mediation efforts by Ambassador Talmiz Ahmed, India's special envoy. India has been extending guarded support to the gradual process of transfer of power to the Iraqi government, elections, constitution making and normalization of the situation in Iraq. India is a member of the Donors Group for Iraq and has made modest contribution for the Iraq Reconstruction Funds. India has also helped Iraq in setting up of field hospitals and in other infrastructure projects. In May 2004 India's special envoy to West Asia Mr. C. R. Gharekhan visited Iraq and offered assistance in the drafting of Iraqi constitution besides help in the rebuilding of Iraqi institutions. After the Iraqi elections in January 30, 2005 for the 275 member National Assembly, the sectarian divide in Iraq has further widened in line with the US policy of divide and rule with religious groups and parties gaining ground thereby undermining secularism which was the basis of Iraqi political system under the Baathist rule. Shias are now dominating Iraq and the Kurds are trying to achieve maximum autonomy. The US has found political sectarianism very useful to control Iraq. The Sunnis continue to be killed and suppressed by the US just like the British who killed and suppressed Shias during and after the First World War.[30]

The US forces it appears will remain in Iraq for the foreseeable future to provide security to the puppet Iraqi governments which will be manipulated and the ten or more military bases being prepared throughout Iraq will form a permanent feature of US military presence in the country. From its presence in Iraq the US finds it easy to implement its regional strategy towards Iran, Syria, Saudi Arabia and others. This will only make Iraq the magnet and training ground for Islamists from all over the world. It might become a more dangerous place than Afghanistan and Somalia. Since Iraqi oil is going to last at least for another fifty years and with growing US demand for oil, Iraqi oil is likely to become indispensable for the US economy. So far the US used to get its job done in the Arab world through Israel, now both Israel and the US will work in tandem to rearrange the whole Arab world according to their strategic needs. As Lord Curzon said whichever state dominates the Arab world, it will be in a position to influence India is coming true. Pax Americana and Israeli domination of the region should be a wake up call for India to devise new policies to prevent fragmentations, violence, wars, instability and terrorism which is spreading fast in the Arab world and whose impact will be surely felt in India as well.

Instability in the Arab world poses a greater threat than ever before, as India's reliance on the Gulf oil is growing. Although the issue of terrorism is also important and imported arms from Israel are vital for India's security, there is no need for India to place undue emphasis on bilateral relations between India and Israel as the NDA-BJP sought to do as per its notions of grand strategy. India must tackle the threat of terrorism to it by itself, but not in cooperation with Israel, a state with a dubious record in this field, to say the least. Many Indians express their solidarity with the cause of the Palestinians and the larger Arab cause, which is only natural. The BJP tilt towards Israel hurt India's relations with Arab countries. India should speak out in favour of the Palestinians and condemn the Israeli atrocities. This is essential not only to repair our ties with the Palestinians but also to restore ties with the Arab and Islamic world.

Another major concern [as seen briefly before] in India's foreign policy towards the Arab world, of course, is the US invasion and occupation of Iraq. That the US plans to keep its forces in place even after 2007 and foist a puppet regime on the people of Iraq is a development that India cannot ignore or give implicit sanction to. The daily killings of innocent Iraqis by the US forces and destruction in holy places are fuelling the Iraqi resistance, which has not only intensified but, as the US has confirmed, has escalated into a full-scale guerilla war. Despite the arrest of Saddam Hussein and his key advisors and killing of the Baath leadership, the Iraqi people have not buckled to US dictates and it is unlikely they will meekly surrender to the US-led occupation of their country. India did a wise thing by not sending troops to strength in the Iraq at the US request. The anti-US sentiments sweeping the Arab and Islamic world are likely to gain strength in coming years due to the US war against Afghans, Iraqis, Palestinians and other Muslims. Rather than supporting these wars, and reaping its share of the backlash, India should work for a speedy end to the US occupation of Iraq and also speak out on the daily atrocities committed by the US occupation forces involving air planes, helicopters, artillery, tanks, APC's, chemical weapons so on. In order to hide its actions the US has barred free media.[31]

The United Progressive Alliance government's common minimum programme stated that "it will maintain the independence of India's foreign policy stance on all regional and global issues even as it pursues closer strategic and economic engagement with the US". But the reality is that in the context of West Asia, US policy is actually affecting India in a gradual way. Pax-Americana in the Arab world has serious implications for India. The US control of Gulf oil sources may in the future affect India's quest for energy security, especially as India imports 70 per cent of its oil from the Gulf. The US support to undemocratic regimes in the region is encouraging these Islamic countries to use violence in the face of reluctance of the rulers to initiate genuine political reforms. The security and future of Indian workers in the region in the wake of continued wars, terrorism and instability has become an issue of concern. And the US desire to involve Pakistan in its strategy in Arab world has implications on India's security and influence in the region. India's close ties with Iran and Syria have come under pressure and if the US intensifies its pressure on these two states, while doing nothing to restrain Israel, which seeks to increase its influence in the region with help from the US, we may see more wars, violence, terrorism and instability.[32]

It is imperative for India to maintain close ties with Iran, [although a country with a very strained relationship with the US], to protect itself against fallout from Afghanistan, to gain access to Central Asian energy resources [natural gas] and to deal with Pakistan. This relationship with Iran is also vital for Iraq and its stability in the Gulf region. Apart from the Presidents of Turkey, Iran and Algeria, [of course Sharon] no other leader has made a State visit to India from this region in recent times. India's pro-Israeli tilt has become a burden and it's high time we pursued a more vigorous policy to strengthen our relations with the Arabs and the wider Islamic world. Peace, security and stability in West Asia are crucial for our own security and prosperity and this calls for new initiatives, dynamism and recognition of the traditionally close historical relationship with the Arab and Islamic world.[33]

India's economic ties are unlikely to suffer with the Arab states in the immediate future, but one needs to be cautious in developing closer ties with Israel until the process of reconciliation gets under way between the Arabs, especially Palestinians and Israelis. Perhaps the Congress led coalition will attempt to balance the traditionally close ties with Arab and Muslim states of West Asia with Israel. We have to safeguard our core interests like import of 70% oil and gas, security and welfare of nearly 5 million Indian workers, over 16% exports to the region, growing trade and investments with the region. On top of these, security and stability in the region is linked with early resolution of the Iraq crisis, (US withdrawal of occupation forces) establishment of a viable Palestinian state and encouraging political reforms and democratization of political systems which alone can contain the growing slide towards religious resurgence, violence, terrorism and instability in the region. In sum, it is possible to have normal ties with Israel, and at the same time, retain the traditionally close ties with Arabs provided New Delhi adopts a pragmatic approach both at home and abroad. At the moment it may appear the Arabs are down and getting the beating at the hands of US and Israel but their sheer population numbers, with over twenty states, enormous oil and gas resources, strategic location and also the historical relations, no Indian government can ignore them. If India ignores the Arabs it will not enhance New Delhi's interests or image in the international arena.[34]

Notes and References

1. See S. Maqbul Ahmed, Indo-Arab Relations (New Delhi: 1978); M.A. Saleem Khan, Early Muslim Perception of India and Hinduism (New Delhi; South Asian Publishers, 1997); S.M. Husayn Nainar, Southern India as Known to Arab Geographers (New Delhi: Cosmo Publications, 2004); M.S.S. Nadwi, Indo-Arab Relations (Hyderabad: 1962); Ronald Watkins, Unknown Seas: How Vasco da Gamma Opened the East (London: John Murray, 2004); N.N. Vohra, ed., *History, Culture and Society in India and West Asia* [New Delhi: Shipra, 2002]; A. K. Pasha, "India and West Asia", *World Focus*, Vol. 25, No. 10-11-12, October-November-December, 2004, pp. 41-46; Beatrice Niolini, Makaran, Oman and Zanzibar: Three-Terminal Cultural Corridor in the Western Indian Ocean [1799-1856] [Leiden: E J Brill, 2004] Surendra Gopal, "India and Oman in Medieval Times", *Journal of Indian Ocean Studies*, Vol. 9, No. 3, December 2001, pp. 391-96; Iftikar Ahmed, "Oman's Commerce with Mughal Empire in 17th Century" Journal of India Ocean Studies, Vol. 9, No. 2, August 2001, pp. 238-248; Afzal Ahmed, Portuguese Trade and Socio-Economic Changes on the Western Coast of India, 1600-63 [Delhi: Originals, DK, 2000].

2. Faleh Abdul Jabar and Hosham Dawod, ed., *Tribes and Power: Nationalism and Ethnicity in the Middle East* [London: Saqi, 2003], pp. 257-306; Madawi al Rasheed, ed., *Transnational Connections and the Arab Gulf* [London: Rutledge, 2005] pp. 59-90; Robert J. Blyth, *The Empire of the Raj: India, Eastern Africa and the Middle East, 1858-1947* [London: Palgrave, Macmillan] pp. 132-69; M. Hamid Ansari, "Iraq-open for business!" AGNI, Vol. 7, No. 4, May-August, 2004, pp. 1-22 [p. 18].

3. A. K. Pasha, "Nehru and the Crises in West Asia", *Détente*, Vol. IX, No. 1, May-June 1990, pp. 4-9; M. S. Agwani, "Nehru and the Arab World", *Secular Democracy, Nehru Number*, 1976, p. 171.

4. A. K. Pasha, *India and West Asia: Continuity and Change* [Delhi: Gyan Sagar, 1999] p. 19 Najma Heptullah, *Indo-West Asian Relations: The Nehru Era* [New Delhi: Allied, 1991].

5. Sudha Rao, The Arab-Israeli Conflict: The Indian View [New Delhi: 1972] pp. 24-29; *India and Palestine: The Evolution of a Policy* [Delhi: MEA] p. 15; Richard J. Kozicki, "India and Israel: A Problem in Asian Politics," *Middle Eastern Affairs*, May 1958, p. 164; see also Prithvi Ram Mudiam, *India and the Middle East* [London: British Academic Press, 1994]; B. R. Nanda, Gandhi: *Pan-Islamism, Imperialism and Nationalism in India* [New Delhi: Oxford University Press, 2002]; See also Jacob Abadi, *Israel's Quest for Recognition and Acceptance in Asia: Garrison State Diplomacy* [London: Frank Cass, 2004] pp. 257-285.

6. Jawaharlal Nehru, *India's Foreign Policy: Selected Speeches, September 1946-April 1961* [New Delhi: 1961] p. 94; see also Raj Krishna Srivastava, *India's Relations with the Arab East [1947-64]*, Ph.D. Thesis, Kanpur University, 1976.

7. A.K. Pasha, *Indian and OIC: Strategy and Diplomacy* [New Delhi: Centre for Peace Studies, 1995], pp. 3-4; S. Gopal, "India, the Crisis and the Non-Aligned Nations", in W. M. Roger Louis and Roger Owen, ed; *Suez 1956: The Crisis and Its Consequences* (Oxford, 1989), p. 173; M.S. Rajan, *India in World Affairs, 1954-56* [New Delhi: 1964] p. 151; Asha Hans, *Indian Diplomacy: The Suez Crises* (Delhi: Amar Prakashan, 1983).

8. Bharat Kumar, "India and the West Asian Crisis," in Surendra Chopra, ed., *Studies in India's Foreign Policy* (Amritsar: 1983) p. 335; M.S. Agwani, *The West Asian Crisis: 1967* (Meerut: Meenakshi Prakashan, 1968); Krishan Gopal, WANA: A Documentary Study of Major Crises, 1947-1978 with particular reference to Indo-Arab Cooperation (New Delhi: V. I. Publications, 1981).

9. Pasha, No. 4, pp. 36-46; Richard Edmund Ward, *India's Pro-Arab Policy: A Study in Continuity* (New York: Praeger, 1992), p. 85.

10. A.H.H. Abidi, "India's Policy Towards the Muslim States: Approach and Problems", *Problems of Non-Alignment*, Vol. 2, No. 1, March-May 1984, pp. 145-56; M.S. Agwani, "India and the Arab World," in B.R. Nanda, ed., *Indian Foreign Policy: The Nehru Years* (New Delhi: 1976) p. 66-77; K. R. Singh, "India and WANA", *International Studies*, Vol. 17, Nos. 3 and 4, June-October 1978, pp. 625-37; Ajay N. Jha, *India's Economic Diplomacy in the Gulf* (New Delhi: ABC, 1998); Moshe Dayan, *Breakthrough: A Personal Account of the Egypt-Israel Peace Negotiations* [New Delhi: Vikas, 1981] pp. 26-32.

11. Girijesh Pant, "Iran-Iraq Conflict and India: A Dimension in south-South Relations," *Quarterly of Strategic Studies*, Vol. 1, No. 1 January 1984, pp. 70-77; R. C. Sharma, ed; *Perspectives on Iran-Iraq Conflict* (New Delhi Rajesh Publications, 1984) p. 99; K. R. Singh, "India and the Gulf Conflicts" in Satish Kumar ed; *Yearbook on India's Foreign Policy, 1990-91* (New Delhi: Tata McGraw, 1991) pp. 16-26; and Maya Chadda "India and West Asia", in Satish Kumar, ed. *Year Book on India's Foreign Policy, 1985-86* (New Delhi: Sage, 1988) pp. 144-45; A.K. Pasha, "Prospects for Peace in the Gulf," *Détente*, May-June 1989, p. 23.

12. A.K. Pasha ed., *The Gulf in Turmoil* (New Delhi: Lancers Book, 1992), A. K. Pasha, "India's West Asia Policy: Continuity and Change", Strategic Analysis, Vol. 16, No. 6, September 1992, pp. 783-804; M.H. Nuri, "India and the Gulf Crisis", *BISS Journal*, Vol. 13, No. 1, 1992, pp. 1-50; C. S. R. Murthy, "The Gulf War and Beyond: The UN," in K. R. Singh, ed. *Post-War Gulf: Implications for India* (New Delhi: Lancers Books, 1993), pp. 17-26.

13. A.K. Pasha, "India and GCC", in Riyaz Punjabi and A.K. Pasha, ed., *India and the Islamic World* (New Delhi: Radiant, 1998) p. 34-48; A. K. Pasha, "Communal Revivalism in India: Its Impact on ties with WANA," in Muchkund Dubey, ed., *Communal Revivalism in India: A Study of External Implications* (New Delhi: Har Anand, 1994) pp. 54-58; and A. K. Pasha, No. 7; and Pasha, No. 4, pp. 86-96.

14. A.K. Pasha, "India and the GCC States: Challenges and Opportunities," *World Focus*, Vol. 24, No. 2, February 2003, p. 9-15; UAE Year Books and MEA Annual Reports.

15. Pasha, n.7; and Pasha, n.4; see also Ajay N. Jha, "Economic Relations between the UAE and India: Genesis, Growth and Prospects," *International Studies*, July-September 1986, pp. 40-62.

16. Pasha, n. 7, p. 29 Dubey, n. 13, pp. 54-58; Girijesh Pant, "Political Economy of Regime Transition in Kuwait," in A.K. Pasha, ed., *Contemporary Gulf* (New Delhi: Détente, 1999) pp. 176-211.

17. Ibid, pp. 95-96; see also A.K. Pasha, ed., *India and Kuwait: Strategic, Economic and Political Developments* (Delhi: Gyan Sagar, 1999), pp. 244-314.

18. Pasha, n. 14, Muhammad Azhar, *Contemporary Gulf Economics and Indo-Gulf Relations* (New Delhi: New Horizon, 1999) pp. 199-220; AHH Abidi, ed., *Indo-Gulf Economic Relations: Patterns, Prospects and Policies* (New Delhi: Intellectual, 1989) pp. 81-118.

19. N. Janardhan, "GCC-India-Pakistan Ties," in *Gulf Yearbook, 2004*, (Dubai: Gulf Research Centre, 2005) pp. 193-202; see also special issue on Iraq in *India Quarterly*, Vol. LX, No. 4, October-December 2004.

20. A.K. Pasha, "Perspectives on Indo-Saudi Relations," in A.K. Pasha, ed., *Perspectives on India and the Gulf States* (New Delhi: Détente, 1999) pp. 208-27; and Pasha n. 4, pp. 143-67; see also Muhammad Azhar, *Ibid.*, "GCC Aid to India," pp. 190-207.

21. Pasha, n. 14, p. 13; see also A.K. Pasha, "India and West Asia: Continuity and Change," in Nalini Kant Jha, ed. *India's Foreign Policy in a Changing World: Essays in Honor of Professor Bimal Prasad* (New Delhi: South Asian Publishers, 2000) pp. 240-69.

22. Janardhan, n.19, p. 196.

23. *Ibid.*, Javed Ahmed Khan, *Indian and West Asia: Emerging Markets in the liberalization Era* (New Delhi: Sage, 1999); see also A.K. Pasha, *India, Bahrain and Qatar: Political Economic and Strategic Dimension* (Delhi: Gyan Sagar, 1999) pp. 674-06.

24. Azhar, n.18, pp. 221-40: Pasha, n.23, pp. 105-82.

25. Bansidhar Pradhan, "Indo-Omani Relations: Political, Security, and Socio-Cultural Dimensions," in A.K. Pasha, ed., *India and Oman: History, State, Economy and Foreign Policy* [Delhi: Gyan Sagar, 1999], pp. 72-90; *Oman in Focus* (New Delhi: Embassy of Oman,) May 2005, pp. 18-21, 50-52 and 56-60.

26. Pasha, n.14, p. 14-15; see also Swami Agnivesh and Valson Thampu, *Harvest of Hate: Gujarat under Siege* (New Delhi: Rupa and Co, 2002); and Siddharth Varadarajan, ed., *Gujarat: The Making of a Tragedy* (New Delhi: Penguin, 2002).

27. A.K. Pasha, "Arafat, Palestinians and the Future", *Mainstream*, Vol. XLII, No. 50, December 4, 2004, pp. 7-12; see also A. K. Pasha, Palestine after Arafat: Struggling to Survive", *Hard News*, Vol. 2, No. 1, December 2004, pp. 60-61.

28. A.K. Pasha, "Post-Arafat Palestine", *World Focus*, Vol. 26, No. 5, May 2005, pp. 1-4; see also A. K. Pasha, "Conflict Resolution and the

Palestinian Peace Process", in Arun Kumar Banerji, ed., *Conflict Resolution in the Post-Cold War Era*, [Calcutta: Minerva Associates, 2000] pp. 72-91.

29. M. S. Agwani, "India and the Palestine Issue", *World Focus*, May 2005, pp. 12-15, see also Avi Shlaim, *The Iron Wall: Israel and the Arab World*, [London: Penguin, 2004].

30. A.K. Pasha, *Iraq: Sanctions and Wars*, [New Delhi: Sterling, 2003]; A.K. Pasha, "The Recent Gulf Crisis: India's Options", *Strategic Analysis*, Vol. XVII, No. 10, January 1995, pp. 127-86.

31. A.K. Pasha, "Iraq and its Future: An Overview", *World Focus*, February 2005, Vol. 26, No. 2, pp. 3-6; M. H. Ansari, "Iraq: The Pace of Reconstruction" *Indian Quarterly*, Vol. LX, No. 4, October-December, 2004, pp. 27-34.

32. A.K. Pasha, "The Iraq Crisis: An Overview", *World Focus*, Post Saddam Iraq, Vol. 25, No. 1, January 2004, pp. 3-6; see also Sukumar Murlidharan, "Intelligence, Incompetence and Iraq or Time to talk of democracy, demography and Israel", *Social Scientist*, Vol. 32, Nos. 11-12, November-December 2004, pp. 21-80.

33. A. K. Pasha, "Why is the Islamic World important for India?" *Hard news*, Vol. 1, Issue 7, June 2004, pp. 56-57; A. K. Pasha, "India, Iran and the GCC States: Common Political and Strategic Concerns", *Encounter*, March-April, 1998, pp. 66-74.

34. Speech by Prime Minister Dr. Manmohan Singh, at the inauguration of the Centre of West Asian Studies, Jamia Millia Islamia, New Delhi, 29 January 2005; Speech by Natwar Singh, Minister for External Affairs at the Indian Association for Central and West Asian Studies [IACWAES], Jamia Millia Islamia, New Delhi, October 6, 2004.

20

India's Relations with Eastern South Asian Neighbouring Countries in the 21st Century: Bangladesh, Bhutan and Nepal

Dr. Parmanand

Establishing or maintaining ideal or even reasonably good relationships with one's immediate neighbours is more often than not a difficult task. Familiarity, inter alia, often breeds contempt and fear. In the South Asian region—where India occupies a position of preponderance in terms of population, area, developmental indices and other resources—various factors constantly contribute to this difficulty.

In fact, this reality also makes this region different from various other regions of the world, where too sufficient attention is attached to maintaining friendly and cooperative relations with one's neighbours. It is within this broad framework that the core state of South Asia, i.e., India, has to conduct its relations with various neighbours—particularly, Bangladesh, Bhutan and Nepal.

A variety of factors often come together in increasing India's problems in dealing with neighbouring countries—including these three—in various manners and degrees. Territorial disputes, cross-border infiltration or terrorism, open borders or open borders-like situations, non-concern about each other's security concerns, uneven economic development, different and incongruous political structures all join together to create this state of affairs. Various similarities on cultural, religious, ethnic and economic planes generally exacerbate problems at state-to-state level relationships. Paradoxically, one finds, at times, that while the government-to-government level relations become worse or tense, the people-to-people relations become strong and vibrant, making the relevant government rethink on the existing state of things.

At the present juncture, the Indian government is making serious attemps to improve or strengthen multidimensional and multipurpose ties with India's neighbours. To a very great extent, this is a continuation of the policy and endeavour of the previous government or governments. It very significantly and unmistakably underlines the adherence to continuity and consensus in conducting relations with neighbours. It is also against this backdrop that we would analyse India's relations with Bangladesh, Bhutan and Nepal.

It would be in order to refer to a brief but striking speech made by India's Foreign Secretary Shyam Saran on February 14, 2005 under the auspices of the Institute of Defence Studies and Analyses at the India International Centre, New Delhi. The speech was very largely a policy statement.

Shyam Saran, inter alia, stressed: "India wishes to reassure its neighbours that it respects their independence and sovereignty. What it regards as unhelpful is the display of narrow nationalism based on hostility towards India that often becomes a cover for failure to deliver on promises made to their own peoples.[1] India's Foreign Secretary also chose the occasion to underline the absence of common security perception in the region and stated: "We must also recognize, regrettable though this may be, that countries of South Asia, while occupying the same geographical space, do not have a shared security perception and, hence, a common security doctrine. This is different from EU or ASEAN". Saran, indeed, went to the extent of emphasizing that in South Asia "at least some of the States perceive security threats as arising from within the region."[2] Explaining "security", Graham Evans and Jeffrey Newnham (1998: 490) view it as a "term which denotes the absence of threats to scarce values". Martin Griffiths and Terry O'Callaghan (2004: 289) state: "To be secure is to be free from harm". Stephanie Lawson (2003: 78), on the other hand, stresses that the traditional concept of security in International Relations "has revolved almost exclusively around the state and its survival as a political community". Indeed, according to him, the "ultimate goal of state behaviour, and its core 'value', is assumed to be the securing of the state itself against anything that may threaten its existence or integrity".

Relevantly, Lawson[3] refers to the United Nations Human Development Report (1994) which talks about a more specific list of seven security concerns: (1) economic security, (2) food security, (3) environmental security, (4) personal security, (5) community security, (6) health security and (7) political security.

True, there seems to be a general consensus among the authors and analysts of International Relations that there can be no such thing as "absolute" security, and it is always a question of "more or less" But states have been conscious of, and concerned about, their security in various ways and degrees. The tragicomedy is that even a relatively regionally strong state like India has to be concerned about its security in the region because of the existing regional and international milieu.

After all, it was forced into intra-regional wars on a number of occasions. And the states of Bangladesh, Bhutan and Nepal—of course, in varying degrees and manners—cannot be taken away from the calculations of India's security concerns. Needless to stress, various other dimensions of foreign relations are, and would be, based on such calculations.

Going back once again to the speech of the Foreign Secretary, which is being viewed by many as a new doctrine vis-a-vis neighbours, one comes across some more significant points. In his presentation, Saran also stated that some members of the South Asian Association for Regional Cooperation (these three eastern South Asian states are also its members) "actively seek association with countries outside the region or with regional or international organizations, in a barely disguised effort to "counterbalance" India within the Association or to project SAARC as some kind of a regional dispute settlement mechanism."[4]

In yet another interesting and remarkable observation, the Foreign Secretary stated: "The challenge for our diplomacy lies in convincing our neighbours that India is an opportunity not a threat, that far from being besieged by India, they have a vast productive hinterland that would give their economies far greater opportunities for growth than if they were to rely on their domestic markets alone."[5]

The Three States and India

India's relations with Bangladesh, Bhutan and Nepal in the 21st century cannot be seen in a vacuum or in isolation. India has been closely associated with each of them in the past. It was very largely responsible for making Bangladesh a sovereign independent—the newest in South Asia—state in 1971, and has made significant contributions in its economic development. But of late several factors have raised questions about the state of Bangladesh-India relations.

India has maintained continuous and close relations with the two eastern Himalayan and landlocked states of Bhutan and Nepal since the pre-colonial days. In the post-colonial phase, too, India, Bhutan and Nepal have been maintaining some kind of "special" ties (which we would examine in the follwing paragraphs), through the "special" ties are, at times, resented by some elements. But a variety of factors keep Bhutan and Nepal coming closer to India. Of course, peculiar circumstances, at times, make Indo-Nepal ties rather sour. The people-to-people relations, though, become much stronger under such circumstances. Bhutan-India ties, though, stand out of all the bilateral ties in question here, they have proved to be most constant and bilaterally beneficial.

Indo-Bangladesh Relations

The border between Bangladesh and India (4,100 km) is the largest in size in comparison to India's border with any of its neighbours. Myanmar is the only other neighbour of Bangladesh apart from India. The Indian states of West Bengal, Assam, Meghalaya, Tripura and Mizoram border this newest South Asian country. By helping the then East Pakistan emerge as a sovereign independent state based on linguistic nationalism and, to a very great extent, secularism, India and analysts had justifiably thought that the relations between the two would be friendly, cooperative and mutually beneficial.

In fact, the first constitution of Bangladesh promulgated on December 16, 1972—which still remains operational with several amendments—talked about "secularism" along with "nationalism", "socialism" and "democracy" as one of the four "fundamental principles of state policy" (Article 8). In fact, the Bangladesh constitution had incorporated the principle of secularism much before India did it through an amendment to its Constitution's preamble in 1976.

On the other hand, the 12-Article "Treaty of Friendship, Cooperation and Peace between India and Bangladesh" signed by Indian and Bangladesh Prime Ministers Indira Gandhi and Sheikh Mujibur Rahman, at Dhaka on March 19, 1972 established the foundation of a special and mutually beneficial friendly ties between the two. The treaty talked about transforming the border into "a border of eternal peace and friendship". One could see for oneself the wide gulf between the desire of the treaty signatories and the existing reality of the present day.

Not less significantly, the treaty had also talked about continuous strengthening and widening their "mutually advantageous and all-round cooperation in the economic and scientific fields". The two states had also undertaken to develop "mutual cooperation in the fields of trade, transport and communications between them on the basis of the principles of equality, mutual benefit and the most favoured nation principle" (See Article 5). The two parties had also promised not to allow "the use of its territory for committing any act that may cause military damage to constitute a threat to the security of the other High Contracting Party" (Article 8).

Things changed for worse soon both in national political structure in Bangladesh and bilateral ties. Sheikh Mujibur Rahman, known as the Father of the Nation, was assassinated on August 15, 1975 and fundamentalist forces got more entrenched in the country's politics and polity. The Proclamation Order No. 8 of 1977 removed "secularism" from the Constitution and substituted it by "Absolute trust and faith in the Almighty Allah" as the basis of all actions. The 8th constitutional amendment effected on June 7, 1988 made "Islam" the "State Religion of the Republic".

The provisions of the treaty that we discussed above also became infructuous in March 1997 on the completion of 25 years. Originally signed for 25 years, the treaty was subject to renewal. The existing domestic politics precluded Prime Minister Sheikh Hasina Wajed, considered close to India, from taking interest in its renewal. And, today various factors are making relations between India and Bangladesh less and less friendly and more and more tense. Indian diplomacy, indeed, is under severe strain in dealing with Bangladesh. Things have only worsened after the October 2001 general elections.

Bangladesh has, for a relatively long time now allowed on its territory the camps of various terrorist organizations of India's Northeast. Such groups include the United Liberation Front of Asom, The NSCN(IM) and the National Democratic Front of Bodoland. India's Border Security Force (BSF) handed over a list of 78 militant camps operating from Bangladesh to the Bangladesh Rifles (BDR) on October 23, 2003 during their meeting in Shillong.[6]

According to the Indian government's estimates, at present there are 99 camps of northeastern insurgents operating from Bangladesh and 88 insurgent camps are housed in different parts of the country.[7] Such groups are not only creating serious security problems for India, but they are now even getting training in Pakistan in sophisticated explosive devices.[8]

Bangladesh has been consistently and emphatically denied the existence of any such camp in its territory. Of course, the arrest of ULFA leader Anup Chetia in Dhaka in the 1990s makes abundantly clear the proof of Indian militants' presence in the country. Such things have not only adversely affected India's security but has also made Bangladesh's ties with India tense. The refusal of Indian Prime Minister Manmohan Singh to visit Dhaka 14 February 2005 to participate in the 13th SAARC summit citing the security situation in Bangladesh as a reason only underlines the increasing bilateral tension on this front. Bangladesh's non-responsive attitude to India's sensitive concerns has made matter only worse.

The problem of illegal immigration from Bangladesh to India and the former's emphatic denial of any such happening has only contributed to increasing tension. It is estimated that about 15 to 20 million illegal Bangladeshis are living in several states of India and posing a serious threat to India's national security. J.R. Mukherjee (2005: 8) is of the view that "Bangladesh also continued with the pre-partition strategy of the Muslim League, and subsequently of Pakistan, to ensure maximum migration into the North-East and Bengal so that, after demographic change, these states would secede to Bangladesh".

True, these two are issues of serious significance and consequence adversely affecting bilateral ties, but there are several other issues that too hugely contribute to relation deterioration and bilateral tension. For instance, though only 6.5 km out of 4,100 km remains undemarcated, it adds to various tensions between the two. The killing of 16 BSF personnel in April 2001 is one such example. On December 12, 1996, the two countries signed a treaty on Ganges Waters for a period of 30 years. New Disputes have emerged in recent times. Bangladesh has been non-cooperative on the front of providing trans-shipment facility to provide movements of goods to and from the landlocked northeastern Indian states. Indeed, Bangladesh Foreign Minister M. Morshed Khan prides himself on harping that India should not forget that India's northeast is Bangladesh-locked.

India, it is true, has been able to maintain good relations with Bangladesh when the country had the governments of the Awami League under Sheikh Mujibur Rahman (1972-75) and Sheikh Hasina Wajed (1996-2001). During the military rule and the rule of the Bangladesh Nationalist Party it has faced problems. The 21st century shows the signs of being full of challenges for Indian diplomacy in Bangladesh.

Indo-Bhutan Relations

Bhutan does not have a very long border with India; it is only 660 km long. But the importance of this landlocked Himalayan Buddhist kingdom remains immense for India's security and foreign policy. On the one hand, Bhutan is sandwiched between the two Asian giants—China and India; on the other, the mountain kingdom is, to a very great extent India-locked inasmuch as it is surrounded by India in the south, east and west. It is bordered by China in the north, thanks to the takeover of Tibet by the Communist state in the early 1950s.

Bhutan is the only South Asian state, besides India, which has not been able to solve its border problems with China though 17 rounds of boundary demarcation talks have gone on between the two since 1984.

Bhutan is the second smallest South Asian state in terms of territory (46,500 sq. km) and population (about 0.6 m), next only to Maldives, but India's four states—Sikkim, West Bengal, Assam and Arunachal Pradesh—border it, making it a very crucial subject for Indian foreign policymakers and security managers.

It would be no exaggeration to suggest that the small kingdom has shown an incomparable concern for India's security thus far. When several Indian terrorist outfits found a safe haven in Bhutan in the late 1990s and established their camps there, the Royal Government of Bhutan lost no time in acknowledging their presence—without indulging in any rhetoric, as other neighbours do. True, it avoided the terrorists' forcible eviction forthwith because of the safety and security concerns of its citizens, who frequent India's Assam and West Bengal for a variety of socio-economic reasons, but from the outset it tried to persuade these terrorists to leave the kingdom.

When it came to the crunch. His Majesty King Jigme Singye Wangchuck himself and his son led the Royal Bhutanese Army in the forcible exit of the terrorists and dismantling their camps in December 2003. In truth, the threat of danger to the personal security of the King and other royals still looms large because of that exemplary historic step. A grateful India, lost no time in acknowledging Bhutan's memorable help on this front.

Speaking at the 12th SAARC summit of the heads of state or Government in Islamabad on January 4, 2004, Indian Prime Minister Atal Behari Vajpayee said: "In this context, I would like to draw attention to the courageous action taken by his Majesty the King of Bhutan and his government against the insurgent groups, which were trying to use Bhutanese territory to launch terrorist activities in India. It is an outstanding example of sensitivity to the security concerns of a neighbour, which is at the same time in the direct long-term security interest of Bhutan itself".[9]

Bhutan's King Jigme Singye Wangchuck, ever since his accession to the throne in 1972, has been taking a keen interest in positively and productively strengthening his kingdom's ties with India. In an exclusive personal interview to me as early as October 21, 1991 at the Thimphu's Tashichho Dzong (the central secretariat of the Royal Government of Bhutan) his Majesty said: "India is our closest friend and neighbour. The foundation of Indo-Bhutan relations was laid by Pandit Jawaharlal Nehru and my father, Jigme Dorji Wangchuck, in the 1950. Since then Indo-Bhutan friendship has grown and flourished."

Indo-Bhutan relations today provide an excellent example of how a large country like India and a small neighbour like Bhutan can coexist in perfect peace, harmony and friendship based on mutual trust, understanding and cooperation.[10]

As time has progressed, Indio-Bhutan ties have only become stronger and more mutually beneficial. Bhutan has very fruitfully and beneficially integrated its economy with that of India. The two have established a free trade area. Indian currency is a legal tender in Bhutan, along with its own Nugultrum, for decades. Bhutan's economy has only become more vibrant after it began collabourating with India in hydropower generation in the 1980s and the scope for more ventures on this front is galore. Indeed, after some further cooperation on this front, Bhutan's economy is likely to become self-reliant.

On the legal front, the bilateral ties are governed by the 10-Article Treaty between India and Bhutan signed in Darjeeling on August 9, 1949. While this treaty does no talk anywhere of the kingdom's sovereignty, Article 2 thereof states: "The Government of India undertakes to exercise no interference in the internal administration of Bhutan. On its part, the Government of Bhutan agrees to be guided by the advice of the Government of India in regard to its external relations".

This particular provision is being resented, of course, thus far *sotto voce*, by various young elements in Bhutan. Some Indians, too, wish this Article to be suitably amended or ended. Several things, though, are quite obvious. This Article has almost become a dead letter. And notwithstanding the status of Bhutan's sovereignty in the Treaty, India has constantly upgraded Bhutan's international status. Indeed, India never hesitated in making the mountain kingdom a member of the United Nations. Today, it is a full-fledge member of various regional and global organizations like the SAARC, the BIMSTEC, the Colombo Plan, the UNO, the WTO and the NAM et al.

In the 21st century, there is every indication of Bhutan and India playing more and more cooperative a role in foreign affairs—both regional and global. There togetherness in foreign and security affairs should become a role model for other countries in the region and outside. India, in March 2005, decided to double the strength of the Sashatra Seema Bal (SSB) on the Indo-Bhutan border along with that on the Indo-Nepal border. This should take care of the problems of security that might surface in the future. Bhutan is one country which has never played the China card with India. On its part, India has always been sensitive to Bhutan's urges and aspirations in various fields.

One hopes this continues in the 21st century, notwithstanding various changes that would occur on various fronts. King Jigme Singye Wangchuck, the Crown Prince, His Royal Highness Dasho Jigme Khesar Namgyal Wangchuck, and the Ministers of the Royal Government of Bhutan have constantly realized the importance of India in Bhutan's all-round development and security. India, on its parts has never failed in realizing the kingdom's importance in its foreign policy. It was not for nothing that King Jigme Singye Wangchuck thus far has become the Chief Guest at the Republic Day celebrations in New Delhi twice. The 21st century, in all probability would make the Indo-Bhutan friendship more meaningful, where the problem of security on Indo-Bhutan border would become less serious.

Indo-Nepal Relations

Indo-Nepal border is 1,750 km long and, like Bhutan, Nepal is also a landlocked state. Indeed, like Bhutan, Nepal, too, is an India-locked state inasmuch as it borders the South Asian core state in the south, east and west. China borders Nepal in the north, as it does in the case of Bhutan. In other words, Nepal, too is sandwiched between the two Asian giants. It is altogether a different matter that this geographical state has helped the non-democratic governing elite of Nepal on several occasions. And Nepal's non-democratic governing elite, in particular, have never hesitated to take advantage of this situation by playing the China card.

There have been so many similarities on the social, cultural, religious, ethnic, linguistic and economic planes between these two South Asian states that many observers tend to conclude from time to time that there are many Nepals in miniature in India and vice versa. Open borders between the two and unrestricted travels on the ground have only contributed to unique people-to-people relations between the citizens of the two countries. Indeed, these facilities and similarities have witnessed a large number of matrimonial alliances between the Nepali and Indian people since times immemorial.

The 10-Article Treaty of Peace and Friendship signed between India and Nepal on July 31, 1950, in Kathmandu—which remains the legal and formal basis of relationships between the two states and governments has only created some kind of special ties between them. Article 6 of the Treaty says: "Each Government undertakes, in token of neighbourly friendship between India and Nepal, to give to the nationals of the other, in its territory, national treatment with regard to participation in industrial and economic development of such territory and to the grant of concessions and contracts relating to such development".

Article 7 of the 1950 Treaty states: "The Governments of India and Nepal agree to grant, on a reciprocal basis, to the nationals of one country in the territories of the other the same privileges in the matter of residence, ownership of property, participation in trade and commerce, movement and other privileges of a similar nature".

Indeed Article 2 of the Treaty establishes special security relationship between the two countries by stating: "The two governments hereby undertake to inform each other of any serious friction or misunderstanding with any neighbouring state likely to cause any breach in the friendly relations subsisting between the two

Governments".

Various similarities and various backgrounds should have normally brought the two governments immensely close to each other resulting in very positive and fruitful cooperation on a variety of planes. Unfortunately, this does not happen most of the time. It is widely believed and stated that there are so many similarities that some difference from India alone give Nepal a sense of independence. Many observers of Indo-Nepal relations also tend to believe that since the days of the 9th Shah, King Mahendra Bir Bikram Shahdev (1955-72), nationalism and patriotism in Nepal are believed to be based on anti-Indianism. With the passage of time this trend, if anything, has only got strengthened. It is altogether a different matter that King Mahendra's father and predecessor, the 8th Shah, King Tribhuvan Bir Bikram Shahdev (1911-55) had begun an era of special ties with India.

What has been happening since February 1, 2005—and one does not know for certain how long would it last—has only generated tension in the Indo-Nepal ties. This time round, Nepal is not only playing the China card, but seems eager to play any card that embarrasses India. The purpose of the present governing elite under the proactive leadership of King Gyanendra Bir Bikram Shahdev seems to concentrate more and more powers and throttle democracy in every possible manner. The state of Nepal has presently got the alibi of the menace of Maoist terrorism to make itself a garrison state by accumulating all kinds of arms and ammunition.

Nepal wishes that India should be constantly concerned about its security without bothering much about any reciprocity. Even the provisions of the 1950 Treaty expect Nepal to do much more on that front. Besides, India's closeness with democratic political elements in Nepal naturally impels the Indian government and people to sympathize with them to promote democracy in the kingdom. The governing elite would like to be left free and alone in the name of internal affairs. It forgets conveniently India's role in 1950-51 in rescuing monarchy from the clutches of the then Rana rulers (1846-1951).

Worse, even democratic governments in Nepal have not been very willing to cooperate for overall socio-economic bilateral progress. They, too, seem to be thinking most of the time that some degree of anti-Indianism is a must. Besides, there is often inter-party scramble for playing to the gallery in the name of anti-Indianism or sham nationalism. All this, in truth, creates a vicious circle and a Catch-22 situation. This nitty-gritty of state-to-state and government-to-government relations leaves much to be desired. Playing to the gallery has harmed Nepal immensely.

In the 21st century India has got to be very careful on the front of the state-to-state diplomacy and relationships. "Give and take" cannot and should not mean that India gives and Nepal takes. Nepal's hydroelectric power potential is second in the world—next only to Brazil. Nepal, according to authentic and undisputed statistics, can generate power to the tune of 83 m. kilowatts. It would, whenever the potential is realized (if at all it is allowed to be realized), change the mountain kingdom's economic profile for the better and beyond recognition. But the big question is: whether Nepal's concern over its "nationalism" and "sovereignty" would allow it to think of its own advantage. It may do well to learn from Bhutan on this front.

So far the Mahakali Treaty—signed between India and Nepal in 1996 and ratified in the same year remains a non-starter. Nepal has, on the other hand, often shown less interest in combating the activities of Pakistan's ISI in its territory aimed at harming India's physical and economic security.

It is not being suggested here that India must be in the right in all its dealings with Nepal. But it seems that the former has been more transparent and willing to help Nepal's economic growth. It is time for all kinds of political elite in Nepal to realize that the days of adhocism in relations with India are over. On its parts, India has tried to have an enlightened and well-meaning policy towards Nepal for a long time now.[11]

Conclusion

Politics—whether national, regional or international—is the art of the possible. But it is also the choice between the disastrous and the unpalatable. There is no point in expecting the existence of an ideal situation in politics: otherwise the "power politics" school of thought or "realism" would not have assumed so much of importance or acceptance in International Relations.

Its size, its population and other available resources have made India capable of helping its three neighbours in question in a variety of ways. Of course, the three neighbours have their significant use, too. But Bangladesh and Nepal have got to show their willingness. And before that India has to be more careful in conducting its foreign policy vis-à-vis them.

The beginning of the 21st century and the new millennium does not appear to be generating much optimism. However, politics is always pregnant with all kinds of positive potentialities. Bertrand Russell, by all accounts the greatest philosopher of the 20th century has (1961: 120) rightly observed "...while hope is possible, despair is a coward's part".

In any case, India has to be very careful in maintaining her security and national interests. At the time of writing India seems to be doing well. The policy-makers and decision-makers of India's foreign relations need not be blinded by the pleasant or convenient past of any bilateral relations—or for that matter existing numerous similarities on the socio-cultural fronts in the present.

India's security, integrity and sovereignty must always of primary concern and considerations. None of the three neighbours in question should take India for granted: nor should India waver in showing reciprocity. But now, it has been proved beyond doubt that any relationship based on sentimentalism and emotionalism per se has not been very enduring and beneficial. Maybe in the new century and millennium, India, Bangladesh, Bhutan, and Nepal give a fresh and serious thought to their relationships making them more positive and productive.

References

1. *Strategic Digest*: New Delhi, Vol. 35: No. 3, March 2005 : 286.
2. See *Ibid.*, 284.
3. *Ibid.*, p. 90.
4. *Strategic Digest*, Vol. 35, No. 3, March 2005 : 284.
5. *Ibid.*, : 285.
6. Anand Kumar, 2003 : 32.
7. Sreeradha Datta, 2003 : 190.
8. "Bangla bogey: Envoy's contention skewered", ed., *The Statesman*, New Delhi, March 28, p. 8.
9. *Strategic Analysis*, Vol. 34, No. 2, February 2004 : 113.
10. Parmanand, 1992 : 236.
11. For an update, see Parmanand, 2005 a&b.

Sreeradha Datta, 2003, "India and Bangladesh: The Border Issue", *Himalayan and Central Asian Studies*, New Delhi, Vol. 7, Nos. 3-4, July-December, pp. 177-95.

Graham Evans and Jaffrey Newnham, 1998, *The Penguin Dictionary of International Relations*, London: Penguin.

Martin Griffiths and Terry O'Callaghan, 2004, *Key Concepts in International Relations*, London: Routledge.

Anand Kumar, 2003, "Indo-Bangladesh Relations", *Himalayan and Central Asian Studies*, Vol. 7, Nos. 3-4, July-December, 29-40.

Stephanie Lawson, 2003: *International Relations*, Oxford: Polity. J.R. Mukherjee, 2005: "North-East In Retrospect", *The Sunday Statesman*, New Delhi, March 27, p. 8.

Parmanand, 1992, *The Politics of Bhutan: Retrospect and Prospect*, Delhi, Pragati.

Parmanand, 2005: "Nepal and the World-I: International Community Becomes Active", *The Statesman*, New Delhi, March 7, p. 8.

Parmanand, 2005, "Nepal and The World-II: Following Pressure, The King Will Do Well To retrace His Steps", *Ibid.*, March 8.

Bertrand Russell, 1961, *Has Man A Future?*, London, Penguin.

21

The Crisis in Nepal

Dr. Sita Kaushik

The recent developments in Nepal are of concern not only to the people of Nepal but to India as well. King Gyanendra's decision to suppress the democratic forces by imposing emergency and taking powers in his hands is condemnable to say the least. The democratic forces were working within their rights and under the overall supervision of the King. They have never opposed the Kingship. It seems, King Gyanendra was having his own planned time-table to grab the power and rule the country as an absolute dictator. As a constitutional head and a head of the state of a nascent democracy of Nepal, he should not follow those states who are prone to military coup. It is unfortunate that the King of Nepal took this decision under the pretext that the democratic government of Nepal was unable to suppress the Maoists. There is no better way to fight the Maoists except by bringing them into the political mainstream. The government of Deuba was only doing that. Like other Communist parties they can be persuaded to join the political process and fight elections on equal level, though it may take time. Suppression of all democratic rights and banning of all political parties in the name of saving the country to get rid of Maoist menace is not the solution of the woes of Nepalese people. What is needed is a stable government which represents the will and aspirations of the people and work for the economic, political and social development.

A country of less than 30 million population, receiving aid and assistance from innumerable sources including the UN and its agencies, US, European countries, China, Pakistan and India, remains one of the least developed among the developing countries till today. King Mahendra and King Birendra had ruled the country as sole authority of power almost for half a century, yet the level of development reached nowhere. Given the will and determination on the part of authorities to develop Nepal, it would not have been difficult and the situation would not have been like the one which is prevailing at this time. Authoritarianism is not a penacea, if it is not a part of an ideology which calls for the development and welfare of the people by equitable distribution of fruits of development.

On February 1, 2005, King Gyanendra took powers of governance in his own hands by imposing emergency and finished the democratic rights of the people of Nepal. But it is not the end of the democratic forces of Nepal. They will challenge the king at the right moment. The unfinished task of democratic revolution of 1950-51 of Nepal will have to be carried now. (I say this because from 1951 to 1959 elections did not take place in Nepal. Initially King Tribhuvan and after him King Mahendra ruled the country by appointing the Prime Ministers on their whims. Essentially the first general election took place in 1959 and within 18 months, i.e., on 15th December 1960 Royal coup took place. King Mahendra took absolute powers in his own hands. The democratically elected government was dismissed and emergency was declared. After a long struggle, democracy was restored in 90's. Now again the experiment is being repeated. That is why I say it is the unfinished task.)

But now the situation is quite different. That time King Tribhuvan himself was leading the democratic movement against the Rana regime. Today his grandson King Gyanendra is suppressing the democratic forces. The declaration of state of emergency on February 1st of this year has once again put Nepal in the dark. True there are insurgents in Nepal, but they can be controlled by the state power within the constitutional framework. It does not require emergency to be imposed and suspend all democratic rights of the people. If some external help is required there are democratic countries like the US, India etc. who are prepared to help, provided there is request from the present government of Nepal. Now the problem is that such a request is not likely to come from the present government. That is the dilemma. The essential problem is how to restore democracy in Nepal without the help of the people there. The people of Nepal will not like to be suppressed for ever. They will come out and seek help from neighbouring countries.

India can be a willing partner for restoration of democracy as well as for cracking down Maoism provided a request comes from the Nepalese side. However the King does not want to talk to India.

Because he knows that India will always be with democratic forces and not with him, formalities apart. Actually, King Gyanendra had rebuffed every Indian effort to persuade him to rope in the political parties to counter the Maoist offensive in the country. India suspected, rightly as it turned out, that the only reason why the monarch wished to come to New Delhi in December-January 2005 was to seek an Indian endorsement for his move to jettison democracy as it existed in Nepal. This alone explains why the visit had to be postponed thrice in a row.

It seems King Gyanendra has some sort of aversion towards India since his childhood because of India's refusal to recognize him as King in 1950-51. This alone explains unlike King Birendra, Gyanendra is always known for his reported hardline views on India related issues.

He was in the midst of a controversy when the Gorkhaland movement set the Darjeeling hills on fire in 1986-88. The West Bengal police held him responsible for fomenting trouble from across the border.

In 1989, he and late Queen Aishwarya were suspected of turning King Birendra against India after the lapse of the Trade and Transit Treaties between the two countries that led to the closure of 22 entry points to Nepal. This caused tremendous hardship to the Nepalese people who finally started a movement for democracy in 1990 that ultimately clipped most of the palace powers.

Therefore 1st February coup was not an altogether unexpected development however, unwelcome it might be to the democratic forces in Nepal or to the well-wishers of Nepali people in the rest of the world. Democracy which means the will of the people comes from within the calling of the people and that needs education, social and economic development and awareness which is still lacking in Nepal. Dictators all over the world have tried to see that the populace do not become aware of their rights. Those who did were overthrown by the people. That is the basic principle. But the people of Nepal have already enjoyed the fruits of democracy and their basic freedom. What the King is doing now is denying them their rights of which they have already become generally conscious. And, therefore, to put a cap on such a cauldron is a dangerous decision of the monarchy. How long can people suffer the deprivation of their rights only time will tell. But it is certain that the King cannot suppress the movement once it has taken shape.

This development shows how states can often be hell-bent on destroying themselves. The conduct of Nepal's monarchy is another example or illustration of this phenomenon. King Gyanendra suspended civil liberties and the modicum of democracy that existed in Nepal on the pretext of saving it from Maoists and ineffectual politicians. He was hoping that this would create enough ambivalence in the international community, in particular in India, to enable him to get away with his stratagem. After all, the prospect of Maoist take over in Nepal makes most governments nervous. If the choice was posed as one between Maoists and the King, the King would win.

Although the international community has asked the King to restore democracy, it is fair to say that it has not acted decisively enough to compel the King to do so. India should have sent strong signals to the King right from the beginning. Instead, it has only now taken a firm position, but what it will do on the ground remains unclear.

To be frank, crisis in Nepal has brought home India's limitations as a major power. Not only did the King blatantly ignore India's advice and concerns, the timing of the dismissal was designed to cause maximum embarrassment to India. But even more importantly, it has exposed how limited India's options are when it comes to dealing with its neighbours. A great power ought to be loved or feared or both. But India does not offer carrots that are attractive enough for its neighbours to love, nor its stick is strong enough for them to fear her. We yet again helplessly watch Nepal drift by. We do not appear to have the military capabilities to transplant democracy or bring the Maoists to heel. Nor do we have other forms of soft power to greatly influence the outcome. We once again are left to pick up the pieces.

Similarly, India do not have enough incentives to offer to make the regimes in Bangladesh more accommodating. On the other hand the threat of force seems at best, empty.

With the SAARC again we are caught in the middle. There may be good reasons to have postponed the summit in Dhaka, but it is difficult to escape the impression that once again we have not been strong enough to read out the act of our neighbours in public. Denying the King a photo-op, or avoiding going to Dhaka in the middle of an Awami League protest against the assassination of a former finance minister may have been sound good reasons to cancel the Summit, but then we should not have been shy to come out openly, instead of giving the excuses like the security concerns in Bangladesh or the crisis in Nepal. Some might think such a stance to be arrogant which is either our humility or incapacity.

To be fair to India, we are surrounded by regimes that are so determined to undermine the welfare of their own people that they do not respond to normal incentives. One is reminded of a Chinese saying that some people pick up rocks to crush their own feet. The actions of the regimes in India's neighbourhood have this quality. Nepal would rather stop development than listen to India. Bangladesh would rather impoverish itself than trade energy with us. Pakistan remains too uncertain about its identity to think long-term. This makes it more difficult for India to offer the usual incentives that countries respond to.

One might think India's relative weakness comes from its reluctance to use force. But the question is whether we have the relative capability to successfully deploy force against our neighbours even if we wanted to. Experience shows that our options on the use of force are limited and the truth is that no nation is feared, unless it has the capacity to use overwhelming force.

Often weak states are capable of creating havoc enough for strong ones. They can partly do this by playing other powers against each other, as Nepal keeps on playing China card or Pakistan card.

China has been largely silent on the developments in Nepal. China has said that "the Nepalese Maovadis have nothing to do with them. To deal with Maoists in Nepal is the internal matter of Nepal". India should not take it on its face value. The Chinese premiere Wen Jiabao visited India on 9th April for four days. This visit gave India-China ties a strategic dimension and also imparted bilateral ties with the mature understanding that the "two Asian emerging superpowers" can grow together instead of being rivals—that there is a lot to learn from each other. Not only this, even Chinese President Hu Jintao is likely to visit India this year.

In the light of Pakistan's open offer to supply arms to Kathmandu, India is reviewing its military assistance to Nepal and wants to keep its options open. In the first week of March 2005 Pakistan's Ambassador to Nepal Jameer Akram announced that Islamabad would be happy to meet Nepal's defence needs. Pakistan has been waiting to fish in Nepal's troubled waters. It seems for Gyanendra any country who is against India is the closest friend. He is playing a dangerous game, and it may not be helpful to him in the end.

Inspite of the earlier decision to stop military supplies to Nepal following the February 1st coup, India is now all set to lift the measures in view of its possible implication for national security. Undoubtedly, Maoist menace is India's biggest security threat. Prime Minister Manmohan Singh told Parliament on 5th March 2005 that 170 districts of India were under Naxal influence. Home Minister Shiv Raj Patil stated in the Parliament that the outlawed KLO in the North East was developing links with the Nepalese Maoists and ULFA. Naxal violence is a great threat to internal security, Indian Army is now going to conduct a crackdown operation along the emerging Naxal corridor from Andhra Pradesh to Bihar and onto the forested Himalayan foothills of Nepal.

It seems Indo-Nepalese crisis has added to the quality of Indo-US dialogue. Donald Camp, US Deputy Assistant Secretary of State for South Asia told a Congressional Committee on 2nd March 2005 while making a case for a budget request that India was the "preeminent power in the region" with whom, US was "consulting closely" on ways to help Nepal resolve its political crisis. It is said that "not a day passes without a meeting between senior Indian and US officials either at Kathmandu, New Delhi or Washington to exchange notes on the situation. Though the US has not taken any public posture on the suspension of the $ 2 million security assistance to Nepal since 1st February 2005 emergency, yet no US military supply has reached Nepal. America's position on Nepal crisis is based on three broad objectives:

(i) King Gyanendra needs to move quickly to reinstate and protect civil and human rights.

(ii) Release those detained under the state of emergency.

(iii) Begin dialogue with political parties intended to restore multiparty democratic institutions under constitutional monarchy.

Let us discuss a brief history of Nepal's democratic movement. The revolution of 1950-51 was epoch making event in the life of the country. The democratic experiment in Nepal has suffered many a setback. Each time it has been able to face the problem and has won. In December 1960, King Mahendra dismissed B.P. Koirala's elected government and established Panchayati Raj System; the system of government more suitable to "the genius of my people". In the words of Rishikesh Shah, King Mahendra's partyless Panchayati Raj was "in practice means of exploiting, under the garb of tutelary democracy, the age old Nepali tradition of unquestioned obedience to autocratic authority of any kind". The three-decade-long experience of "partyless democracy" in fact destroyed whatever little possibility there was for development of a democratic culture in Nepali polity. The partyless Panchayat system came to a sudden end in the early months of 1990 after an escalating political protest, that led the decision by King Birendra to allow the reestablishment of multiparty democracy. A new constitution was enacted and a new hope sprang in many hearts that

Nepali polity had got a second chance to evolve into a parliamentary multiparty democracy with a constitutional monarch as head of the state, "acting as a friend, philosopher and guide to the politicians and as a father figure to his people".

But leaders of almost all political parties squandered away their second chance and the monarch could not resist the temptation of playing parties against each other in the hope that ultimately he could get back the power he had lost to the upsurge of popular will. A glance at the political developments in Nepal since the lifting of the ban on political parties by King Birendra in April 1990 will testify the above statement.

On April 16, 1990 he appointed an interim government paving the way for major political reforms. It led to multiparty parliamentary system with King as the constitutional monarch. Krishna Prasad Bhattarai was appointed Prime Minister who was to head an interim cabinet representing Nepali Congress, United Left Front (ULF) and King's nominees. By November 1990, i.e., on 9th November. King proclaimed a new constitution establishing a multiparty democracy under a constitutional monarchy. Nepal's first free election since 1959 was held in May 1991 and Congress party came out with clear majority. Girija Prasad Koirala became the first popularly elected Prime Minister after 30 years. 18 months before the schedule, i.e., on 11th July 1994, King Birendra had to dissolve the Parliament as Koirala lost the vote of confidence on the floor of the house because of squabbling in the party.

In November 1994 another general election took place. The Communist United Marxist Leninist (UML) won most of the seats but failed to gain an outright majority. UML Chief Manmohan Adhikari was appointed first elected Communist Prime Minister at the head of a minority government on November 29, 1994. Even before the completion of one year, he had to resign as he lost the vote of confidence, i.e., on September 10, 1995. Next day Sher Bahadur Deuba of the Nepali Congress was appointed Prime Minister to lead a coalition government in alliance with the formerly royalist Rashtriya Prajatantra Party (RPP) and Nepal Sadbhavana Party (NSP). It did not last long. By March 6, 1997 Deuba had to resign as he lost the confidence motion.

On March 10, 1997 RPP's leader Lokendra Bahadur Chand was appointed as the Prime Minister to head a coalition with UML and NSP. Within six months, i.e., on October 4, 1997 Lokendra Bahadur Chand was voted out. On 6th October 1997 RPP Chief Surya Bahadur

Thapa became the Prime Minister with the support of Nepali Congress. On January 8, 1998 Thapa recommended the dissolution of Parliament fearing opposition move to topple him. The dissolution did not take place. Thapa resigned in a pact with Nepali Congress on 10th April 1998 and on 12th April Nepali Congress leader G.P. Koirala was appointed as Prime Minister of a minority government. To make his position strong Koirala inducted Communist Marxist Leninist party members into his cabinet on August 26, 1998. On December 10, 1998, the Communist Marxist-Leninist party left the cabinet accusing Koirala of violating the power sharing agreement. Then Koirala resigned on December 21, 1998. He was reappointed as Prime Minister to head a coalition with the UML and NSP on December 23, 1998.

On January 15, 1999 King Birendera dissolved the Parliament. Elections took place in May 1999. Voters went to poll amid tight security and unrest because of Maoist rebels fighting for one party communist republic. On 29th May 1999 second time Krishna Prasad Bhattarai was appointed as Prime Minister of Nepal as the Congress party got the majority. This was the ninth time that King Birendra had appointed Prime Ministers since April 1990 (and six persons had intermittently taken the chair). Before the completion of one year again K.P. Bhattarai had to resign as Prime Minister, because on 14th March 2000 a petition signed by sixty-nine members of Parliament of Nepali Congress presented a memorandum calling Bhattarai to step down, saying that he failed to deliver on election promises. After Bhattarai's resignation on 16th March, G.P. Koirala was appointed as Prime Minister on 20th March 2000, i.e., 4th time he became Prime Minister in nine years. He was Prime Minister as well as elected President of Nepali Congress. On November 9, 2000 dissident Nepali Congress leader Sher Bahadur Deuba said he would challenge Koirala for party presidency. Again on December 28, 56 rebel Nepali Congress leaders signed a petition seeking to replace Koirala saying he failed to keep election promises to stamp out corruption and Maoist revolt in which more than 1670 people had died since 1996. By January 2001 Koirala managed to win the vote of confidence and also succeeded in getting elected as President of the party for the second time. After the palace shoot out of June 2001, Koirala was replaced with Deuba by King Gyanendra. But within no time Deuba was sacked (i.e., on 4th October 2002) by King Gyanendra accusing him of not being able to provide effective governance.

This time while dismissing Deuba on 1st February 2005, King Gyanendra charged him with having failed "to make necessary arrangements to hold elections by 2005 and to protect democracy, sovereignty of the people and life and property". This is not the first time Deuba has been removed from office by King Gyanendra. But the difference is that then Deuba was accused of having failed to provide effective governance, but now the sovereignty of people and life and property of the country as well as not being able to conduct election by April 2005 at the height of Maoist menace was given the main reason for his removal as well as for taking all powers in his own hands.

Let us discuss in brief the problem of Maoism in Nepal, how it came up and who are its ideologues and what is its agenda. The movement started in Jhapa in the far-eastern Terai region of Nepal and was the direct fall out of West Bengal's Naxalbari movement of the late 60's. When democracy was restored in 1990s a group of extreme leftwingers in the Communist Party of Nepal (CPN) had formed a United People's Front (UPFN) and fought election in 1991. It emerged as the third largest group after the Nepali Congress and Communist Party of Nepal. The UPFN split up and two of its leaders led a group which called itself the Communist Party of Nepal (Maoists). It's main leaders are Baburam Bhattarai and Pushp Kumar Dahal, better known as Comrade Prachand. This group came out of the Parliamentary mainstream by 1995 and decided to take the path of armed revolution. In fact before 1996, Baburam Bhattarai made a last ditch attempt to join the mainstream politics when he presented a memorandum of 40 demands to the then Nepali Congress Prime Minister Sher Bahadur Deuba. Besides demanding the scrapping of the 1950 Indo-Nepal treaty, the memorandum demanded an end to monarchy by restricting the royal family's lavish life style and a switch through a constitutional amendment from a Hindu nation to a secular one. The government did not react, but the Maoists had their ready reply, i.e., on February 13, 1996 they struck simultaneously in seven districts; Rukum, Rolpa, Ramechap, Sindupalchok, Rhotang, Sinduli, Panchthar. These districts are seemingly so distant from governance and development that they have cradled the movement that is now the bane of the Nepali government; the dreaded shadowy Maoist uprising.

Factors like poverty, deprivation, bad governance and political instability have over the years helped the communists emerge as a formidable force. While the Maoists have launched fierce "People's War" since February 1996 to establish a republic, the CPN (ML), an aggressive mainline party, wants a national government comprising all parties including the Maoists, to frame a new constitution. The

UML, the largest Left faction, since April 15, 1999 took control of streets in Kathmandu and other major towns to press for the resignation of Prime Minister G.P. Koirala on grounds of corruption.

In the last 14 years, the Kingdom has seen more than a dozen governments established with the help of money power, political treachery and as stooge of the King. This has made a negative impact in popular consciousness about the credibility of democracy for which the people fought against the palace for 30 years. No matter how much the King and the Nepali Congress defend the existing system, a majority of the population in Nepal are in search for an alternative arrangement. This could be only through the democratic system.

What has frustrated the people even more is the fact that no government has sincerely tried to improve their lot, despite the abysmal conditions of human survival. The per capita income of Nepal is still not more than $ 200, one of the lowest in the world. The ceaseless pattern of migration to other countries for employment, especially to India, has remained the same as it was 160 years ago. The basic infrastructure of development for industry is still missing. The country is surviving on trade and smuggling and providing mercenaries to various countries.

Literacy figure comes around 25 to 30 per cent. Basic medical facilities and health care are almost negligible. The mortality rate of children below five in Nepal is quite high.

From 1996 onwards, the trigger happy Maovadis have been striking successfully in various parts of the country. In the initial phase the violent attacks were on petty landlords, greedy shopkeepers and small institutions holding public funds, such as local treasury, post offices and banks in the far-flung western zones of Kathmandu. Now it has engulfed more than 75 per cent of the district of Nepal. Insurgent Maoists have been successful in blockading access to Kathmandu Valley. Never before in their long history of underground movements the Reds were so confident about their strength as Maovadis are having these days. Today its "people's government" are found in various districts of western Nepal, where the police with their traditional guns could not venture out to face them. Definitely Nepalese need outside help to tackle this problem. India is the main country which can help but India will not do it unless request comes from Nepalese side. That is the problem of India and I think it is rightly so. After all interference in the internal affairs of a country with a traditional society like that of Nepal will not tolerate any external interference which is uncalled for by them. So the democratic forces of Nepal will have to come together once again to get what they want. Suppression by a monarch cannot be the justification for the suspension of all democratic rights of the people. After all the will of the people is supreme. How long the people will wait how long will they stay suppressed in their houses. I am sure the people of Nepal will get together to challenge the power of the monarch and that too very soon. Nepal is a conservative and traditional country. It is difficult for her to meet the challenges of the modern world. For Nepal, Maoism is just a problem of a few hard headed people in the country. To my mind it is a wider problem. In the UP, Bihar border the Maoists are sneaking through and are creating problems in India with the help of Indian Maoists. Indian state power can suppress them but it seems Nepalese state power is unable to suppress them. Given the seriousness of the problem, the democratic forces of Nepal would have suppressed them but the King made it an alibi for imposing the emergency and taking away the rights of the people. This is an unfortunate development which needs condemnation by the comity of nations. May I add the present situation in Nepal has created a difficult security problem for India. Let us hope India will rise to the occasion to look after its own security and in the process will look after the security problem of Nepal. It is because the threat of Maoism both in the underbelly of Nepal and adjoining border areas of UP and Bihar is great. It has to be tackled jointly rather than taking such unilateral action by the king of Nepal. The Nepalese government should have gained the confidence of Indian government to face the problem. Unfortunately it did not do so.

22

India's Policy in South East Asia

Dr. Udai Bhanu Singh

In the beginning of the present century Asia has seen a churning which could lead in time to a profound change in the manner in which nations conduct relations among themselves. India is making an attempt to reshape its relations with the countries to its east and is in turn being shaped by their aspirations and needs. Additionally there exists the influence of the international environment which is also in a state of continual change. In this dynamic situation it is still possible to identify the nation's objectives though they may be reassessed in the light of the interests of other states.

These national interests of various nations are concretized as objectives pursued by the government of the day in each country and are crystallized in the public consciousness as abiding and not to be forfeited at any cost. But in doing so, realism demands that the interests of other states will also have to be taken into consideration while formulating and implementing one's foreign policy. Moreover, certain norms and principles—sometimes influenced by the cultural traditions of the country—guide the objectives that a nation chooses to pursue.

India has had some abiding national interests but it has sought to fine-tune its objectives to the changing national, regional and international environment.[1] In the post-Cold War period a new strategic and economic scenario began to emerge in which the importance of Asia Pacific had begun to be recognized. On the one hand was India's own importance as the second most populous nation in the world, a large economy and a civilization of 5,000 years standing. On the other was the emergence of ASEAN with its population of about 550 million and a combined GDP of US $ 735 billion and a combined trade turnover of US $ 720 billion. India's declining defence expenditure, reduced naval modernisation and its holding of joint naval exercises served to reassure ASEAN States and Australia. Together with these developments, the rise of China could hardly be ignored.

Strategic Objectives

The strategic reason prompting closer cooperation includes the factor of geographic proximity. India has maritime boundaries with Indonesia, Myanmar and Thailand. It has a land border with Myanmar. The four Indian states which share a land border with Myanmar are: Arunachal Pradesh, Nagaland, Manipur and Mizoram. The borders with the three South-East Asian neighbours have been officially demarcated. Nicobar island and Aceh (Sumatra, Indonesia) are close enough to be a matter of concern to the Indian government in the context of recent convulsions in Aceh. India's large dimension and common maritime boundaries with some South-East Asian states posits both a challenge and an opportunity for New Delhi. There is the need to protect offshore resources like fisheries, oil and gas. India is a pioneer investor under UN Convention on the Law of the Sea (UNCLOS) and hence it has an interest in Indian Ocean. From South-East Asia's perspective since nine out of ten countries have a coastline (only Laos being landlocked) they have a vested interest in promoting trade through maritime route and seeking maritime security. In this sense our interests coincide.

Protection of Sea Lanes of Communication

Much of India's trade is conducted through the sea; hence, it is important that movement of its ships is secure and unimpeded. Hence the need to protect the Sea Lanes of Communication (SLOCs). SLOCs have been witness to several threats in recent times: piracy, drug trafficking, gun running, human smuggling, pollution, accidents, mines, closure of choke points, inter-state disputes, territorial disputes.[2] South-East Asia also has some crucial Straits: Malacca, Sunda and Lombok. Through these straits a high density of marine traffic passes and these are important energy supply routes as well. It has been suggested that joint maritime centres be established at important ports for rapid response to maritime incidents of different kinds.[3]

Dealing with the Major Powers

China factor is a recurring subtext in any discussion about South-East Asia. China looms large over both South and South-East Asia. According to a study, India and China will be amongst the six largest economies in the world by 2050.[4] Another report 'Mapping the Global Future' released by the National Intelligence Council (think tank of

CIA) predicts the rise of Asia by 2020 under the leadership of China and India.[5] It is a source of concern for South-East Asia for a myriad of reasons, but their response has generally been restrained and veiled. There is no reason why our reaction should be overt. Yet the concern cannot be brushed aside. It can be measured by various yardsticks: China's economic strides, its military modernization, its claims over the South China Sea, its growing influence in Myanmar[6] and use of its territory to access the Indian Ocean, the economic dominance of the Chinese ethnic community in South-East Asia. Some states have resorted to a policy of 'congagement' (containment plus engagement) in dealing with China. The option before India, in practical terms implies learning from the experience of those ASEAN members who have had to directly deal with China.

Combating Transnational Terrorism

The series of events starting with the terrorist attacks of September 11, 2001 in the US, the Bali bombing on October 12, 2002 and the Marriott Hotel in Jakarta in August 2003 galvanized the ASEAN States into cooperating against terrorism. India and ASEAN foreign ministers signed the joint declaration on terrorism, which envisages exchange of information, cooperation in legal matters, cooperation in enforcement matters and training.[7] It is clear that Aceh on the tip of Indonesia's Sumatra island is close enough to Great Nicobar for New Delhi to be concerned about disturbances there. Some earlier reports had said that Osama bin Laden was looking to Indonesia as a springboard for terrorist operations.[8]

Nuclear Issues

Even though on many nuclear issues India and ASEAN do not see eye to eye, India has sought to reaffirm its commitment to the goal of a nuclear weapon free world. Despite the fact that all ASEAN States have ratified or acceded to the NPT and India has not, possibilities for cooperation on nuclear issues are emerging. Former Prime Minister Vajpayee said, "The security of India and that of ASEAN are closely interlinked. We believe that a multipolar world order would provide the best guarantee of equal security for all states. We respect the status of South-East Asia as a Nuclear Weapons Free Zone and, as a nuclear weapon state, we are willing to convert this recognition into a de jure commitment."[9] Perhaps that was the reason India offered to sign the Protocol to the South-East Asia Nuclear Weapon Free Zone Treaty even though none of the Permanent Five have come forward to sign it.

Reform of the United Nations ASEAN Support on Crucial Issues

Vietnam has supported India's candidature for permanent membership of the UN Security Council and membership of all important economic and political fora of the region. Laos too has extended support for India's candidature for UNSC seat.[10] Jakarta too backs India's claim for permanent membership of UN Security Council.[11]

Cooperation in dealing with natural calamities: Indian Navy was prompt in speeding relief and rehabilitation to friendly nations affected by the December 26 tsunami. The devastating impact of the tsunami of December 26, 2004 highlighted the need for cooperation in not just relief work but also in disaster warning mechanisms.[12]

Defence Cooperation

In order to achieve its security objectives, India has undertaken defence cooperation with some South-East Asian countries.

Indonesia: India and Indonesia signed five agreements including the formation of a Joint Commission and defence cooperation. Under the agreement on defence, India could supply some naval patrol boats and provide repair facilities and supply spares to Indonesian naval vessels. India could supply ammunition, batteries for submarines and torpedoes and chemical explosives for the Indonesian Navy. This agreement was possible, as the US and the European Union have imposed sanctions on supply of defence equipment to Indonesia. This pact will also counter Australian influence in Indonesian establishment. Australia had sought to exploit Indonesian concern following Pokhran II tests. Indonesian officers have received training in India since the fifties but the numbers have dramatically increased. Many Indian ships (Delhi, Aditya, etc.) visited Jakarta in October 2000 and participated in joint exercises with the Indonesian Navy. One Indonesian ship, KRI Singa, participated in MILAN 99 exercise at Port Blair in March-April, 1999. The Indonesian Chief of Naval Staff visited India in 2000.[13] Mr. Vajpayee during his Indonesia visit also carried forward the prospects of Defence cooperation particularly the Navy. The Indonesian proposal for a defence pact among Indonesia, China, India and Russia did not figure in Mr. Wahid's talks with Mr. Vajpayee. The Indian Chief of Naval Staff Adm. Sushil Kumar visited Indonesia from 28-31 August 2001.

Malaysia: It may be recalled that under an MoU signed with Malaysia their pilots began receiving training on MiG 29s in India. There was in fact a desire to raise the level of cooperation to that of joint production of defence equipment. The Malaysia-India Defence Committee (MIDCOM) met in Kuala Lumpur in January 2001. The

Indian side was represented by the Defence Secretary Mr. Yogendra Narain, the Vice Chief of Air Staff and the deputy chiefs of Army and Naval Staff. There was information sharing on operations relating to MIG-29 which both countries possess. The meeting of the MIDCOM was only the third such since it was set up in 1992. The first meeting was held in February 1993 when the then Defence Minister Mr. Sharad Pawar went to Kuala Lumpur. The second such meeting was held in May 1997. There is even some speculation on a "regional consortium" for the building of the Light Combat Aircraft" in which India may involve some ASEAN members.[14]

Singapore: India is providing missile testing range in Chandipur, Orissa to Singapore. Indian Navy also conducted joint exercises in February-March 2005 with Singapore Navy in the South China Sea.

Vietnam: PM Vajpayee's visit had been preceded by visits by Defence Minister George Fernandes and External Affairs Minister Jaswant Singh a few months earlier. During Defence Minister Fernandes' five day visit to Vietnam starting from March 26, 2000 training in Vietnam of Indian officers in 'jungle warfare' was agreed upon. He was the first Indian Defence Minister to visit Vietnam. India sought Vietnamese help to get its army personnel trained in Vietnam on counter insurgency tactics to deal with problem areas in northeast, Kashmir and Naxal affected areas. It is quite appropriate to have reached agreement to have training of their military personnel in each other's countries. The other area which was included 'in the high level security dialogue was piracy on the high seas. "Vietnamese officers received training at the National Defence College. New Delhi also has naval cooperation with Vietnam, with India ready to supply the Petia class boats to Vietnam.

Participation in naval fleet review off Mumbai in February 2001 included Indonesia, Malaysia, Singapore and Thailand. Port visits to South-East Asia are part of maritime diplomacy. For instance by sending mostly indigenously built ships to East Asian countries the progress in India's shipbuilding industry was sought to be conveyed. Secondly, the ability of Indian ships to withstand typhoons on the Chinese coast also conveyed in a sense the strength of the Indian Navy.[16]

Multilateral Ties: India's security objectives cannot be realised single-handedly and a cooperative approach is a necessity. It was with a view to achieving these goals in a holistic and regional sense that India opted to join and participate in multilateral institutions in South-East Asia like ASEAN, ARF and CSCAP. What has India's role in these structures been and to what extent has it been able to further those objectives through its participation in them. To what extent has India's participation in these help promote India-South-East Asia relations? What has New Delhi's role been and what we would like it to be?

One of India's economic objectives has been to be part of multilateral economic institutions in the Asia Pacific region. India needs to link up with the global economy and towards that objective it must harness the opportunities in the Asia Pacific and South-East Asia. There are regional economic and other groupings with which India can integrate Indian PM assured Vietnamese leader that India fully supported Hanoi's entry into the World Trade Organisation.

From Sectoral Dialogue Partnership to Summit-level Interaction

India became sectoral dialogue in 1992 consequent to the decision taken at the 4th ASEAN Summit held in Singapore in January that year. It enabled India's participation in four sectors viz., trade, investment, science and technology and tourism.[17] This was formalised through an Exchange of Letters between the then ASEAN Secretary General Dato' Ajit Singh and India's Minister of External Affairs, Dinesh Singh.

India's sectoral dialogue status was upgraded to that of a full dialogue partner in 1995. In the 1970s and 1980s this was restricted to aid donors belonging to the developed world and only in 1991 was its ambit broadened.[18] This was a major development firstly, as it vindicated the success of India's 'Look East' policy and the strength of its sectoral dialogue partnership and the growth in cooperation between India and ASEAN that this had led to. Second, India's full dialogue partner status cleared the way for enhanced interaction in the future. Third, when India graduated to the level of full dialogue partner ARF membership too was within attainable distance. Critics have pointed out that India's decision to recognize the Phnom Penh regime in 1981 "put India-ASEAN relations into a coma for the next 12 years. ASEAN immediately suspended India's bid to become a dialogue partner... India would have already been at the forefront of Asia, not as isolated as it is today. India could have been a leading member of APEC and of ASEM.[19]

The Full Dialogue Partnership status cleared the way for India to secure the membership of the ASEAN Regional Forum in 1996 as the 20th member. Mr. I.K. Gujral attended the Third ARF and the Post-Ministerial Conference held at Jakarta.[20] Pakistan succeeded in its efforts when it was granted membership of the ARF on July 2, 2004.[21] ASEAN had initially hesitated because it had yet to arrive at a decision on two other applicants for membership (i.e., Bangladesh and East Timor). In the context of improving Indo-Pak bilateral relations Pakistan's ARF membership is being seen in a positive light especially in the light of Islamabad's undertaking to ASEAN to refrain from raising bilateral issues at the forum. In the post May 1998 scenario, the membership of the two nuclearised states of South Asia is seen more as a confidence building measure and as a welcome development. Fear of sensitive issues being raised at this forum cannot prevent India from playing an energetic role in ARF. On balance it will only help promote India's interest.

India became a Summit level partner in 2002, taking its engagement with ASEAN thereby to a higher plane. India participated in its first summit level interaction with ASEAN on November 5, 2002 at Phnom Penh in Cambodia. ASEAN conducts the ASEAN+3 dialogue with three key partners—China, Japan and South Korea. India had sought to enlarge this dialogue into ASEAN+4 with its inclusion. That did not happen. Instead a dialogue at the India-ASEAN Summit level was initiated in 2002. The ASEAN+3 is the summit level meeting between ASEAN and three countries (China, Japan and South Korea) together. Taken together their two-way trade with ASEAN approximated $ 196 billion in 2004, while China' two way trade with ASEAN was about $ 50 billion which is targeted at $ 100 billion for 2005. With the success of the India-ASEAN Summit and with growing confidence in the India-China relationship, the ASEAN+4 may yet become a reality.

The 1st India-ASEAN Summit was held in Phnom Penh on November 5, 2002 attended by the then Indian PM Vajpayee. The 2nd India-ASEAN Summit was held on October 8, 2003 at Bali, Indonesia, which was again represented by Mr. Vajpayee. It was notable for three documents which emerged from its deliberations: the "Framework Agreement on Comprehensive Economic Cooperation"; the accession document to the ASEAN Treaty of Amity and Cooperation; and adoption of the Joint Declaration on Cooperation in Combating International Terrorism.

The Framework Agreement signed by the leaders of India and ASEAN initiates the process for the establishment of an India-ASEAN Regional Trade and Investment Area, which includes a Free Trade Area in goods, services and investment.[22] "The negotiated FTA would commence from January 2006."[23] The 3rd India-ASEAN Summit was held on November 29, 2004 at Vientiane, Laos. India's Prime Minister Dr. Manmohan Singh led the delegation. The two documents which ASEAN and Indian leaders signed were: 'ASEAN-India Partnership for Peace, Progress and Shared Prosperity' and the 'ASEAN-India Plan of Action.'[24]

India's Participation in Other Important Regional Fora

BIMSTEC: The regional grouping BIMSTEC (which now stands for Bay of Bengal Initiative for Multi-Sector Technical and Economic Cooperation) has broken the artificial boundaries of South and South-East Asia. It brings together five states of South Asia (Bangladesh, Bhutan, India, Nepal and Sri Lanka) and two states of South-East Asia (Myanmar and Thailand) to optimize complementarities through trade and investment linkages. BIMSTEC has a combined market of 1.3 billion consumers and an aggregate GDP of $ 800 billion.[25] Trade among the seven BIMSTEC countries stands at just over $ 7 billion. BIMSTEC has the target of achieving regional free trade by 2017.[26] The potential for intra-BIMSTEC trade remains large as the current figures are rather low. BIMSTEC earlier stood for Bangladesh-India-Myanmar-Sri Lanka-Thailand Economic Cooperation (BIMSTEC)[27] and was formed on June 6, 1997.

India's economic and strategic objectives could be promoted through BIMSTEC. India's trade with BIMSTEC stand's at $ 3.7 billion which constitutes only 4 per cent of its total trade.[28] India's PM Manmohan Singh participated in the first BIMSTEC summit (Bangkok, July 29-30, 2004) in which he made several proposals to enhance cooperation.[29]

The BIMSTEC Economic Ministers Retreat held in Bangkok in August 1998 prioritized six areas of cooperation among member countries, of which technology; transportation and communication were to be India's responsibility and energy was to be Myanmar's responsibility.[30] BIMSTEC would help in the early operationalisation of the southern corridor of the Trans-Asian Highway project. The trans-Asian railway will help link up this region to China, Russia and Central Asia. These projects could be of immense importance to landlocked Laos. International organisations like ESCAP have played an important role in conceptualizing the plan for these projects; India's expertise in highway and railway construction could contribute to the early completion of these projects.[31]

India can introduce issues of common concern into BIMSTEC like intellectual property rights as when it hosted a WIPO Sub-regional Forum on Intellectual Property Rights among BIMSTEC Countries in November 1999. India also held the first BIMSTEC Transport and Communication Experts' Meeting on 23-24 April 2001. Strategically, by being part of BIMSTEC, India is able to be in close touch with the mainland ASEAN countries in the immediate neighbourhood of China.

It may in fact be a good idea to extend BIMSTEC to the Indochina countries.

MGC: The Mekong Ganga Cooperation[32] forum (MGC) brings together India with five ASEAN members (Cambodia, Laos, Myanmar, Thailand and Vietnam) with the object of promoting tourism, culture and education. It provides an opportunity to reactivate the civilisational link between India and ASEAN. India also suggested including a transport and communications component (the ESCAP Asian Highway project) within its ambit so that eventually greater trade and investment flows within the region. The inaugural session was held in Vientiane where the Vientiane Declaration was issued on November 10, 2000.[33] The Declaration calls for cooperation in knowledge based sectors, transport and infrastructure development. MGC comprises (other than Thailand and India) LMCV countries which were late comers to the ASEAN. The Vietnamese Foreign Minister Nguyen Dy Nien said that India, because of its interest and progress achieved, occupied an advantageous position. It could help bridge the development gap between the new and older ASEAN member countries, including the digital divide through implementation·of the Initiative for ASEAN Integration (IAI) and through the MGC.[34] The Asian highway project will link New Delhi to Singapore via Ho Chih Minh city, Phnom Penh, Bangkok, Vientiane, Chiang Mai, Yangon, Mandalay, K. Alemyo, Tamu, Dhaka and Calcutta.[35] India completed its segment of the proposed highway when India's External Affairs Minister Mr. Jaswant Singh inaugurated the 160 km. long Tamu-Kalewa-Kalemyo road on February 13, 2001. MGC tourism has a great potential because tourism in South-East Asia has remained restricted to the main ASEAN cities like Bangkok, Singapore and Kuala Lumpur. If Indian Department of Tourism taking advantage of the civilisational linkages ties up with the travel agents in these MGC countries, it will be able to provide Indians with new tourist destinations in ASEAN and in reverse promote tourist inflow into India.

IOR-ARC: There is yet another forum but one which has a far larger membership than BIMSTEC or the Mekong-Ganga Project. The Indian Ocean Rim-Association for Regional Cooperation (IOR-ARC) was formed on March 5, 1997 to promote inter-governmental economic cooperation among the rim countries and began with 14 members (including India, Indonesia, Malaysia and Singapore) and has a potential of an unwieldy 35 members.[36] During his visit to Indonesia earlier this year the Indian PM, Mr. Vajpayee called upon Indonesia to play an important part in pushing forward the Indian Ocean Rim Association for Regional Cooperation.[37]

CSCAP: Second track diplomacy constitutes an important component of any nation's overall international diplomacy. India secured membership of the Council for Security Cooperation in the Asia Pacific (CSCAP) in 1994, at first as an Associate Member only and thereafter in June 2000 as a full fledged member. The Indian Council of World Affairs provides the Secretariat for CSCAP India (previously provided by the IDSA). The CSCAP is a process parallel to the ARF process and deals with security issues. It supports the ARF with inputs. So what kind of an approach should be adopted by New Delhi in dealing with CSCAP? While it can be no one's case to advocate a policy of isolation, India cannot afford to rush into commitments at the Track Two level, which it may find hard to uphold at the Track One level. Secondly, it is important to remember that India suffers from a further handicap. A similar level of government-non-governmental interaction so critical to Track Two activities has not developed in India, and we need to be equally well equipped to meet the requirements of frequent and regular interaction. This is easier said than done: it presupposes a close link between the government and the nongovernmental sector. A break in the channels of communications, often leads to their working at cross-purposes.

India's exclusion from important regional fora: India is in the footprints of the Asia Pacific Economic Cooperation (APEC) region and it had quite appropriately sought its membership. It is already an outside member of two workshops: science and technology; and energy. But because of the moratorium on membership, its aspirations could not be fulfilled. Similarly when the inaugural Asia-European Union summit took place in 1995, India was pointedly excluded by ASEAN though China, Japan and South Korea were invited.[38] When the first Asia-Europe Meeting (ASEM) to bring together two of the world's important centres of economic activity, was held in Thailand in 1996 India was excluded. India, though an important economic player in Asia, remains excluded from this important grouping.

Economic Objectives

India has had the experience of working with ASEAN. India also has tremendous goodwill in South-East Asia. India's Look East policy has coincided with the introduction of economic liberalization. India's many economic objectives for wanting cooperation with ASEAN include the need to tap alternative energy sources (to look east to South-East Asia and not to be solely dependant on West Asia) and to ensure their supply. India seeks to improve its bilateral trade with countries of South-East Asia as its sizable population could provide a viable market. Besides, India seeks to attract investment from those countries with surplus capital. There is a potential for Indian businessmen to investment in the reverse direction and they have a wide choice since the ASEAN membership has a diverse profile.

The serious consequences of growing transnationalization of economic life were witnessed when South-East Asia was in the grip of an economic crisis which began with the currency crisis affecting Thailand on July 2, 1997. Electronic commerce which enabled swift manipulation of the currency prices contributed to the crumbling of the economy. It reduced the price competitiveness of Indian goods vis-a-vis South-East Asian exports due to devaluation of their currencies. Secondly, Indian exports to South-East Asia reduced because of their reduced buying capacity. This demonstrated clearly the need for India and ASEAN to have a holistic view of security.

(a) Trade

India's trade with ASEAN has grown from about $ 3.1 billion in 1991 to about $ 13 billion in 2004. It is targeted for $ 15 billion for 2005 and $ 30 billion for 2007.[39] The rising trend in India-ASEAN trade coincides with phase two of our Look East Policy which is distinguished, among other things, by the signing of free trade area (FTA) agreements.[40] India and ASEAN signed a framework agreement for a free trade area when Mr. Vajpayee went to Bali for the ASEAN-India summit in October 2003. India and Thailand signed a Framework Agreement on October 9, 2003. Singapore and India signed a Comprehensive Economic Cooperation Agreement (CECA) on June 29, 2005 which was truly a giant step forward in economic relations between the two countries because of its wide ranging implications.[41] Malaysia too is keen to sign some form of free trade agreement with India.[42]

Among the less developed LMCV countries of ASEAN Laos stands out as an example of a country with which trade volumes have been modest. The investment linkages have similarly been tenuous.[43] Yet there is hope. Because Laos is a landlocked state, Indian companies could make use of that country's surface links with Vietnam and Thailand thereby using it as a base to supply to other ASEAN countries. The full potential will be realised once either the Asian Highway Project or the railway link (Singapore to Kunming) becomes operational. India being ASEAN's full dialogue partner should call for an early completion of this project. Secondly, Indian companies could provide scaled down technologies (which they have developed) which are appropriate to small ASEAN countries. For example, small paper mills and rural telecommunications.[44] Thirdly, Indian banking system could have joint ventures with Laos as that country needs a reliable system which can be relied upon when others trade with Laos.

A comparison of the trade figures of China-ASEAN on the one hand and India-ASEAN on the other hand is very telling. For instance, Vietnam's two-way trade with India stands at only $ 500 million whereas that with China stands at $ 5 billion.[45] India and Vietnam agreed to raise their two-way trade value to $ 1 billion by 2006.[46] Vietnam and China on the other hand aim to raise their two-way trade value to $ 10 billion by 2010.[47]

(b) Investment

Foreign Direct Investment is defined "as a form of long-term international capital movement made for the purpose of productive activity and accompanied by the intention of managerial control or participation in the management of a foreign firm." It differs from indirect or portfolio investment which is concerned only with yields on securities. FDI brings with it not only capital, but also managerial skill and technical know how.[48] India seeks to improve its investment relations with South-East Asia. Foreign Direct Investment from ASEAN was at an insignificant level in 1990. But the approved FDI rose to $ 4 billion (Rs. 14,000 crore) over the period January 1991 to May 2002 though the actual FDI inflow over the same period was lower at $ 620 million.[49]

Indian businessmen could invest in the medium and small sectors in countries like Laos. When the Laos PM Boungnang Vorachit visited India (June 15-21, 2003) he informed that with a stable political situation and lower taxes in Laos, India's investment in Laos had considerably improved. He invited Indian businessmen to invest in Laos agriculture, forestry, garments, finished leather and hydropower transmission, tourism and infrastructure development.

The Vietnamese President Tran Duc Luong had visited New Delhi in December 1999. He invited investment by Indian business and industry in Vietnam. When Mr. Vajpayee went to Vietnam he took along with him a FICCI delegation to show Indian private sector participation. Mr. Vajpayee also addressed a meeting of the India-Vietnam Joint Business Council in Hanoi. Three agreements were signed by the business representatives of India and Vietnam.[50] The Oil and Natural Gas Commission-Videsh is already prospecting for oil and gas in Vietnam. It plans to invest a further $ 238 million in

Vietnam, its largest ever investment abroad. Mr. Brajesh Mishra pointed out that if India wanted to import crude from Vietnam then we "want security of sea lanes". The close linkage between economics and security becomes quite clear from this one fact.

(c) Infrastructure Development

Road and railway links constitute important elements of infrastructure in any country's economy. Myanmar being the only South-East Asian country with which India shares a land border, participating in road building activity in Myanmar is significant from several perspectives.

- It opens new linkages to South-East Asia.
- It will potentially boost trade and tourism which are crucial for the development of India's North East. This region has somehow been left out of the national mainstream in terms of development.
- Good road network on our borders with Myanmar could reduce the response time in dealing with insurgents. It could help deal with problems of law and order.
- Roads are an important factor in view of Myanmar's strategic location between India and China.

On February 13, 2001 Mr. Jaswant Singh inaugurated the 160 km long Tamu-Kalewa-Kalemyo road. It links Moreh town in Manipur to central Myanmar. It would constitute a segment in the proposed Asian Highway linking Singapore with Istanbul. The then Myanmar Foreign Minister U Win Aung suggested the possibility of India and Myanmar developing a deep sea port at Kyaukpyu, providing a linkage to Mizoram. The two countries are already cooperating in the field of hydel projects and in information technology.[51] Rail link between New Delhi and Hanoi is also envisaged.

(d) Tourism

One major Indian objective should be to attract tourist traffic from South-East Asia. This would include both local South-East Asians and foreigners who come to visit South-East Asia. Packages can be worked out with travel agents in South-East Asia, particularly in the Buddhist circuit. While new air routes between Indian and South-East Asian cities will need to be started, there is a potential to develop the sea route as well. Aggressive marketing and use of information technology will enable India to develop this industry and increase its foreign exchange earnings.

Secondly, support to tourism can be seen as an offshoot of India's look east policy. Increased travel and tourism will increase understanding between the peoples of the two regions. Tourism can be seen as an educating process, which would have a beneficial impact on other sectors of the economy.

India has not developed its tourism sector despite the fact that tourism is the second highest net foreign exchange earner. The travel and tourism industry accounts for 5.6 per cent of the GDP and supports 5.8 per cent of the total employment. According to a WTO study, East Asia and the Pacific will become the second most favoured tourism destination and South Asia itself will attract 19 million tourist in 2020. The growth of tourist traffic to India has been slow: inbound traffic has increased from 1.7 million in 1990 to 2.5 million in 1999. During the same period the figures for Malaysia are 7.5 million and 7.9 million. According to WTO figures for 1998, tourists tend to stay longer in India (22.7 days) than in a South-East Asian country like Malaysia (5.5 days) and spends less in India (US $ 52.8 per day) than in Malaysia (US $ 73.6).[52]

Thailand is a prominent tourist destination but Laos or Vietnam are not equally well-known. Indian tourists could be persuaded to go to Laos and Vietnam through aggressive marketing by the private sector and through the aegis of the MGC. India and Vietnam signed an agreement on travel and tourism cooperation during PM Vajpayee's three day visit to Vietnam in January 2001.[53]

There is great scope for tourism with Laos which is as yet untapped. Laos has many historic sites of importance but the Bangkok-Vientiane and the Bangkok-Angkor Vat sectors are more costly than the New Delhi-Bangkok sectors. As yet Laos and Vietnam are not on our air map. Direct flights between New Delhi and Vientiane and New Delhi and Hanoi should be considered. Once these links are established it could help tourism in India as we could promote the Buddhist circuit in India. India has a rich cultural and natural heritage. The Buddhist circuit holds great appeal in South-East Asia and can be developed.

A step in the right direction to promote greater appreciation of each other's cultures was the launching November 29, 2004 of the first India-ASEAN motorcar rally from Guwahati, India which ended in Batam, Indonesia in which about 60 cars participated. This raised hope in the benefits that a good road network could bring.

(e) Energy

India is the fourth largest oil consumer in the Asia-Pacific.[54] India's demand for petroleum product is set to increase from 96 million tonnes currently to 195 million tonnes per annum by 2011-12. India has opened the exploration and development of oil and gas reserves to foreign companies and they can also establish refineries and pipelines. India would have to reduce its dependence on West Asian oil and gas, and diversify its sources of energy. India's overall import dependence for energy which is currently 14 per cent and likely to increase to around 40 per cent by 2010 would increase still further by 2020. Similarly our import dependence on oil is around 40 per cent which is likely to increase to 70 per cent by 2010. Our import dependence on natural gas is likely to rise to 43 per cent by 2010.[55] South-East Asia will become an important producer of natural gas.

Simultaneously, as South East Asia becomes an important energy source for India (including coal, oil, and gas from Indonesia and natural gas from Australia, Malaysia, Myanmar and Indonesia), it will become increasingly important to ensure the security of Straits of Malacca Hydroelectric projects with neighbouring Myanmar (such as Chindwin River project) would provide the much needed power to India's north-east.

During PM Vajpayee's visit to Vietnam in January 2001 an agreement on utilisation of atomic energy for peaceful purposes was signed: MoU between India's Department of Atomic Energy and the Vietnamese Science Ministry. India would also provide equipment for a nuclear science laboratory in Dalat. Vietnam would contribute $ 200,000 and India $ 400,000 in the forms of grant by way of equipment and other interrelated backup for this laboratory. India would also provide support in the exploration and exploitation of uranium.[56] Vietnamese scientists have already trained at Indian facilities dealing with peaceful uses of nuclear energy. That Vietnam was keen on having its nuclear scientists trained in India was raised by Hanoi during the India-Vietnam Joint Commission meeting in November 2000. The basis for the latest MoU lay in an agreement signed in 1986, valid till May 2002.

(f) Human Resource Development

Productivity has not received adequate attention in some of the ASEAN States. India could collaborate with Singapore (where productivity movement is strong) in setting up HRD centres in countries like Myanmar and Laos and equipping them with productivity tools and techniques. Studies on India-ASEAN HRD have already been conducted. The Vietnamese Foreign Minister Nguyen Dy Nien recalled India had offered 100 slots a year to ASEAN under its ITEC programme for the ASEAN-India Human Resources Training Programme. He said India could contribute to HRD especially in the areas of IT training, English language training and application of science and technology.[57]

As part of its initiative to establish Entrepreneurship Development Centre (EDC) in each CLMV country, the first EDC was opened in Vientiane during the 10th ASEAN Summit with similar ones to be opened in Cambodia, Myanmar and Laos in 2005.

(g) Information Technology

The high literacy rate in South-East Asian countries presents a good opportunity to India to invest in Information technology and other education related activities. India could develop software for various South-East Asian languages. A joint institute on Information technology has been suggested. India has provided a Rs. 100 million grant for a software and training centre for Vietnam. Earlier in December 1999 India had given a $ 5 million credit to set up two centres for software and human resources development. Indian institutions having expertise on the subject like the Institute of Applied Manpower Research could offer their services to ASEAN while scientific and technological cooperation could be promoted through CSIR.

Cultural Cooperation: A leader from South-East Asia once noted: "The countries of South-East Asia and India have had a long-standing relationship that dates back to several centuries. The historical and cultural linkages and the existing traditional ties form the basis or foundation on which strong ASEAN-India relations can be built."[58] But there is need to exercise caution: the South-East Asians do not like a patronising attitude. They may have borrowed from India but they have worked on that tradition and indigenised it. In a sense because of the value-added it has become something different. However, we should not go to the other extreme and become ashamed of these links.[59] If anything these links should be fostered. Just as India helped in the restoration of Angkor Wat, it could help in the restoration of UNESCO World Heritage site of Wat Phu in southern Laos.[60]

During Prime Minister Atal Behari Vajpayee's three day visit to Vietnam in January 2001 the two countries signed a protocol on cultural exchange.[61]

The Indian Technical Economic Cooperation (ITEC) programme begun in 1964, is a major vehicle of Indian economic diplomacy. Under it, scholars from many countries are received by India. Improved links between the think tanks of India and South-East Asia are required. India should establish cultural centres in South-East Asian countries on the lines of the British Council. A greater sensitivity towards South-East Asia will develop if their culture becomes more easily accessible to the Indian public at large. For instance films and books from ASEAN should become available to Indian public as easily as from the developed world.

It must be remembered that high level visits (such as the PM's) are not a panacea for everything: the promises made during these visits have to be followed up with concrete action and the nitty-gritty of the agreements have to be seen through.[62] For instance, if we want closer interaction with a country like Vietnam we should see to it that the Vietnamese language is taught in some of our universities. Once we have sorted out details such as these, we will begin to see the Look East policy of the early nineties.

One aspect of the globalisation phenomenon has been the spread of communication and information technology which is sometimes viewed as a threat to the cultural integrity of a nation state. At another level, domestic entertainment industry faces a danger from blockbuster Hollywood films, India and ASEAN could formulate a coordinated response to this.

Indian minority community: The Indian presence in South-East Asia amounts to 2.5 m only whereas the Chinese minority community is over ten times that. Indians constitute 8 per cent of the population in Malaysia, but own only 1.5 per cent of wealth. Indians comprise 7 per cent of the total population in Singapore. The Indian minority community is better adjusted in the land of their adoption than the Chinese community, because they neither practice cultural exclusivity nor are they economically powerful in a conspicuous way.[63] The same sensitivity has to be applied when dealing with the people of Indian origin in South-East Asia. They can definitely act as a bridge if their unique and independent identity is recognized. They understand the region well and usually know the local language also. Subhash Chandra Bose sought their cooperation in India's freedom struggle. However, it is not enough to advise the Indian community to identify themselves with the land of their adoption. The Indian Government should be willing to stand by them in their problems.[64]

It may also be recalled that people of Indian origin have occupied important positions in South-East Asia—Malaysia and Singapore for instance. In reverse, some South-East Asians have made India their home. On some rare occasions these residents have been a source of some tension between India and some South-East Asian countries. Indian government should utilise the talent of those qualified among them to develop language skills in India (especially with regard to Vietnamese, Indonesian etc.).

Prospects for the Future

As India and ASEAN becomes increasingly interconnected they will be attracted or repelled by concentric power circles that extend further afield. Both India and ASEAN may need to readjust their relations in the context of the pulls and pressures experienced in their respective relationships with other powers. New Delhi might need to do more to facilitate the business community do its work of trade and investment. It can do this by providing information about business conditions and opportunities in ASEAN for the benefit of the Indian business community and similar information about India for the ASEAN business community. ASEAN is harmonising its products, trading, and customs procedures. It would seek extension of these arrangements to India and in turn offer to make the required changes in its system.

India will have to work along with South-East Asian regional organisations, which will be called upon to offer suitable response/ solutions to regional crises/problems. Regional organisations will invariably come up with new formulations. New multilateral institutions or structures may take shape and older ones lose their importance. The long experience of interacting with each other would help India and South-East Asia overcome the difficulties that an uncertain international environment might bring with it in the distant future.

References

1. This paper covers the period beginning 1991.

2. Vijay Sakhuja, "Indian Ocean and the Safety of Sea Lines of Communication", *Strategic Analysis*, Vol. XXV, No. 5, August 2001, pp. 689-702.

3. P.K. Ghosh, "Maritime Security Environment in SE Asia and the Indian Ocean Region", Paper presented at the Tenth CSCAP Maritime Cooperation Working Group Meeting, Kuala Lumpur, May 31, 2001.

4. Goldman Sachs' report Dreaming with BRICs: The Path to 2050 at http://www.gs.com/insight/research//reports/99.pdf. Also see Rahul Sen, *Regional Economic Integration: Case for a Regional Export Credit Agency for Asia*, New Delhi, ISEAS, Capital Publishing Co., 2005.

5. Refer report at http://www.cia.gov/nic/NIC globaltrend2020.html.

6. Chinese naval threat in the South China Sea and in the Indian Ocean through Myanmar came to be increasingly recognised. There were several indicators: Chinese support of the crushing of the Myamnarese pro-democracy movement in 1988; Chinese military aid to SLORC/SPDC; ingress by Chinese immigrants from Yunnan province leading to demographic changes in Myanmar, modernising Myanmarese infrastructure (road and rail) to link China to the Indian Ocean. Besides this there was the ASEAN need to diversify

relations. A similar need to diversify relations was felt by India following the collapse of Soviet Union.

7. Sujit Chatterjee, "India, ASEAN in big trade pact, to fight terror", Redifcom <www.rediff.com/money/2003/oct/08vajtour.htm>

8. "Bin Laden Moves in on Indonesia", *The Australian*, September 4, 2001 (on the internet).

9. Prime Minister Vajpayee, "India and ASEAN-Shared Perspectives", Address to the Institute of Diplomatic and Foreign Relations, Kuala Lumpur, May 16, 2001.

10. "India-ASEAN relations taking on a new dimension: Manmohan", *The Hindu*, November 29, 2004.

11. Amit Baruah, "Jakarta backs India's claim for Security Council seat". *The Hindu*, January 11, 2001.

12. "Floating hospital on mission to Indonesia", January 10, 2005.

13. Shishir Gupta, "Australian influence in for competition: Jakarta Defence Pact", *Hindustan Times*, January 14, 2001.

14. Amit Baruah, 'Engagement' with Malaysia a continuing process, *The Hindu*, January 24, 2001.

15. Jay Raina, "Vietnam training Indian troops in jungle warfare", *Hindustan Times*, January 9, 2001 and "George for Vietnamese help in guerrilla tactics", *Hindustan Times*, March 27, 2000.

16. *Times of India*, September 30, 2000.

17. For details, Udai Bhanu Singh, *ASEAN Regional Forum and Security of the Asia-Pacific*, Delhi Paper No. 15, IDSA, New Delhi, 2001.

18. Rodolfo C. Severino, "ASEAN and India—A Partnership for Our Time, "Eleventh India-ASEAN Eminent Persons Lecture, January 9, 2001 (Research and Information System for the Non-Aligned and Other Developing Countries, New Delhi).

19. Kavi Chongkittavorn, "Brotherly Engagement: India, China and ASEAN," Fourth India-ASEAN Eminent Persons Lecture, August 13, 1998 (Research and Information System for the Non-Aligned and Other Developing Countries, New Delhi).

20. "India to join ASEAN Forum", *Jane's Defence Weekly*, 28 February 1996.

21. Fazal-ur-Rahman, "Pakistan and the ASEAN Regional Forum", *Strategic Studies*, Vol. 24, No. 4, Winter 2004. Also see editorial, "Welcome Entry", *The Hindu*, July 6, 2004 and P.S. Suryanarayana, "Pakistan keeping its fingers crossed on admission to ASEAN forum", *The Hindu*, April 24, 2004.

22. Seema Gaur, "Framework Agreement on Comprehensive Economic Cooperation between India and ASEAN: First Step Towards Economic Integration", *ASEAN Economic Bulletin*, Vol. 20, No. 3, (2003), pp. 283-91.

23. "South East Asia and the Pacific", *MEA Annual Report*, 1 January 2003, 31 March 2004, p. 119.

24. Refer "Deepening ASEAN-India Partnership", Chairman's Statement of the 3rd ASEAN India Summit, Vientiane, 30 November 2004 < http://www.aseansec.org/16745.htm>

25. Bhutan Broadcasting Service web site, Thimphu, July 29, 2004 as cited in *BBC Monitoring Global Newsline—Asia Pacific Political*, July 30, 2004.

26. PTI news agency, New Delhi, July 31, 2004 as cited in *BBC Monitoring Global Newsline Asia Pacific Political*, August 1, 2004.

27. It was known as BISTEC until Myanmar joined it in December 1997.

28. Intra-BIMSTEC trade is important for countries like Nepal (43 per cent of its total trade) and Myanmar (27 per cent). Doordarshan DDTV, New Delhi, July 29, 2004, as cited in *BBC Monitoring Global Newsline—Asia Pacific Political*, July 30, 2004.

29. These included a ministerial conference on energy, sharing experience in remote sensing and a tourism round table.

30. The other areas allotted were: trade and investment; tourism; and fisheries.

31. V. Jayant, "The Mekong-Ganga Initiative", *The Hindu*, November 28, 2000.

32. The six foreign ministers decided to drop the name proposed earlier 'Ganga-Mekong Swarnabhoomi project' in favour of 'Mekong-Ganga Cooperation'.

33. "East meets east", *Pioneer*, November 20, 2000.

34. Nguyen Dy Nien, "ASEAN-India Dialogue Relations: Present and Prospects', India-ASEAN Eminent Persons Lecture, September 15, 2001 (Research and Information System for the Non-Aligned and Other Developing Countries—FICCI, New Delhi).

35. Mekong-Ganga project signed, boost to ASEAN economic ties," *Hindustan Times*, November 11, 2000.

36. Rahul Roy Chaudhury, IOR-ARC: The Indian Ocean Rim-Association for Regional Cooperation," *Asian Strategic Review*, 1996-97.

37. *The Hindu*, January 11, 2001.

38. Ravi Velloor, "ASEAN not impressed by India's economic status", *Indian Express*, April 2, 1995.

39. N. Ram, "Catching up in the East", *The Hindu*, November 29, 2004.

40. C Raja Mohan, "Look East Policy: phase two", *The Hindu*, October 9, 2003.

41. "India, Singapore sign economic pact", *The Hindu*, June 30, 2005.

42. This was suggested by Malaysian PM Abdullah Ahmad Badawi during his visit to India in December 2004. See "Badawi suggests trade agreement", *The Hindu*, December 21, 2004.

43. There has been cooperation in agriculture with India providing a US $ 2 million soft loan to Laos to purchase water pumps from India and another loan to improve irrigation for the entire country. Refer, Thaatsaphone Noraseng, "India-ASEAN Economic Cooperation with special reference to Lao PDR-India Economic Relations", Paper presented under RIS/ITEC Programme, New Delhi, July 9, 2001.

44. Dr. Nagesh Kumar of RIS at Seminar on India-ASEAN Economic Cooperation, July 9, 2001.

45. *Diplomatist*, Vol. 8, Fourth quarter, 2004. In his January 2001 visit to Vietnam, India's PM Vajpayee had set a target of $ 500 million two way trade to be achieved within the next three years.

46. "Vietnam-India to strengthen economic cooperation", Voice of Vietnam text website, Hanoi, October 18, 2004, cited in *BBC Monitoring Asia Pacific*, Economic, October 19, 2004.

47. *BBC Monitoring Asia Pacific Political*, October 19, 2004.

48. India's FDI data is available from two sources: the Ministry of Industry which disseminates only FDI Approvals and the RBI which disseminates actual *FDI-inflow data*. See Sanjiv Kumar, FDI In India, BR Publishing Corp., New Delhi, 1996.

49. MEA, *Visit of the Prime Minister to Vientiane, Lao PDR to attend 3rd India-ASEAN Summit, November 28-30, 2004* (Ministry of External Affairs, Government of India, November 25, 2004).

50. *Hindustan Times*, January 10, 2001.

51. Amit Baruah, "We will help combat insurgency: Myanmar", *The Hindu*, February 17, 2001.

52. For data presented here the author has made extensive use of data provided in CII *Malaysia-India Business Forum*, May 15, 2001.

53. Amit Baruah, "India to assist Vietnam in nuclear research", *The Hindu*, January 9, 2001.

54. The top three are Japan, China and South Korea.

55. G. Parthasarathy, 'Look East for Energy Security", *Pioneer*, 5 July 2001.

56. Jay Raina, "Terrorism poses threat to Asia: PM", January 9, 2001.

57. Nien, n. 34.

58. Mahathir bin Mohamad, Speech at the First India-ASEAN Lecture, December 21, 1996, New Delhi.

59. Vishal Singh, India and South-East Asia," in Bimal Prasad, ed., *India's Foreign Policy: Studies in Continuity and Change*, Vikas, New Delhi, 1979.

60. N. Ram, "India's role in a changing ASEAN", *The Hindu*, November 30, 2004.

61. Amit Baruah, "India to assist Vietnam in nuclear research", *The Hindu*, January 9, 2001.

62. P.S. Sahai, "India and ASEAN: VVIP Visits and Beyond", Talk at India International Centre, New Delhi, February 27, 2001.

63. For details refer, I.J. Bahadur Singh, *Indians in South-East Asia*, Sterling, New Delhi, 1982.

64. Refer Singh, n. 59.

Select Chronology: India-South-East Asia Bilateral Relations 1991-2005

1991

January 3-6: India's Foreign Secretary visits Kuala Lumpur.

April 24-28: India's President visits Vietnam.

April 28 May 1: India's President visits the Philippines: The first ever by an Indian head of state to that country.

August 12: India's Minister for External Affairs visits Singapore.

October 3-5: Prime Minister Hun Sen of Cambodia visits India.

November: The Fifth Meeting of the Indo-Thai Joint Trade Committee held in New Delhi.

December 5-6: Singapore's Foreign Minister Wong Kan Seng visits India.

December 12-15: India's Minister of State for External Affairs visits Cambodia.

1992

March: Malaysian Defence Minister Dato Sri Najib visits India.

March 21-27: The Foreign Minister of Vietnam Nguyen Manh Cam visits India.

March 22-27: Singapore's Deputy PM and Minister of Trade and Industry, Brig Gen Lee Hsien Loong, accompanied by a high powered delegation visits India.

April: HRH Maha Vajiralongkorn, the Crown Prince of Thailand visits India.

July: Foreign Minister of Indonesia Ali Alatas visits New Delhi.

August: Brunei Darussalam establishes a Resident Mission headed by an Acting High Commissioner in Delhi.

September: India's PM attends the NAM Summit in Jakarta, Indonesia.

September: Sultan of Brunei visits India.

September 8-13: The General Secretary of the Communist Party of Vietnam Do Muoi, led a high level delegation to India.

November 2-3: First session of the Indo-Malaysian Joint Commission held in Kuala Lumpur. Co-chaired by the Malaysian Foreign Minister and India's Minister of State for External Affairs.

1993

January 29-31: India's Foreign Secretary visits Malaysia.

February: India's Minister of State for External Affairs Salman Khurshid visits Vietnam.

February 1-2: India's Foreign Secretary visits Thailand.

February 1-7: India's Defence Minister visits Malaysia.

April: India's PM Narasimha Rao visits Thailand.

May: Archaeological Survey of India team returns after 7 year project for restoration of the Angkor Vat Temple in Cambodia.

September 22-28: India's Vice-President KR Narayanan visits Vietnam.

November 2-5: The Second India-Thailand Joint Commission session held in New Delhi. Co-chaired by Thai Foreign Minister Sqn. Ldr. Prasong Soonsiri and the Indian Minister of External Affairs Dinesh Singh.

December: Malaysian PM Mahathir Mohammad visits India during the G-15 meeting.

December: Indonesian President Suharto visits India.

1994

January 23-30: PM Goh Chok Tong visits India as the Chief Guest for the Republic Day Celebrations. Leads a delegation of businessmen and others.

Lao Foreign Minister Somsavat Lengsavad visits India.

September: Indian Prime Minister PV Narasimha Rao visits to Singapore.

September: Indian Prime Minister PV Narasimha Rao visits Vietnam.

October: Thai Deputy Foreign Minister Dr. Surin Pitsuwan visits India.

October 24: Cambodia applies for Observer status in ASEAN.

November: India-Indonesia Joint Business Council meeting held in New Delhi.

1995

January: Singapore's PM Goh Chok Tong visits India; also attends the Centenary celebrations of the Confederation of Indian Industries (CII) in Calcutta.

January: Thailand's Deputy PM Dr. Supachal Panitchpakdi, attends the Centenary Celebrations of CII in Calcutta.

January 27: Secretary level talks between India and Thailand, held in New Delhi.

January 16-18: Indo-Vietnam Joint Working Group meets in New Delhi.

1996

March: India and Indonesia hold Joint Business Council meeting, and office of FICCI opened in Jakarta.

March 3-13: India and Singapore hold Anti-Submarine Warfare Exercises off Visakhapatnam. Chief of Naval Staff of Singapore Rear Adm. Kwek Siew Jin participates.

April 10: Vietnamese petroleum enterprise concludes a contract with the US company Conoco for joint development of oil wells in the South China Sea.

May: Chief of Naval Staff Admiral V.S. Shekhawat visits Vietnam.

May 1-2: India's Secretary (East) K. Raghunath visits Brunei: attends the Second Meeting of the Indo-Brunei Joint Committee at Secretary level set up in 1995.

June 20: Chief of Naval Staff Admiral V.S. Shekhawat and Air Marshal K.B. Singh attend the inauguration of the Indonesia Air Show, held in Jakarta.

June 25: Secretary (East) K Raghunath visits Thailand for Senior Official level dialogue with the Thai Foreign Office.

August 18-19: Minister of External Affairs visits Malaysia.

August 20-21: Minister of External Affairs visits Singapore.

September 12-13: Second Meeting of the India-Philippines Joint Business Council held in New Delhi.

December: Malaysian PM Mahathir Mohamad visits India to receive the Jawaharlal Nehru Award for International Understanding for the year 1994. Delivers First India-ASEAN Eminent Persons Lecture on 21 December.

December 16: Cambodia's First PM Prince Norodom Ranariddh visits Bodh Gaya, Patna on a pilgrimage.

1997

March 3-5: Philippines President Fidel Ramos visits India.

January 16-17: The Third Meeting of the India-Vietnam Joint Working Group is held in New Delhi.

March 7-9: Vietnam's PM Vo Van Kiet visits India.

April 4-6: Indonesian Foreign Minister Ali Alatas visits India.

May 1-5: Lao PM Khamtay Siphandone visits India.

July 6-11: Lao Foreign Minister Somsavat Lengsavad visits India to Co-chair the First Session of the India-Laos Joint Commission in New Delhi.

August: the 8th session of the India-Vietnam Joint Commission (JCM) held at Hanoi.

August 28-29: India's Secretary (Economic Relations) AN Ram visits Singapore for bilateral talks.

December 23: India and Indonesia sign a MoU to establish a Joint Consultative Forum (JFC) for bilateral consultations (on bilateral and international matters).

1998

February 2-5: India's Chief of Air Staff, Air Chief Marshal S.K. Sareen visits Thailand at the invitation of his Thai counterpart.

February 11: India-Brunei Third Joint Committee meeting held in New Delhi.

May 11 : India carries out three underground nuclear tests at Pokhran with a fission device, a low yield sub-kiloton device and a thermonuclear device at 1545 hrs.

May 13: India carries out two more tests with sub-kiloton devices at 1221 hrs. Thereafter, it announces completion of the planned series of tests.

May 28: Pakistan matches India's tests by carrying out five tests at Chagai hills range in southwest Pakistan.

May 30: Pakistan carries out one more test. All the tests were reported to be fission devices using highly enriched uranium (U-235).

Minister of State for External Affairs, Ms. Vasundhara Raje visits Vietnam, Singapore and the Philippines to counter the negative fallout of India's nuclear tests.

December: The Filipino and the Chinese navies confront each other over Mischief Reef in the South China Sea.

1999

June 29: 4th round of the Indo-Philippines Foreign Office consultation held in New Delhi.

July 6-9: India's Minister of State for External Affairs Smt. Vasundhara Raje visits Thailand.

October 16-19: India's Chief of Naval Staff Admiral Sushil Kumar visits Singapore.

October 11-13: Philippines Defence Secretary (Minister) Mr. Orlando Mercado visits India. Led delegation to DEFEXPO INDIA 1999.

November 12-13: First meeting of the India-Indonesia Joint Consultative Forum held in New Delhi.

December 1-5: Vietnam's President Tran Duc Luong visits India.

2000

January 17-22: Singapore PM Goh Chok Tong visits India.

February 8-9: Indonesian President Abdurrahman Wahid visits India.

February Cambodian PM Samdech Hun Sen visits India.

March: India's Defence Minister George Fernandes visits Vietnam.

April : Brunei Sultan's sister HRH Princess Masna, Ambassador-at-large Ministry of Foreign Affairs, visits India.

June 1-3: India's External Affairs Minister Jaswant Singh visits Singapore. Speaks on "India and ASEAN: Security Paradigm AD 2000".

July: Malaysia takes over as country coordinator for India's interaction with ASEAN, for a period of three years.

July 8-10: Thailand's Foreign Minister, Dr. Surin Pitsuwan visits India.

September 17-21: Indonesian Naval Chief Admiral Achmed Sutjipto visits India.

October 5-8: Ships of the Indian Navy, INS Delhi, INS Aditya and INS Kuthar pay goodwill visit to Jakarta.

October 9-11: The Second Session of the India-Malaysia Joint Commission held in New Delhi. Malaysia's Foreign Minister Datuk

Seri Syed Hamid Albar and India's External Affairs Minister Jaswant Singh co-chaired the Meeting.

November 8-11: India's External Affairs Minister Jaswant Singh visits Laos at the head of the Indian delegation to the third India-Laos Joint Commission Meeting and 3 participates in the launching of the Mekong Ganga Cooperation at Vientiane.

November 6-8: India's External Affairs Minister Jaswant Singh visits Vietnam. Co-chairs the 10th session of India-Vietnam Joint Commission for Economic, Scientific and Technical Cooperation in Hanoi.

November: India's President K.R. Narayanan visits Singapore.

November 14-21: SPDC Vice Chairman Maung Aye visits India.

November 21, New Delhi: India-Myanmar Joint Statement.

2001

January 10-14: India's PM Atal Behari Vajpayee visits Indonesia.

January 17: India-Singapore Foreign Office Consultations held in New Delhi.

January 7-10: India's PM Atal Behari Vajpayee visits Vietnam.

February: India's External Affairs Minister Jaswant Singh visits Myanmar. Inaugurates the 160 km long Tamu-Kalewa-Kalemyo road.

2003

October 8-12: India's PM Atal Behari Vajpayee visits Thailand.

2004

January 12: Singapore's Deputy PM Lee Hsien Loong visits India.

July 8-11: Singapore's PM Goh Chok Tong visits India.

Singapore's Navy Chief visits India.

October 15: India's PM Manmohan Singh visits Vietnam.

October 24-29: Chairman of Myanmar's SPDC, Senior General Than Shwe visits India leading a high level delegation.

December 19: Malaysian PM Abdullah Ahmad Badawi's first state visit to India. He was accompanied by a trade and industry delegation. A dozen agreements and MoUs were signed.

December 26: Tsunami waves causes widespread damage to life and property in South-East Asia, India and beyond.

2005

June 3: Thailand PM Thaksin Shinawatra in New Delhi on a day long visit. An MoU on education was signed.

June 28: Singapore PM Lee Hsien Loong arrives in New Delhi on a three day visit. He concludes the CECA with India.

Select Chronology: India-South-East Asia Multilateral Relations 1991-2004

1991

October 21-23: India's Minister for External Affairs participates in the Paris International Conference on Cambodia (PICC).

1992

January 27-28: The 4th ASEAN Summit in Singapore decides that a Sectoral Dialogue with India be established.

May: India's Minister of State for External Affairs visits Indonesia for the NAM Ministerial Meeting in Bali.

June: India's Minister of State for External Affairs attends a Ministerial Conference on the Rehabilitation and Reconstruction of Cambodia held in Tokyo.

1993

March: India's Sectoral Dialogue relationship with ASEAN is formalised through an Exchange of Letters between ASEAN Secretary General Dato' Ajit Singh and India's Minister of External Affairs Dinesh Singh.

March 16-17: Sectoral dialogue inaugurated with the Indian side led by External Affairs Minister Dinesh Singh at New Delhi. ASEAN Secretary General Dato' Ajit Singh leads an ASEAN delegation.

May: India's Minister of State for External Affairs R.L. Bhatia visits Indonesia for the NAM Ministerial meeting.

June: The Council for Security Cooperation in the Asia Pacific (CSCAP) founded.

July 23: Laos and Vietnam attend as Observers and Cambodia as Guest for the first time the 26th AMM held until July 24 at Singapore. Laos was represented by its Foreign Minister Somsavat Lengsavad, and Vietnam by its Foreign Minister Nguyen Manh Cam. Cambodia was represented by its Foreign Minister, Prince Norodom Sirivudh.

September: India's Minister of State for External Affairs RL Bhatia visits Indonesia as PM's Special envoy to extend invitation to President Suharto for G-15 Meeting to be held in New Delhi.

1994

January 6 : The ASEAN-India Joint Sectoral Cooperation Committee (AIJSCC) convenes its First Meeting in Bali, Indonesia.

March: Indonesia's President Suharto visits India for the reconvened G-15 Summit.

March: Malaysia's PM Mahatir Mohamad visits for the reconvened G-15 Summit. Indian PMs visit to Vietnam and Singapore.

July 22-23 : 27th AMM at Bangkok. Laotian Foreign Minister,

Somsavat Lengsavad, and Vietnamese Foreign Minister, Nguyen Manh Cam, attended the 27th AMM as Observers. While Cambodian Foreign Minister Prince Norodom Sirivudh and the Myanmar Foreign Minister, Ohn Gyaw attended the AMM as Guests.

July 25: First session of ARF at Bangkok with 18 participants including the six ASEAN members (Brunei, Indonesia, Malaysia, Philippines, Singapore and Thailand), the seven dialogue partners (US, European Union, Australia, Canada, Japan, Singapore, Korea and New Zealand), the two Consultative partners (China and Russia), and the three Observers (Papua New Guinea, Vietnam and Laos).

October 17: Vietnam applies for ASEAN membership.

December: Institute for Defence Studies and Analyses (IDSA), New Delhi, admitted as Associate Member of CSCAP.

1995

February 13-17: The AIJSCC holds its Second Meeting in New Delhi and Goa.

August 2-3: ASEAN PMC held in Brunei.

December 1995: The 5th ASEAN Summit decides to admit India as a full dialogue partner.

1996

March 15: Laos applies for ASEAN membership.

July: India participates for first time in the Post-Ministerial Conference and the Third ARF held in Jakarta. India's Minister of External Affairs I.K. Gujral represents India as Full Dialogue Partner of the ASEAN.

November: ASEAN's First Informal Summit.

November 14: The First ASEAN-India Joint Cooperation Committee is held which is led by on the ASEAN side by Michael Cheok, Director General of ASEAN Singapore while the Indian side is led by Amar Nath Ram, Secretary (Economic Relations) of the Ministry of External Affairs at New Delhi through November 16.

1997

March: Treaty on the South-East Asia Nuclear Weapons Free Zone (Bangkok Treaty) enters into force. ASEAN calls upon NWS to accede to the Protocol of the Treaty.

April 6-8: Thai Foreign Minister, Mr. Prachuab Chaiyasan visits India to participate in the NAM Foreign Ministers' Meeting.

April 6-8: Philippine Secretary (Minister) of Foreign Affairs, Mr. Domingo L. Siazon, Jr., visits India to participate in the NAM Foreign Ministers' Meeting.

June: Bangladesh-India-Sri Lanka-Thailand Economic Cooperation (BISTEC) is launched.

July: India participates in the ASEAN-PMC and the fourth ARF, held in Kuala Lumpur. Led by Finance Minister P. Chidambaram.

1998

February 5: ASEAN-India Workshop on Development Cooperation (later referred to as "ASEAN-India Working Group Meeting") in Jakarta. Aimed to streamline the approval and implementation of ASEAN-India projects.

February 9: First ASEAN-India Senior Officials' Meeting (SOM) in New Delhi as part of the Dialogue Partnership.

April: The ASEAN India Joint Cooperation Committee Meeting held in New Delhi provided important mechanisms for implementing various decisions.

April 28-29: The Second ASEAN-India Joint Cooperation Committee (JCC) meeting at Singapore. It was decided to establish a Working Group on Trade and Investment.

June 18: The Chairman of the ASEAN Standing Committee said ASEAN would not insist on Pakistan's participation as an adhoc member or as a guest.

July 1998: Jaswant Singh, then Deputy Chairman, Planning Commission and a special envoy of the PM led the Indian delegation to the 31st ASEAN PMC and the 5th ARF meetings held in Manila. After India's nuclear tests it was the first security related forum in which all nuclear weapons States were interacting.

December 15-16: The 6th ASEAN Summit in Hanoi. The 'Hanoi Plan of Action' for 1999-2004 period is drawn up indicating measures aimed at enhancing intra-regional economic integration, trade liberalization and financial cooperation and the establishment of AFTA by 2002.

1999

January 13-14: The second meeting of the ASEAN-India Working Group, in Jakarta. AFTA-India linkages, Information Technology, Biotechnology, human resource development, tourism and the Hanoi Plan of Action were discussed.

February 25: The 2nd India-ASEAN SOM at Singapore discusses political, economic, cultural and functional cooperation. The economic crisis, ARF, South Asian developments, South China Sea, Treaty of Amity and Cooperation in SEA, disarmament and international economic and trade issues, were also discussed.

May: The 6th ARF SOM at Singapore. Attended by India's Secretary (ER) ST Devare.

July 26: India participates in the 32nd ASEAN-PMC and the Sixth ARF Session held in Singapore. Led by External Affairs Minister Jaswant Singh.

2000

November 8-11: The 3rd India-Laos Joint Commission Meeting. India's External Affairs Minister Jaswant Singh leads the delegation and participates in the launching of the Mekong Ganga Cooperation at Vientiane.

2001

July 27: India participates in the 7th ARF session held in Bangkok.

2002

November 5: The 1st ASEAN-India Summit at Phnom Penh, Cambodia.

2003

September 4-6: 2nd India-ASEAN Business Summit in New Delhi and Mumbai. An India-ASEAN web portal is launched.

October 8: The 2nd ASEAN-India Summit at Bali, Indonesia. PM Atal Behari Vajpayee led the Indian delegation. Three agreements signed: Framework Agreement for Comprehensive Economic Cooperation; India accedes to the ASEAN Treaty of Amity and Cooperation; Adoption of the Joint Declaration on Cooperation in Combating International Terrorism.

December 2003: Twenty-two professors from ASEAN Universities Network visit India.

2004

February 7: Trade and Economic Ministers' Meeting.

February: 6th Ministerial Meeting of BIMSTEC at Phuket, Thailand when Nepal and Bhutan join BIMSTEC.

March 25-26: 6th India-ASEAN SOM held in Vientiane, Laos at which India submits a draft Track-I Vision document.

July 30-31: BIMSTEC Summit is held in Bangkok with seven members. Dr. Manmohan Singh presents several new initiatives which India would organize.

November 22: The first India-ASEAN Motorcar rally.

November 29: 3rd ASEAN-India Summit at Vientiane, Laos.

23

Globalisation of Economy and India

Dr. R.K. Wadhwa

Globalisation is an old phenomenon. The history of globalisation can be traced back to as long as human civilisation. As the man has progressed since ages, the definition of globalisation got extended. According to the World Bank, "though the term (globalisation) has been so widely used, there does not appear to be any precise, widely agreed definition. Indeed the breadth of meanings attached to it seems to be increasing rather than narrowing over time, taking on cultural, political, and other connotations in addition to the economic."

According to Tomas Larsson "Globalisation is the process of world shrinkage, of distances getting shorter, things moving closer. It pertains to the increasing ease with which somebody on one side of the world can interact, to mutual benefit, with somebody on the other side of the world". Over many millennia, there has been a dramatic rise in cross-border trading of goods, people, ideas, and cultures. The rise in international trade in terms of imports and exports, multinationals, and specialization, combined with comparative advantage, are indicators of an increasingly global economy. Although definitions of globalisation range from too broad to too narrow, it is enough to know that globalisation and increasing interconnectedness of exchange, customs, laws, and politics are related in order to embark upon a study of globalisation's history.

Beginning of Globalisation

Man has progressed over time—from hunter-gatherer, to nomad, through agricultural improvements to the development of villages and cities in each region. There have been improvements in technological skills—from wheels, kilns, sails, architecture, to new professions like weavers, masons, shipbuilders, and goldsmiths. Irrigation, ploughing, pottery, and accounting are skills that led to development. Minining, oil, and gas have also been drivers for trade. Development occurred when it became possible to produce more food than for local consumption.

The invention and development of matters such as coinage, language, and political and legal systems allowed a framework and a context for many nations. These allowed some degree of commonality between different states. But there were many regional markets (whether it be within countries like China, or the freedoms of the Holy Roman Empire), and goods were sold where they were produced, much like in the developing world today. Some items travelled easily, such as ironware, tin, pottery, marble, and horses. It was not until improvements in transport arrived, that trading expanded to include more vulnerable produce.

Globalisation increases as countries progress through the transitional stages. Three common transitional stages or 'revolutions' are recognized: agricultural, industrial, and technological. The first was the use of enclosures, which, in England, occurred during 1750-1860. The industrial revolution led, through the factory system, to mechanization, urbanization, migration to the cities, vast population increases, and an eventual concern for education, sanitation, greater international trade, and specialization. The technological revolution, starting in the latter part of the twentieth century, with its emphasis on electronics, complex machinery, computing, the internet, and efficiency has simplified today's world and allowed a more integrated globe.

Lack of Global World System

By the middle of the second millennium, though there were increasing links between countries, due to a lack of transport, plus certain areas such as Africa, America, Oceania, and China, being barred as too distant or undeveloped, there was no one global world system. If this world system were the case then technology and different ideas would have spread so much more rapidly, rather than allowing the disparities that existed. In order to ensure that the trade that did exist was financially profitable, it was primarily in 'luxury' goods such as silk, rather than mass transit of goods.

Two things changed this lack of a world system: firstly the European era of discovery, which can be described as starting in the last years of the fifteenth century; secondly, advanced maritime navigation. Both were a result of the outward looking tendencies of Europe during the fifteenth century as the rules of the more powerful nations, especially Spain and Portugal vied with each other for power and territory. Christopher Columbus and other explorers wanted to reach the East for spices, trade and power, and for Christendom to become more dominant than Islam.

By the seventeenth century, the Dutch were the key European nation in promoting trade and beginning the proto-globalisation of Europe. Trading companies, joint-stock companies, public banks, and the stock exchange were all Dutch initiations. Joint stock-companies pooled funds and put them under common ownership for a specific venture or series of ventures. England was also a trading nation during the same period, especially through its global imperialist network based upon its Caribbean territories and Americas, and later expansion into India and Canada.

Setback to Globalisation

The incidence of the protectionist measures increased after the First and Second World Wars and the Great Depression thereby hampering the globalisation. The failure of the Treaty of Versailles and the impotence of the League of Nations meant that economic nationalism, reparations, and the loss of territory were inflicted on Germany. The cost of the Great War was estimated at $ 380 billion (in present prices) from the destruction of infrastructure. Human capital was lost permanently.

Post-1918, inflation in Austria, Hungary, Greece and other countries reduced the value of their currencies dramatically. These issues were combined with the tariff wars during the Great Depression, such that one country's problems affected their trading partners. This was economic nationalism rather than freedom and cooperation, which should have happened to relieve the effects of the depressed economy. Also, there was no international intention to return to the previous free trade situation. Instead various conferences were held without successful outcomes. The global situation in the mid-1920s, with the Union of Soviet Socialist Republics (USSR) mired internal difficulties and Western Europe stagnating, did not promote the globalized world of free trade, dreamed about by Richard Cobden and others in the mid-nineteenth century.

Developments Towards Globalisation in the Second-Half of Last Century

In 1944 the leaders of the world met at Bretton Woods to establish International Monetary Fund (IMF), World Bank, and the International Trade Organisation (ITO). The establishment of International Trade Organization did not see the light of the day due to non-endorsement by the US Congress. However, in place of ITO a charter treaty, i.e., General Agreement on Tariffs and Trade (GATT) was signed in 1948 to bring in reduction in the tariff barriers.

US have been the dominant player in the global economy in the last century. Because of the presence of World Bank and International Monetary Fund headquartered in US, the Washington consensus prevailed upon the developing countries to bring in reform process in their policies. The shift in the global economy took place from imperialism to neo-imperialism and the countries started investing heavily in other countries.

The globalisation is said to have gained momentum in 1980s with a number of developments that took place in mid-80s like onset of Uruguay Round of Multilateral Trade Negotiations in 1986; collapse of Berlin Wall in 1989; disintegration of USSR in 1990; convergence of ideologies, i.e., democracy and communism; shift from social democracy to free market economies in the west; growth and emergence of Trade Blocs like NAFTA, and the establishment of World Trade Organisation in 1995—a rule based Trading System.

During the past three decades or so, the process of globalisation is said to have taken place in the following phases:

Political Globalisation :	Convergence of political ideolo-gies
Economic Globalisation:	Entry of MNCs
Techno-Globalisation:	Revolution in the Telecom and IT Sector bridged the gap between the developed and developing nations
Cultural Globalisation	The current phase of globaliza-tion does not believe in any cultural barriers.

Effects of Globalisation

Globalisation today is a fact of life. The effects of globalisation are apparent everywhere. It has played a major role in sustaining the economic expansion of the global economy in the second half of the 20th century. Globalisation, the integration of national markets through international trade and investment, offers infinite possibilities, greater freedom and new hope for the world's poor. Since globalisation emerged in the 70s, world infant mortality rates have fallen by almost half, adult literacy has increased by more than a third, primary school enrolment has risen and the average life span has shot up by 11 years. Due to successful efforts to lower global barriers, international trade and investment have become a primary engine of world growth. And growth is responsible for reducing poverty. In fact, studies indicate that developing countries with open economies grew by approximately 5 per cent a year in the 70s and 80s, while those with closed economies grew less than 1 per cent annually.

Today, 24 developing countries representing about 3 billion people, including China, India and Mexico, have adopted policies enabling their citizens to take advantage of globalisation. The result, their economies are catching up with rich ones. The incomes of the least globalized countries, including Iran, Pakistan and North Korea, have dropped or remained static.

If remaining world merchandise trade barriers are eliminated, potential gains are estimated at $ 250 billion to $ 550 billion annually. About two-thirds of this would accrue to developing countries—more than twice their annual level of aid. Helping the world's poorest countries become globally integrated will position them for greater growth in the 21st century.

Free trade encourages efficiency in the national markets through competition and the division of labour—that allows people and economies to focus on what they do best. Examples have been there that economies which have embraced free trade under globalisation have progressed faster than economies that have been the latecomer.

In the words of Mexican President Ernesto: "In every case where a poor nation has significantly overcome its poverty, this has been achieved while engaging in production for export markets and opening itself to the influx of foreign goods, investment and technology that is, participating in globalisation."

Indian Perspective in Globalisation

The world changed, and India changed even more: from an aid dependent country, notable chiefly for its past glory and current poverty, to an economic powerhouse widely expected to grow into not just one of the largest but also the most dynamic economies of the world.

For more than four decades since Independence, India had adopted a highly protected, regulated, restricted, and controlled policy towards an inward market approach and did not seem to have a policy of globalisation as such. There have been policy attempts from time to time which either directly or indirectly had implications for globalisation.

The year 1990-91 marked the end of the most protected trade regime phase in India and the country ushered into an era of globalisation. The continued deterioration in the economy due to the political instability, turmoil in Punjab, Kashmir, Assam and the rest of north-east, and overspending by the central and state governments in an attempt to meet the new exigencies during 1980s had a worsening impact on fiscal sector and the external sector. In the fiscal sector, the current account deficit went up from 0.2 per cent of the GDP during 1974-79 to 1.6 per cent in 1980-85 and further to 2.3 per cent during 1989-90. The negative trends in the external sector accentuated by the fall of the Soviet Union and the sharp rise in oil prices led to drop in India's exports to Eastern Europe from 20 per cent of total in 1989 to 11 per cent by 1991-92. Further the attack on Kuwait by Iraq disrupted the long-term supply contracts of oil to India from Iraq and led to a sharp rise in oil import bill for over two years. The net effect of these developments on India was that the import cover of the foreign exchange reserves came down from around five months in the mid-eighties to just 1.8 months by 1989-90. Short-term debt, which was 6.1 per cent of the total debt in March 1989, was pushed up to 9.9 per cent of the total debt in March 1990, and further to 10.2 per cent by March 1991. The ratio of short-term debt to total foreign exchange reserves excluding gold and SDR—was 90 per cent in March 1989. By March 1990 it was 2.2 times the reserves, and by March 1991 it went up to 3.8 times the foreign currency reserves.

As the situation continued to worsen, India's international credit ratings were downgraded. India, therefore, had no other option except to mortgage 46.9 tonnes of its gold reserves to raise additional funds from the international markets to meet international obligations. In order to meet the above crisis, the Government of India initiated the reform process in 1991. The reforms included a programme of micro-economic stabilization, changes in industrial and trade policies with the aim of improving the efficiency, productivity and international competitiveness of Indian economy. Further, in order to get the Indian economy integrated with the world economy, the government announced structural changes in its economic policies relating to exchange rate determination and management, industrial licensing, foreign collaborations, investment by NRIs, portfolio investments by foreign institutional investors, mobilization of funds by Indian commercial and industrial corporates from foreign countries, reduction in the tariffs (peak customs duty on nonagricultural imports has decreased from 300 per cent in 1990 to 15 per cent in 2005), simplification of export-import procedures, and so on.

Some of the key indicators of the reforms introduced by the government directed towards globalisation include:

• The launch of the New Industrial Policy in July 1991 which led to dereservation of the sectors kept in the domain of public sector in favour of private both domestic and foreign players. The effort towards opening of the economy can be gauged from the fact that out of the 17 sectors reserved for the public enterprises as many as 15 sectors have been opened for private participation. The two sectors viz. Atomic Energy and Railways have been kept reserved for the public sector because of strategic importance. Even within the railways the peripheral services like catering, maintenance of platforms, palace on wheels, etc. have been opened up.

• To improve the efficiency and cut down the public expenditure investment norms have been liberalized to attract inflow of capital from domestic and foreign enterprises including institutional investment in various sectors like banking, insurance, transport, real estate, retailing etc. The inflow of private capital has not only improved the competitiveness of the Indian manufacturing sector but has generated large employment opportunities leading to rise in the standard of living of the people.

• The opening of the telecom-IT sector has resulted into India's presence in the global marketplace and has been rated among the world's best. It is wrong to say that the fortune is confined to information technology and BPO, the growing increase in India's exports even without the help of a weak currency has led India to emerge as a powerful economy in the Asian region.

The reforms thus introduced in the policy frames have accelerated the growth rate from 5.7 per cent in the eighties to what could well be a new trend growth rate of 7 per cent now. The quality of this growth has improved remarkably: whether measured in terms of the units of capital required to produce a unit of output, foreign borrowings needed or the quality of the output, an indication of which is how much of it can be sold abroad.

India's export performance in the post-liberalisation period, i.e., 1991-2005 has been much better than the pre-reform period. From a negative growth of 0.55 per cent during 1991-92, the value of exports in dollar terms witnessed a growth rate of 25.98 per cent in 2004-05. In terms of openness of Indian economy, that is trade measured as percentage of value of GDP, the degree of openness almost doubled from a level of 13 per cent in 1990-91 to 22 per cent in 2002-03.

Exports from India registered a continuous increase from a modest 2.79 per cent growth in 1992-93 to 20.91 per cent in 1995-96. A declining trend in the export growth started in 1996-97 and witnessed a negative growth of 5.14 per cent in 1998-99. The negative growth in exports could mainly be attributed to the recession in world economy caused by East Asian crisis. Exports, however, picked up in 1999-2000 and witnessed a growth of 19.84 per cent in 2000-01 at USD 44 billion from USD 37 billion in previous year. The volume of exports has touched the level of USD 80 billion in 2004-05 from USD 18 billion in 1990-91 an increase of 344.44 per cent. India's share in global exports has also risen from the lowest level of 0.4 per cent in 1992-93 to around 1 per cent in 2004-05. The 25 per cent growth in exports witnessed during 2004-05 over the previous year coupled with firming up of domestic manufacturing activity and India's growing export competitiveness give clear indications that the target set by the Department of Commerce at USD 150 billion by 2009-10, and USD 300 billion by 2015 can be achieved without any difficulty.

A notable feature in India's export performance is that it had achieved 18 per cent growth at a time when the global economy was struggling to revive and even many of the developed countries found it difficult to achieve growth in their export. Besides, as per the WTO Report 2002, the country achieved 15 per cent growth, next only to China (22 per cent), among the 30 leading exporters in world merchandise trade during 2002. Export performance of many countries during this period has either been negative or in single digit, for example, USA (5 per cent), Canada (3 per cent), Japan (3 per cent), UK (1 per cent), Hong Kong (5 per cent), Korea (8 per cent), Singapore (3 per cent), Thailand (5 per cent), and Indonesia (0 per cent).

Growing integration of India's financial sector with that of the rest of the world, along with growing integration of the economy as a whole, has brought down interest rates and input prices. Venture funds, private equity and a booming stock market have enabled enterprise to flourish, overcoming earlier limitations of having to accumulate initial capital either through inheritance or loot. The foreign exchange reserves of the country are now at a very comfortable level at USD 130 billion against a mere USD one billion in 1990.

Myths about Globalisation

Globalisation Eliminates Jobs. One of the misconceptions about globalisation has been that it eliminates jobs. It is not true. For example, had India not embraced free market economy the number of jobs that have been created in the BPOs and other sectors would not have taken place.

Globalisation Causes a Race to the Bottom in Environmental and Labour Standards. Another fallacy is that capital flows where environmental and labour standards are lowest. However, the facts are Investors invest where returns are greatest, which tends to be where labour is most productive, which is where people are correspondingly richer—and richer people tend to demand better, not worse, environmental amenities and working conditions. The same is true of working standards. Jobs in foreign-owned enterprises are usually greatly sought after, because they both pay higher money wages and offer better working conditions than the domestic alternatives.

Globalisation Creates Inequality. The causes of rising or falling inequality are complex, but there is substantial truth to the claim that globalisation causes inequality: the wealth gap between countries that have closed economies and those that have free trade keeps growing. That's not the inequality the anti-globalizers have in mind. Within countries that have opened their economies to trade and investment, middle classes have grown, which means less income inequality, rather than more.

Globalisation Leads to Loss of Sovereignty. Another fallacy is that globalisation leads to loss of sovereignty. It is said that with the entry of large number of MNCs, the economic power of the country shifts from domestic companies to foreign companies. That is not so, if a country encourages entry of MNCs, they help in creation of job opportunities, exploration of untapped resources and make optimal use for the economic growth and development, besides bringing in new technology to increase surplus production for exports.

Benefits of Globalisation

Globalisation Leads to Peace by Diminishing the Incentives for Conflict. Protectionism is based on a mentality and a corresponding set of policies that emphasize the opposing interests of nations. Free trade, in contrast, links nations together in peace. There's an old adage when goods cannot cross-borders, armies surely will.

Trade Creates Wealth. Imagine that someone created a machine that would allow you to push through one door things you can make cheaply and through the other door would come things you'd like to have but that cost you more to produce. Australians could herd sheep in one door and out of the other door would come cars and photocopiers. And Japanese could push VCRs and stereos through one door and pull petroleum, wheat, and aircraft through the other. India could push its software skills through one door and pull hardware technology through the other.

Trade Leads to Benefits for All. The most common error of protectionists is to confuse absolute advantage with comparative advantage. Even if the person in the front row is better at everything than you, both of you benefit from trade if he specializes in what he does best and you specialize in what you do best. The old example of the typist and the lawyer applies across-borders as well as within offices. The lawyeı can both write legal briefs and type better than the typist, but both benefit by the lawyer specializing in writing legal briefs, which cost less in terms of lost typing output, and the typist typing them up, which costs less in terms of lost legal argumentation, since the typist is better at typing than at arguing law. Total joint output is higher and each receives more income. That's one reason why trade is so closely connected with peace, as well. It's because people can see their fellow humans as partners in mutually beneficial cooperation, rather than as deadly rivals, that human society is possible in the first place. Trade is at the very foundation of human civilization.

Free Trade is the Fastest Route to the Elimination of Child Labour. Around the world approximately 250 million children labour, the percentage of children who labour has fallen—not risen—with rising trade and globalisation, and for pretty obvious reasons. Poor countries are not poor because children work. Children work because they are poor. When people become richer through production and free exchange, they send their children to school, rather than to the fields. Global trade is the fastest route to the elimination of child labour and its replacement by child education.

Free Trade is a Fundamental Human Right. The anti-globalizers and protectionists start with the assumption that they have the right to use force to stop you and me from engaging in voluntary exchange. But fundamental rights should be equal for all humans, and the right to engage in trade is a fundamental right, one enjoyed by all humans, regardless of on which side of a border they may live. Free trade is not a privilege, it is a human right.

> "Protectionism should, therefore, be rejected not merely because it is inefficient. It should also be rejected because it leads to conflict and war, because it is immoral, and because it is uncivilized".

Conclusion

The challenges introduced by globalisation are similar to those introduced by the industrial revolution. Just as the Internet eliminates distance, we relive what the railroads and electricity brought to an earlier age. But with change comes controversy. And just as the industrial revolution's detractors spawned Marxism, it is essential to correct globalisation's defects before counter forces destroy its promise.

As globalisation has progressed, living conditions (particularly when measured by broader indicators of well being) have improved significantly in virtually all countries. However, the strongest gains have been made by the advanced countries and only some of the developing countries. It is also a fact that among developing and LDCs those countries that have opened up their economies to get integrated with the global world have progressed faster than the protected and closed economies. No country, least of all the poorest, can afford to remain isolated from the world economy.

To succeed in this highly technical environment, seize the benefits of globalisation and reduce the risks. To ensure that all people in all countries have access to the benefits of globalisation, the international community should endeavour to help the poorest countries integrate into the world economy, grow more rapidly, and reduce poverty. Workers in the advanced countries must continually learn new skills, developing countries must welcome global integration, and all nations must provide safety nets. By teaching people and their nations to fish in the waters of globalisation, billions will achieve the means to obtain a higher quality of life. Thus, the Chinese proverb "Give a man a fish and you feed him for a day; teach a man to fish and you feed him for a lifetime," has become more relevant in the globalisation context.

References

1. World Bank, www.worldbank.org
2. Larsson, Tomas, The Race to the Top: The Real Story of Globalisation.
3. Smith, Adam, The Wealth of Nations.
4. Spruiell, Stephen, Protectionism: Tariffs, Subsidies, and Trade Policy.
5. Rippon, Mathew J., History of Globalisation.
6. Martin Chris, Gains from Trade.
7. *The Economic Times*, New Delhi (various issues).
8. Wadhwa, R.K., An Overview of India's Foreign Trade in the Pre- and Post-Liberalization Era.
9. Exports—A Success Story, Ministry of Commerce and Industry, Government of India, New Delhi.
10. India's Foreign Trade Policy 2004-09, Ministry of Commerce and Industry, Government of India, New Delhi.
11. Globalisation, Free Trade, Foreign Aid—www.newsbatch. com.
12. www.aworldconnected.org
13. www.imf.org.

Index

D

E

F

G